the **Social Organization of Juvenile Justice**

the **Social Organization** of **Juvenile Justice**

Aaron V. Cicourel

Transaction Publishers
New Brunswick (U.S.A.) and London (U.K.)

Library of Congress Catalog Number: 94-17406
ISBN: 1-56000-779-6
Printed in the United States of America

Library of Congress Cataloging-in-Publication Data

Cicourel, Aaron Victor, 1928–
    The social organization of juvenile justice / Aaron V. Cicourel ; with a new introduction by the author.
        p. cm.
    Originally published : New York : Wiley, 1967.
    Includes bibliographical references and index.
    ISBN 1-56000-779-6
    1. Juvenile justice, Administration of—California—Case studies. 2. Sociolinguistics. I. Title.
HV9105.C2C53   1994
364.3'6'0973—dc20   94-17406
                                                               CIP

To Gregg, Denise, and Eric

CONTENTS

INTRODUCTION TO THE TRANSACTION EDITION

In designing and implementing a study of juvenile justice in two California cities of approximately the same population size, I sought to contrast an official view of cases known to the police with my day-to-day observations of how police, probation, and court officials interact with juveniles and arrive at decisions (courses of action) about the youth in question. The cases known to the police provided a basis for questioning official statistics. Many problems emerge when aggregated rates are used as a point of departure for discussing juvenile justice and delinquency. Observing the daily activities of police and probation officers and court officials led to discussions and documents that both summarized and elaborated complex events. These events provide us with a representation of unofficial and official statistics on juvenile justice and delinquency.

By focusing on those occasions where decisions are made by bureaucratically designated officials in the system of juvenile law enforcement and justice, I tried to make visible how local events and circumstances contribute to the way delinquent careers achieve recognition and action. Restricting myself to official and unofficial organizational encounters meant that I could seldom report on direct observations of family activities, peer social interaction, school behavior, or the juvenile's personal account of her or his actions and motivations. But many of the activities I could not witness directly were often examined directly or indirectly by law enforcement and court officials and reported to me orally or included in bureaucratic records.

A central focus of my research was the way in which I came to know and describe what I perceived to be the social organization of juvenile justice. My preoccupation with methods was quite deliberate. I felt that official statistics and the records kept by the police and probation departments contained normal idealizations that masked many of the complex events that came to be aggregated and called rates of delinquency. I wanted to clarify the research process by observing the way police, probation, and court personnel transform their experiences with juveniles and each other into verbal and written documents or texts that are then used as evidence for events or activities called delinquent, illegal, suspicious, or dangerous.

Research problems help us understand the unexamined ways we idealize the experiences of those we study and our own activities as researchers when what we call social structure gets packed into selectively organized and remembered discourse and textual representations. The focus on discourse and text is necessary if we are to understand how the agencies responsible for detecting, processing, reporting, adjudicating, and disposing of persons called delinquent document their claims about juvenile delinquency and juvenile justice. This focus helps us understand claims about the distribution and causes of delinquency by the media, government agencies, and researchers using official statistics and written records.

Recent developments in the study of legal activities have underscored the importance of cognitive and linguistic aspects of the reasoning and language used in the administration of civil and criminal justice.[1]

Sociolinguists are preoccupied with the way language is used in particular contexts. The term *context* can include: the setting in which a speech event occurs, the participants present, who can speak or chooses to remain silent, the local spatial and temporal aspects of the interaction that takes place, the goals that appear to be explicit or that emerge, and the social or status relationships that are implicit, can be observed, or are identifiable over the course of the exchange.

Speech Communities

The idea of a speech community presumes that its members have developed idealized and practical cultural mental models about verbal and nonverbal behavior but where actual displays are inherently embedded in ecological settings in which others are always a prominent aspect of real performances.[2] The members of a work group expect and either tacitly or explicitly demand that peers or co-workers employ particular types of speech on particular occasions of interaction. The existence and continuity of a speech community, therefore, is contingent on both its diversity and homogeneity at different levels of abstraction and language use in mundane settings.

Speech Events

Speech events in everyday life settings provide information on the way socially defined activities shape and are shaped by verbal displays while participants pursue one or more tasks. Hymes has identified categories by which speech events can be characterized.[3] The first refers to a situation or a local setting or scene. The situation will include various kinds of participants who may be called speaker, hearer, or audience as well as different possible outcomes or goals. The speech event will include the form and content of a message and norms that prescribe and proscribe the kinds of interaction and interpretation expected or sanctioned. Finally, there can be different kinds or genres of speech events. The focus is always on the use of language in practical settings.

Within legal and police settings, speech events are often highly ritualized activities even when a suspect or defendant is being mistreated.[4] The way novices are socialized into these activities is a rich source of information about how speech events can tell us about complex legal and social control processes and structures.

The identification of such activities is often known to observers but it is often difficult to obtain systematic data on these events. The research analyst must become something of an "insider" while simultaneously trying to maintain a level of objectivity that will generate observations about routine and delicate matters.

Utterances or Speech Acts

The term *utterance* or *speech act,* unlike a sentence, refers to the pragmatic force of speech in the sense of both describing and constituting an action in the world. In Austin's notion of utterances with illocutionary force, the general idea was to underscore the shared conventions needed for speakers to use words in particular contexts.[5] An important aspect of Austin's work is that many utterances cannot be described by reference to their truth conditions but primarily by the local conditions of use. The mention of local conditions of use, however, is not to be understood as meaning the study of local ethnographic conditions but what Austin and the participants producing speech acts assume are the appropriate conventions governing their verbal activities.

A more general view of speech acts revolves around the intentional aspects of utterances studied by Austin and the conversational postulates and cooperative principle of Grice.[6] According to Grice, speech acts inform a hearer or audience of one's informative intention. Speakers are expected to be as informative as necessary without saying more than needed, not say anything false or for which one lacks adequate evidence. In addition, the speaker should be relevant, not obscure or ambiguous, brief and orderly. The hearer is expected to be able to choose the implications of the explicit content of an utterance such as those conveyed implicitly by the local context.

Within legal and police settings, many local conventions emerge and become bureaucratically routinized and ritualized as when particular speech acts signal that the court is now in session. Specific speech acts are required in order to obtain speaking rights. When interrogating suspects, particular speech acts may be required before questions can be posed. Speech act theory, as developed by Austin, Grice, Searle, and others, provides the student of legal and police or criminological processes with useful guidelines for understanding the formal aspects of language use in speech communities or during speech events.[7] These idealizations, however, must be modified by ethnographically informed sources of knowledge about the way complex bureaucratic organizations function on a daily basis and the kinds of locally instantiated speech events that mark decision-making processes.

Eyewitness Testimony

In Anglo-American law, an area that remains obscure is the law of evidence. In particular, the reliability of eyewitness statements or accounts. It is difficult to identify clear rules that govern what witnesses say about what they have heard or seen. In addition, as noted by Loftus, the evidence obtained from eyewitnesses can be quite unreliable.[8] In the United States, mistaken eyewitness testimony has been associated with the conviction of innocent people. The fact that this kind of information is unverifiable is aggravated by the kind of people often called upon to be eyewitnesses. Lawyers seek persons who are considered of good character and who also speak with conviction about their accounts. Such information tends to be readily accepted by the members of a jury.

Loftus draws upon the psychology of perception, memory, and the recall of complex events to address the issue of eyewitness testimony. She refers to a three-stage process:

1. The first stage refers to the acquisition of information about an event that is perceived and about which information is initially stored in memory.

2. The second stage refers to the retention of information in memory about the event.

3. The third stage refers to a search for relevant information in memory that can be retrieved and communicated to others.

Different variables are said to affect the three stages. For example, the way a question is posed or phrased and the kinds of assumptions associated with the questions can have subtle yet serious impact on information stored in memory. Let me illustrate Loftus's experimental research on eyewitness testimony. A movie is shown to a group of subjects about an automobile accident. The subjects were then asked questions about the accident. The key question of the experiment was asked in two different ways to two different groups of subjects. One of the groups was asked, "How fast were the cars going when they smashed into each other?" The second group was asked, "How fast were the cars going when they hit each other?"[9] The subjects were asked to return a week later and at that time they were asked, "Did you see any broken glass in the accident?"

The wording of the two questions, however, produced different responses in the way the two groups answered the question about broken glass. The group that had been given the tern *smashed* were most likely to say, incorrectly, that they remembered the presence of broken glass. The group given the term *hit* were less likely to report having remembered seeing broken glass.

Experiments like the automobile accident led Loftus to raise a number of issues about the way witnesses are questioned by the police before a trial or by an attorney or counsel during a trial. The point is that the kinds of questions asked can influence the organization of the witness's memory and affect subsequent testimony.

The perception of an event by a witness can lead to experiences that focus on several types of activities that can occupy the witness. For example, experiencing a robbery can mean the witness may focus on the individual features of the robber's face, or appear to be looking at the face but in actuality the witness is thinking more about how to escape from a situation that is quite unpleasant. The kinds of activities in which a witness becomes involved can be important in how well he or she may remember different aspects of an incident.[10]

There are many problems associated with the use of eyewitness testimony. Loftus notes that even when instructions are given to a jury by a judge, they do not help much in assessing the reliability of any one eyewitness's remarks. Members of a jury often do not pay attention to the judge's instructions. (In my experience, jurors often not only do not understand the judge's instructions—because they are often ambiguous—they also are reluctant to challenge them.)

For present purposes, several serious issues revolve around the kind of research that has been done on eyewitness testimony. Most of it has been based on careful experimental research on the perception of events, their retention and retrieval. There have been few empirical studies of eyewitnesses in natural settings. Our lack of knowledge about the role of witnesses in natural settings suggests that the kinds of issues raised and discussed carefully by Loftus are highly relevant for understanding on-line behavior, but that many more problems associated with language use in locally managed settings need to be addressed. These issues include the local circumstances in which the police make an investigation and begin to search for witnesses as well as other information. The knowledge base of police investigators is often impressive from a practical point of view, but they are not easily able to interrogate a cross-section of a population with the same level of skill and depth. Their training is not as sophisticated as a lawyer's with respect to language use and they can become unsure of their actions when interviewing persons of higher status.

Lawyers often lack the practical experiences that police officers have of dealing with suspects in their natural settings. But lawyers are skilled at recognizing that a witness's credibility and ability to withstand cross-examination in a courtroom can vary by a number of factors that Loftus has mentioned. The lawyer's education can often be a barrier to the interrogation of witnesses from lower socioeconomic groups and different ethnic or racial backgrounds.

In contrast to scholars who examine the relation between question and answer as part of the general structure of conversation, or the way questioning in courtrooms is related to legal functions of language use, Philips seeks to link general and legal concerns between questions and answers to broader societal issues.[11] For example, she looks at patterns of courtroom discourse in terms of the way persons respond to questions by building on these same questions in constructing their answers. In general terms, Philips argues that responses to questions reveal patterns that are part of a hierarchy of status, power, and authority differentiation. These patterns, notes Philips, can be described as situational (or locally managed in the courtroom) and as reflective of the larger society in which the activities occur. The patterns of discourse, therefore, are not peculiar to courtrooms but should be found in all hierarchically organized social activities or role relations, especially in bureaucratic settings in the United States and in European or European-derived contexts.

The basic question posed by Philips is "Who asks and who responds?" Philips found that the court cases she recorded (forty-two in all) followed the expected normative pattern for the most part, with the judge being the person who mediated all discourse. For example, the judge asked most of the questions (1,433 of 1,488 or 96 percent of the time). The judge also asked more questions of the lawyers than they did of him. Most of the questions asked of the lawyers by the judge are of a "Wh" format (questions like who, when, where, what, and how). Noting that her findings are consistent with Danet et al.,[12] Philips states that Wh-questions are viewed as less coercive than yes-no questions and they are more likely to be used when the person asking the questions is not so worried about controlling the respondent.

A general point made by Philips is that in criminal proceedings, the view exists that the defendant's speech should be restricted and controlled in contrast to the speech of a lawyer. The legal folk wisdom that seems to motivate this viewpoint is that defendants or others unfamiliar with the close relationship between the law and words used in court are more likely to make mistakes or damage their testimony or their case if they are not controlled. In addition, defendants or others unfamiliar with law and court procedures may jeopardize their case by saying something that can harm the legal validity of the procedure. Philips suggests that perhaps the control exercised over defendants or other nonspecialists is due to their lower status in the courtroom. Philips found that only 5 percent of the questions asked by the lawyers of the judge were Wh-questions.

An important consideration for the reader is the fact that most of the time, language use in institutionalized contexts, such as police stations, courtrooms, lawyer's offices, and the judge's chambers, are interrelated. That is, the questioning presumes knowledge about the nature of the criminal or civil justice system and involves persons who have had different amounts of experience interrogating different people or being interrogated. These experiences lead to various kinds of routines of questioning that often give the expert or professional a degree of predictability and control over what the listener (defendant, witness, lawyer, judge, police officer) will produce as a response. The routines developed are designed to help the questioner feel comfortable with the exchange.

The application of cognitive and sociolinguistic concepts and methods to law enforcement and the administration of criminal and civil justice is in its infancy and cannot be expected to solve major problems easily. It will take considerable time before we can begin to understand the way that status and power relations are associated with the structural arrangements of legal institutions and the day-to-day implementation of legal statutes, rituals, communication strategies, and daily confrontations between persons with different expertise and the ability to put their knowledge into practice.

My daily activities with police, probation, school, and court officials, as well as juveniles and their families, required that I describe details that also produced selectively organized and remembered discourse and texts. This meant asking the reader's indulgence when judging my observations and assumptions about rude or impolite conduct by juveniles or policemen, aggressive or passive behavior, laughter or tears, and the like, when trying to convince the reader that my remarks should be honored. Thus, I had to make many judgments that I assumed would be clear to any reader despite the idealization inherent in all description. I had to rely on unexplicated judgments to claim that bureaucratic accounts I presented as data were misleading or prejudicial in their characterization of a juvenile's conduct, background, or family situation. I wanted to reveal the experiences I acquired for understanding a decision by the police to file a petition requesting a court hearing. The reader should be able to read the probation officer's characterizations of a juvenile's career when recommending probation or incarceration so that I could explain how prior encounters between the juvenile and the officer shaped a particular biographical sketch. I felt it important to reveal how the probation officer's textual account was used to persuade the judge or referee that the juvenile should be treated leniently or severely.

The importance of discourse and text or text and discourse, depending on the sequence and availability of materials, becomes clear when we recognize that police, probation, and court personnel's implicit classificatory schemas or typifications are only partially displayed in official reports that are then used by others for inference and action. The language used by law enforcement and court personnel in reports and legal documents must interface with legal statutes. We can seldom have access, however, to the dialogues or discourse that occurred at the time of arrest, during interrogation of witnesses and the suspect, the possible consultations with others in deciding to file a petition, the discussions of probation officers with the suspect, his/her family, school officials, and so forth. Unless we seek an independent study of the discourse that precedes reports by the police and probation, and unless we elicit information from these officials about their decisions and their use of terms in the writing of reports, we cannot understand the meaning of aggregated information like official records and statistics.

Throughout this book, I assume the researcher and reader are familiar with my use of American English. I force the reader to rely on his or her imagination or memory to understand my remarks that a juvenile's tone of voice is often the basis for a police office or probation officer or judge calling the juvenile's behavior "in defiance of authority" or an indication of a "bad attitude." Other problems include agreement on the meaning of gestures and dress, physical posturing, linguistic expressions suggesting double meanings, jokes, anxiety, and the like. The researcher, therefore, makes many unexamined assumptions and judgments in converting his experiences, thoughts, observations, and elicited and official records into materials that are viewed as "objective" data.

In subsequent chapters, I present and interpret materials on the social organization of juvenile justice by using verbatim conversations or reports whenever possible. The materials making up the data of the present study consist of police and probation reports, conversations I observed and sometimes recorded, a few conversations recorded but not observed by me, and regular participant observation for over four years of two police and probation departments and juvenile court settings. I tried to follow each case from initial exchanges between juveniles and police and probation officials to subsequent reports and interviews, trying to show how different experiences and activities are rendered as familiar scenes and depictions of juveniles, their families, and general behavior by law enforcement and court officials. The discursive and textual accounts provided the basis for creating or transforming the juvenile in question, his or her peers or family life, into objects of interest to the police and probation officials in order to make descriptive accounts of "what happened" appear convincing and justifiable vis-à-vis evaluations and dispositions. The oral and written accounts by police and probation officers standardize the routine and erratic business of juvenile and familial encounters or the exchanges interviewers have with witnesses to make the accounts meaningful to themselves and others. The selectivity and organization of the material included in the accounts, therefore, provided the basis for transforming a juvenile, his peers, his family, or his neighborhood into an object that justified particular actions and/or inferences. The selectivity of a descriptive account permits an observer to manipulate unstated details or observations by forcing the reader to imagine a particular type of atmosphere or one damaging to the suspect or favorable to the decisions made by an official. I have attempted to show that what is included in a report provided the basis for various constructions of "what happened" by interested parties, for example, how participants of a setting perceived and interpreted "authority relationships," accomplished decision-making activities, satisfied the observer's notion of "punitive supervision," and achieved the behavioral features that enable us to say that someone "conformed" to rules that satisfied organizational procedures.

The researcher's attempts at measurement require a theory of the construction of documents and how documents or textual accounts reconstruct discourse or conversations. I tried to show how the police or probation officer used encounters with juveniles or others connected with the case to organize a report that could then be used as documentary "evidence" of a "bad attitude," "poor risk for probation," or some similar or more favorable characterization. Thus, in analyzing conversations and reports, the researcher must approximate a "rewriting" of the dialogue or prose to reveal how selective attention, memory, and unstated but presumed common knowledge or understandings were integral features of a report that could be used by others as definitive or strong evidence of "what happened."

The study of the social organization of juvenile justice directs the researcher to how police and probation officers come to recognize juvenile activities (sequential and parallel stimulus conditions) as relevant to their circumstances of work, how these officials become oriented to a course of action, and how they organize the behavior in a way that is assumed to be consistent with an imagined appropriate course of action that others in law enforcement and the courts can recognize as meaningful. My observations suggested that police and probation officers developed perspectives that followed typifications held by members of the community. Each city was divided into areas where the officers expected to receive difficulty or "difficult" elements, areas where little trouble was expected, and areas where most care should be taken in dealing with the populace because of socioeconomic or political influence or ethnic concentrations. The typifications can result in quick inferences about "what is going on" in some setting despite the absence of factual information that must be used sooner or later in oral or written form. At the beginning of an encounter, officers often attributed typical circumstances, social causes, and outcomes to juveniles and thereby projected "careers" that different delinquent types would be likely to follow.

The concern with daily decision making by law enforcement organizations was designed to reveal how police, probation, and court officials conceive of the settings they must address. Hence, their conception of the situation and their ways of thinking about their encounters with suspects or juveniles adjudicated as guilty have both an unfolding situated character during the encounters and a more formal status as evidenced by written reports. I wanted to call the reader's attention to each successive stage of decision-making because of the legal consequences of each encounter and written report. Each encounter and written report affects the juvenile, and events considered illegal in such a way that the contingencies in which the participants interpret what is going on, the thinking or "theorizing" employed, are progressively altered or eliminated or reified as the case is reviewed at different levels of the legal process and reaches a hearing or trial state. At each stage, the participants must rely on their selective attention and memory in making use of an interpretive schema to filter available "facts" or in creating interpretations about motives, intent, trustworthiness, family support, and the like. Participants attempted to produce propositions that were to be accorded a factual status from the various perspectives of the police, witnesses, lawyers, or a referee or judge. Hence, law enforcement definitions of deviance and their distribution and occurrence cannot be viewed as "obvious" descriptions of existing "social problems." The existence of different interest groups in the community, including law enforcement policies and practices and the juvenile's family resources, are key elements for understanding the day-to-day activities whereby official versions of deviance are generated and discussed.

Throughout my study of juvenile justice practices I was sometimes unable to obtain the kinds of details that seemed essential for the methodological strategy I followed. These problems are described in several parts of the book. I was often unable to obtain verbatim tape recordings of discourse that would reveal pauses, interruptions, extralinguistic particles like "uh," "oh," "ah," and specific lexical items, phrases, and other semantically significant utterances that can provide us with a glimpse of the contingent character of police-juvenile or police-probation encounters. These details are necessary if we are to indicate how materials based on official records that sociologists use as a point of departure for inferences and policy recommendations can create misleading constructions of social reality. Transcriptions of audio- and videotapes can also capture otherwise taken-for-granted behavioral or emotional conditions, but these may not seem relevant to a reader interested in more macro issues associated with crime and delinquency.

Normatively organized ways of processing information can create a problematic data base that most sociologists ignore in their rush to begin an analysis of aggregated materials that possess a suppressed history. I have, therefore, focused on the aspects of discourse and the changes, deletions, or transformations that occur when an initial encounter is summarized in a subsequent report. There are many research settings where we cannot obtain the details of discourse that preceded the writing or formal reports, are not permitted to attend informal sessions that are preliminary to official meetings, or cannot be present when family interaction occurs that leads to decisions we learn about after the fact. We are often forced to deal with statistical outcomes of complex events or textual materials that conveniently help investigators to span complex details in order to achieve practical solutions to routine and special problems. But these statistical and textual conveniences mask the constraints of information processing and the limitations imposed by socially organized interpretive schemas we use routinely when making research decisions and which govern the members of a group or organization we study. Our routine use of interviews and questionnaires to elicit information poses similar problems. The many participant observer studies of industrial bureaucracies, hospitals, or special groups generate field notes that are like textual summaries that cover a broad range of unspecified detail about appearances, voice intonation, and the selectivity of their presentation.

I have tried to stress a basic issue in social-behavioral science research; how do we decide the minimal adequacy of a data base to begin making claims to knowledge about crime and delinquency, political power, imperialism, class conflict, and the like? An important first step would be the study of different strategies for assembling a data base. We need an explicit model that describes the structure of everyday communication so that we can achieve some control over our elicitation strategies, field notes, and audio and video recordings. How we represent what we call information is a basic part of the use of all research procedures and our analysis of data.

The present study differs from previous and current research on juvenile justice by calling attention to routine organizational conditions that help create the cognitive and social selectivity of a data base. A second point is to recognize that our definition of crime or delinquency, imperialism or class conflict, requires theoretical and methodological conceptions that are integrated and that make the researcher's interests and ways of eliciting and organizing materials a basic part of the description of the research problem. Hence, the researcher's interests are as much a part of the study as the way participants describe their interests and actions through the research strategies employed.

Concluding Remarks

Before concluding this introductory chapter, I think it appropriate to review a critique by Barry Hindess.[13] The critique provides an opportunity to clarify a number of problems that readers may have encountered in their past or current examination of the research presented here.

Hindess unfortunately links his critique of my work to work by Douglas, as if our views are equivalent and hence can be quoted interchangeably.[14] There are serious theoretical and methodological differences between us that Hindess chooses to ignore because he can avoid the details of my research materials by focusing on epistemological issues, which he selectively quotes to buttress his critical remarks. He charges that we are guilty of "a complete relativism and...a necessary agnosticism" instead of a serious concern with "objective knowledge."[15] Douglas's work on suicide employed a perspective that was similar to my own earlier theoretical remarks on the use of official statistics but these works are different from the empirical study I present in this book. In recent work unavailable to Hindess when he wrote his critique, Douglas attacks me for stressing the role of language as a topic and resource in sociological research and insisting that situated language use be part of any sociological model of the actor. Hindess's claim that we both deny the possibility of universal features in our discussion of "background expectancies and tacit knowledge" ignores some of my work that was available to Hindess and that stresses the importance of invariance in social organization.[16]

A central feature of Hindess's critique is the curious notion that the foundation of knowledge is not derived from human experience. The form of research advocated by Hindess pretends that the key issues have to do with the system of categories and the conjunction of conceptual and technical instruments. His point is that my work denies the relevance of "concepts and...rationalist forms of demonstration" in making claims to knowledge. This is a weak and misleading charge. Demonstrations of the adequacy of description and the relationship between formal theoretical conceptions and evidence are central to the present work. Hindess would have us believe that official statistics are not linked to the experiences and situated decisions of census workers or survey interviewers. He is convinced that the key element to an understanding of any distribution of official statistics is an unexplicated notion of a "determinate process or production of knowledge" that conveniently combines "conceptual and technical instruments."[17] Presumably, the consciousness of respondents and enumerators or interviewers is not an issue, but instead "the structure of the system of categories" as determined by concepts and rationalist forms of demonstration.[18] Hindess does not elaborate his position. He does not indicate how this utopian situation comes about whereby the researcher's ideas of how to construct his categories and interpret the responses of respondents to his questions in some cultural-historical context, is to be divorced from the experiences of all parties to the research and the organization and analysis of findings. Hence, he ignores the point that our oral and written accounts reflect our experiences.

Those we interview or observe and our use of a classification system to subsume objects and events are not determined by an abstract algorithm. The use of "rationalist forms of demonstration" seems to mean divorcing oneself from the difficult fieldwork and decisions and simply examining those products that result in official statistics being called "objective knowledge."

Hindess fails to understand the relationship between the ideas and experiences of the researcher and the construction of the system of categories. Further, how do conceptual notions acknowledge or ignore the influence of the researcher's experiences as a member of some group? How do technical instruments reflect or distort the historicocultural and interpersonal context of eliciting information? For example, the police or probation officer's report employs a vocabulary that is designed to convey "the facts," yet the language used also provides the reader with a subtle or obvious suggestion of guilt or innocence based on the selective use of experiences and other information. Interview schedules and questionnaires provide a more obvious case in point. If Hindess had addressed the research strategies and materials obtained in the present study, he would have seen that the theoretical terms I used were not as important as how I defined the limits of my study and actually pursued and reported the research. Hindess does not go beyond his provocative statement that official statistics must be seen as a "product" that requires examination by reference to "the conditions and instruments of their production,"[19] nor has he participated in an actual research situation involving a survey or census study as the basis for his remarks. Instead, he relies on a "safe" but careful critique of the 1951 Census of India on the distribution of persons engaged in agriculture for his view of an adequate research strategy. He does not address the field research conditions associated with "the assignment of cases into classes." He acknowledges problems of reconciling the classification system used by officials of the Indian Census and the categories used by classical political economy theory and also notes that an ideally trained team of observers would not eliminate certain basic problems appreciably. But despite recognizing that the system of categories supplied to enumerators determines the types of ambiguity that can appear in the classification of individuals, Hindess persists in locating the problem only in the set of categories.[20] He does not also locate the problem in the observer's stated and often unstated conceptions of "appropriateness" of categories and how all enumerators and survey interviewers are left with ambiguous decision-making situations in attempting to use any set of categories.

The present study attempts to show some of the consequences of providing law enforcement officials with legal categories that require constant negotiation to deal with juveniles suspected or considered guilty of legal infringements. I have stressed the inherent difficulties of the law enforcement process by examining the day-to-day social organization associated with the assembly of unofficial and official statistics, and of central importance, how the organizational decisions affect the careers of individual juveniles in the context of interpersonal encounters and family background.

Hindess's confusion about my discussion of official statistics stems from his failure to recognize how normative common sense categories inherent in our use of language influence the conceptual and technical instruments we use in the assembly and interpretation of official statistics. Hindess does not clarify his assertion that my position denies what he calls a "pre-theoretical observation language." In his abstract epistemological critique he fails to address the difficult issues of how research gets done and how findings are often fortuitously linked to theory. Hence, the ad hoc theorizing of the researcher during questionnaire construction, interviews, observation and coding practices, versus the way the police work, is never examined by Hindess. He merely pretends to address the theoretical-research nexus, but his analysis of the 1951 Indian Census conveniently avoids the decisions of technicians and bureaucrats who conduct a census and the decisions required in actual research situations.

Another related assertion by Hindess claims that I advocate a comparison of an observer's report with that of some mysteriously produced account of a more "real" environment of objects. This charge stems from a quote from Douglas's work exhorting sociologists to provide each other with "accurate descriptions of real phenomena" as an alternative to official statistics. Hindess fails to compare the programmatic statements in *Method and Measurement in Sociology* with the actual research of the present book.[21]

Hindess claims that my position makes research so problematic that all studies will deteriorate into infinite regress problems. Had Hindess taken the time to examine the research materials carefully and the theoretical focus of my work, he would have seen that his claim that the outcome of my orientation means an infinite regress problem never materializes. My concern is with how laymen and researchers create and settle for different levels of descriptive adequacy when making decisions about arresting juveniles, how a report is written that recommends incarceration or probation, or how documents or official statistics are used as a data base for making inferences and claims to knowledge.

Contrary to remarks by Hindess, my research on juvenile justice can be used to improve crime statistics and to estimate and to control possible sources of error. But such improvements would not eliminate the problems inherent in using official statistics, nor would such improved statistics take the place of controlled field research on crime and delinquency. My concern with the limitations of descriptive statistical accounts and the observer's reports are designed to call attention to routine and normal sources of error or misclassification that are inherent in data-reduction procedures. Hence, claims to knowledge must acknowledge and include efforts to understand the collection and organization of research materials. These procedures involve similar information-processing activities in the transition from discourse between law enforcement official and juvenile, to a written report that becomes a legal document summarizing and evaluating the juvenile's conduct, prospects, and possible disposition. The contrasts between different levels of descriptive accounts help to reveal aspects of invariant and variable processes of social organization.

For readers unfamiliar with Hindess's book, his careful review of the inadequacies of the 1951 Indian Census classification system for determining the distribution of persons engaged in agriculture is not a refutation of a position attributed to my work. My work is not based on the ambiguous notion of the consciousness of the enumerator as described by Hindess. The system of categories devised by the members of a legal bureaucracy and their interpretation in actual settings is examined in the present work. Hindess does not tell his readers how Indian Census enumerators used a classification system while actually engaged in interviews. Work on the influence of bias on suicide rates suggests that we will have to devise careful studies of the ways in which bureaucratic personnel employ official systems of categories.[22] I indicate how police and probation officers must link their situated experiences to the legal categories and the descriptions necessary to justify an arrest or detention at Juvenile Hall or accept a petition for a court hearing. Chapters 3-7 provide a large corpus of materials that reveal many details on the interaction between a legal system of categories and actual encounters between juveniles and law enforcement officials. Hindess did not examine the research materials to criticize my work, nor does he provide his own research materials to refute my study of how the observer and observed make claims about who are delinquent and how they are processed. But we agree on at least one point. Censuses or other surveys cannot be improved by resorting to technical modifications.

Hindess's basic misconception of my work can be found in the conclusion of the critique where he claims that I seek "to establish human experience" as the "foundation of knowledge."[23] The point he makes is that I stand guilty of wanting to eliminate the distortions of "background expectancies, tacit knowledge, and the like" from sociologists' theoretical statements and findings. I have never taken this position, but instead have insisted that our tacit knowledge, interests, typifications, and use of language as members of some cultural group are always part of our claims to knowledge. We can recognize their effects but we cannot avoid their influence. We cannot as researchers avoid using concepts and making reference to rationalist forms of proof and demonstration, but we can recognize that formal languages presuppose and invoke tacit knowledge when linked to descriptions of our experiences and when we use any system of categories to subsume objects and events by rule or procedure. Unfortunately, most of Hindess's critique is a play on words and not a serious effort at examining the difficult empirical issues of field research on juvenile justice.

In more recent work there has been considerable change in the way theoretical and methodological issues are presented.[24] In traditional research, the representational system we call oral language is assumed to be a standardized indicator of past, present, and future settings. But these standardized auditory-oral displays presuppose unexplicated ideas about a memory system, internal representations and normative conceptions of "normal" thinking, and social activities. My current research has continued the focus of this book on the relationship between discourse and text in socially organized settings by examining the role of cognitive processes in the study of social structure. This means achieving greater control over the elicitation and analysis of information on discourse and textual materials.

The present work on juvenile justice seeks to clarify the interaction between the sociologist's concepts, legal categories, folk concepts as used by law enforcement personnel and those they interview, and the official statistics that are often used as a point of departure for depicting the distribution and causes of juvenile delinquency. Thus, the interaction I seek to clarify includes how decisions are made to arrest someone, how the conditions of an arrest are reported by the police, how the police decide to file a petition requesting that a court hearing be held, how the probation officer decides that a preliminary hearing to consider the acceptability of the petition is warranted, how the probation officer negotiates a relationship of trust with the juvenile, and so on.

The present study of juvenile justice was motivated by a desire to address problems sociologists share with members of the group he or she studies. But at the same time, I have underscored the importance of making the researcher's interests and the interests of those he or she studies a problematic feature of the research project. My intention was to interest the reader in theoretical and methodological issues that are often ignored in traditional research in the hope of also calling attention to the fact that our definition and pursuit of research problems requires a reflexive perspective that is often blurred by our preoccupation with formal statements and our unspecified involvement as members of the society we study.

NOTES

1. Some of the recent literature includes: Brenda Danet, "Language in the Legal Process," *Law and Society Review* (1980) **14**; Brenda Danet and Bryna Bogoch, "Fixed Fight or Free-for-All? An Empirical Study of Combativeness in the Adversary System of Justice," *British Journal of Law and Society* (1980); and William O'Barr, *Linguistic Evidence: Language. Power and Strategy in the Courtroom* (New York: Academic Press, 1982).
2. Alessandro Duranti, "Ethnography of Speaking: Toward a Linguistics of the Praxis," in F. J. Newmeyer (editor), *Linguistics: The Cambridge Survey* (Cambridge: Cambridge University Press, 1988).
3. Dell Hymes, "Toward Ethnographies of Communication," chapter 1 in *Foundations in Sociolinguistics* (Philadelphia: University of Pennsylvania Press, 1974).
4. Susan Urmston Philips, "The Social Organization of Questions and Answers in Courtroom Discourse: A Study of Changes of Plea in an Arizona Court," *Text* (1984) **4**.
5. J. L. Austin, *How to do Things with Words* (Cambridge, Mass.: Harvard University Press, 1962.
6. H. P. Grice, "Logic and Conversation," in P. Cole and J. L. Morgan (editors), *Syntax and Semantics: Speech Acts* (New York: Academic Press, 1975).
7. John R. Searle, *Speech Acts* (Cambridge: Cambridge University Press, 1969).
8. Elizabeth F. Loftus, *Eyewitness Testimony* (Cambridge, Mass.: Harvard University Press, 1979).
9. *Ibid.*, p. xii.
10. *Ibid.*, pp. 48–49.
11. Philips, "The Social Organization of Questions and Answers," *op cit.*, p. 226.
12. Danet and Bogoch, "Fixed fight or Free-for-All?" *op. cit.*
13. Barry Hindess, *The Use of Official Statistics in Sociology: A Critique of Positivism and Ethnomethodology* (London: Macmillan, 1973).
14. Jack Douglas, *The Social Meanings of Suicide* (Princeton, N.J.: Princeton University Press, 1967).
15. Hindess, *The Use of Official Statistics in Sociology, op. cit.*, p. 12.
16. *Ibid.*, p. 26.
17. *Ibid.*, p. 41.
18. *Ibid.*, p. 44.
19. *Ibid.*, p. 12.
20. *Ibid.*, p. 36.

21. A. V. Cicourel, *Method and Measurement in Sociology* (New York: The Free Press, 1964).

22. L. Guralnick and C. B. Nam, "Census-NOVS Study of Death Certificates Matched to Census Records," *The Milbank Memorial Fund Quarterly* (April 1959) **36**, 144-153; D. P. Phillips and K. A. Feldman, "A Dip in Deaths Before Ceremonial Occasions: Some New Relationships between Social Integration and Mortality," *American Sociological Review* (December 1973) **38**, 678-696; D. P. Phillips, "An Empirical Study of the Influence of Bias on Suicide Rates: 1. The Case of Occupational Suicide" (unpublished manuscript), 1974.

23. Hindess, *The Use of Official Statistics in Sociology, op. cit.,* p. 43.

24. A. V. Cicourel, "Elicitation as a Problem of Discourse," in H. von Ulrich Ammon, N. Dittmar, and K. J. Mattheier (editors), *Sociolinguistics: An International Handbook of the Science of Language and Society* (Berlin: Walter DeGruyter, 1988); "The Interpenetration of Communicative Contexts: Examples from Medical Encounters," in A. Duranti and C. Goodwin (editors), *Rethinking Context: Language as an Interactive Phenomenon* (Cambridge: Cambridge University Press, 1992); "Cognitive and Organizational Aspects of Medical Diagnostic Reasoning," *Discourse Processes* (1987) **10**; "The Reproduction of Objective Knowledge: Common Sense Reasoning in Medical Decision Making," in G. Bohme and N. Stehr (editors), *The Knowledge Society* (Dordrecht, Holland: D. Reidel, 1986).

PREFACE

This book and a subsequent volume on fertility and family organization in Argentina stem from my earlier work: *Method and Measurement in Sociology*. In the present volume, as in the method book, I have tried to show the relevance of methodological issues to different theoretical problems and to substantive areas in sociology.

My primary interest, however, has not been in showing how much better we can understand commonly accepted substantive areas in sociology. I am concerned with the development of methods (which I view as basic to theory construction) for particular theoretical issues, while making both the researcher's and the actor's rules of procedure problematic elements in all research. How do both the researcher and the actor come to know, understand, predict, or categorize an environment of objects and consequently arrive at findings or socially distributed knowledge? The researcher's activities must be as much an object of study as the actor's ways of "knowing" or "explaining" his environment (Chapter 1). A primary assumption of my work has been that sociological research problems have been influenced too much by everyday social problems such as, for example, crime, delinquency, over-crowded slums, and political reform (Chapter 2). Basic questions about how social order (or concerted social action) is possible need not be limited by the traditional views that a common value system and network of norms provide consensus in society, and that the problems that sociologists must focus upon stem from special-interest groups, inadequate pursuit and realization of basic values, and the implementation of accepted norms. (This problem is discussed in some detail in my forthcoming book on fertility and family organization in Argentina.)

I have not ignored conventional sociological problem-oriented research. I have chosen to give equal (if not more) attention to how the "problem" is generated by the everyday activities of professionals and laymen in contact with juveniles, without denying the concern of sociologists, professionals in law enforcement and corrections, and laymen interested in "law and order" regarding what are taken to be the "facts" of rising delinquency rates and its demoralizing and disorganizing influence on the socialization of youth and the "future" of the United States. The decision-making activities that produce the social problem called delinquency (and the socially organized procedures that provide for judicial outcomes) are important because they highlight fundamental processes of how social order is possible. This book (hopefully) is one of a series of progress reports on basic issues in social organization; that is, it is an attempt to recast traditional problems so that they will illuminate the foundations of social order or the structure of social interaction. Subsequent volumes will move progressively away from conventionally defined social problem areas. My initial choices of substantive areas such as delinquency, fertility, and family organization were prompted by an interest in providing the reader with familiar subject matter for reexamining basic issues. All studies of social problems presuppose solutions or theories about how communication is possible (including communication among lower animals), about how social meanings are generated and "understood" thereby permitting further inference and action, and about how language and rules develop—in short, how social organization is generated, sustained, and altered over time. In this volume I barely touch upon the concepts that would help illuminate basic issues of how social order is possible, but my intention is to initiate, at least, a modest beginning.

This study required several years of field work. Field work means bothering many people and enlisting their cooperation. I was fortunate in obtaining the help of two men—Chief Probation Officers in "County A" and "County B" —who made possible access to probation materials and the daily activities of Probation Officers. Without the help of these two men the study could not have started. One of them helped me become a Probation Officer without pay so that access would be facilitated. Each one gave me the benefit of his years of experience, the help of his entire staff, and an introduction to the Police Chief of his "City." There are many Probation Officers, Juvenile Hall supervisors, and assistants that I also would like to thank (but, again, anonymously). Their cooperation was always friendly and generous.

My contacts with the police were not always as fortunate. Access always depended upon continual and renewed personal contacts with individual officers despite official approval. Several officers in City A and three in City B made the "police" portion of this study possible. More than three years was required for certain kinds of information from one police department, and my relationships with officers did not seem to be "close" until the final months of the study. Nevertheless, the help was indispensable for the completion of this book.

In addition to my acknowledgments of the help I received from the probation and police authorities (whose names remain undisclosed) in City A and City B, I must stress the fact that they agreed to allow me access to materials (access that was sometimes rather intimate), knowing full well that I had negative observations to make about their work, despite my feeling that there were very few practices motivated by direct malicious interests. I am sure that I have offended one or more of these people who were so important in my being able to do the research, and I apologize here for any possible misunderstandings of my intentions. All names and places are fictitious and I made every attempt to conceal information that inadvertently would reveal the possible identity of the persons involved.

The research reported here initially began as a small pilot project supported by the Small Grants Section of the Ford Foundation's Youth Development Program. I began by studying probation records in City A (see Chapter 2). As this pilot study was drawing to a close, I was enabled to continue the work as one of the group of researchers participating in the Delinquency Studies Program of the Center for the Study of Law and Society, University of California, Berkeley. This program was supported by a grant from the Office of Juvenile Delinquency and Youth Development, Welfare Administration, U.S. Department of Health, Education and Welfare in cooperation with the President's Committee on Juvenile Delinquency and Youth Crime, under Public Law 87-274. As a member of the Delinquency Studies Program group, I was provided with research assistance and one semester of half-time teaching, culminating in a year at Berkeley where most of my time could be devoted to preparing the present manuscript. This work is, therefore, one of the continuing series of research monographs sponsored by the Center for the Study of Law and Society.

Throughout the study I was fortunate in being able to discuss my work with a number of individuals who are knowledgeable about the substantive and theoretical areas covered in the book. I thank Donald Cressey, John Kitsuse, Edmin Lemert, David Matza, Sheldon Messinger, Lloyd Ohlin, Philip Selznick, and Carl Werthman. I am particularly grateful for the helpful comments on an earlier version of Chapter 1 by Peter McHugh and Fritz Sack, the continual accessibility and very useful discussions of Sheldon Messinger, and the advice of William Chambliss, John Kitsuse, and Roy Turner on reorganizing the first draft of the manuscript.

A number of students helped me obtain the data given in Chapter 3. It is a pleasure to thank Laura Ferguson Appleton, Jennie Barrett, William Blischke, Robert Heeron, and Linda Spratt. William and Sharon Blischke and Tim Lehman performed the difficult coding operations, and William Blischke carried out the computer runs and assembled the initial cross-tabulations. William Blischke was especially helpful throughout the study because he not only did all work assigned to him exceptionally well but also had continual contact with the data throughout the study, and was therefore able to raise critical questions about their relevance. Finally, I am grateful to Mary Alden, Lydian Clapp, Paula Marshall, and Gloria Neal for excellent typing services.

AARON V. CICOUREL

Santa Barbara, California

Chapter 1

PRELIMINARY ISSUES OF THEORY AND METHOD

In studying the agencies of social control in a "community"—empowered with the authority to prevent disorder and restrain or punish—I am able to provide an empirical setting for raising basic issues by focusing on how juveniles are labeled "delinquent." The present study of juvenile justice stems from general interests in a theory of social organization. My purpose is to go beyond agencies of social control (such as the school, the police, probation services, and the juvenile court) and ask how any set of activities we often label "bureaucratic"—punishment or otherwise—routinely processes persons. I assume all socially organized activites labeled "complex" or "bureaucratic" are bounded in similar ways: General procedural rules are laid down for members, and members develop and employ their own theories, recipes, and shortcuts for meeting general requirements acceptable to themselves and tacitly or explicitly acceptable to other members acting as "supervisors" or some form of external control. Case studies, therefore, should be designed to reveal invariant properties of the social arrangements observed and interpreted. To suggest there are invariant properties discernible in case studies means the researcher must search for and demonstrate the generalizability of his findings as applied to all forms of social organization.

I have, of course, not avoided but have pointedly discussed the theoretical and empirical problems studied under the labels of delinquency, crime, justice, broken homes, social class, and the like, since they can be primarily utilized to portray basic elements of social organization in general bureaucratic processing.

Because the most prominent theories of deviance (and, for the present purposes, delinquency) have stemmed from writers with a structural-functional perspective,[1] this chapter outlines an alternate perspective and critically discusses theoretical and methodological positions structural-functionalists utilize for recommending their work. The theoretical and methodological

1

issues are difficult to separate but include (1) the sociologist's depiction of how the actor makes sense of an environment of objects so that his (the actor's) inferences and action produce the activities the sociologist labels "social structures," and (2) the alternative ways in which sociologists achieve solutions to problems of objectification and verification when studying social organization. The theoretical and substantive issues discussed throughout the remainder of the book presume a knowledge of these two problems.

Objectification and Verification

I use the term objectification to denote the observer's *and* the actor's attempts to convince the reader (or listener) of the credibility of the properties or elements being attended and labeled "data" for purposes of making inferences and taking further action. To objectify some event or object or "mood," therefore, is to convince someone that sufficient grounds exist or existed for making specifiable inferences about "what happened." The basic question becomes, therefore: How does the subject and the observer preserve or seek to preserve the environment of objects he or others attended or presumably attended and used to generate something called "data?" Notice how the problem of verification—interpreting the materials labeled data as supporting a prior or *ad hoc* proposition about why and how something happened or is constituted according to specifiable procedural rules—may appear to be trivial if the problem of objectification is simplified by labeling the results of a questionnaire (the "answers") or the tables produced by the Census Bureau as objectified data. Throughout this book I seek support for the assertion that most sociologists, and particularly structural-functionalists, are glossing over the core of sociological research by utilizing oversimplified procedures for objectifying the collection of materials labeled "data," and verifying propositions called hypotheses. If we agree to accept census materials as adequate descriptions of specifiable phenomena, then the problem of verification is trivial even if there are competing theories as to the meaning of the results. But if we assume (for purposes of discussion) that our "best" efforts at objectification consist in the use of multiple video tapes of the same environment of objects over time to depict or "bottle" adequately the phenomena under study, then the problem of verification becomes complicated. The complication arises because we must attend to the problem of how the observer (subject or researcher) utilizes tacit knowledge (background information or what anyone "knows") in identifying and selecting materials from the video tapes, and recommending interpretations (as straight descriptions or coded shorthand accounts) of "what happened." Three or more video tapes, presumably of the same environment of objects, do not resolve the problem of objectification. There would be difficulties in presenting a convincing argument to a reader who has access to the video tapes while he reads the researcher's account of what happened. What sorts of agreements must both the researcher and the reader achieve as conditions for deciding the various meanings being rendered? Assuming both the researcher and the reader are members of the same society, it might be easy to agree on the meaning of physical items like chairs and tables, but I am interested in how we assign unequivocal meaning to the juvenile's tone of voice when a police officer or probation officer or judge labels such behavior "in defiance of authority" or an indication of a "bad attitude." Other problems include agreement on the meaning of gestures and dress, physical posturing, linguistic expressions suggesting double meanings, jokes, anxiety, and the like. The complications are enormous. I raise them in connection with video tapes to underscore their significance when the reader must rely on accounts far more complicated; when he seeks to understand how a set of questionnaire items impinged on a set of respondents, how each respondent interpreted each question, depending on what kinds of tacit knowledge vis-à-vis what kinds of personal experiences and situational contexts or abstract imagined contexts not revealed by the fixed-choice response categories provided. Also, in the same or a different situation where the descriptions, rendered by a researcher of action scenes he witnessed and now portrays for the reader, must be taken as "clear" because of the authority of the researcher. The problem is equally complicated when the researcher utilizes written reports by members of a complex organization and must determine the relevance of attributions such as social class, social character, mental illness, intelligence, and the like, made by members of the organization in the routine course of their daily activities. Unless the respondent's and researcher's decoding and encoding procedures are basic elements of the research enterprise, we cannot make sense of either the phenomena being studied or the materials labeled "findings."

Tacit Knowledge and Everyday Activities

I have stressed the problems of objectification and verification because sociologists seldom concern themselves with the properties of everyday social life, but take for granted the properties of daily life built into their identification and study of various collections of activities they label "social problems," or the "dynamics" of "social systems," or the "variables" crucial to the maintaining of a "system of social stratification." Both the "natural" and "laboratory" events studied by the sociologist are not established by asking first what a "natural order" is like, and then what would it take to generate activities members of the society would label as "unnatural" or "natural." Instead, the problems taken as points of departure are assumed to be "obvious" instances of *the* "real world." Any sociologist, insisting that the study of social order and disorder, society, or community, must begin with an examination of the properties of routine practical activities in everyday life, is not likely to meet the approval of colleagues who have already decided what the "real world" is all about, and they have been studying "it" for a long time. The following quotation from Charles C. Fries, a linguist recommending linguistic innovations to conventional grammarians, has a similar implication:

> The point of view in this discussion is descriptive, not normative or legislative. The reader will find here, *not* how certain teachers or textbook writers or "authorities" think native speakers of English ought to use the language, but how certain native speakers actually do use it in natural, practical conversations carrying on the various activities of a community.
>
> The scientific linguist doesn't attempt to investigate the creation of great literature; he has devoted himself to the difficult task of discovering and describing the intricate and complicated mechanisms which the language actually uses in fulfilling its communicative function and which the literary artist also must take as basic in his expression.
>
> As a general principle I would insist that, in linguistic study and analysis, any use of meaning is unscientific whenever the fact of our knowing the meaning leads us to stop short of finding the precise formal signals that operate to convey that meaning.[2]

The central issue succinctly raised by Fries is natural social interaction, and how natural occurrences provide us with the raw material from which we infer or impute the existence of structure or patterning to everyday life. The use of English by native speakers in natural practical conversations provides the linguist with a basis for comparing formal structure with usage of communication in a community and also provides the sociologist with materials from which he can infer and construct descriptions of social structure. The crucial issue is how the observer objectifies the raw material he observes so that others can arrive at similar inferences. The structural-functionalists short-circuit the issue by the use of an unexplicated vocabulary that recommends structure by fiat; they take for granted the existence of activities they describe formally and presume no further explanation is necessary as to how they come to know their existence.[3] The abstract vocabulary displaces both the objectification and description of the day-to-day social interaction from which inferences about social structures are made. The issue is sometimes resolved by the use of impressionistic accounts requiring the indulgence of the reader in what "any sophisticated social scientist knows" to be true about the way organizations operate, or by the use of "indicators" (for instance, census materials, attitude scales, rates) presumed to stand for a "known" behavioral environment of objects and events. But in both cases (impressionistic observation couched in elegant language about things that "anyone knows," or "indicators" based upon procedural "leaps" from census materials or surveys) the correspondence between what is claimed as observed and the language used to describe objects and events is never clear to the reader nor available for independent verification. The accounts are always truncated expressions the reader must fill in to make sense of presumed intended meanings. The standard response to this issue is that it is impossible to present the reader with such detail. This answer presupposes that details of decoding and encoding descriptions and questionnaires are technical problems. In this book I want to demonstrate the problem is not simply one of better methods or a better technology. It is a problem requiring a more elegant theoretical apparatus for making sense of what we have and are doing methodologically, and for showing how substantive studies change accordingly.[4]

The referents for our observations and inferences provide the reader with grounds for evaluating what we report as findings. Field research (which includes films of natural occurrences where not only linguistic features of conversations are preserved but also paralinguistic elements such as voice intonation, physical gestures or general body motion, and ecological setting and physical distances between participants) at least demands an explicit theoretical apparatus from researchers. But even work using verbatim transcripts seems to question unequivocally the credibility of impressionistic accounts, as well as the significance of information based upon attitudinal questionnaires about hypothetical social interaction divorced from the contingencies of actual encounters between actors. Attitudinal accounts, such as structural descriptions by fiat, idealize the actor's environment of objects, so that *how* the observer decides the behavioral properties and meaning structures (assumed to be present to infer that the "goals," "values," or "rules" of the organization are being achieved, violated, or changed) remains obscured by the procedures employed. Verifiability is truncated. Recommending the same procedures when they are truncated does not guarantee the "same" findings, but merely suggests a practical solution to an obscure problem. How the observer decides what he "knows" and "observes"—much less how the actor accomplishes the same tasks—is not a variable feature of conducting and reporting conventional sociological research. Recent trends in psycholinguistics, componential analysis or ethnoscience or ethnographic semantics, the ethnography of communication, the analysis of conversation, and ethnomethodological studies have sought to provide rules for moving from the actor's experience to verbal and nonverbal communication, and from an act or event or sequence of events to a description of activities that can be examined independently by other researchers.[5]

But recent work in psycholinguistics and the several anthropological approaches to the study and use of language for ethnographic work seldom examine a prior problem: How are natural sequences of descriptive accounts recognized as meaningful by members of a group or collectivity? How do members decide that particular accounts (in specifiable sequential form) are "adequate" for understanding what is being communicated, so that a response, also taken as "adequate," is forthcoming? How can we show certain conversations reveal agreements between speakers about particular issues, even though there is no manifest evidence for such agreements in the actual utterances being analyzed? Or that antinomies establish quite a different meaning from the immediate apparent semantic presentation? (Notice that the observer's view is always dependent upon the actor's conception of objects and events even though an outside model is invoked.)

Our task is similar to that of constructing a computer that would reduce the information obtainable by means of the perspectives of differently situated video tapes, so that the information (or parts of it) could be retrieved while maintaining intact the fidelity of the original natural occurrence. Sacks[6] speaks of this problem as one of constructing an apparatus capable of producing conversational sequences that could be recognized by members of the society as "correct" or "appropriate" utterances of known objects and events. Such an apparatus would also analyze various categories members of the society use in everyday descriptive accounts. The researcher is interested in how such categories, as used by members in specifiable sequences, signify events and allow members to recognize "what happened." The analysis of conversations within a paralinguistic context (1) makes explicit the problem of objectification, and (2) provides a basis for both researcher and reader to compare the inferences made without having merely to urge the reader that the observer's remarks are to be taken on faith as accurate portrayals of "what happened."

A vital assumption of the above discussion is that the syntactic information, contained in a descriptive account by a member of a tribe or society, is not adequate for understanding how members generate or transform accounts into a meaningful interpretation of what is happening or "what happened." Nor, therefore, can the researcher merely content himself with the syntactic information assumed to be inherent in the account, regardless of its form (that is, as a one-word utterance or a lengthy text). Any and all information imputed or extracted from members' descriptive accounts requires the utilization and assumes the existence of "background expectancies"[7] or tacit knowledge.

Chomsky and Halle assert that for a grammar to be descriptively adequate, it must account for "the tacit knowledge (linguistic intuition) of the native speaker."[8]

Without reference to this tacit knowledge there is no such subject as descriptive linguistics. There is nothing for its descriptive statements to be right or wrong about. Taxonomic linguistics has been unhappy with this state of affairs. Since Bloomfield conferred upon linguistics the first place among the social sciences for having freed itself of the yoke of the "elusive spiritistic-teleologic words of our tribal speech" (Bloomfield, 1927), it has been thought undignified to pay attention to such a "mentalistic horror" as linguistic intuition. Nevertheless, tacit knowledge of the speaker's language is at every stage and every point precisely what the linguist is dealing with. No one, surely, is content simply to rearrange the data in a corpus. Every linguistic description attempts, at least, to extract "patterns" or "regularities" from a corpus, or to abstract from it principles that will apply to other linguistic material as well. But statements of "patterns," "regularities," and "underlying principles" go beyond the data. They are based on some assumption about the nature of linguistic patterns or regularities. Without such assumptions (which, unfortunately, are rarely made explicit), innumerable "patterns" and "regularities" can be found in any data, all mutually conflicting, and most of them, for some reason, quite ridiculous. All linguistic work is, obviously, guided by certain assumptions about the nature of linguistic structure and linguistic patterns; and such assumptions, which are the heart of linguistic theory, can be tested for adequacy in only one way, namely, by determining whether the descriptions to which they lead are in accord with tacit knowledge concerning the language. Whatever may have been said in methodological discussions, this ultimate reference to the speaker's tacit knowledge of his language is quite apparent in all actual linguistic work.[9]

The remarks by Chomsky and Halle underscore the necessity of building into one's theory of how members understand and communicate knowledge and experience about any environment of objects the existence of "tacit knowledge" about what is intended by the appearances, and how the appearances are described, both by the actors (or native speakers) and the observer. What is presumed to be "understood" or "left unstated" by the actor or observer can be made observable by textual or experimental analysis or manipulation.[10] Notice, therefore, how the problems of objectification and verification cannot be resolved by merely claiming to have "bottled" all of the relevant information by the use of films and tape recordings. Background expectancies (tacit knowledge) are integral to any kind of analyses and include much more than implied by Chomsky and Halle.

The member of the society uses background expectancies as a scheme of interpretation. In their terms, actual appearances are for him recognizable and intelligible as the appearances of familiar events. Demonstrably he is responsive to this background. At the same time he is at a loss to tell us what specifically the expectancies consist of. When we ask him about them he has little or nothing to say. . . . The anticipation that persons *will* understand, the occasionality of expressions, the specific vagueness of references, the retrospective-prospective sense of a present occurrence, waiting for something later in order to see what was meant before, are sanctioned properties of common discourse. They furnish a background of seen but unnoticed features of common discourse whereby actual utterances are recognized as events of common, reasonable, understandable, plain talk.[11]

The key element of Garfinkel's remarks is the insistence that all of the properties making up the concept background expectancies "are sanctioned properties of common discourse." Members not only routinely assume the properties outlined, but demand their presence and use by others. Thus, what members and researchers label "data" and "findings" can only be understood by reference to the background expectancies.

But the above discussion of objectification and verification, as part of the problem of depicting how the actor makes sense of an environment of objects so that his inferences and action produce the activities we label "the social structures," is resolved by sociologists routinely in other ways. Some minimal discussion of the alternate ways is necessary if the remainder of the book is to be meaningful.

Solutions to Objectification and Verification

Let me characterize loosely the ways in which sociologists actually resolve the problem of objectification-verification by reference to the types of research strategies they employ routinely in the course of obtaining and recommending their findings to others. At the risk of violating particular researchers' mixed strategies, I shall describe the "solutions" in ideal typical terms as follows:

	Macro Theories	Micro Theories
Impressionistic Data	A	C
"Hard" Data	B	D

A. Research in this category usually involves familiarity with the society being described via participant observation as a lay member or researcher, and the use of documents, diaries, depth interviews, and similar media. The problem of verification is not viewed as an issue, because how the actor and observer understand their environments is not made an issue and, therefore, the factual or objective character of the material is not problematic. When material is questioned, the researcher provides various *ad hoc* and illustrative reasons for believing or disbelieving different parts of the data.

This group of researchers is seldom interested in making an issue out of the factual character of their data, but is especially concerned with treating the data as a vehicle for demonstrating the relevance of their theoretical and substantive interests. Those doing this kind of work are not equivalent, but their work does exhibit an absence of clear statements about the problem of verification, suggesting the implicit assumption that extensive discussion is not warranted, the material presented as data being sufficiently obvious to preclude elaboration of the problem. The details of day-to-day participation are not reported. The credibility of the description is to be found, instead, in the depth of the theoretical and substantive conclusions, not in the "richness" of the documents or participation with which depictions are offered. Quotations from documents or respondents are used as illustrative material for the deeper theoretical and substantive conclusions. The environment of objects, which is part of the actor's visual field and his background expectancies, is not taken to be an integral feature of the actor's point of view; his oral or written remarks are interpreted by the researcher under the assumption that the language used carries *prima facie* meanings, or that they can be explained by reference to *ad hoc* "underlying patterns." The descriptive accounts are merely illustrative of the researcher's interpretation of the action scene and not the source of his interpretation as part of some clear correspondence to an explicit model of the actor. It is the researcher's implicit model of what is going on that is critical, for he supplies the interpretive schema by a vocabulary that assumes a correspondence between his understanding and the actor's understanding of the same action scene. The actor's and the researcher's meaning structures are treated as if they are the same; it is only the researcher's conceptual framework for making sense of them that differs in that it seeks a "deeper" analysis of the meaning of the activities of the group, organization, or society.

The analysis is a constructed superstructure that represents the researcher's attempt to characterize a network of social relationships with a vocabulary presumed to be a clear-cut depiction of the organization's activities and purposes. The verification of what is observed or inferred is recommended without reference to the interpretation of the actor or the researcher of each other's environment of objects according to their separate and joint common sense and scientific rules of procedure. The reader is invited to indulge in the adequacy of the rendered interpretations without explicit recourse to the steps that were followed in deciding the relevance of the materials quoted or observed by both actor and observer. But adequacy here means what "sense the interpretation makes," given some general concepts in conjunction with the illustrative quotations. The conceptual analysis leads to inferences of the underlying structure of "things" that the illustrative materials themselves can only suggest or reveal indirectly. The *post hoc* "underlying patterns" constitute the social reality of interest to the researcher, not the illustrative materials. The illustrative materials, in fact, can be "misleading" because they seldom reveal much about the underlying patterns unless one is armed with the *implicit* conceptual framework of the researcher.[12] The ways in which both actor and observer attach social significance to their visual field and their experiences in actual encounters are not considered to be empirically problematic, much less critical to an understanding of how each accomplishes the task, assigns meanings to events, or resolves the problem of verification. The macro theorist's structural analysis is not concerned with the "logic-in-use" of "act meaning," but the "reconstructed logic" of the "action meaning."[13] The concern with action meaning is an attempt to impute *post hoc* motives to the actor by the sociologist's conceptual constructions, and not how the actor routinely decides "what happened" or attaches meaning to objects and events in the course of their occurrence.

The verification procedures of the impressionistic structural sociologist are to be found in the elegance with which he tells his story, its "convincing" character, and how well it seems to fit a "reasonable" explanation of what happened. Thus it takes another expert such as the literary critic, the drama critic, or someone who is also familiar with the "inside" view of the events in question, to support (and, therefore, "verify") the adequacy of the account given.

B. The macro theorist who seeks "hard" data (for example, census materials, vital statistics, surveys) shares the impressionistic theorist's disregard for the difference between how actors' logic-in-use generates actual behavior while his reconstructed logic is used to speculate about past and future action and attitudes. How the actor makes sense of his environment and constructs courses of action over time are not issues of verification that concern the quantitative-oriented macro theorist, except as they are squeezed into the asserted objectivity of census materials and vital statistics (after the appropriate qualifications about sampling problems, poor reporting, and assorted errors).[14] In the case of surveys, the procedures are assumed to depict the courses of action the actor would take or has taken according to the hypothetical or factual type of questions posed. There is seldom any way of independently verifying the extent to which the actor in fact performed as indicated by him, or that he would perform in the stated way at some future date. How the actor interprets the stimulus question, or the possibility that the respondent's answer was motivated by the question and disengaged from his past experiences and daily activities, and thus generated "data" relevant only to the immediate questionnaire and situation, are not matters that are more than technically problematic for this group. The problem of verification revolves around setting up a correspondence between demographic categories or precoded questions, the tables that emerge, and the general ideas that led to the formulation of the questionnaire. The documentary method is very much in evidence because the general ideas provide the rationale for the formulation of particular questions with alternative responses and, depending upon how the responses become coded and tabulated after the fact, the general ideas are then elaborated. The general macro ideas relate the actor's attitudes as elicited by fixed-choice questionnaire items to the researcher's conception of societal values and norms. The researcher moves from general conceptions about values, norms, institutions, and similar categories, to individual expressions that are operationally tapped by the attitude questions, and then back to the general conceptions. The macro notion of public consensus or public opinion provides the theoretical rationale for plumbing the depths of community sentiment. The basic assumptions of survey solutions to the problem of verification are as follows: The questions posed to the respondent are inherently meaningful to any cross section of the population; the responses are responses to the same stimuli, that is, any single item is understood identically by all respondents; the respondent's conception of the stimuli is identical to that of the researcher, as the latter intended the construction of the questions; and the researcher's coding of the responses faithfully reflect the respondent's intentions. While admitting that the survey "skims" the manifest surface of the actor's attitudes, it is the analysis of response patterns at the level of latent structures that provides this point of view with the presumed "real" meaning of the actor's responses. The actor's perspective is revealed by way of the constructions (questionnaire items) of the researcher, but we have no way of knowing how the actor accomplishes his answers, what is seen as relevant or meaningful in the stimuli presented to him, or what he would do in actual social interaction.[15] Pretesting may eliminate gross misusage of terms, but does not avoid the problem of assuming that because the respondent *was able* somehow to answer all questions "successfully" (that is, the appropriate spaces were filled), the various meaning structures employed by some sample of respondents correspond identically (with some presumed minor margin of error) to the intended meanings of the researcher. The tacit knowledge or background expectancies invoked during the course of interaction (logic-in-use) cannot be equated to the respondent's use of such expectancies when the questionnaire items are disengaged from the action scenes and the responses are constructed imaginatively. Whereas the actor's stock of knowledge is fundamental to his conception of social reality and is employed *in the course of interaction* to make sanctioned sense of the immediate social scene (including written material), the structural-functional notion of underlying pattern refers to the researcher's unexplicated construction of some kind of deep level of organization in the actor's social character, viewed as an internalized and stable property or set of properties.[16]

C. The group I shall call processual theorists is usually more systematic in its participant observation and reporting of the day-to-day activities of the groups or organizations they study. They often believe the basic social processes of everyday life cannot be quantified directly without losing the essential features of the interaction, and that the ongoing features of social interaction cannot be captured at more abstract levels of analysis, for instance, the structure of the entire society. Great stress is placed upon the unfolding and unpredictable character of social interaction, although their research reveals many apparent regularities in the way in which the fleeting character of process unfolds. Considerable attention is given to the problems of entering and leaving the research setting and maintaining appropriate social relationships with members.[17] In contrast to the structural theorists, the processual theorists are not interested in the analysis of documents as much as in observing the actual encounters over time of the members of the groups or organizations they study. There is a lack of systematic theorizing, but there is preoccupation with the details of "what happens" among the processual theorists. They are concerned with the actor's point of view (and attempt to reveal it by quoting the respondent) and with preserving the natural setting of the social scene. But there is no conceptual distinction given between the actor's point of view, his vocabulary, how he assigns meaning to his environment, and the observer's procedural rules for accomplishing his research and analysis of these matters. As with the structural theorist, there is no interest in asking what the appropriate rules are for explaining the "normal" sequencing of human activities, so that each participant recognizes each other's remarks as "adequate" indications of meaningful action. Or in asking what are the categories of language to which actors typically attend in assigning social meanings to each other's intentions and those of others. The systematic student of social process seems overly concerned with the danger of reifying his observations and inferences by "too much" abstract theorizing and prefers to let his descriptions and questions "speak for themselves." Thus the problems of objectification and verification are handled by adopting what appears to be a very straightforward methodology. This methodology consists of seeking entrance to a group or organization by means of explicit explanation to a few members or by presumably natural circumstances so that this presence can be accounted for on independent grounds. In either case, the object of the study is to become familiar with the group or organization from the "inside" in order to become conversant with daily activities in much the same way as actual members of the group or organization. The problem of verification consists in making the reader feel he is a witness to the inner workings of the group or organization because of the particular access provided by detailed description and revealing quotations. There have been allusions to a desire for a kind of natural history of the research and the observer's participation, but such a procedure has not been clarified in the literature, though its approximation has been stated as a goal.[18] While some critics of this strategy question the representativeness of the procedure, few complain about the extent to which we can take for granted the presumably convincing character of the accounts. A problem for proponents of this viewpoint, therefore, is how to make the information that is available to the researcher accessible to the reader so that we have some way of disentangling the actor's perspective and observer's point of view from an interpretation that appears to fuse them both. The environments of both the actor and the observer are described in terms which assume both are obvious to the reader, and that both make sense of their social worlds in the same way. The problem of verification is resolved by seeking to convince the reader he has been privileged to witness an exposure that preserves the actor's daily existence by virtue of the observer's special vantage point in penetrating the routine and esoteric activities of the group or organization.

D. Processual theorists, seeking quantitative data, insist they seek the actor's point of view, but rely primarily upon survey questionnaires or small-group experiments. In neither case is it clear how the actor decides upon courses of action, nor is there concern with the behavioral environment of the actor when the researcher asks how the actor decides what alternatives are perceived and interpreted. Objectification and verification are resolved in the one case by the use of questionnaire items seeking to elicit the actor's choices from alternatives the researcher has provided him. The researcher's construction of the questionnaire items is assumed to correspond to the actor's interpretation of his environment, so that the language employed is considered to have the same meanings for all respondents. The actor's objectification and verification procedures are not at issue, but what is assumed to be important is the dynamics of the role-taking of social interaction. The meaning of the sequences and content perceived by the actor is assumed to be "obvious" to both the actor and the observer. The observer's task is to use the questionnaire items to measure the substantive outcomes of a hypothetical role-taking sequence. The issue is not so much what role-taking is, or how we objectify its properties, but given a "reasonable" account of what different writers seem to agree upon is role-taking, the questionnaire items provide an operationally "convincing" solution by fiat. The fiat is in the unknown ways in which the actor completes the instrument; the researcher accepts the completion without making the subject's actions problematic. For the researcher, the fact that the subject fills them out is taken to mean the respondent's thinking about content follows theoretical views of role-taking, and the structure of the items is "correct" because the correspondence is thus documented by the very act of completing the instrument. The small-group researchers, however, seek experimentally created situations that attempt to simulate actual occurrences or basic properties of social interaction. In small-group research when participants are supplied with instructions for the task or simulation that is to occur (and the observations made by the researcher or judges determine the realization of some previously stated objective, or a "realistic" task is devised and then incongruities introduced to disrupt the participants' expectations), reliance upon the actor's verbal reports or physical movements are not viewed as problematic. Quantitatively oriented processual theorists seek objectification by eliminating actors' "subjective" reports in favor of his "objective" responses to a machine, a paper and pencil questionnaire, a task described by the experimenter, or meter readings of machines that the subjects manipulate "objectively." The actor, as a direct source of information on how he perceives, learns, and reasons[19] during the course of social interaction, is rejected, while every attempt is made to objectify the actor's actions by providing him with "objective" instructions on how to conduct himself, during which time the experimenter faithfully records the "objective" products of the action. In seeking act meaning or the actor's logic-in-use, the experimenter seeks to eliminate the actor's "subjective" accounts, substituting the observer's or the machine's accounts. "Confusion," "rationality," and "affect" (substantive meanings) are all supplied by the researcher after examining the "objective" data; the reader is not exposed to the actor's environment of objects as opposed to the observer's environment, much less how both arrived at their respective conclusions about "what happened." The experimenter's accounts of the action scene are no more "objective" than the field researcher's, inasmuch as both rely upon accounts the reader must accept as faithful descriptions of the action scenes. The experimenter claims an edge, however, because his experiments presumably can be replicated. But in sociology, such experiments remain less convincing than the field researcher's descriptions because most of the laboratory-created settings seem far removed from anything the reader can identify with, in spite of the so-called "objective" findings. The simple fact is that the experimenter cannot objectify even his laboratory setup for the reader, so that the latter has access to the same data available to the researcher at the time of the experiment. The experimenter must urge the reader to accept his account of "what happened" or "what it was all about." The language used in the experiment does not carry with it any necessary "objective" character, any more so than that of the field researcher. The quantitative processual theorists have sacrificed intuitive convincement for contrived "hardness."

An Alternate Perspective

In criticizing macro and micro theories and their solutions to the problems of objectification and verification, I stress an alternate view that assumes (1) that when we use one or more of the strategies outlined above (as I have done throughout this study), we must view the strategy as an object of inquiry in order to become aware of its limitations and its implicit reliance upon the background expectancies, and (2) the social structures sociologists seek to understand presuppose a knowledge of the background expectancies members of a society must utilize as a scheme of interpretation for making an environment of objects recognizable and intelligible. The problems of objectification and verification cannot be resolved by appeals to technical skills in capturing or "bottling" the phenomena invoked as observational sources of data. The sociologist must come to grips with the problem of making the background expectancies visible[20] to the reader when describing or reporting the results of his investigations if the shortcomings of sociological research are to be overcome.

In subsequent chapters, I present and interpret materials on the social organization of juvenile justice by using verbatim conversations or reports whenever possible. I assume the critical task of the researcher is to show the reader how the research materials are always understood by reference to unstated and seen (but unnoticed) background expectancies both members *and* observers *always* employ to recognize and to understand their activities.

The materials making up the data of the present study consist of police and probation reports, conversations I observed and sometimes recorded, a few conversations recorded but not observed by me, and regular participant observation for over four years of two police and probation departments and juvenile court operations. The significance of background expectancies is continually underscored by reference to the following kinds of analyses: (1) the examination of verbatim materials to show how the researcher makes sense of the subject's remarks, while also invoking features of the action scenes or past scenes felt to be relevant to the subject and observer in deciding what is happening, or how some descriptive account by either the subject or researcher was reached; and (2) revealing unstated and the seen but unnoticed background expectancies included or left out as a particular case (a juvenile considered to be potentially or actually delinquent by the police and probation officials) is analyzed over time.

As a case is reviewed over time, from its initial exchanges between juvenile and police and probation officials to subsequent reports and interviews, I claim the object of interest (the juvenile and the descriptive accounts) are transformed so as to produce familiar scenes and depictions of juveniles, their families, juvenile activities, and the like, in order to prepare the object for definite evaluation and disposition. The transformation of the object, therefore, is always part of the manipulation of background expectancies in order to make the descriptive accounts of what happened convincing and justifiable vis-à-vis evaluations and dispositions. Oral and written descriptive accounts by police and probation officers standardize the business at hand so that activities falling under their domains of interest could be made meaningful to themselves and others. The selectivity of descriptive accounts, therefore, presume and utilize the unstated and the seen but unnoticed background expectancies to render social activities meaningful. In analyzing conversational and written materials, the researcher must commit himself to interpretive descriptions of the materials and not allow the data to "speak for themselves." The alternate perspective assumes that use of categories by members serve to depict their perception and interpretation of the social environment. Further, members of a group methodically employ categories for depicting their life circumstances and the grounds for their action.[21] The conversational and written materials must be used to show how particular interpretations were intended by the speaker or writer, forcing the researcher to relate the narrow or broad limits to the alternative interpretations permissible, given a specifiable contextual setting. By continual reference to the materials themselves (and the unstated, as well as the seen but unnoticed background expectancies imputed to members and assumed by the observer), the researcher specifies how the actors subscribe to interpretations typical of the categories employed and thereby achieve rational (for the actor) decisions. The categories provide both the actor and the researcher with a means for making sense of the other's communication, and these categories can be located in specifiable collections of activities presumed to be "known" to enable the observer to restrict the meanings intended. The reader can then decide for himself how the researcher goes about assigning meaning to data by reference to verbatim materials, and how there is necessary reliance upon unstated and seen but unnoticed background expectancies both members and researchers employ to make the action scenes visible or recognizable and intelligible.[22]

The police and probation officer (like many bureaucratic officials) are faced with the problem of transforming their conversations with juveniles and adults into oral and written reports in order to dramatize and justify their participation and decisions. How do their reports reflect the social scenes when read by others unfamiliar with the exchanges reported? How does the report stand as a depiction of objects and events not subject to review? Notice that the material is used as "evidence" for making decisions binding upon the actions of others, with consequences that are independent of a researcher's description of "what happened." In my analysis of such materials, I attempt to show that what is included provides the basis for various constructions of "what happened" by interested parties. In later chapters, I discuss how members perceive and interpret "authority relationships," accomplish decision-making activities, satisfy the observer's notion of "punitive supervision," achieve the behavioral features that come to be labeled as "conforming to rules that maintain organizational structure," and so forth.

The kinds of problems confronting the field researcher are similar to those encountered by students of dramatic arts. Consider the following quotation from a book initially published in 1931 and recently reissued:

> You cannot, in any case, transfer casual conversation to the stage. You may produce the effect of having done so, but that is quite another thing. You must—all else apart—set in order and condense. If there were no more matter and method in ten minutes' dramatic talk than in an hour's round the average luncheon table, no one would ever guess what the play was about and it would never be over. It may be that ten minutes' actual talk by a man to his lawyer at some crisis in his affairs, or an Ambassador's to a Minister with peace or war in balance, might make pretty good drama as it stood. But note what would make it so: the emotional tension produced by precedent events and a strict mental ordering of what must be said in the ten minutes if precious time was not to be wasted. Even then, give the dramatist such matter to make fully effective on the stage, and he will find redundancies to prune—leaving a few of them to suggest the redundancy of spontaneous talk—and in their place he will slyly add a little information about these precedent events. The man and the lawyer, the Ambassador and the Minister, each knows all about them and knows that the other knows, and they need not refer to them. But this new third party to the talk, the audience, knows nothing, and must be informed. Very slyly, though, the information must be slipped in, or all effect of spontaneity will be gone. And if so much dramatizing is still needed of what life has already dramatized, how much more will have to go to the converting of the slack, haphazard happenings of every day? Besides which, all dramatic talk, at pedestrian level or climax, must be tuned to concert pitch.[23]

The use of a dictionary for the analysis of written reports or documents assumes the researcher can legitimately impute the abstract or disengaged meanings of the dictionary to the text, thus suspending the relevance of meanings in their situational context. Many fictional works appear to seek explicitly a type of language that could be described as having dictionary relevance, particularly when it is the author's attempt to comment directly about the meaning of what is going on, while other parts of the same work may present dialogue that intends meanings to be understood in the context of the actual usage of language. But if we follow Granville-Barker's remarks, the dialogue of a literary work, as in the example of dramatic talk, cannot maintain the fidelity of spontaneous conversation. The researcher must identify the normative or idealized or formal features of literary works, organizational reports, and documents so as to compare them with the properties of spontaneous speech. The empirical problem is complicated by our inability to specify neatly "pure" spontaneous usage as opposed to "pure" normative, idealized, or formal language forms. But the analysis of casual conversations, as opposed to formal documents, reports, poetry, and the like, provide a defensible point of departure for studying forms of social organization, as well as providing a basis for measurement. The use of seemingly explicit categories by members suggests a kind of "matter-of-factness" to utterances or documents that permit "cut-off points" to social organization. The researcher's attempts at measurement require a theory of the construction of documents and the ways in which they reconstruct conversations. Thus, in analyzing conversations and reports, the researcher must approximate a "re-writing" of the dialogue or prose so that he can communicate the unstated and seen but unnoticed background expectancies for the reader. Such a procedure would enable the reader to understand how the participants and observer made sense of their environments as portrayed by the researcher.

NOTES

1. Cf. Robert K. Merton, *Social Theory and Social Structure*, revised (New York: The Free Press, 1957, Chapters 4 and 5) ; see also Merton's remarks in *New Perspectives for Research on Juvenile Delinquency*, H. Witmer and R. Kotinsky (editors), U.S. Government Printing Office, 1956; Albert K. Cohen, *Delinquent Boys* (New York: The Free Press, 1955) ; and Richard A. Cloward and Lloyd E. Ohlin, *Delinquency and Opportunity* (New York: The Free Press, 1960).
2. *The Structure of English* (New York and Burlingame: Harcourt, Brace and World, 1952), pp. 3 and 4, and footnote 6 on p. 8.
3. I am saying that both impressionistic and quantitatively oriented structural-functionalists *necessarily* require knowledge from *within*. The actor's perspective, his linguistic code, the meaning of his gestures, voice intonation, are all built-in features of the analysis, but not viewed as integral to securing, coding, and analyzing data.
4. Notice that the argument is not simply the possibility of objectifying the details of practical activities, but that such phenomena are integral to an understanding of what structural-functionalists mean by social organization or social structure. The presuppositions of common-sense reasoning are built into structural arguments, and any reading of their propositions necessarily requires that everyday meanings be supplied to render the statements meaningful. But the empirical and conceptual properties of such meanings remain unstated. Thus, studies that have followed a macro level of analysis, even when explicitly concerned with "dynamics," assume the observer's depiction of social organization stands outside of any participant's (or

observer's) interpretation of "what happened." Other studies are explicitly concerned with how participants' views from "within" inform the observer's analysis. For examples of studies from the "outside" see P. Selznick, *TVA and the Grass Roots* (Berkeley: University of California Press, 1949); Selznick, *The Organizational Weapon* (New York: McGraw-Hill, 1952); A. W. Gouldner, *Patterns of Industrial Bureaucracy* (Glencoe, Ill.: Free Press, 1954); P. M. Blau, *The Dynamics of Bureaucracy* (Chicago: University of Chicago Press, 1955); while an example of the "within" view can be found in Melville Dalton, *Men Who Manage* (New York: Wiley, 1959).

5. Cf. Ward H. Goodenough, "Componential Analysis and the Study of Meaning," *Language*, **32**, 195-215 (1956); Floyd G. Lounsbury, "A Semantic Analysis of the Pawnee Kinship Usage," *Language*, **32**, 158-194; Charles O. Frake, "The Ethnographic Study of Cognitive Systems," in T. Gladwin and W. C. Sturtevant (editors), *Anthropology and Human Behavior* (Washington, D.C.: The Anthropological Society of Washington, 1962), pp. 72-85; Dell H. Hymes, "The Ethnography of Speaking," *ibid.*, 13-53; Roger Brown, *Words and Things* (Glencoe, Ill.: Free Press, 1958); Ward H. Goodenough (editor), *Explorations in Cultural Anthropology* (New York: McGraw-Hill, 1964), pp. 25-55, 111-129, 167-177, 221-238; Harold Garfinkel, "Studies of the Routine Grounds of Everyday Actions," *Social Problems*, **11**, 225-250 (1964); Aaron V. Cicourel, *Method and Measurement in Sociology* (New York: Free Press, 1964, Chapter 8); also two recent special issues of the *American Anthropologist*, Vol. 66, No. 6, December 1964, edited by John J. Gumperz and Dell H. Hymes, and Vol. 67, No. 5, October 1965, edited by E. A. Hammel; Harvey Sacks, *The Search for Help: No One to Turn To*, doctoral dissertation, Department of Sociology, University of California, Berkeley, 1966; Harold Garfinkel, "Remarks on Ethnomethodology," paper presented at the American Sociological Association annual meeting, Chicago, September 1965; and B. N. Colby, "Ethnographic Semantics: A Preliminary Survey, with CA Comment," *Current Anthropology* (February 1966) **7**, 3-32.

6. My reference to sequences or sequential sentences or events is taken from unpublished lecture notes by Harvey Sacks.

7. Cf. Alfred Schutz, *Collected Papers I* (The Hague: Martinus Nijhoff, 1962); and Garfinkel, "Studies of the Routine Grounds of Everyday Actions," *op. cit.*, for detailed discussions of the phrase "background expectancies."

8. Noam Chomsky and Morris Halle, "Some Controversial Questions in Phonological Theory," *Journal of Linguistics*, 1 (No. 2), 97-138 (1965).

9. *Ibid.*, p. 103.

10. Cf. Garfinkel, "Studies of the Routine Grounds of Everyday Actions," *op. cit.*

11. *Ibid.*, p. 226 and p. 229.

12. The search for meaning in "underlying patterns" has been called the "documentary method of interpretation," and a detailed account of its features can be found in Harold Garfinkel, "Common Sense Knowledge of Social Structures: The Documentary Method of Interpretation," in J. M. Scher (editor), *Theories of Mind*, New York: Free Press, 1962, 689-712.

13. Cf. Abraham Kaplan, *The Conduct of Inquiry*, San Francisco: Chandler, 1964, p. 8 and p. 32.

14. For examples of work under this section see Emile Durkheim, *Suicide*, (translation by J. A. Spaulding and G. Simpson) (Glencoe, Ill.: Free Press, 1951); S. M. Lipset, *Political Man* (Garden City: Doubleday, 1960); and O. D. Duncan and L. Schnore, "Cultural, Behavioral, and Ecological Perspectives in the Study of Social Organization," *American Journal of Sociology* (September 1959) **65**, 132-146. For a refreshing reexamination of the relation between "hard data" as used by the above authors and the problem of social meaning, see Jack Douglas, *The Social Meanings of Suicide* (Princeton: Princeton University Press, 1967).

15. Cf. Irwin Deutscher, "Words and Deeds: Social Action and Social Policy," *Social Problems* (Winter 1966) **13**, 235-254; and Deutscher, "Public vs. Private Opinions: The 'Real' and the 'Unreal'," unpublished paper read at the Eastern Sociological Association meeting, Spring 1966.
16. A detailed account of this position can be found in the following quotation:

> Although much has been said about the relation of psychoanalysis to sociology, and some important interdisciplinary work has been done, little attention has been devoted to the logical or procedural convergence of the two fields. The psychological interpretation of social events is not at issue here. The suggestion is, rather, that the logic or mode of analysis associated with dynamic psychology may be similar in essential ways to the analytical logic of sociology, at least when coherent, adaptive social organisms are being studied.
>
> The characteristic quest of the interpretive analyst is not for a mere description or history. Nor is he interested in how selected variables are related to each other. The protocol of a free-association interview, or a life history, is scrutinized for "revealing" symptoms. What is revealed? The relation between id impulses, ego structure, and social pressure will form, it is presumed, a constellation inferable from the individual's overt behavior, including his verbal responses. The patient is studied for signs which reveal an underlying (latent) pattern. To expose this pattern, by way of the analysis of symptoms, is the goal of interpretation.
> . . .
> Similarly, interpretation in sociology scrutinizes a mass of data to find indicators of an underlying pattern. There is nothing interpretive about a public opinion poll until an inference is made about a latent structure. Even this is a low-order interpretation if it does nothing more than assess the validity of attributing a specific attitude to a population, say hostility or indifference toward a particular government program. We move toward fuller interpretation as we look for evidences of a constellation of attitudes, or at least of a single orientation so powerful that it shapes many aspects of behavior. Studies of apathy or impotence, or of the "mind" of military or political elites are interpretive in this sense. The essence of the interpretive process is the drawing of conclusions, from the study of observable "indicators," that some underlying pattern or configuration exists. The sentiments, self-images, and dispositions of a population are, of course, not the only kinds of latent patterns that may be identified.

The quotation is taken from Philip Selznick, *The Organizational Weapon* (Glencoe, Ill.: Free Press, 1960), vii-viii.
17. See the informative appendices in W. F. Whyte, *Street Corner Society* (Chicago: University of Chicago Press, 1955), and Dalton's *Men Who Manage, op. cit.*
18. Cf. Howard S. Becker, "Problems of Inference and Proof in Participant Observation," *American Sociological Review* (December 1958) **23**, 652-660.
19. For a view that contrasts with the quantitative micro theorists see Peter H. Greene, "An Approach to Computers that Perceive, Learn, and Reason," Publ. Institute of Radio Engineers, New York, pp. 181-186 (1959).
20. Garfinkel, "Studies of the Routine Grounds of Everyday Actions," *op. cit.*, p. 226.
21. Descriptive accounts by members contain structural references to their relations with others by specifying objects and events, but the same account can also be read as providing the grounds for action. Sacks uses the term "membership categorization device" to discuss how members use categories paired with population members according to rules of application to show how members classify one another and depict conditions of social interaction. See his *The Search for Help . . . , op. cit.*
22. It is of more than passing interest to note that students of nonhuman social behavior rely upon an implicit phenomenal world imputed to animals, and a tacit use of

background expectancies when describing action scenes. For an illuminating account of this problem see Henry Elliott, *Animals and Man: Notes on Animal Behavior Studies as a Model for Scientific Sociology,* master's thesis, Department of Sociology, University of California, Berkeley, 1966. See also C. H. Schiller (editor), *Instinctive Behavior* (New York: International University Press, 1957); I. De Vore (editor), *Primate Behavior: Field Studies of Monkeys and Apes* (New York: Holt, Rinehart and Winston, 1965); and A. M. Schrier et al. (editors), *Behavior of Non-Human Primates* (New York: Academic Press, 1965), Vol. 2.

23. Harley Granville-Barker, *On Dramatic Method* (New York: Hill and Wang, 1931), pp. 37-38.

Chapter 2

THEORIES OF DELINQUENCY AND THE
RULE OF LAW

Studies of juvenile delinquency seldom view such activities as products of the agencies of social control. Juvenile contacts with police, probation, and court officials are integral parts of the community's legal system. The rule of law, as activated vis-à-vis juveniles, reveals more than an analysis of problems of delinquency, but also tells us something about the articulation of members' notions of legality and justice with the social organization of daily existence. The articulation of legality and justice with the social organization of every-day life presupposes a common reference to the importance of rules (legal and nonlegal), and to the interaction of both types when members of a given community engage in activities considered deviant. The interaction of legal and nonlegal rules implies that what is considered deviant by some members of the community (including the police) is not always obvious to the suspect or his supporters, and that what ends up being called justice is negotiable within the boundary conditions of established organizations.[1] The negotiable character of justice suggests that a study of the social organization of law-enforcement activities vis-à-vis juveniles can reveal something about the practiced and enforced nature of the legal order, and members' conceptions of morality in the community.

Community Social Problems

Community-defined social problems such as crime, delinquency, poverty and alcoholism have supplied many sociologists with their research problems and the relevant data. The substantive area of the sociology of law has been characterized as a concern for the legal system as an authoritative set of rules which are designed to handle community defined social problems. The definition of the community "problem" must be separated from the sociologist's interests in such problems as data, in order to avoid the danger of allowing community definitions and the sociologist's lay perspective as a member of

22

the community to define the distinctively sociological perspective to be employed.

The sociologist, in separating the various perspectives (yet incorporating them as concepts and data into his theoretical and substantive analysis), can then indicate how certain actors, groups, and ecologically defined areas, come to be designated as ill, criminal, competent, stable, disorganized, etc. The separation of perspectives enables the observer to specify the interaction of folk or commonsense notions about "right," "wrong," morals, and the like, with the articulation law-enforcement officials make between legal rules and conduct as reported and observed by others and themselves, and how the interpretations stemming from the emergent interaction is linked to members' conceptions of community political intrigues, special interests, social class groupings, and the past activities of courts on the issue in question. Specifying the ways in which the members of a community define or initiate, sustain, and alter imputations of competence, illness, and criminality, provides an empirical context for clarifying abstract jurisprudential concepts on the rule of law.[2]

The past 70 years of the juvenile court movement is often viewed as an attempt to improve the ways in which juveniles should be handled and treated by police and correctional agencies. The movement has been shifting its emphasis over time so as to include more and more factors; "causes" now include everything from disorganized neighborhoods and families to the lack of educational and occupational opportunities, personality, and characterological problems. Recent changes in juvenile court laws now emphasize the legal rights of juveniles. Community definitions of the "problem" now seem to have entered a phase whereby the sheer quantity of delinquent acts publicized by law-enforcement and mass media has led increasingly to characterizations of alarming increases in "irresponsible" youth.

The concern with juvenile delinquency has often led to a view that delinquents are responsible for their acts and should be held accountable and be punished for them, although the conceptions of what are "good" adolescents and what the punishment should be have changed. A second view holds that adolescents are continually having "natural" problems growing up, and since a certain amount of permissiveness is necessary, their acts therefore should not be viewed within the context of adult activities, but treated as temporary outbursts to be controlled gradually when "maturity" is reached in adulthood. This second view translates "natural" problems into environmental, community, familial, or personal problems and absolves the juvenile from serious responsibility. Whereas the first view sees juvenile outbursts as "signs of" future trouble and basic defects that must be corrected now, the second view considers outbursts a natural part of growing up and learning how to understand and explore the world with more or less impunity from the sanctions imposed upon adults. The same types of activities are viewed differently, with different remedies proposed and different conceptions about the moral responsibilities of youth. The juvenile court law, therefore, can be viewed as a social movement designed to standardize and regulate procedures for articulating rules governing juvenile conduct with their "natural" problems as delineated by the second view.

In following an ethnomethodological perspective, this book directs the researcher's attention to the theories of delinquency employed by laymen and particularly to theories employed by police, probation, and court officials when deciding the existence of delinquency. The foregoing remarks on different theories of delinquency that may exist within Western legal systems resembles Bohannon's analysis of Tiv law.[3] Bohannon's concern for treating both Western legal traditions and Tiv (or any other) conceptions of law as "folk-systems" means such theories become sources of data, particularly when used to label behavior delinquency. Gluckman's response to Bohannon —in answer to Bohannon's charge that Gluckman has elevated western "folk-system" categories and theories to an analytic status in examining African native law—does not neutralize or undercut the view that Western legal traditions remain folk systems. Yet Gluckman's response has merit when he claims Bohannon does not indicate how we are to compare various types of legal traditions. What is needed are studies showing how folk theories articulate with actual practice, adequate descriptions of the environment of objects attended by members, and the organizing features of their practical activities. How natives describe events and objects provides a basis for contrasting abstract notions such as "contract," "debt," "crimes," and "rape" with folk or members' categories.

Theories of Delinquency and Official Statistics

Sociological theories of delinquency have been couched traditionally in loosely construed motivational and organizational terms. The actor's socialization in family, peer, and neighborhood forms of social organization is said to provide the conditions for an implicit "negative" or "positive" "attitude toward authority," "good" or "bad" parental models after which to pattern his own conduct, "good" or "bad" friends who hold an important influence over his behavior, a "good" or "bad" neighborhood which exposes him to the moral and decent elements of everyday life, or the disorganized, criminal, evil side of life. Finally, there is the notion of the actor's adjustment and reaction formation to "growing up," and the working-class boy's "problem" with social status and his perception of future opportunities.[4]

The emergence of these theories presumably followed the changing conceptions of youth developed during the latter part of the nineteenth century when elements of American and English communities became concerned with the impact of urban life and industrialization on the family and the conduct and activities of youth. It has been suggested that the increasing concern with problems of youth, leading to the establishment of the juvenile court law, was primarily a feminist movement, dedicated to helping the children of the poor, the immigrant, the broken family, the abandoned.[5] The articulation of motivational and organizational variables in sociological theories of delinquency appears quite "natural." The fact that this union almost always implied it was the children of slum dwellers who are most likely to become delinquent also seems to follow quite "naturally." The development of welfare legislation, settlement houses, the juvenile court, and sociological theories attributing delinquency to youth from poverty-ridden, disorganized neighborhoods with unstable homes and gangs with nothing "constructive" to do, all in a context of rapid industrialization and urbanization, seems "natural." The use of the term "natural" is intended to underscore the congruence between sociological and lay theories of delinquency.

By way of introducing my critical discussion of delinquency theories, I want to begin by describing two apparently unrelated "social problems."

1. Throughout the latter part of the nineteenth century, the early part of the twentieth century, and down to present times there have been many works pointing to the "irresponsible" and often illegal activities of public officials and corporation owners, managers, and others in positions of trust. Sutherland's work on white-collar crime underscored that the illegal activities in question were done during routine business activities.[6] Journalistic and academic reports on illegal activities in every branch of local, state, and federal government argue the same point. The men involved were always viewed as responsible members of the community, active in charities, elders in the church, and so on. The amount of corporation and public white-collar crime does not seem to have diminished even though it does not always receive extended publicity.

2. A parallel development to white-collar crime, namely middle-to-upper-class delinquency, has had a much shorter history, for it is only within the past ten years that occasional publicity and some research has referred to such activities. The idea of middle-to-upper-class delinquency has achieved modern salience, even though it does not necessarily follow that there is any causal correspondence between white-collar crime and delinquency in the same social classes. A safe assertion, however, seems to be that both white-collar crime and middle-to-upper-class delinquents enjoy the historical association between illegal conduct and middle-to-upper-class advantage within the legal system.

In this section, I criticize traditional sociological theories of delinquency, as theories of crime were questioned by Sutherland in his work on white-collar crime, by reference to the meaning of official statistics, the organizational practices of law-enforcement officials, and the prevalence of middle-to-upper-class delinquency. Some preliminary data from a pilot study in one of the two counties studied provide a limited empirical context for showing how the larger study was conceived and altered to include a specific concern with the social organization of juvenile justice.

Community definitions of juvenile delinquency assume important socio-logical significance when it can be argued that such activities are common to all segments of the community (with comparable rates of occurrence), and expose a large sector of youth to community meanings of legality and justice in a context which is outside of due process considerations and the formal machinery of the courts. This socialization to the legal system includes a middle-to-upper-income population which presumably has few criminal con-tacts with the police as adults, and provides such youth with an image of the rule of law noticeably divorced from the ideals of due process. The study of juvenile justice becomes more than a concern with youth who have gone astray, or juveniles primarily from disorganized homes, neighborhoods, and personal problems of adjustment. Lay and sociological notions about "tradi-tional" adult crime and white-collar crime seem to be fused and confused in activities we label juvenile delinquency. In both cases the abstract conceptual-ization is seldom articulated with the everyday activities of law-enforcement officials and members of some community.

The Meaning of Official Statistics

Sociological conceptions of delinquency stem primarily from two sources: (1) sociologists' own commonsense conceptions of traditional slum or lower-class delinquency, that is, the idea of lower-class disregard for middle-class norms, and delinquency as part of ecologically "disorganized" sections of urban areas, and (2) the availability of official statistics at the local, state, or federal level, showing a high correlation between delinquency and lower-income groups with broken homes, alcoholism, and similar problems. Viewing delinquency in "disorganized" areas as the major social problem to be cor-related with traditional variables of density or urbanization, social class, family marital status, educational opportunity and participation of youth, ethnicity, and other factors, has been exaggerated. The sociologist has been so accustomed to viewing notions about the transitional stages of urbanization and industrialization as producers of social problems, that his research is oriented toward demonstrating the validity of his lay conceptions of delin-quency, rather than contrasting members' theories of social problems with his own general theories about social order. By accepting members' and his own commonsense definitions of social problems, the sociologist has also accepted the official statistics about who are the delinquents. The explanatory power of delinquency theories are, therefore, neat retrospective accounts which fit both the popular conceptions about how adolescents become delinquent, and how official rates are distributed.

A word of caution is in order concerning the significance of official statistics. Law-enforcement officials, statisticians attached to rate-producing agencies, criminologists, and sociologists have long known and commented on official statistics as misleading. Many corrections and refinements have been suggested and used. But regardless of whether corrections have been used, the official statistics are utilized nevertheless as indicators of the prevalence and significance of delinquency, and the net result has always been to use the findings (the "social facts") as documenting the theoretical position derived from commonsense or lay conceptions. An understanding of how official statistics are assembled informs the researcher as to how "delinquents" are produced by the socially organized and socially sanctioned activities of members of the community and representatives of law-enforcement agencies. A knowledge of the "praxiology"[7] of the various actors involved in the rate-producing process would presumably supply the researcher with a program for adequately describing how persons in the community come to be defined and processed as "delinquent." The data for demonstrating the cogency of the sociologist's program consist of his and members' descriptions of observed events, an account of the environment of objects attended, and the progressive transformations that can be affected by initial encounters between suspects and victims, suspects and the police, the writing of an official report based on interrogation and observation, subsequent probation interviews and reports, court performances, and the like. The analysis of oral and written material presupposes a seldom mentioned contextual relevance based on linguistic and practical reasoning principles as they are used in different social groupings.

The meaning of official statistics is similar to the problem of rumor generation and transformation; demonstrating how socially organized activities produce such outcomes as rates, for example, parallels the transformations that occur in everyday events when members transform vague and disconnected pieces of information into an ordered "happening." The meaning of the law depends upon a model which breaks down the successive transformations whereby alleged deviations from general rules, as imputed to juveniles by members of the community or police officers and described by members of the community and law-enforcement officials, come to be recognized, acted upon, so that the legal system is activated. The subsequent oral and written reports and hearings continually simplify or "round," abstract, and reinterpret the original event or act so that it "fits" the kind of logic used by legally oriented members accustomed to standardized recipes for explaining relationships between legal rules and conduct. Legal thinking and a legal view of social reality remove the contingent features of everyday life in the course of successive transformations over time from the original event or act to final adjudication. The net result is an "obvious" and "clear" picture of causality and "what happened." Legal reasoning formalizes the premises of commonsense thinking about the world as taken for granted and known in common by "everyone" and understood by "anyman," and "closes" ambiguities in the language to create a two-valued logic as a means of making decisions and arguing the validity of concrete events in terms of taken-for-granted assumptions about everyday life.

The statistical models and materials utilized by students of delinquency and crime, amount to a premature specification of "dependent" and "independent" variables. The ready-made "variables," provided by official bureaucratic organizations charged with certain bookkeeping operations, have no "obvious" correspondence with the daily events and practical reasoning that led to the production of rates. The statistical model employed or presupposed restricts the problem to that of determining the "right" fit between an obscure collection of findings and some formalized categories or equation. The amount of variance "explained" by the variables employed provides the criteria for determining success or temporary failure.

The meaning of official statistics, therefore, must be couched in the context of how men, resources, policies, and strategies of the police, for example, cover a given community, interpret incoming calls, assign men, screen complaints, and routinize reports. Several studies provide evidence for demonstrating how criminal justice becomes problematic when we examine the ways persons come to be labeled suspects and victims, and how labels assigned are articulated with some kind of statutory equivalent.[8] The discretion found in the administration of juvenile justice is striking in the juvenile court law and those charged with administering it because of the dilemma of viewing the juvenile in criminal and clinical terms. An offender's record, then, may never reflect the ambiguous decisions, discretion, accommodations of law-enforcement personnel, familial assistance or hindrance, or actions by the victims. Therefore, the use of statistical accounts must seek those images suggested and acted upon by lay and law-enforcement personnel or sociologists, and compare these images with the networks of social action by which the actor becomes officially known as a delinquent or criminal. The set of meanings produced by *ex post facto* readings of statistical records cannot be assumed to be identical to the situational meanings integral to the various stages in the assembly of the official statistics.

Because the official line intended by the juvenile court law is not to view the labeled delinquent as a criminal, but as an adolescent who is either "misdirected," "disturbed," or from a "poor or unfortunate environment," among other influences, the legal concept of an adversary system is notably absent. The absence of an adversary element continues in spite of a parellel movement in juvenile justice to that in adult justice, considerable debate, and changes over problems of due process during arrest, search, and seizure. The early work of Paul Tappan on juvenile court practices, the California Special Study Commission on Juvenile Justice, and Nathan Goldman's study of juvenile offenders clearly indicates the many variations in organizational procedures and personnel interpretations, and how they differentially influence the administration of juvenile justice.

Theories of Delinquency

The growing literature on middle-class delinquency suggests such activity is "another" kind of "social problem" rather than of general significance reflecting the operation of legality and justice in a given community.[9] The theories proposed by Cohen, Miller, Cloward and Ohlin, Short, and others, and the plausible theoretical alternatives proposed by Matza on how adolescents perceive their predicaments and "drift" into delinquent acts, view community definitions of delinquency as fairly clear and, in doing so, assign little significance to the community political structure and the variations in law-enforcement social organization that provide the context for the bureaucratic and professional-legal validation of activities that come to be defined as delinquent. But some implicit theory of "the delinquent" is presupposed in the organizational viewpoint taken here, and although I do not address this problem explicitly in the research reported below, the reader is entitled to some indication of my biases and their relevance for the organizational emphasis of my thesis.

Questioning the generality assumed in theories of delinquency directed toward explaining higher incidence in lower-income families, or as a reaction against middle-class society and the lack of opportunities, or a separate subculture with its own values, poses problems about how adolescents come to engage in community-law-enforcement-defined-delinquency. Matza's book *Delinquency and Drift* develops a convincing abstract statement about the actor's point of view in the sequence of events leading to community-official definitions of delinquency.[10] Matza's discussion of how a mood of fatalism, the neutralization of legal norms in the criminal law leading to a periodic breaking of the "moral bind to law," a sense of injustice, and the "drift" into delinquency that follows provides the elements of an implicit theory of delinquency not necessarily tied to the class-based assumptions in conventional theories.[11] Consider the following quotation from an earlier statement by Matza and Sykes:

> To speak of juvenile delinquency in general, as we have done in this paper, should not obscure the fact that there are different types of delinquency and the differences among them cannot be ignored. Yet it seems worthwhile to pursue the idea that some forms of juvenile delinquency—and possibly the most frequent— have a common sociological basis regardless of the class level at which they appear.
>
> One such basis is offered, we believe, by our argument that the values lying behind much delinquent behavior are the values of a leisure class. All adolescents at all class levels are to some extent members of a leisure class, for they move in a limbo between earlier parental domination and future integration with the social structure through the bonds of work and marriage. Theirs is an anticipatory leisure, it is true, a period of freedom from the demands for self-support which allows room for the schooling enabling them to enter the world of work. They enjoy a temporary leisure by sufferance rather than by virtue of a permanent aristocratic right. Yet the leisure status of adolescents, modified though it may be by the discipline of school and the lack of wealth, places them in relationship to the social structure in a manner similar to that of an elite which consumes without producing. In this situation, disdain of work, an emphasis on personal qualities rather than technical skills, and a stress on the manner and extent of consumption all can flourish. Insofar, then, as these values do lie behind delinquency, we could expect delinquent behavior to be prevalent among all adolescents rather than confined to the lower class.[12]

Matza and Sykes emphasize that delinquency should be explained by the similarity of the offender's perspective and behavior with the features of the society that produced him. Thus the delinquent (presumably some generic type) is a reflection of the community from which he comes and the prevailing practices of adults who support the idea of subterranean values rather than some normative conception of legality and justice.

The delinquent's routine activities and world view produce what Sykes and Matza call "techniques of neutralization." For example: (1) the juvenile denies responsibility because it was an "accident," or due to forces beyond his control; (2) he denies injury so that vandalism is defined as "mischief," theft as "borrowing," or a general and vague notion that the act is not that harmful even though it is illegal; (3) he denies that the victim has been wronged by transforming him into a wrongdoer who deserves injury or by assigning to the victim a trivial status, as in acts against property; (4) he rejects those who disapprove of his acts by noting they are motivated by questionable interests or are of questionable moral character; and (5) he neutralizes social controls by appealing to the more "important" loyalties of the gang, the clique, and the like, which may have led to illegal activities but deemed "necessary" because the special group's norms are accorded higher loyalty or precedence.[13] Thus the delinquent or potential delinquent, who is subsequently labeled and treated as such by law-enforcement officials, enters into encounters with ideas about police or probation officers and his own conceptions of legality and justice, and the ways in which he can expect to be handled. To the remarks by Sykes and Matza must be added the notions that the projects of action that produce a certain deference and demeanor, physical appearance, language categories, and general definition of the situation by juveniles, interact with the organization of police activities: the day-to-day routines law-enforcement agents employ for stopping, interrogating, arresting, and referring youth to the juvenile bureau for further investigation according to the social types and conceptions juvenile officers invoke when evaluating a case and deciding to file or not to file an application for a petition requesting a court hearing. Subsequent encounters with probation officers are influenced by the official police reports that may be sent to probation and the situation as related by the youth directly to his probation officer. Each encounter in the administration of juvenile justice, beginning with the initial police-juvenile contact, produces a dialogue whereby social objects and events are interpreted, given meaning, labeled, and categorized, so that some mutual comprehension of "what happened" may be produced even though there may be several versions of the official statement and many differences in interpretation of the same event or act.

Notice that the previously mentioned theories by Cohen, Miller, Cloward and Ohlin, et al. do not seek an explanation of the juvenile's conduct by reference to the actor's conceptions of legality and justice or perceived responsibility and involvement, nor is there any attempt to show how the "man-on-the-street" and law-enforcement officials, through the former's conceptions of "wrongdoing" and the latter's policies and day-to-day decision-making, are key elements in how juveniles come to be known as delinquent.[14]

Some Preliminary Findings

Middle-class delinquency provided a point of departure for examining more general problems of practical decision-making. Before the present study was conceived the chief of police of a wealthy Chicago suburb revealed his unofficial files and statistics on delinquent activities to John Kitsuse and myself. The chief noted his files included everything from drug addiction, shoplifting, and burglary to alcoholism, drunk driving and truancy, suggesting that the adolescents in this community engaged in delinquent acts on a par with those of the worst areas of Chicago. He noted that drinking, drunk driving, and traffic problems hold a slight edge over other offenses because of the easy access adolescents in his community had to such activities.

The usual pattern of delinquency, according to the chief, consisted of four or five offenses of a similar type over a period of many months with each offense leading to a brief discussion between the police, parents, and the child, and terminating with the vows of careful future supervision and more responsibility on the part of the offender. After the fourth or fifth offense, depending upon its seriousness according to police criteria, the youth and his family were asked to appear before the local county judge for a hearing. The chief noted that by this time both the parents and the offender would appear quite concerned about the matter and viewed the impending hearing with pessimism. The court hearing was described as an amiable setting with the family seriously attentive to the judge, and the offender neatly dressed and displaying the "proper" demeanor and deference. To the chief, the families almost always appeared as a kind of ideal of the "good family." The judge's actions were described as those of a kind but serious disciplinarian who scolded the offender and reminded the family of their responsibility to the child. The disposition was said to be a stern warning and some trivial punishment like six months of mowing the huge lawn surrounding the family house.

Perhaps the chief's descriptions were exaggerated, but he repeated many times that he and his men felt that they had no control over delinquent conduct in the community because of the high social and economic standing of the families and their willingness to "cooperate" with the police. The offenders were described as articulate and well-behaved. The chief felt that the judge undermined his position and that of his men and department because of a "soft line" after the police had spent time building up the seriousness of the offenses and the possible dispositions available to the judge. The chief felt the parents and child tended to minimize the seriousness of the delinquent acts after the hearing and the authority of the police therefore was undermined. Finally, even if the offenses continued and the judge became more punitive in his dispositions, the chief reported the average family could easily send their child off to some private school or to relatives until he reached eighteen or entered college.

The present study began by exploring the content of official materials before doing fieldwork with law-enforcement personnel. An initial lack of resources for a larger study led to a pilot study based on probation records in one of the two cities. I wanted to examine the extent to which official records revealed or did not reveal the incidence and form of middle-to-upper-class delinquency as compared with lower income groups. A second objective was to determine the extent to which such materials revealed the nature of decision-making that led to dispositions.

The pilot study consisted of 100 cases taken at random from the probation files. I began with 1960 and selected twenty cases each from 1960, 1959, 1958, 1957, and 1956. Because of companion cases the sample increased to one hundred and fifty-three. Throughout the period during which material was being extracted from the files, I was able to spend considerable time observing and speaking with probation officers about the sequence of events before and after they entered the picture. The observations and informal discussions helped to clarify and inform me about the nature of day-to-day activities and obscure details not available in the official records.

The court record was not always available nor was it possible to transcribe it from the original shorthand. Because each probation file often contains extensive notes and reports on the offender and his family, it was possible to extract some information pertaining to the number of offenders by marital status of parents and a crude conventional estimate of social class standing in the community. The information is tentative because it is not possible to know how decisions about such evaluations of the home life as "good," "bad," or "adequate" were made. All official data are used under the dubious assumption that the probation officer's remarks, because they reflect decisions and grounds for action by him, may be taken at face value and assumed to be relevant regardless of the criteria and interpretations originally placed on the observed events that were not evident in the language used.

The distribution of the offender's family by some notion of class[15] (using father's occupation) reveals that most of the cases fell into the skilled, semi-skilled, and unskilled manual worker groups (see Table 1). Thus, category 7 (hereafter the "lower class" group), the "lowest part" of the occupational hierarchy, accounts for about one third (N = 42) of the classifiable cases. Inquiries to probation officers about nonclassifiable cases suggested that the absence of information invariably implied a poor employment record and probably cases of "the lower class element" or chronically poor families who might be migratory workers or transient families. If these nonclassifiable cases are added arbitrarily to the unskilled category the "lower-class" character of the sample increases considerably (N = 67 or about 45 percent of the total sample). Hence the sample would appear to be similar to conventional official statistics about the prevalence of lower or the lowest income groups in community-law-enforcement-defined cases of delinquency.[16] Categories 5 and 6 (henceforth called the "upper-lower" and "lower middle" classes, respectively) account for 35 percent of the sample, while categories 1, 2, 3, and 4 (henceforth called the "middle and upper" class group) account for only 20 percent of the sample. The distribution is of interest because even for such a small sample, the probation data represent only a fraction of the cases known to the police, but higher social class cases are not a trivial part of the sample. Yet

Table 1

Juvenile Offenders Social Class Grouping
by Hollingshead's Occupational Measure

Class Grouping	N
1. Higher executives, proprietors of large concerns, and major professionals	7
2. Business managers, proprietors of medium-sized businesses, and lesser professionals	2
3. Administrative personnel, small independent businesses, and minor professionals	14
4. Clerical and sales workers, technicians, and owners of little businesses (valued under $6000)	8
5. Skilled manual employees	26
6. Machine operators and semiskilled	27
7. Unskilled employees	42
Total	126[a]

[a] Twenty-seven cases with inadequate information (and suspected by the Probation Department to be persons with poor employment records).

such cases are not as likely to be referred to the courts. Thus the preliminary findings suggest caution in accepting conventional conceptions about the class distribution of delinquency. The idea of poverty-ridden, disorganized families, and neighborhoods that affect the personality and character of youth, to the extent that delinquency is a frequent form of behavior, is a narrow view. But the analysis of information from official files cannot be used to address the problem adequately.

A standard factor used for explaining the prevalence of delinquency is that of broken homes. Probation records permit a construction of the marital status of the offender's parents and the information for the present sample is found in Table 2. The finding that 27 per cent (N = 39) of the offenders

Table 2

Status of Offender's Family

	Percent	N
First marriage for both spouses intact	42	(61)
Second or more marriage for either spouse and intact	31	(45)
Broken home	27	(39)
Totals	100	(145)[a]

[a] No information for eight cases.

came from broken homes differs from the figure of 42.5 percent reported by Shaw and McKay.[17] The table also reveals that 31 percent (N = 45) of the families have had two or more marriages for one or both spouses even though the present marriage is intact. One could argue that this latter finding suggests another basis for "disorganization" or negative influence on the child in question, and thus becomes another important structural indicator supporting the relationship between delinquency and broken homes. But when the social class groupings are cross-tabulated with the three marital status categories, the picture changes somewhat.[18] Table 3 reveals the highest concentration of

Table 3

Social Class (by Hollingshead's Occupational Measure)
and Marital Status of Offender's Family

	Broken Home	Second or More Marriage Intact	First Marriage for Both Spouses Intact	N
Middle and upper class	(6)	(16)	(9)	(31)
Upper lower and lower middle class	(11)	(15)	(27)	(53)
Lower class	(22)	(14)	(25)	(61)
Totals	(39)	(45)	(61)	(145)[a]

[a] No information for eight cases.

broken homes is to be found in the lower-class groups and decreases by one half in moving to the next and then final class groupings. The second-or-more-marriage-intact category is similar in absolute numbers for all of the class groupings. Hence this latter category does not necessarily figure as an important supporting indicator for the broken-home argument in the case of lower-income groups alone, for the middle-to-upper-class group has its largest concentration of cases in the second-or-more-marriage-intact category. Even if the broken-home and second-or-more-marriage-intact categories are combined as some indication of family instability that is current or has occurred in the past, the conventional argument about the lower social class causes of delinquency does not appear convincing here because all of the social class groupings fare similarly, with the middle-to-upper-class group appearing the most "disorganized."

Even putting aside the arbitrary decisions made in coding the information presented in Tables 1 to 3, and granting the measures are crude, they are certainly as relevant as the official statistics commonly employed by sociologists and others to document the sources and etiology of delinquency. The use of simple dichotomies or trichotomies are misleading here because they are gross and truncated categories that obscure the elements of social organization within families that presumably contribute or cause youth to become motivated to engage in community-defined delinquency. Herein lies a critical problem in the use of official statistics: the sociological categories are so constrained or so dictated by the available data, with the result that our concepts of process and structure are not articulated by a derivation of the theory whereby appropriate data are generated before the fact, but the theoretical concepts are stretched, altered, or distorted in order to fit the "facts" whose own status is highly questionable. I assume the sociologist's common sense or lay conceptions of community-defined social problems tend to be equated with his sociological conception of the same problems, and that official statistics are then used to "document" this conception. The technical errors leading to truncated categories and the weak force attributed to the influence of the social organization of law-enforcement agencies in conventional theories for managing the data call for a different strategy in obtaining data.

An alternative interpretation of Tables 1 to 3 might be, therefore, that it is the probation officer's use of the layman's or the sociologist's theories (broken homes and disorganized neighborhoods produce delinquency) that accounts for the preliminary findings. Any imputed history of "disorganization" influences the probation officer's decision to accept the application for petition. Juveniles with similar offense records become singled out for "treatment" and court hearings because of lay theories of delinquency causation. Thus commonsense or lay theories are transformed into semiprofessional interpretation after many conversations with probation officers during the course of the preliminary data-gathering period during which the officers invoked negative comments about the home, peer, etc., when justifying placements of juveniles in juvenile hall, a county boys' ranch, or a foster home "for his own good." The imputation of "disorganization" (to personal, family, and neighborhood activities, for example) provides the rationale for organizational decisions that open the door to *ad hoc* professional interpretation and remedial action for the offender.

Juvenile Justice and Theories of Delinquency

Although recent studies of community-defined crime and delinquency have suggested the discretion, ethnic bias, political motives, interpersonal differences, and bargaining that occurs in the administration of criminal justice, few sociologists have separated clearly theories about how and why persons come to engage in community-defined deviance, from commonsense or lay conceptions that orient law-enforcement policies and bureaucratic procedures. Pointing out that the rates discernible from official statistics are worthless or contain errors that can be corrected, or distortions that can be balanced with tempered inferences, is to overlook the heart of the matter: the use of such data to document conventional theories of individual delinquency obscures the view that official statistics reflect socially organized activities divorced from the sociological theories used retrospectively for explaining the same statistics. Members of the community, law-enforcement personnel, attorneys, judges, all respond to various behavioral or imputed symbolic or reported acts and events by juveniles with commonsense or lay conceptions, abstract legal rules, bureaucratic procedures, and policies.

Studies of community-defined delinquency yield material for demonstrating the cogency of a social organization view of juvenile justice. The paper by Toby, cited earlier, provides some instructive remarks. Toby suggests one explanation for the relationship between broken homes and delinquency in the Shaw and McKay data:

> . . . is that such variation is an artifact associated with court cases. Perhaps police are reluctant to refer a girl or a young boy to juvenile court unless they regard the family situation as unfavorable. . . . As a matter of fact, Shaw and McKay sought to account for the unexpectedly high incidence of broken homes among pre-adolescent male delinquents in precisely this way. [There follows a quote from Shaw and McKay] '. . . juvenile police officers of Chicago are instructed to refrain from taking legal action against boys under the age of 12 years, except in those cases where the home situation requires the supervision of the juvenile court.'[19]

In discussing a study by Thomas P. Monahan, Toby similarly notes that

> True, the Philadelphia study showed that, even among first offenders, the lowest percentage of broken homes occurred among children whose cases were adjusted informally; a higher percentage occurred among children whose cases were dismissed by the court; a still higher percentage characterized children placed on probation; and the highest percentage was observed among children committed to an institution.[20]

Although Toby's comments were made in a different context for other purposes, he cites data linking broken homes to delinquency, but these data do not demonstrate how the internal organization of the family causes delinquency; instead a "bad" home situation is said to be associated with delinquency cases referred to the juvenile court. It is difficult to find research explicitly linking data on internal social interaction of the family to motives for delinquency, even though the literature often includes case histories written in a way that such an inference could be easily made. The research literature invariably suggests a broad relationship between family organization and delinquency, retrospectively, after correlating "broken homes" or "bad neighborhoods" with law-enforcement records or self-reporting of delinquent activities. By suggesting that the relationship between broken homes and delinquency may be an artifact, or that court policy is interpreted after the fact as a kind of causal relationship, Toby's work suggests a broader problem: research that uses global concepts fitted loosely to abstract data whose coding procedures are unknown or at best arbitrary or *ad hoc*. Reaching different stages in the administration of juvenile justice is associated with negative or positive imputations made by the probation officer about the offender's family. The preliminary data suggest how the ideologies and policies of law-enforcement officials selectively assemble juveniles for probation evaluation according to existing theories shared by the community and social scientists: delinquent youth from broken homes or homes with a history of separation or divorce are viewed as products of a "disorganized" environment. Thus court jurisdiction and authority over the future disposition of the juvenile is "best" for the youth in question.

To pursue the broken home argument and the alternate interpretation suggested above, the probation officer's reports were examined again for information about the officer's evaluation of the juvenile's home situation. The probation officers' reports suggested that about one half of the "lower class" group and "lower-middle and upper-lower" group were described as having "poor home conditions," while about one third of the "middle-to-upper-class" group were labeled similarly. The equivocal rule of thumb used was to note the presence of comments such as "bad home," "poor home conditions," or "bad environment." Few families were described as socially and emotionally "adequate," although most were described as "adequate" as far as such things as "clean" or "livable" home with enough to eat and things like "proper" clothing and shelter are concerned. The following excerpts from the probation officers' reports provide illustrative material on the kind of evaluations that occur:

(From middle- to upper-class cases)

. . . parents suspected of indulging in alcohol to excess . . . poor supervision and permissive attitude . . . attitude is lackadaisical . . . are creating a true delinquent and must assume the full responsibility for their shameful deed.

. . . mother agreed that minor stable or dependable . . . marital difficulty. Both parents are aware that this conflict undoubtedly has something to do with the minor's behavior and even more so because the minor is aware of it. Both parents appear very concerned . . . and want to help. They are moving, selling house "all this to help Keith."

. . . mother . . . states that any misbehavior is probably due to the very insecure life thrust upon them by her marriages and divorces. Both parents showed much maturity and intelligence regarding their son's problem. There was no typical stepfather apathy apparent. . . . The consensus was that Gary was having a difficult time accepting his mother's way of life and he gave as hard a time as he could get away with. This is typical behavior for a boy with no stability and no masculine guidance in his life.

(From lower-middle and upper lower-class cases)

By all indications [the father] has not been fulfilling responsibility of a parent. [The parents] often go out on weekends to drink and leave the children unattended. The relationship that exists between the minor and his father is inadequate. . . .

. . . mother states that she and her husband were glad Frank was caught . . . as this lesson will prove to him that he must obey the law . . . [the parents] will cooperate fully with any plan of supervision and will also add further disciplinary action to this plan. . . . Parents' relationship appears to be relatively stable and happy . . . both admit to consuming beer quite frequently but maintain the drinking is not to an excess . . . [the offender] was disgusted with the drinking problem and wanted to return to his former home . . . has definitely been affected by financial pressures at home, as well as the habits of his parents of which he does not approve.

(From lower-class cases)

. . . minor "is being picked on by authorities." Home situation is very poor and both parents are very apathetic . . . a very unstable family due to the father's drinking problem and the apathy of the mother.

. . . parents give the impression of wanting to do the right thing, but do not know . . . mother complained that her husband failed to understand the boy and related that he is demanding but never takes the trouble of explaining anything to the boy. Although [the offender] is not a seriously delinquent problem he is well on his way as an exploiter of society. It is apparent that this boy's adolescent needs are not met in the home. . . .

The descriptions of family conditions point to the imputed relation between broken or negatively evaluated homes and delinquency, and to its impact on the probation officer's written and oral recommendation to the court. The language employed by the probation officer is important because of the way the offender, his home life, his parents, and future prognosis are easily classified and each is assigned motives and typical consequences that will follow. The thrust of the evaluation clearly puts the problem in the home environment—not the peer group or neighborhood. Notice that the probation officer's categories ("attitude is lackadaisical," "typical stepfather apathy," "unstable family," "exploiter of society") all "close" the activities being described so that decisions about the juvenile and home life are made easily, but the reader must supply the imagery to comprehend the categories and terms employed. The reader and researcher must assume the categories and terms have consistent meanings for the probation officers and others who are called upon to pass judgment on the materials.

A complex factor throughout the pilot study, therefore, was the kind of language utilized by the different participants in both oral and written communication. Listening to interviews between probation officers and offenders provided impressionistic information about variations in the ways probation officers seemed to be aware of language differences when conversing with certain offenders. Some probation officers seemed to use colloquial speech as a means of "reaching" the offender, as if sensing some kind of social distance. Court proceedings seemed to be a dialogue between judge and probation officer even though the offender was asked questions. Adolescents from lower income families did not seem to understand what was being said in the courtroom nor even care.

Language usage by juveniles can be the means of "convincing" the police or probation officer or judge the offender has been misunderstood, wronged, was unable to control himself, or has engaged in acts for which he cannot be blamed entirely because of difficulties beyond his control at home, in personal problems, and the like. On the other hand, language categories may be viewed as "signs of" guilt, poor "upbringing," a "bad attitude," arrogance, and can enter as an unstated source of "evidence" in deciding the legal features of some act or event. The decision to arrest, file a petition, and recommend, for example, probation, a foster home, a boys' ranch, or the youth authority seemed directly influenced by oral remarks and physical gestures which are difficult to document and may never appear on official records.

Juvenile cases, like adult cases, fall under the rule of law according to decisions concerning typical, "normal," or "strange" appearances at each stage of the judicial process that mark the administration of justice. Labels are applied, persons are "pushed into" or seem to fall "naturally" into categories, all of which provide officials and public alike with the "documentary evidence" of "guilt" or "innocence." The language and physical behavior employed by different types of adolescents provide law-enforcement officials with the "evidence" or "data" for employing a typology of typical delinquents and "good kids" whereby juveniles are labeled, and categorized for further action. Therefore, I now turn to a closer look at the general organization and activities of police departments to provide a broader context for locating the materials presented in subsequent chapters.

Law Enforcement Bureaucracy and Juvenile Justice

Skolnick traces the development of police departments and poses the dilemma of "why a police force?" in terms of whether they should serve as an agency of social control, or concern themselves with the ideals of a legal system and the rule of law. Skolnick notes it is the accountability of the police to the rule of law which remains to this day the concern of laymen and professionals.[21] A recent characterization of the criminal process as two models, a "due process model," and a "crime control model" provides a convenient framework for understanding the dilemmas faced by law-enforcement practitioners.[22] The due process model is concerned with problems of legality, and questions of guilt are addressed vis-à-vis procedural rules developed by a legal system. Thus jurisdiction, timing, and the like are stressed and become legal (not factual) problems connected with the handling of the suspect. The crime control model is concerned with factual questions and emphasizes efficient administration of justice. Thus the typical beliefs of the police officer, entrapment procedures, legal and illegal methods for obtaining information, vague circumstance, and the general articulation of the officer's personal experience and competence with legal criteria are stressed in this model. Skolnick summarizes the reasons why the control model applies so well to policemen as follows:

The policeman views criminal procedure with the *administrative bias of the craftsman*, a prejudice contradictory to due process of law. That is, the policeman tends to emphasize his own expertness and specialized abilities to make judgments regarding the measures to be applied to apprehend "criminals," as well as the ability to estimate accurately the guilt or innocence of suspects. He sees himself as a craftsman, at his best, a master of his trade. As such, he feels he ought to be free to employ the techniques of his trade, and that the *system* ought to provide regulations contributing to his freedom to improvise, rather than constricting it. . . .

To further understand the consequence of his craftsman's bias, it must be understood that the policeman draws a moral distinction between criminal law and criminal procedure. . . . The distinction is drawn somewhat as follows: The substantive law of crimes is intended to control the behavior of people who willfully injure persons or property, or who engage in behaviors eventually having such a consequence, as the use of narcotics. Criminal procedure, by contrast, is intended to control authorities, not criminals. As such, it does not fall into the same *moral* class of constraints as substantive criminal law. . . .

In contrast to the criminal law presumption that a man is innocent until proven guilty, the policeman tends to maintain an administrative presumption of regularity, in effect, a presumption of guilt. When he makes an arrest and decides to book a suspect, the officer feels that the suspect has committed the crime as charged.

He believes that as a specialist in crime, he has the *ability to distinguish between guilt and innocence.*[23]

Skolnick notes the police feel they are merciful administrators of justice even though they only charge people who are guilty, suggesting the "administrative presumption of regularity" may be a general phenomenon among all persons in the legal system.[24]

Skolnick's study is concerned with the tension between a concern for maintaining order and efficiency—a kind of control model orientation, and principles of legality—a kind of due process orientation. His study is valuable for the way it calls attention to the kinds of problems that arise in day-to-day police work in the context of a professional department dedicated to initiative among its employees, and some form of presumed rationality in carrying out the administration of justice. A series of studies have argued and documented similar problems that include the police, the courts, the prosecuting and defense attorneys, juries, and defendants. The following statements are designed to summarize in a brief manner, the significance of the problems that arise in the day-to-day activities of law-enforcement practitioners, their importance for the present study, and how they stress the significance of social encounters within a bureaucratic context of presumed legality and justice.

1. The contingencies of arrest and search and seizure suggest the negotiable character of who comes to be defined as "criminal." Fortuitous circumstances, combined with the nature of the encounter itself, become crucial determinants of possible outcomes. Skolnick presents empirical material from his study showing the ambiguities inherent in legal theory and practice when "reasonable cause" to make an arrest exists. The basic issue revolves around adequate evidence before arrest which would permit a search for other evidence about the crime. It is not clear when *post facto* search and seizure of evidence is the basis for retrospectively justifying an arrest actually made without "reasonable cause." Problems of due process or legality immediately complicate the concern of the police with controlling the behavior of others.[25]

2. Research has suggested many contingencies associated with guilty pleas and the kind of charge that will be made by the district attorney. The negotiable character of the plea and the charge provides the police officer with further evidence that his hands are "always tied" in his attempts to control crime and convict the guilty. Thus police annoyance with court procedures and decisions actually extends to all of the legal machinery that is activated after the arrest has been made. As Skolnick notes, the policeman "operates as one whose aim is to legitimatize the evidence pertaining to the case, rather than as a jurist whose goal is to analyze the sufficiency of the evidence based on case law."[26]

3. The basic dilemma of the police revolves around their seeking to

control deviant acts in the community, using whatever means available to justify their actions and present some simulation of legality, while the courts, on the other hand, seek to maintain some semblance of due process. Yet the prosecuting and defense activities of district attorneys and private council inevitably include economic and political-career overtones in the community. The police in a "clean" and professionally oriented department may often be excluded from the political, economic, and social consequences of their activities, but prosecuting and defense officials are always included. Nor is the judge excluded from indirect pressures in the community as Peltason's study argues, for he must still live in the community and carry out a social existence which is linked inextricably with the lives of others who have definite political, economic, and social interests to protect and foster.[27] The judge is likely to seek and have social encounters with other lawyers representing both prosecution and defense. The police are more likely to be isolated socially unless they have wider ambitions. The fact that most criminal cases are decided at the level of the local community where municipal and superior court judges are usually put into office because of prior political associations and activities, and then reelected when applicable almost without any opposition or difficulty, underscores the problematic features of the administration of justice. There are few decisions not linked to community-wide context, depending upon the suspect, the act in question, and the resources the suspect can mobilize. Skolnick touches upon this issue when he notes that the appearance of innocence can vary markedly with the type of neighborhood in which the police operate and their own theories about the probability of deviance being present or practiced.[28] Skolnick's discussion argues persuasively that the exclusionary rule often depends on *ex post facto* readings of "what happened" and, typically, on whether or not incriminating evidence was in fact obtained which now seems to join with other "suspicious" factors to "document" a previously hypothetical assumption about wrongdoing.

4. The literature reveals that police work necessarily includes close contacts with many people engaged in criminal or illegal activities, people the police may not be able to arrest because of inadequate evidence, but who are used as informers with or without payment. A common observation is that such arrangements can and have led to illegal activities on the part of the police, but law enforcement officials take the view that such relationships are unavoidable if police work is to be successful and "serious" crimes controlled. References to such activities imply that controls over illegal police activities are difficult to maintain because there is a large element of discretion. To cite one example, it is often impossible for administrative superiors to determine that funds for informers have actually been used for the purpose of obtaining useful information. But then administrative superiors are not immune to

corruption. Also, ranking police officials are likely to develop corrupt activities tied to political ambitions and "safe" illegal contacts with "respectable" members of the community.

5. The formally organized activities of the police include an environment where policemen obviously become concerned with their own careers within the department. Such concern can affect their actual work habits and their law enforcement contacts with members of the community. Further, there is concern with their self-image as policemen charged with particular duties.[29] Skolnick argues that in a professionally oriented police department, there is a concern for initiative and a pride in work which runs counter to principles of legality because the occupational demands and identification with the work itself leads to illegal arrest, and search and seizure activities. Westley argues that the policeman's identification with his work and his concern with obtaining the approval of others and sustaining or enhancing his self image lead to violence in daily work activities. Both Skolnick and Westley note the importance to the police of maintaining a position of authority vis-à-vis the public, particularly those he must view as suspects or criminals. The internal working conditions of police bureaucratic practices have been stressed by many writers[30] and constitutes another source of influence on police practices with the public.

6. The relation of the police to the local community is crucial for understanding day-to-day practices. Skolnick suggests that the dilemma of the police—caught between administrative efficiency and order or control in the community on the one hand, and the demands of legality or due process on the other—is a basic dialectic which cannot be resolved but is pushed in one direction or the other by the courts, for example, being more indulgent with the accused, or by more community support for stronger police action. Skolnick argues the police "know" that administrative efficiency or scientific management will not improve their work dramatically or make it easier to obtain legal convictions under due process considerations. The police, according to Skolnick, feel they are primarily dependent upon their contacts and their influence with informers and others in the community, including probation officers, judges, the district attorney, and the like, for achieving convictions and control.[31] Yet the problem of civic interest is not only apathy, but is also an interest in keeping the police squarely in the "middle" of the social control-due process dilemma since it serves particular and very general community interests. Two problems emerge here. Skolnick mentions the substantive issue of how a corrupt political community leads to police corruption. A second problem revolves around the sociologist's interest in how, for instance, a formal system of rules, precedents, statutes, and customs achieves implementation within the contextual settings of daily bureaucratic

activities and the decisions based upon varied practical interpretations of rules, precedents, and other factors.

The work of legal scholars needs to be articulated with the everyday social organization of legal institutions and agencies of control because such scholars presume a knowledge and clarity of the everyday workings of the legal system which is never demonstrated. Questions about the legality of police work or court interpretations and decisions do not make problematic legal labels, and types of legal reasoning that are articulated with the referents for the different vocabularies being used. Uniformity in legal vocabulary does not insure that the meanings used in practical actions remain standardized. When reference is made to the importance of standardized rules, stability of the law, congruence between declared rule and official action, promulgation of laws, and the like,[32] it is assumed that specifiable common understandings exist among practitioners and students of jurisprudence as to the meanings intended by the enormous volume of statutes, precedents, customs, and internal decisions called the legal system. A basic theme in all references to a legal order and the agencies of control is the problem of rational decision-making when statutes, precedents, or legal rules are interpreted.

Rationality and Practical Decision-Making

Throughout the present chapter I have emphasized the importance of decision-making as it occurs within the practical circumstances of police, probation, and court activities. In this final section I turn to the basic organizational problem of rationality in everyday decision-making to underscore the basic theme of the book: how the organizational decisions of law-enforcement personnel can be made understandable by a necessary use of the properties of practical reasoning, that is, background expectancies governing all social interaction.

Persons involved in deciding matters of legality and justice carry with them a stock of knowledge about social types they encounter in different positions in the community, and their social actions reflect conceptions of what is normal, strange, acceptable, safe, likely, usual, and so forth. The elements of social interaction are integral to notions like legality and justice as set forth in theories of jurisprudence or legal statutes, precedents, and customs. Thus, even though the police, probation, district attorney, defense attorney, judge are presumably all oriented to the same legal system, the articulation of the "orientation" with actual events and decisions is an empirical issue basic to sociological interests in social organization.

The study of large-scale organizations emphasizes the importance of rules for developing and regulating the activities of the organization, but the different meanings of the term bureaucracy, as March and Simon, Gouldner, and Crozier[33] have pointed out, often refer to different types of problems and interests and none seem to cover the whole range of activities that seem to arise in large-scale organizations.[34] Social psychologically oriented students of organizations have emphasized the "human" problems that emerge from the work situation itself and how human conditions and motivations affect work productivity and efficiency.[35] The interest in large-scale organizations by political scientists has moved from an earlier formal view of governmental activities that was empirically derived but not verifiable (i.e., a form of "inside-dopesterism"), to an emphasis upon reputational studies and then to an interest in the motivational structure of decision-making of key personnel or executives.[36] The widespread interest in rules or decision strategies has not precluded treating rules as obvious, rather than asking how the actor receives and processes information based on interpretations of imputed or factual conditions, his position in the organization, and notions like vague, ambiguous, or explicit individual goals and perceptions. Students of bureaucracy are concerned with so-called advantages and dysfunctions of rules governing recruiting, production procedures, structural relationships, and policies, yet reject some idealized model of the actor as a rational prototype of the computer, and a few stress the personality or clinical features of the actor's concern with such rules. But it is never clear what is meant by choice (rational or otherwise) on the part of the actor, how such choices are the same as (or differ from) commonsense choices, even though considerable attention is given to the presumably objective factors that the actor is often exposed to, having presumed calculable elements, for example, production schedules, costs versus profits, policy commitments that are translatable into votes or power, etc. A brief examination of the problem of rational choice in everyday life, particularly as imputed to officials charged with law-enforcement and administration, will provide the reader a basis for understanding empirical outcomes to be described later. The problem is especially acute in the case of the law because of the necessary articulation between formal, abstract legal statutes, customs and precedents, and the concrete situations that reflect particular cases and events as they arise in the community. The concept of rationality is pivotal because its ideal-type formulation contrasts sharply with practical decision-making in everyday life. For present purposes, rationality means the observer's model of how the actor decides what is "reasonable," "proper," "logical," "acceptable," "legal," and so forth, during the course of action.

The idea that trained personnel interpret a community's legal order by resolving the practical problem of implementing a set of rules that appear explicit is of limited value unless the implementation specifies the relevance of tacit knowledge or "rules" not written or discussed explicitly in written and oral reports. The ways in which police, probation, court utterances, and written reports reflect compliance with legal rules require the study of rationality as a collection of practical activities. The following statement by Blau and Scott appears to lend support to the position I have just described:

> . . . administrative decisions are highly complex, and rationality is limited for various reasons: all the consequences that follow from a given course of action cannot be anticipated; the consequences of action lie in the future and thus are difficult to evaluate realistically; and rationality requires a choice among all possible alternatives, but many of these will never even come to mind and so will not be considered. In short, individuals are not capable of making complex decisions rationally. The function of the organization is to limit the scope of the decisions that each member must make; only in this way can rationality be approached.[37]

For Blau and Scott the idea of rationality is approachable but not achievable. The authors suggest some of the properties of rationality when they state that "all consequences that follow from a given course of action cannot [but presumably could if rationality held] be anticipated," and that "rationality requires a choice among all possible alternatives." The authors suggest the totality of alternatives may never occur to the actor. Rationality cannot be achieved unless an organization (presumably through formal arrangements) delimits the scope of decisions so that "manageable" alternatives are available to the actor. Organizational rules or policies, such as legal rules or precedents, serve as abstract guidelines within which practical decisions locate evaluations of actual arrangements as falling under or fitting a general or particular policy. The rationality presumably is decided by consulting the "fit." The type of organization, therefore, becomes an important determiner of the kind of guidelines that will serve as criteria of rationality in deciding appropriate "fit." Students of complex organizations suggest separating the notion of rational administration from bureaucratic administration, where the former emphasizes the efficiency and skill or expertness of administration, as opposed to hierarchical authority, a special administrative staff, and rewards differentiated according to a hierarchical level.[38] The law-enforcement official's professional role presumably is consistent with the notion of rational administration, while operating within a bureaucracy that is military-like in structure. The official must coordinate this professional-like task within a military-like bureaucracy, while invoking general and abstract legal rules in social settings involving discretion and considerable *ad hoc* interpretation. The lowest ranking police officer must make decisions that are basic to the entire organization, while attempting to follow complicated legal rules and organizational goals that continually reflect the tension between control and due process objectives.

Organizational theorists have not produced operational methods for assessing the rationality of convincing a police officer, a probation officer, a witness, a jury, or a judge, about the credibility of objects and events. Consulting organizational or legal policies will not clarify the rationality of practical decision-making. Lawyers—like adversaries in corporate or governmental bodies—have the task of minimizing or maximizing the problematic features of decisions contained in the descriptions given by suspects, witnesses, policemen, and the "facts" any of them offer as evidence. The adversary principle is a sort of license to lobby for a particular or general rule or policy, or to reorganize the rationality of particular everyday and legal practical actions so as to provide for the possibility of outcomes that will be shared by others (for example, judge, jury, witness), and give coherence, plausibility, clearness, and the like, to the accent of social reality to which the lawyer (or corporate or governmental advocate) seeks to produce and convince others.

Sociologists typically employ the following simplified explanation of rationality:

> Rational behavior may be viewed as consisting of means-ends chains. Given certain ends, appropriate means are selected for their attainment; but once reached, the ends often become the means for the attainment of further ends, and so forth. . . . The important point about organizational behavior is that the hierarchical structure permits all decisions, except those defining ultimate objectives, to rest on factual rather than on value premises, that is, to be decisions about means rather than ends. Once the objectives of the organization are formally established, the hierarchical organization of responsibilities serves as a framework for means-ends chains—specifying for each official the ends of his tasks and thus confining his duties to the selection of the best means for achieving these ends.[39]

The remarks by Blau and Scott describe an implicit model of organizational behavior, but fails to specify how the member and researcher decide on appropriate means and ends. Distinguishing between factual and value premises suggests both notions can be explained vis-à-vis members' and researchers' unstated (in Blau and Scott) knowledge, perception, and interpretation of an environment of objects. If adversary principles are viewed as natural properties of any form of social organization, then the appropriateness of means is rational, relative to some value-based designation of ends by each advocate of policy. The designation of organizational ends as the pursuit of a social control or due process model of criminal process does not delimit the means, so that their rationality is contained in the meaning of a truncated term like "appropriateness."

The meaning attributed to the concept of rationality in the remarks of Blau and Scott are too imprecise to discuss the practical decision-making of members involved in law-enforcement and the administration of justice. A more elegant theoretical point of departure can be found in the work of Alfred Schutz. The term "rational action," according to Schutz, "as a chief principle of the method of social sciences is nothing else than the level of theoretical observation and interpretation of the social world."[40]

But what are the conditions under which we may classify a deliberated act of choice as a rational one? It seems that we have to distinguish between the rationality of knowledge which is a prerequisite of the rational choice and the rationality of choice itself. Rationality of knowledge is given only if all the elements from which the actor has to choose are clearly and distinctly conceived by him. The choice itself is rational if the actor selects from among all means within his reach the one most appropriate for realizing the intended end.

We have seen that clearness and distinctness in the strict meaning of formal logic do not belong to the typical style of every-day thought. But it would be erroneous to conclude that, therefore, rational choice does not exist within the sphere of every-day life. Indeed, it would be sufficient to interpret the terms clearness and distinctness in a modified and restricted meaning, namely as clearness and distinctness adequate to the requirements of the actor's practical interest.[41]

The quotations from Schutz suggest that conventional characterizations of the notion of "rational behavior" or "rationality" are not to be confused with their ideal-type characterizations such as Weber's reference to "rational act" as opposed to "traditional" or "habitual" acts, for their empirical forms are seldom addressed by sociologists.[42] The appropriateness of a means for realizing an intended end is not simply a matter of presumably clear organizational objectives, but must be understood as relative to the member's typified conceptions of practical adequacy. But the rational properties of everyday experience and action are not to be confused with the postulate of rational choice as employed in scientific inquiry which operates as an ideal for the scientific researcher.[43]

The rational properties of everyday activities, inside or outside of bureaucratic or rational administrations, as rules of corporate bodies or public law statutes or, for example, as properties governing decisions about household budgeting by housewives, always occur in the context of the actor's typifications, projects of action, definitions of the situation, linguistic and paralinguistic behavior, and layers of taken-for-granted meanings attributed to a world known in common with fellowmen. The properties of rational action in everyday experience and action can be summarized as follows:

1. Rational often is used in the same way as the term "reasonable" as in the case of deliberately following previous experiences or recipes. What worked before might well work now.[44]

2. Seeking new ways of doing things that avoids the use of certain mechanical procedures and now deliberately rehearsing in imagination various (and possibly competing) lines of action, as described by Dewey and Mead, but doing so routinely, without any necessary weighing of alternatives carefully.

3. When the actor categorizes and compares experiences and objects.

4. Examining consequences that follow from various alternative courses of possible action. Planning or projecting.

5. A concern with the expectations that follow from the scheduling of events.

6. Allowing some possibility of choice and entertaining various grounds upon which some choice is made.

7. References to what is predictable in terms of likelihood of occurrence as estimated by the actor.[45]

But a critical element of everyday life is the way the actor attends to the "fringes surrounding the nucleus within the stream of thought" because it is "the relation of the fringes which attach the nucleus to the actual situation of the thinker." Schutz continues:

> This is clearly a very important point. It explains why Husserl classifies the greater part of our propositions in daily thought as "occasional propositions," that means, as valid and understandable only relative to the speaker's situation and to their place in his stream of thought. It explains, too, why our every-day thoughts are less interested in the antithesis "true-false" than in the sliding transition "likely-unlikely." We do not make every-day propositions with the purpose of achieving a formal validity within a certain realm which could be recognized by someone else, as the logician does, but in order to gain knowledge valid only for ourselves and to further our practical aims.[46]

Schutz' remarks suggest the actor makes sense of his environment by creating loose equivalence classes (not clear-cut true-false categories), joining the "nucleus" with the fringes so as to concretize what is likely or unlikely. What is not clear here is how both the actor and researcher create conditions in legal and everyday activities that presume their activities are subject to confirmation by a formal validity recognized and binding upon themselves and others. Decision-making in organizational contexts suggests constraints on members' activities, but also the practical circumstances of their situation, knowledge sought and available, and practical aims.

It is the articulation of the style of everyday thought, projected for the actor's practical purposes, with a formal body of legal rules, that evokes and confuses the image of rational action in the scientific sense with the rational properties of everyday experience and action. The various meanings of rational action in everyday life do not mean that "occasional propositions" are irrelevant for understanding the rule of law, but that accounts by law-enforcement personnel, lawyers, judges, and legal theorists, represent progressive transformations of occasional propositions so that they can be *viewed as falling under* legal rules.[47] But the actor's remarks (be it as witness, suspect, or policeman), treated as evidence, are to be understood as containing nuclei and fringes that are integral features of the actor's situation and their place in his stream of thought. The lawyers, judges, or legal theorists who pass judgment over (or decide) "what happened" in order to validate the inclusion of the case as falling under a given statute or precedent, are removed from the time and space of the original member's utterances and the others around him with whom he is intimate and with whom he shares time and space. Legal personnel are only capable of an indirect knowledge based upon writings, reports, managed testimony in a particular setting and, above all, are oriented by their typifications of the events under review.

The lawyer provides particular interpretations for occasional propositions and a particular rationality to the actor's motives and actions, depending upon the prosecution or defense position. The judge may seek to cut into the staged or dramatized legal perspectives presented to the court by his own questions in court or in his chambers, relative to his personal and political interests as well as his ability to question legal strategies and assume the posture of an impartial observer. The rational properties of the policeman's actions involve the articulation between particular readings of legal statutes and a concern with the practical circumstances of social control in the community. His reports and comments will always reflect this concern. The police are, above all, very practically minded and their descriptions of objects and events provide commonsense or lay typifications that are intended as declarative statements to be accepted as "fact." Thus, they are likely to employ a traditional logic that eliminates the fringes of the definitions of the situation and to base their remarks on readings of situations that fuse the nucleus with the "fringes" by experiential fiat, that is, "that's the way it happened."

The earlier quotation from Blau and Scott assumes that the rational properties of organizational decision-making establish formal objectives, according to some hierarchical organization of responsibilities, that provide the boundary conditions under which tasks or ends are specified and the "best" means for achieving them can be evaluated. But this view assumes that the ends are clear-cut and identical for all, and that the means are equally "obvious" so as to pinpoint which are best suited for achieving the end result "rationally." Organizational theory focuses upon problems that trade upon the imagery of economics, but differs from an interest in the economic theory of the firm, for the latter seems to include more problems of social organization as integral for understanding how, for instance, the setting of output levels and the determination of advertising expenditures are elements woven into daily social relationships. But even if Blau and Scott intend by their remarks such economic activities as the determination of prices, production, demand costs, market competition, students of the area are not clear that such matters can be handled that rationally, although many are interested in decision-making models that presume unstated conditions of rationality. In discussing various theories of the firm, Cyert and March indicate the problematic character of the economic theory of the firm:

> In the debate over the theory of the firm, we can identify two major difficulties perceived by economists who view the basic theory as deficient. First, the motivational and cognitive assumptions of the theory appear unrealistic. Profit maximization, it is commonly alleged, is either only one among many goals of business firms or not a goal at all. . . . On the cognitive side, both the classical assumption of certainty and its modern equivalent—knowledge of the probability distribution of future events—have been challenged.
>
> Second, the "firm" of the theory of the firm has few of the characteristics we have come to identify with actual business firms. It has no complex organization, no problems of control, no standard operating procedures, no budget, no controller, no aspiring "middle management. . . ."
>
> The assumptions of rationality in the theory of the firm can be reduced to two propositions: (1) firms seek to maximize profits; (2) firms operate with perfect knowledge. Of course, a number of attempts have been made to adapt these assumptions to make them somewhat more sophisticated. Thus, we can assume that firms maximize the discounted value of future profits, and that firms have perfect knowledge only up to a probability distribution of all possible future states of the world. We are not concerned at this point with such adaptations, for we wish first to consider a set of more frontal assaults on the assumptions. . . . First, is profit the only objective of business firms? Second, does maximization describe what the business firms do about the profits? . . . For example, Rothschild has suggested that the primary motive of the entrepreneur is long-run survival. In this view, decisions aim to maximize the security level of the organization (i.e., the probability that the organization will survive over the indefinite future) . . . . Gordon, Simon, and Margolis have all argued that profit maximizing should be replaced with a goal of making satisfactory profits. Satisfactory profits represent a level of aspiration that the firm uses to evaluate alternative policies. The aspiration level may change over time, but in the short run it defines a utility function with essentially only two values—good enough and not good enough . . . .
>
> Within such a model of the firm [as a cooperative system], Papandreou sees certain areas of psychology playing a helpful role. The goals of the firm are strongly influenced by both internal and external forces. The internal influences come from such entities as stockholders, unions, government, and so forth. . . .
>
> Second, the way in which the theory [Papandreou's] portrays the process of decision making in business firms has been criticized. It is alleged that firms, in fact, do not equate marginal cost and marginal revenue in deciding on either output or price; rather they follow one or another of a series of rules of thumb . . . .[48]

There are further remarks by Cyert and March which would make the comments by Blau and Scott problematic in precisely that area of everyday life—

the economic operations of business or corporate organizations—to which they (Blau and Scott) impute the greatest rationality, but the above quotations should be adequate to point to the necessity of seeking an organizational context for understanding how law-enforcement justifies practices that may have little to do with the implied rationality of ideals of legality and justice abstractly discussed by legal theorists. Specifically, therefore, the actor in law-enforcement organizations makes decisions in terms of his situation and way of thinking that govern his encounter with suspects. These decisions may vary with subsequent encounters, and the accounts of "what happened" will vary accordingly, especially as they assume a formal written status.

Each successive stage of legal decision-making transforms the object or event (as, for example, with rumor transmission) so that the contingencies, the situation in which the actor interprets what is going on, the kind of "theorizing" or thinking employed are progressively altered, eliminated, and reified, as the case proceeds "up" the legal machinery and reaches the stage of a hearing, trial, or appellate jurisdiction. At each stage the various participants select from available "facts" or created interpretations about motives, intent, and the like, those propositions which are to be accorded a factual status in their particular explanation, whether this be from the standpoint of the police, witnesses, lawyers, members of the jury, or judge. The following chapters will examine decision-making through the different stages of the legal process, and show how the background expectancies enable members to search for "valid" explanations of "what happened" and justify decisions.

NOTES

1. The definition or organization I utilize throughout this book is in Harold Garfinkel, "Some Sociological Concepts and Methods for Psychiatrists," *Psychiatric Research Reports* (October 1956) **6**, 181-195:

> . . . the term "an organization" is an abbreviation of the full term "an organization of social actions." The term "organization" does not itself designate a palpable phenomenon. It refers instead to a related set of *ideas* that a sociologist invokes to aid him in collecting his thoughts about the ways in which patterns of social actions are related. His statements about social organization describe the *territory* within which the actions occur; the *number* of persons who occupy that territory; the characteristics of these *persons*, like age, sex, biographies, occupation, annual income, and character structure. He tells how these persons are *socially related* to each other, for he talks of husbands and wives, of bridge partners, of cops and robbers. He describes their *activities*, and the ways they achieve social *access* to each other. And like a grand theme either explicitly announced or implicitly assumed, he describes the *rules* that specify for the actor the use of the area, the numbers of persons who should be in it, the nature of activity, purpose, and feeling allowed, the approved and disapproved means of entrance and exit from affiliative relationships with the persons there (pp. 181-182).

2. Cf. H. L. A. Hart, *The Concept of Law* (Oxford: Oxford University Press, 1961) ; and Lon L. Fuller, *The Morality of Law* (New Haven: Yale University Press, 1964).

3. Max Gluckman, *The Judicial Process Among the Barotse of Northern Rhodesia* (Manchester: Manchester University Press, and New York: Humanities Press, 1955) ; Paul J. Bohannon, *Justice and Judgment Among the Tiv* (London: Oxford University Press, 1957) ; Gluckman, *The Ideas in Barotse Jurisprudence* (New Haven and London: Yale University Press, 1965) ; Laura Nader, "The Anthropological Study of Law," *American Anthropologist* (special publication on "The Ethnography of Law") (December 1965) **67**, 3-32; and P. J. Bohannon, "The Differing Realms of the Law," *ibid.*, 33-42.

4. Austin Porterfield, *Youth in Trouble* (Fort Worth: Leo Potishman Foundation, 1946) ; James S. Wallenstein and C. J. Wyle, "Our Law Abiding Law Breakers," *National Probation* (March-April, 1947), 107-112; F. Ivan Nye, J. F. Short, and V. J. Olsen, "Socioeconomic Status and Delinquent Behavior," in *Family Relationships and Delinquent Behavior* (New York: Wiley, 1948), pp. 23-33; Albert K. Cohen, *Delinquent Boys* (Glencoe: Free Press, 1955) ; Walter B. Miller, "Lower Class Culture as a Generating Milieu of Gang Delinquency," *Journal of Social Issues* **14** (No. 3), 5-19 (1958) ; *Report to the Congress on Juvenile Delinquency*, Children's Bureau, National Institute of Mental Health (U.S. Printing Office, 1960) ; Richard A. Cloward and L. E. Ohlin, *Delinquency and Opportunity* (Glencoe: Free Press, 1960) ; David J. Bordua, "Delinquent Subcultures; Sociological Interpretations of Gang Delinquency," *The Annals of the American Academy of Political and Social Science* (November 1961) **338**, 119-136; Bordua, "Some Comments on Theories of Group Delinquency," *Sociological Inquiry* (Spring, 1961) **32**; Gresham Sykes and D. Matza, "Techniques of Neutralization," *American Sociological Review* (December 1957) **22**, 664-670; David Matza and G. Sykes, "Juvenile Delinquency and Subterranean Values," *American Sociological Review* (October 1961) **26**, 712-719; Albert J. Reiss, Jr. and A. L. Rhodes, "The Distribution of Juvenile Delinquency in the Social Class Structure," *ibid.*, 720-732; Nathan Goldman, *The Differential Selection of Juvenile Offenders for Court Appearances* (New York: National Council on Crime and Delinquency, 1963) ; and Matza, *Delinquency and Drift* (New York: Wiley, 1964).

5. Cf. Anthony Platt, *The Child Savers: The Emergence of the Juvenile Court in Chicago* (Berkeley: School of Criminology, unpublished doctoral dissertation, June 1966).

6. Edwin Sutherland, *White-Collar Crime* (New York: Dryden, 1949).

7. Cf. Henry Hiz, "Kotarbinski's Praxeology," *Philosophy and Phenomenological Research* (Dec. 1954), pp. 238-243; Harold Garfinkel, "Some Sociological Concepts and Methods for Psychiatrists," *op. cit.*, pp. 191-192; Tadeusz Kotarbinski, "Praxiological Sentences and How They are Proved," in E. Nagel, P. Suppes, and A. Tarski (editors), *Logic, Methodology and Philosophy of Science* (Stanford: Stanford University Press, 1962), pp. 211-223; and A. Kaplan, *The Conduct of Inquiry* (San Francisco: Chandler, 1964).

8. Cf. Donald J. Newman, "The Effects of Accommodations in Justice Administration on Criminal Statistics," *Sociology and Social Research* (January 1962) **46**, 144-155; Goldman, *The Differential Selection of Juvenile Offenders for Court Appearances, op. cit.*; Wayne R. La Fave, *Arrest: The Decision to Take a Suspect into Custody* (Boston: Little, Brown, 1965) ; and Jerome H. Skolnick, *Justice Without Trial* (New York: Wiley, 1966).

9. Cf. the references in footnote 4 and A. V. Cicourel, "Social Class, Family Structure, and the Administration of Juvenile Justice," in *Estudios de Sociologia* (Buenos Aires: Bibliografica Omeba, 1965).

10. Cf. Matza, *Delinquency and Drift, op. cit.*, pp. 139-149, for general remarks on how the activities of agents of social control help to sustain a sense of injustice in the subcultural delinquent.

11. *Ibid.*, Chapter 6.
12. Matza and Sykes, "Juvenile Delinquency and Subterranean Values," *op. cit.*, pp. 718-719.
13. Sykes and Matza, "Techniques of Neutralization," *op. cit.*
14. The notion of societal reaction is relevant here by emphasizing both lay and law-enforcement responses to "wrongful " or "illegal" activities. But work derived from the notion of societal reaction fails to specify the observable and tacit properties making up the practical decision-making both lay and law-enforcement officials utilize when deciding some act or sequence of activities is "wrong" or "illegal." Cf. Edwin M. Lemert, *Social Pathology* (New York: McGraw-Hill, 1951); and Jack P. Gibbs, "Conceptions of Deviant Behavior: The Old and the New," *Pacific Sociological Review* (Spring 1966) **9**, 9-14.
15. Hollingshead's occupational factor was used to establish some measure of social class. Cf. August B. Hollingshead, "Two Factor Index of Social Position," dittoed, no date, pp. 1-9.
16. Cf. *Report to the Congress . . . , op. cit.* Much of the material for this section is taken from Cicourel, "Social Class, Family Structure . . . ," *op. cit.*
17. Discussed in Jackson Toby, "The Differential Impact of Family Organization," *American Sociological Review* (Oct. 1957) **22**, 505-512.
18. The reader should note that the entries of each table do not represent frequencies which can be said to constitute independent events since each category is always relative to a variety of coding operations that are not standardized but nevertheless produce a "closing" of the activities or objects described so as to provide the appearance of a set. The coding operations are *ad hoc* procedures for attending conventional theories of delinquency and comparing present results with past findings for the particular problem at hand. Later chapters will reopen this problem in detail.
19. Toby, "The Differential Impact of Family Organization," *op. cit.*, p. 507.
20. *Ibid.*, p. 508.
21. Skolnick, *Justice Without Trial, op. cit.*, Chapter 1.
22. Cf. Herbert L. Packer, "Two Models of the Criminal Process," *University of Pennsylvania Law Review* (November 1964) **113**, 1-68; and Skolnick, *op. cit.*, Chapter 9.
23. Skolnick, *Justice Without Trial*, pp. 196-197.
24. *Ibid.*, pp. 197-198.
25. *Ibid.*, Chapter 10.
26. *Ibid.*, p. 214.
27. J. W. Peltason, *Fifty-Eight Lonely Men* (New York: Harcourt, Brace and World, 1961).
28. Cf. Skolnick, *Justice Without Trial*, Chapter 10. For extensive discussions of the general problem of how typifications enable members to typify and standardize their perception and interpretation of environments, the reader should consult the following: Alfred Schutz, *Collected Papers I* (The Hague: Nijhoff, 1962); Harold Garfinkel, "Studies of the Routine Grounds of Everyday Activities," *Social Problems* (Winter 1964) **11**, 225-250; Aaron V. Cicourel, *Method and Measurement in Sociology* (New York: Free Press, 1964); Max Gluckman, *The Judicial Process Among the Barotse, op. cit.*; Gluckman, "The Reasonable Man in Barotse Law," in *Order and Rebellion in Tribal Africa* (New York: Free Press, 1963), pp. 178-206; Harvey Sacks, "Methods in Use for the Production of a Social Order," dittoed, no date, pp. 1-21; and David Sudnow, "Normal Crimes: Sociological Features of the Penal Code in a Public Defender Office," *Social Problems* (Winter 1965) **12**, 255-276.
29. Cf. William A. Westley, "Violence and the Police," *American Journal of Sociology* (July 1953) **49**, 34-41.
30. See also Arthur L. Stinchcombe, "Institutions of Privacy in the Determination of Police Administrative Practices," *American Journal of Sociology* (September

1963) **69**, pp. 150-160; and Michael Banton, *The Policeman in the Community* (London: Tavistock, 1964).

31. Skolnick, *Justice Without Trial*, Chapter 11.
32. Cf. footnote 2 above.
33. A. W. Gouldner, "Organizational Analysis," in R. K. Merton, L. Broom, and L. S. Cottrell, Jr., *Sociology Today* (New York: Basic Books, 1959), pp. 400-428; J. G. March and H. Simon, *Organizations* (New York: Wiley, 1958) ; and M. Crozier, *The Bureaucratic Phenomenon* (Chicago: University of Chicago Press, 1964).
34. R. K. Merton, *Social Theory and Social Structure* (rev. ed.) (Glencoe: Free Press, 1957) ; A. W. Gouldner, *Patterns of Industrial Bureaucracy* (Glencoe: Free Press, 1954) ; P. M. Blau and W. R. Scott, *Formal Organizations* (San Francisco: Chandler, 1962) ; March and Simon, *op. cit.;* and R. M. Cyert and J. G. March, *A Behavioral Theory of the Firm* (Englewood Cliffs, N.J.: Prentice-Hall, 1963).
35. Cf. W. F. Whyte, et al., *Money and Motivation* (New York: Harper, 1955).
36. Cf. Nelson W. Polsby, "The Sociology of Community Power: A Reassessment," *Social Forces* (March 1959) **37**, 232-236; N. W. Polsby, "Three Problems in the Analysis of Community Power," *American Sociological Review* (December 1959) **24**, 796-803; Raymond E. Wolfinger, "Reputation and Reality in the Study of Community Power," *ibid.* (Oct. 1960) **25**, 636-644; and E. C. Banfield and J. Q. Wilson, *City Politics* (Cambridge: The Joint Center for Urban Studies, 1963).
37. Blau and Scott, *Formal Organizations*, pp. 36-37.
38. *Ibid.*, 206-209.
39. *Ibid.*, 37.
40. Alfred Schutz, "The Problem of Rationality in the Social World," *Economica* **10**, 134 (1943) (and reprinted in Schutz, *Collected Papers I, op. cit.*).
41. *Ibid.*, 141-142.
42. *Ibid.*, 142. The postulate of rationality as described by Schutz implies the following:

(a) Knowledge of the place of the end to be realised within the framework of the plans of the actor (which must be known by him, too).

(b) Knowledge of its interrelations with other ends and its compatibility or incompatibility with them.

(c) Knowledge of the desirable and undesirable consequences which may arise as by-products of the realisation of the main end.

(d) Knowledge of the different chains of means which technically or even ontologically are suitable for the accomplishment of this end, regardless of whether the actor has control of all or several of their elements.

(e) Knowledge of the interference of such means with other ends or chains of means including all of their secondary effects and incidental consequences.

(f) Knowledge of the accessibility of those means for the actor, picking out the means which are within his reach and which he can and may set going (142).

Schutz then includes the following as necessary when speaking of "rational choice":

First: The interpretation or misinterpretation of his own act by his fellow man.
Second: The reaction by the other people and its motivation.
Third: All the outlined elements of knowledge (a to f) which the actor, rightly or wrongly, attributes to his partners.
Fourth: All the categories of familiarity and strangeness, of intimacy and anonymity, of personality and type, which we have discovered in the course of our inventory of the organization of the social world (pp. 142-143).

43. Harold Garfinkel, "The Rational Properties of Scientific and Common Sense Activities," *Behavioral Science* (January 1960) **5**, 72-83.

44. See footnote 28 above.
45. Cf. Schutz and Garfinkel, footnotes 40 and 43.
46. Schutz, "The Problem of Rationality . . . ," *op. cit.*, pp. 139-140.
47. Cf. John Rawls, "Two Concepts of Rules," *The Philosophical Review* (January 1955) **54**, 3-32.
48. Cyert and March, *A Behavioral Theory of the Firm, op. cit.*, pp. 8-13.

Chapter 3

DELINQUENCY RATES AND
ORGANIZATIONAL SETTINGS

In this chapter, materials on delinquency and delinquents taken from police and probation files are examined to reveal how official statistics are assembled. My object is to show how conventional sociological explanations are constructed by researchers using these materials—explanations that sometimes conflict with those available in the literature discussed in the preceding chapter. I shall argue, first, that conventional sociological explanations rely upon tacit assumptions about how the governments and law-enforcement agencies of particular communities work and that these assumptions are too often unexamined. I shall argue, second, that conventional sociological explanations do not take sufficient account of the encoding operations necessarily employed by both those persons who assemble official statistics *and by the researcher*. These two arguments will lead me to question not only the sociological explanations already reviewed, but those I shall construct in the course of presenting materials in this chapter. Chapters 4, 5, 6, and 7 will report the results of participant observation that specifically focused on the problem of how law enforcement agencies encode daily activities, or how official statistics are produced. These latter results will in turn provide a basis for reexamining the materials presented in this chapter.

The Community and Organizational Settings

Of the two California cities studied, City A has a mayor–city-manager–city-council plan. The Chief of Police is appointed by the city manager after recommendations are made by a special board which usually includes outside law-enforcement officers. In City B, there is a mayor–city council plan and the mayor recommends a candidate to the city council. The chief in City B must resign his lower civil service position on the force unless he agrees to an "acting" appointment. The following generalizations were made on the basis of my own impressions of the two cities after discussions with law-enforcement officials and various members of each community, including professionals and businessmen: City A is run with a minimum of "normal" corruption—its employees have seldom been involved in public scandals, and the "corruption" that does exist must be labeled "legal," even though many feel it is not within the "spirit" of the law; City B, on the other hand, has a history of corruption, vice, and underworld elements in both city and county government, and in both sets of law-enforcement agencies (sheriff and police departments). It would be difficult to objectify my characterization of the two cities even if I included remarks made by informants throughout the study. In the case of City A, I was unable to pinpoint corruption in the police department or city political administration, and the same was true of the Board of Supervisors for the county, the sheriff, and the probation department. The discussions of corruption in City A did not include the use of the term "corruption," but referred to "deals" and the lack of ethical responsibility on the part of the city council. The daily newspaper of City A reported frequently about city council changes in zoning laws, sale of city land to developers, and other real estate action which favored certain parties, including firms that city council members were connected with contractually or through family ties.

City B, on the other hand, has been noted locally for corruption in virtually all areas of city and county life, including state and federal representatives. My informants in City B were primarily police and probation officials I had come to know well during a period of several years. There had been several publicized scandals in the newspapers over illegal activities by the police. Police informants revealed that the public information that appeared in the daily newspaper, as would be expected, was but a small part of the illegal activities that occur. An additional complication stemmed from informants' claims that the daily newspaper was a party to the corruption. At the end of my field work, a reform mayor and a new chief of police (a key informant throughout my study) took office in City B. Interviews with both men revealed a wider pattern of corruption than previously suspected, and this included many highly placed city officials, important businessmen, and high-ranking police officers.

But to understand how municipal and law-enforcement bureaucracy and administration is reflected in the social organization of juvenile justice, a few remarks about the organization of any city (or larger unit of analysis) are required.

A useful idea here is that of viewing city politics, governmental agencies, business enterprises, voluntary associations, and the like, as an ecology of games,[1] each with its authority and power bases, administrative organization, and bureaucratic problems in the pejorative sense, used by Crozier and others interested in the "human relations" or natural system problems of large-scale organizations.[2] The assertion that City A emphasizes the city manager-city council type of local government with little patronage and an efficient and rather corruption-free police department, while City B has a mayor-city council plan with patronage and a police department, known locally for its dishonesty, provides two contrasting settings for understanding how different organizations concerned with juvenile delinquency and justice act or fail to act on similar problems.

The essential idea in the ecology-of-games notion is that power is not centrally organized around one person or an elite that more or less decides how the "pie is to be divided," but there are different centers of power in the community in imperfect communication with each other, and imperfectly utilizing their resources to the extent that some groups, therefore, appear to be powerful or exercise more power than others by default.[3] There are many "games" such as banking, business, newspapers, local government, education, police, the district attorney and the courts, rackets, and the like—all in a kind of union or intersection as suggested by, but not equivalent to, the set-theoretic sense of the terms.[4] The "games" cooperate or are in conflict over the exercise of influence. There is a kind of economics of imperfect competition in that some types of interest are viewed as "naturally" falling within certain "games," while other areas are problematic. The idea of unstated rules of cooperation underscores the idea that all parties benefit from playing the game regardless of the formal "sides" they are on officially. For example, in City A, school officials cooperated better with the police than with probation officers even though school personnel identified more with the better educated and more professional probation officer (and vice versa). The practical problem for the schools was that of controlling "kids," and there was not much interest in the "rehabilitation" or "adjustment" orientation and activities of probation officers if the juvenile was considered a "troublemaker" at school.

The organization of the political game in local government obviously can affect the ways in which other games will operate internally and vis-à-vis some product or client. Thus the police are dependent upon their law-enforcement mandate from their chief, the extent to which he will protect them from political pressure, and the way they carry out policies as delegated to them. If the chief is appointed in terms of patronage, as in City B, then his tenure of office is not likely to be long (it has seldom been long in City B with many chiefs maintaining acting appointments to preserve their civil-service status) and many day-to-day routines will be affected each time there is a change in local politics and the office of the chief. In such a situation, a concern with the notion of administrative efficiency can seldom be the focal point of day-to-day routines, nor will there be much interest in resolving problems connected with work activities or interpersonal problems between staff and line. Most of the daily activities focus upon practical solutions to immediate problems (for example, the complaints of clients) and the development of individual interests and "payoffs."

I have asserted that political influence on law enforcement is minimal in City A, yet no civil service system exists even though its merit system operates like one in practice. City B is based upon civil service procedures. In both City A and City B, the merit and civil service systems operate similarly in that it is difficult to dismiss anyone. Outside review boards for promotion are common in City A, while in City B, informants reported considerable manipulation by the police commission. While City A has very orderly promotions with long tenure in office for ranking police officers and city officials but retains the merit system, City B retains its lower-level police and city personnel, while frequent changes occur at the top. In City A, there is less politicking on the part of law-enforcement heads, as far as their personal ambitions are concerned, their political activities often being restricted to seeking more budget allowances for their departments. Police officers below the chief in City A occasionally join fraternal orders if they are ambitious within the community and department, but are seldom involved directly in city politics. The obverse is true of City B where even nonranking detectives are politically active and seek and obtain some measure of community power independent of their police position. Such activities serve not only to give them independence within the department but, combined with their official position, augments their power outside of the force. Many detectives in City B are able to command better income and influence outside of the force (using the office as a base of operations) through independent business interests or political activities. Such activities are not only sources of mobility (within and outside of the force), but they also weaken the hierarchical organization of the department. It is not uncommon in City B for a sergeant to become an acting chief of police for a period of time and then return to his former position below men he previously commanded. This has never occurred in City A. Even moonlighting activities in the two cities follow the pattern described above: In City A, most off-duty police activities are organized through the police department, for example, policing dances and football games, while in City B, such arrangements are made individually and usually include many types of outside work such as security work at department stores.

The ecology of games, therefore, obviously differs for different cities and provides several rough boundary conditions for understanding the kinds of interaction that are likely to occur between different power groups. The extent to which different games operate, through individual or collective activities during interaction, depends upon the political system in operation. It is often assumed that employees of agencies and departments work through their chief officers, but there are usually key actors who break out of rigid bureaucratized

channels of communication to coordinate organizational activities more effi-
ciently. But when key actors are "in business for themselves," direct action
obviously weakens the authority of each separate department head and encour-
ages contacts between subordinates and outside power figures. City B is riddled
with a multitude of coalitions that cross-cut the various "games" of the community.[5] In City A, in contrast to City B, there is pride in the professionaliza-
tion of the police department, and individual officers form something of a
social ingroup described by Skolnick, while staying away from city politics.
Therefore, internal police decisions in City A are less likely to be questioned
by the district attorney, defense attorney, probation officer, and judge, than
is the case in City B.

District attorneys, defense attorneys, and judges in both cities are always
politically involved—as would be expected in any city—with local affairs and
often state and even national affairs. In both City A and City B, the district
attorneys seemed more concerned with the possibility of success in particular
cases and reluctant to prosecute when some doubt exists as to winning, even
though they may be convinced personally that the suspect is guilty. I stress the
point that the hesitation and "deals"[6] that occur are not based on due process
considerations or whether the case falls under some legal jurisdiction, but
seem to be based on extralegal factors such as the District Attorney's reputation for winning, his political ambitions within and outside the community,
and his interest in "getting along" with particular elements in the city.

The Implementation of a Complex Policy

The organization of juvenile justice is complicated by different and often
conflicting philosophies and policies. The police are theoretically bound by the
philosophy of the juvenile court law, but changes in the law in California have
come about because of abuses attributed primarily to the police. The Governor's Special Study Commission on Juvenile Justice (1960) in California led to
many changes in the law, many of which were designed to protect the minor's
rights. The Commission's recommendations were not always far ahead of
rapid changes in several of the more professionally oriented police departments
in the state, but the reports and subsequent legislation did validate those practices and introduce innovations into administrative procedures vis-à-vis
juveniles.

The different and conflicting issues here revolve around what I take to be a
basic dilemma in police and probation work—the use of punishment-oriented
views during encounters with "difficult-to-handle," "rough," juveniles who do
not seem to respond to the essentially "clinical" orientation some juvenile
police and, especially, probation officers assume should be used. Police officers
appear to be least interested in adopting this "clinical" orientation even though

juvenile officers do formally claim to identify with the principles of the juvenile court law. At state and regional meetings of the California State Juvenile Officers Association, there are frequent remarks acknowledging both the criticism or jokes made by other police officers and the indication of increased desirability of working in juvenile bureaus. But the clinical-control cleavage stems from juvenile officers' attempts to implement simultaneously both a "clinical" or permissive approach (where the notion of a "permissive approach" does not always imply imputations of illness), and social control orientation practiced by their colleagues in patrol or the detective bureau. The probation department and the court, various community agencies, and the juvenile court law-created Juvenile Justice Commission of each county remind the police of the special or "civil" nature of the juvenile court law and the importance of "rehabilitating" youth who get into trouble. But the professional orientation of the police department emphasizes the repression and control of criminal activities regardless of age and relies upon typified imputations of "disorganized" or "bad" environments for seeking offenders. For the police, "robbery" or "rape" has little to do with the age of the offender or his life circumstances. The two departments studied provided both a professionally oriented organization (City A) and one more or less patterned after the model of the corrupt big city force (City B), intimately associated with political and criminal graft and corruption, vividly illustrating the conflicting orientations the police employ. The following general statements, based upon my impressions, will give the reader a rough idea of how the administration of juvenile justice proceeds and the organizational context of police and probation activities:[7]

1. The apprehension of juveniles involves an almost immediate disregard for the procedures of criminal law; adult arrest, and search and seizure rules are seldom followed.

2. There are few formal legal procedures followed, and the problem of evidence seldom poses a serious issue, inasmuch as a presumption of guilt is often an integral part of the investigative process.

3. Although the issue of advising the suspect of his constitutional rights was a controversial issue in California during the period of this study, the two departments studied did not routinely advise the juveniles accordingly. In rare and serious cases the suspects would be advised. (In a nearby large city, however, both juveniles and adults were usually advised of their rights by juvenile officers. The policy in City A and City B was handed down by different judges in the two counties and was assumed to be consistent with the intent of the juvenile court law.

4. The police utilize a rather strict social control model for juveniles they

feel are guilty and repeaters; the juveniles are handcuffed and treated as adults.

5. The police investigation of a case invariably includes a meeting between the suspect, his family, and the officer, and separate interrogations with both the juvenile and his family. The mood appears "serious" and the simulated use of legal rules of procedure varies with particular cases.

6. Probation investigation also includes a meeting with the family, but here the atmosphere is clinical in orientation. Legal rules of procedure are notably absent. The conversation always revolves around "helping" the juvenile, and there is explicit interviewing concerning family problems and the personal adjustment of the offender.

7. The court hearing always includes a (sometimes quick, unclear or perfunctory) reference to the right to counsel by the juvenile and his family, even though the hearing itself represents a fairly cut-and-dried operation which is seldom challenged. The "hearing" (or occasionally simulated "trial") has been settled by way of unofficial communications between the probation officer, his supervisor, the offender and his family, and the court referee or judge. The hearing is sort of a ritual ceremony that provides an abstract operational validity to underscore the seriousness of the matter. The hearing enables the probation officer, the judge, or the family to underscore particular or general features of what has happened and the consequences that may follow if it happens again.

8. Neither the offender nor his family take the suggestion of the right to counsel seriously unless there is a fear (hinted at by the probation officer beforehand) that the juvenile may be placed outside the home. In the latter case, the family is often middle- to upper-class in the socioeconomic scale. A due process format may then be introduced into the proceedings.

All parties in the administration of juvenile justice formally assume their task is to "help" the youth in question; therefore, promoting a concern with constitutional rights is difficult to enforce. One source of changes in the California juvenile court law has been motivated by legally minded partisans who felt that the police were routinely adopting a punishment-oriented view toward the suspect known to be a recidivist, where the presumption of guilt was common, and where the lack of due process procedures was felt to necessitate the inclusion of changes to protect the juvenile. The argument is clearly similar to the continuing debate in adult cases over arrest and search and seizure procedures. An understanding of police "rationality" requires an appreciation of their practical circumstances.

A basic dilemma of juvenile justice is the belief in individualized "treatment" so that the offender may be helped back to a "normal" life, but the professional orientation of police departments emphasizes social control and an efficient administrative operation that does not include the allocation of time for a "treatment-oriented" approach to "helping" youth. The juvenile officer is ambivalent because he seeks to embrace a semiprofessional view of juvenile activities that includes a justification of the juvenile court law, but his daily work activities are oriented by the adult penal code, so that his cases are not seen always as falling under the juvenile court law. By invoking the punitive, social control model of the police department, the juvenile officer is caught between general administrative policy and practice, and the particular, more special type of case the juvenile offender implies. The matter is complicated because the semiprofessional juvenile officers' association officially sanctions the "special treatment" approach implied in the juvenile court law.

The probation department, on the other hand, is somewhat less troubled by the same dilemma. Probation officials, when dealing with particular types of juveniles, often employ a similar solution, but for different reasons and with less severity—but with their own professional image and professional objectives. One group seems oriented toward social work, while another group seeks to avoid complete identification with social work and to develop an independent professional orientation. Inasmuch as the clinically oriented social work position is more developed, is organized professionally, and is invariably invoked as a needed set of procedures for handling delinquent youth, it is difficult for the probation officer to avoid at least a superficial usage of clinical terminology in describing a youth's problems and his family context. The case load assigned to the probation officer and the organization of the staff along professional-supervisory lines, with less hierarchy than the police, tends to force the probation department into a kind of social work organizational structure. The use of secretaries for dictating the results of interviews, a standard type of outline for writing up the interview, frequent staff meetings to discuss cases and policies that give a professional atmosphere to the department, and considerable autonomy and personal freedom in carrying out work assignments and accounting for time—all contribute to the desire on the part of the probation officer to generate professional appearances.

But the professional aspirations of both police and probation officers are dampened by the fact that salary scales are fixed, and social mobility within the organization is limited. Most police departments, regardless of whether they operate on a civil service or merit system, are slow to promote their men, and a series of tests and interviews are constant obstacles. The fact that officers are neither always motivated nor feel they have the time to study for examinations, are often "nervous" about board interviews, realize that promotions will invariably take them out of their present assignment, put them on nights more often, or work more weekends, means that the monetary rewards and added responsibility accompanying promotions are not always very attractive. Thus the daily routine of work occurs within a setting that does not offer many changes, surprises, or aspirations, except for a few who are willing to undergo the difficulties of moving up in the system. Some dissension results from younger men successfully passing examinations and interview boards, and then moving up faster than the men who "broke them in." Even in the relatively honest department of City A, promotions always implied some type of internal political influence or favoritism. Inasmuch as seniority is a critical factor for maintaining a particular position and level of pay, it is very difficult for a police officer to change jobs and move to other departments except as a chief. The latter often is not done until he has accumulated enough years in one department so that he can later receive retirement pay at the age of 60 or 65, thereby lessening the danger of getting fired as chief. The police officer, therefore, is fairly "locked" into his job and must adjust to the circumstances of the particular department he is in. For officers who do not move "up" very far—the bulk of them—everyday police work takes on a routine character. The officer develops his theories about individuals and groups, morality and immorality, good and bad people, institutions, practices, and typifications of community settings, and such theories or conceptions are employed in routine ways according to recipes not likely to make due process features of his work problematic. An administrative organization demanding standardized reports and standardized procedures readily suggests a social control model as the central orienting ideology for everyday police activities, but where rationalities of action are fused with the problems of limited mobility and the practical circumstances of restricted ingroup relations that seldom change.

The average probation officer's college degree gives him a broader base from which to claim professional status, but the organizational structure of the probation department leaves him few possibilities for change and little difference in pay. The probation department pyramids faster than the military-like police, so that a regular deputy probation officer is restricted in his internal social mobility. The emphasis is upon professional work orientation, and there are few higher positions whose occupancy he can achieve. Civil service or merit system seniority requirements make it difficult to move to another department, except early in the game, because one must start at the bottom again, as in the police department. Therefore, within the probation department, there is little excitement generated by the cases handled, and personalized or individualized attention is difficult because of heavy caseloads, court appearances, investigative interviews, or routine calls. Keeping up with bureaucratic ritual and administrative demands leaves little time for more professional activity, for example, additional training, quality control of interviews and reports, and professional discussion about theories and trends in crime and delinquency, even though the state and county organizations seek to supply some of these activities at annual or more frequent regional meetings. Those probation officers interested in professional development recognize the discrepancy between their aspirations and the practical circumstances of achieving the necessary activities. Both police and probation departments have a difficult time obtaining the necessary funds from city councils and county supervisors for the kind of in-service and outside training which they would like and which they feel is necessary for continued professional growth, as well as minimal information flow into the departments. Few officers (among the police as well) are interested in taking the time away from other activities they enjoy and from their families for "re-tooling" periodically or regularly. The fact that professional activities do not guarantee rewards in the form of pay, promotion, or change in duties has not helped this picture. But there are demands for giving lectures or appearances before various civic groups and voluntary associations interested in "youth" or community "betterment." Success with regional or state-wide organizations is not necessarily correlated with success or rank in the local organization, and participants and elected officers of both juvenile officer associations and probation, parole, and corrections officers' associations are not always of higher rank in the police or probation department.[8]

My observations suggest police and probation perspectives follow community typifications in organizing the city into areas where they expect to receive the most difficulty from deviant or "difficult" elements to areas where little trouble is expected and where more care should be taken in dealing with the populace because of socioeconomic and political influence. The partition of the city into areas of more or less anticipated crime provides both police and probation officers with additional typifications about what to expect when patrolling or making calls in the areas. Thus the officer's preconstituted typifications and stock of knowledge at hand leads him to prejudge much of what he encounters, which an independent observer does not always "see." Thus, particular ecological settings, populated by persons with "known" styles of dress and physical appearance, provide the officer with quick inferences about "what is going on" although not based upon factual-type material he must describe sooner or later in oral or written form.

The officer's typifications about social types, causation, and typical outcomes enable him to construct "careers" based on what different delinquent types are likely to follow, contingent upon the kinds of decisions made at given points in time. Thus, at a certain point, the officer may narrow the possible alternatives down to one: commitment to the California Youth Authority. The prior activities of the youth, his family situation, his "attitude," the kinds of resources available to him and his family, and the likelihood they will be used and may prove effective narrow the possibilities of the disposition decision.

The officer's imputation of "career" (for example, "this kid is a real loser") is revealed by the oral and written remarks made about the suspect and is to be distinguished from the "career" that the sociologist constructs as a consequence of tracing the different conceptions of the same youth, revealed by official records of the police, the family, the school, and probation department. Each of the latter have their own notion of "career" or the short-run and long-run courses of action the suspect is likely to pursue. The sociologist's imputation of a composite career is intended to show how each separate career is produced, and how the composite career can be an unintended product that is independent of the various careers taken singly, or "historicized" by whoever chooses to interpret the meaning of the juvenile's actions after the fact.

Each career-generating agency maintains and selects "facts" for interpretation by means of its own ideology, theories, organizational policies, and practices. Therefore, categorization into "points of no return" or the view that "nothing more can be done" or "the right foster home will do the trick" or the "right peer group will change him," and so forth, are rooted in the kinds of structural arrangements the agency feels are possible, and the particular encounters a representative of the agency maintains with the juvenile in question.

But the careers generated by different agencies are also dependent upon the particular way information is obtained and the resources available to the police, probation, the school, the family, and so on. The school information may only include an official transcript of grades, omitting relevant comments about behavior in class, truancy, and other factors, or simply stress the existence of a behavioral problem in class.

The juvenile officer is a detective armed with a variety of theories about different areas of the city, the kinds of "kids" who "get into trouble," a network of informers and sources of information, written and mental notations about possible suspects and "shady characters," various fragments of information about persons he feels are guilty of different offenses, but against whom he does not have the evidence necessary to convince the probation department or the district attorney, and so forth. The policeman's network or "map" of community activities is, therefore, much more extensive than the information obtainable from observations of concrete action he undertakes for initiating, and following through with, judicial procedures designed to convict persons of law violation. The maintenance of written and mental "dossiers" include persons who may be "clean" now, and with respect to whom no action is now possible, and those for whom there is insufficient evidence, but the perspective which guides the officer's actions is that at any point in time the information might be instrumental in suggesting "leads" and evidence for conviction and clearing cases.

Probation officers employ a kind of quasi-social work or psychiatric interview that—in contrast to the police—takes into account such factors as establishing "rapport" with the subject and utilizing more abstract interrogative procedures. The probation officer's training and sources of information are more limited and do not have the aura of "inside dopesterism" that is implicit in police contacts and information. Whereas police and probation officers seldom take systematic notes, the latter follow a fairly standard outline which resembles a clinical sheet often found in social work agencies or in the files of psychiatric clinics. The language used to describe the suspect or offender's life and behavior is full of global phrases and often empty remarks that are designed to be "objective" and detached, but are often based upon vague notes and impressions about the subject. The simulation of a professional interview appears more successful on paper than when it is observed or overheard, and the final product contains little documentation and many labels, clichés, and vaguely used global-type concepts designed to "explain" the subject's predicament. But the reader must always be aware of the truncated nature of police and probation files. Thus, tables constructed from files are even more truncated abstractions of the original events leading to the assembly of the files. It is not the abstractions themselves about which I am complaining, but the lack of theories and procedures in sociological studies for moving from original events to files and then to tables. Tables derived from police and probation records, census materials, vital statistics, and other organization sources are invariably disengaged from the original events, and there is an absence of theories and procedures that would show what meanings are preserved, distorted, and transformed by the abstraction process. To ignore members' and researchers' abstraction processes is to ignore the heart of the problem.

Before turning to the tables assembled from the two cities studied, I want to underscore how their interpretation *necessarily presumes* a knowledge of the impressionistic descriptions given in this section. Yet it is common for social scientists to utilize delinquency rates from local, state, or national sources and construct inferences that never clarify what is presumed about community and law-enforcement organizations. The "findings" of the next section, therefore, are typical of the current practice of using statistical rates *disengaged from* the everyday practices of the organizations producing them. Subsequent chapters will make such rates and findings problematic by examining the everyday decisions of law-enforcement personnel in active cases.

Delinquency Rates in City A and City B

The data presented in this section were assembled by standard sociological procedures for generating the information necessary for examining the kinds of arguments cited earlier in my review of delinquency theories. These data strongly question the theories described earlier and structural notions presented by theorists like Merton.[9]

The tables represent the routine results of police and probation work, whereby unclear policies, procedures, and imputations (taken for granted by the researcher) produce suspects, delinquents, victims, and the like, according to socially organized and accepted practices of police, probation, and laymen pursuing their everyday affairs.

An examination of Tables 1 and 2 reveals differences in the number of

Table 1

Number of Offenders and Offenses
in City A and City B (1962)

	City A	City B
Number of offenders	446	498[a]
Number of offenses	1028	768

[a] Original samples of 500 from each city. Fifty-four and two cases, respectively, were not used because of lack of information.

Table 2

Offenders by Number of Repeated Offenses
in Cities A and B (1962)

	City A		City B		Percentage Difference
	N	%	N	%	
1	258	58	385	77	+19
2	84	19	60	12	−07
3	43	10	19	4	−06
4	18	4	10	2	−02
5	10	2	11	2	00
6+	33	7	13	3	−04
Totals	446	100	498	100	

offenses and offenders in the samples taken from the two cities studied. City A appears to have the larger number of recidivists. The differences seem to be associated with extensive organizational differences for there were large differences in the actual number of offenders carried in the files of the two police departments (8000 cases for City A and 3200 for City B in November 1962) at the time the samples were drawn.

Given the roughly equivalent population of 100,000 for each city, another explanation could be generated by reference to the fact that City A had more juvenile officers with which to investigate and apprehend suspects (three officers in City B to five in City A). An additional sample of 1615 new individuals (with 1873 offenses), taken from the entire 1964 records of City B (see Table 3), can be contrasted with 3036 new cases in City A for 1961, 3162 cases for 1962, 4088 cases for 1963, and the 2021 cases handled during the first six months of 1964 in City A (see Table 4). It should be added that the Juvenile Bureau in City A increased its staff in 1963 (from five in November 1962) to

Table 3
Total Number of Offenders in City B
for 1964 by Number of Offenses

	N
Number of cases	1615
Number of offenses	1873

Table 4
Total Offenders for City A
During 1961-1964

Year	N
1961	3036
1962	3162
1963	4088
1964	2021[a]

[a] First six months only.

a total of seven officers.[10] An obvious remark here is that we should expect the cases handled to increase as the number of officers increases. But I am also suggesting that there are qualitative differences in the type of "net" and how many "fish" will be caught. The meaning of the rates is contingent upon the number of law-enforcement officials as well as unexplicated criteria concerning who will be stopped, interrogated, and detained as an offender.

The information contained in Table 5 reveals a fairly similar breakdown for both cities vis-à-vis the sex ratio of offenders suspected or known to the police. Table 6, based upon the 1964 material for City B, also reveals an almost identical sex ratio for that city. The sample taken from City B in November 1962 and the total recorded universe of 1964 appear comparable and the former can be viewed as representative of the city. Although 1873 entries are recorded for 1964 in City B, with 1615 different individuals involved, it is not the case that multiple offenses are always recorded. Police discretion in the field and office and in record keeping pose insoluble problems for the researcher seeking measurement devices that will yield precise rates of delinquency. More about this problem later; here I shall only repeat that police detection and investigation invariably complicate the assembly of rates because of discretion over who is apprehended, who will talk, and how incidents are reported and recorded.

The figures presented in Table 7 are of interest because of differences in the distribution of male offenders in the two cities. The prevalence of repeat offenders in the last year of junior high school and throughout high school suggests more "hard core" cases. City A has more recorded repeaters than City

Table 5

*Sex Ratio of Offenders in
Cities A and B (1962)*

	City A		City B	
	N	Percent	N	Percent
Male	312	70	378	76
Female	132	30	120	24
Totals	444ª	100	498	100

ª No information on two cases.

Table 6

Offenders by Sex Ratio in City B during 1964

	N	Percent
Male	1200	74.3
Female	415	25.7
Totals	1615	100

B and fewer first offenders, at least in the later junior and senior high period. (The cases for ages 0-6 are usually child neglect or similar problems.) Differences in the two police departments suggest that organizational procedures could account for the recorded differences, with the larger and more professional staff of City A expected to produce more repeaters. The fact that there are 97 males for whom there is no information in City B, however, precludes a "convincing" argument. The information from the 1964 City B material provides additional information because it reveals the bulk of the offenders were 13 years of age and over, heaviest at the high school age levels (see Table 8).

Table 9 shows that most of the offenses were first contacts (1420) in 1964 for most of the offenders in City B. The differences are in the "expected"

Table 7

*Number of Offenses by Age and Sex
in Cities A and B (1962)*

Sex	Age	City A Offenses							City B Offenses						
		1	2	3	4	5	6+	Totals	1	2	3	4	5	6+	Totals
Male	0-6	23	4	—	—	—	—	27	25	—	—	—	—	—	25
	7-8	13	2	1	—	1	1	18	16	—	—	—	—	—	16
	9	17	—	—	1	—	—	18	13	2	—	—	—	—	15
	10	16	6	—	—	—	—	22	10	4	—	—	—	—	14
	11	17	2	1	1	—	1	22	12	—	—	—	2	—	14
	12	11	4	3	—	—	—	18	18	3	2	—	—	—	23
	13	21	9	5	1	—	2	38	15	1	2	1	—	1	20
	14	19	5	4	2	—	3	33	20	6	2	—	2	2	32
	15	14	11	8	5	—	7	45	25	10	2	1	4	—	42
	16	8	6	4	2	3	3	26	20	9	3	2	—	2	36
	17-18	5	12	3	1	3	8	32	18	12	3	3	2	6	44
Female	0-6	14	8	3	1	—	—	26	17	2	—	—	—	1	20
	7-8	6	—	—	—	—	—	6	7	—	—	—	—	—	7
	9	7	1	—	—	—	—	8	2	—	—	—	—	—	2
	10	6	—	—	—	—	—	6	2	—	—	—	—	—	2
	11	3	3	—	—	—	—	6	6	2	—	—	—	—	8
	12	5	2	1	—	—	—	8	6	2	—	—	—	—	8
	13	9	1	—	—	—	—	10	10	1	1	—	—	—	12
	14	8	3	2	—	—	1	14	9	2	1	—	—	—	12
	15	9	2	1	—	1	3	16	14	2	1	1	1	—	19
	16	1	1	4	—	1	—	7	7	1	2	—	—	—	10
	17-18	6	1	3	4	2	2	18	3	—	—	1	—	—	4
	Totals	238	83	43	18	11	31	424ª	275	59	19	9	11	12	385ᵇ

ª No information on 22 cases (7 females and 15 males).
ᵇ No information on 113 cases (16 females and 97 males).

direction: "loose" reporting and a lack of interest in pursuing delinquency in City B leads to less reportage of repeat offenders.

The material from Table 10 does not suggest a strong case for arguing that City B produces more Negro and Mexican-American offenders than City A. The 1960 Census shows that the nonwhite population for City A was 4.67 percent, while it was 7.4 percent in City B. The Mexican-American population of City B is reportedly higher (data not available) than that of City A (which for the 1960 Census was estimated at 8.53 percent). I shall assume that a disproportionate number of ethnics was handled in City B, and that the differences in Mexican-American population are similar to those reported for

Negroes, because of impressionistic data from informants (including police officers) that ethnics in City B are beaten and not always picked up officially. Patrol and detective officers do not want such incidents recorded because juvenile officers would complain. There are several *ad hoc* possibilities for

Table 8

Age at Present Offense
in 1964 for City B

	N	Percent
01	5	0.3
02	2	0.1
03	3	0.2
04	5	0.3
05	6	0.3
06	19	1.0
07	6	0.3
08	8	0.4
09	15	0.8
10	25	1.3
11	57	3.0
12	91	4.9
13	149	8.0
14	265	14.2
15	350	18.7
16	398	21.2
17	373	20.2
18	17	0.9
19	2	0.1
20	2	0.1
No information	70	3.7
Totals	1873	100

Table 9

Number of Police Contacts for
Juveniles in City B for 1964

		N	Percent
	1	1420	88
Total contacts	2	153	9.5
for year 1964	3	28	1.7
	4	7	0.4
	5	7	0.4
Totals		1615	100

Table 10
Offenders by Race in Cities A and B (1962)

	City A		City B[a]	
Race	N	Percent	N	Percent
White	358	80	303	61
Mexican-American	48	11	133	27
Negro	26	6	55	11
Other	14	3	2	—
Totals	446	100	493	99

[a] No information: 5 cases.

explaining the overrepresentation of ethnics, but I shall assume that City B's police department is more likely to perceive ethnics as "trouble-makers." The differences (in Table 10) between Mexican-American and nonwhite reported offenders, as opposed to white offenders in City A, do not fit official statistics or lay impressions that nonwhite offenders are overrepresented in contrast to the white population. But in the 1964 material (see Table 11) for

Table 11
Offenders by Race in City B for 1964

Race	N	Percent
White	930	57.6
Mexican-American	427	26.4
Negro	255	15.8
Indian	2	0.1
Other	1	0.1
Totals	1615	100

City B, the Mexican-American offender population remains high and is almost identical to that reported for the general sample from 1962. The Negro figure (15.8 percent) is higher—exactly double the reported 1960 Census figure of 7.4 percent nonwhite for City B. City B's police department has been depicted by ethnic informers as negative toward Negroes, and the percent of Negro offenders is high, but not as dramatic as popular conceptions and official statistics imply. Informants' conceptions of City A is that of a well-policed, nonghettoized community, while City B has been described in opposite terms by residents and outsiders alike. In Table 12 (City B), notice that females seem to be overrepresented among Mexican-American and Negro offenders, but City B's figures lack information for 93 males as opposed to 16 females. (See Tables 13-15 for further details.)

Table 12
Offenders by Race and Sex in Cities A and B (1962)

| | City A | | | | City B | | | |
| | Male | | Female | | Male | | Female | |
Race	N	Percent	N	Percent	N	Percent	N	Percent
White	254	85	98	78	180	63	51	49
Mexican- American	29	10	18	14	74	26	35	34
Negro	16	5	10	8	31	11	18	17
Totals	299[a]	100	126[b]	100	285[c]	100	104[d]	100

[a] "Other" and no information = 15.
[b] "Other" and no information = 6.
[c] "Other" and no information = 93.
[d] "Other" and no information = 16.

Table 13
Number of White Offenses by Age, Sex,
in Cities A and B (1962)

| | | City A | | | | | | | City B | | | | | |
Sex	Age	1	2	3	4	5	6+	Totals	1	2	3	4	5	6+	Totals
Male	0-6	18	3	—	—	—	—	21	16	—	—	—	—	—	16
	7-8	11	2	—	—	1	1	15	12	—	—	—	—	—	12
	9	11	—	—	1	—	—	12	7	1	—	—	—	—	8
	10	15	5	—	—	—	—	20	9	3	—	—	—	—	12
	11	17	2	1	1	—	1	22	9	—	—	—	1	—	10
	12	10	3	2	—	—	—	15	11	2	1	—	—	—	14
	13	15	7	5	2	—	1	30	10	—	—	1	—	—	11
	14	19	4	4	3	—	—	30	13	3	1	—	1	1	19
	15	14	10	8	5	1	3	41	18	7	1	1	—	—	27
	16	8	4	3	2	1	3	21	14	4	2	2	—	1	23
	17-18	5	11	2	1	3	5	27	12	9	2	1	—	4	28
Female	0-6	10	6	3	1	—	—	20	10	—	—	—	—	—	10
	7-8	4	—	—	—	—	—	4	3	—	—	—	—	—	3
	9	5	1	—	—	—	—	6	1	—	—	—	—	—	1
	10	6	—	—	—	—	—	6	1	—	—	—	—	—	1
	11	3	2	—	—	—	—	5	3	1	—	—	—	—	4
	12	4	1	1	—	—	—	6	3	1	—	—	—	—	4
	13	7	1	—	—	—	—	8	6	1	—	—	—	—	7
	14	6	1	1	—	—	1	9	4	1	1	—	—	—	6
	15	7	—	—	—	—	1	8	6	2	1	—	1	—	10
	16	2	1	4	—	—	1	8	3	1	—	—	—	—	4
	17-18	8	1	2	4	1	2	18	—	—	—	1	—	—	1
Totals		205	65	36	20	7	19	352	171	36	9	6	3	6	231

Table 14

*Number of Mexican-American Offenses by
Age, Sex, in Cities A and B (1962)*

Sex	Age	No. of Offenses in City A							No. of Offenses in City B						
		1	2	3	4	5	6+	Totals	1	2	3	4	5	6+	Totals
Male	0-6	3	1	—	—	—	—	4	5	—	—	—	—	—	5
	7-8	1	—	—	—	—	—	1	2	—	—	—	—	—	2
	9	3	—	—	—	—	—	3	3	1	—	—	—	—	4
	10	—	—	—	—	—	—	—	1	1	—	—	—	—	2
	11	1	—	—	—	—	—	1	3	—	—	—	1	—	4
	12	1	—	—	—	—	—	1	4	1	—	—	—	—	5
	13	3	1	—	—	—	—	4	5	1	1	—	—	1	8
	14	3	1	—	—	—	1	5	6	2	1	—	1	—	10
	15	1	1	1	—	1	—	4	4	2	1	—	3	—	10
	16	1	1	1	—	—	—	3	5	4	1	—	—	1	11
	17-18	—	—	—	—	—	3	3	3	2	1	3	1	3	13
Female	0-6	1	1	—	—	—	—	2	2	1	—	—	—	—	3
	7-8	—	—	—	—	—	—	—	4	—	—	—	—	—	4
	9	—	—	—	—	—	—	—	1	—	—	—	—	—	1
	10	—	—	—	—	—	—	—	—	—	—	—	—	—	—
	11	—	1	—	—	—	—	1	3	1	—	—	—	—	4
	12	1	1	—	—	—	—	2	2	1	—	—	—	—	3
	13	2	—	—	—	—	—	2	2	—	1	—	—	—	3
	14	3	1	1	—	—	—	5	3	1	—	—	—	—	4
	15	2	—	—	—	—	2	4	5	—	—	1	—	—	6
	16	—	—	—	—	1	—	1	4	—	1	—	—	—	5
	17-18	—	—	—	—	—	1	1	2	—	—	—	—	—	2
	Totals	26	9	3	0	2	7	47	69	18	7	4	6	5	109

Conventional theories of delinquency (high rates for ethnics and lower-income families) become problematic when we examine Table 16 where lower-income groups do not dominate the cases; in City A the argument does not hold, while in City B it appears that the conventional argument obtains some support but is certainly not convincing. (*Note:* the missing cases are primarily families living outside the 1960 city limits, annexed since then.) While this could mean lower-income areas in the county, that is, unincorporated areas, there were high-income areas also annexed, and it would be difficult to argue that for City A the general results of Table 16 would be affected greatly. In City B, it also could be argued that many of the outside-of-city cases were high-income areas of the county. Table 17 reveals that in City A and City B, it would be difficult to argue that middle- to upper-income families were underrepresented among whites, even if all the missing cases were dis-

Table 15

Negro Offenses by Age, Sex, in
Cities A and B (1962)

Sex	Age	No. of Offenses in City A							No. of Offenses in City B						
		1	2	3	4	5	6+	Total	1	2	3	4	5	6+	Total
Male	0-6	2	—	—	—	—	—	2	5	—	—	—	—	—	5
	7-8	1	—	1	—	—	—	2	2	—	—	—	—	—	2
	9	2	—	—	—	—	—	2	3	—	—	—	—	—	3
	10	1	1	—	—	—	—	2	—	—	—	—	—	—	—
	11	—	—	—	—	—	—	—	1	—	—	—	—	—	1
	12	—	1	1	—	—	—	2	3	—	1	—	—	—	4
	13	1	1	—	—	—	—	2	—	—	1	—	—	—	1
	14	1	—	—	—	—	1	2	1	1	1	—	—	—	3
	15	—	—	—	—	—	—	—	3	1	—	—	1	—	5
	16	—	—	—	—	1	—	1	1	1	—	—	—	—	2
	17-18	—	—	1	—	—	—	1	3	1	—	—	1	—	5
Female	0-6	3	1	—	—	—	—	4	5	1	—	—	—	—	6
	7-8	2	—	—	—	—	—	2	—	—	—	—	—	—	—
	9	1	—	—	—	—	—	1	—	—	—	—	—	—	—
	10	—	—	—	—	—	—	—	1	—	—	—	—	—	1
	11	—	—	—	—	—	—	—	—	—	—	—	—	—	—
	12	—	—	—	—	—	—	—	1	—	—	—	—	—	1
	13	1	—	—	—	—	—	1	2	—	—	—	—	—	2
	14	—	—	—	—	—	—	—	2	—	—	—	—	—	2
	15	—	—	1	—	1	—	2	3	1	—	—	—	—	4
	16	—	—	—	—	—	—	—	—	1	—	—	—	—	1
	17-18	—	—	—	—	—	—	—	1	—	—	—	—	—	1
	Totals	15	4	4	—	2	1	26	37	7	3	—	2	—	49

tributed among the lower-income groupings. City B reflects a high proportion of ethnics picked up, whereas in City A, this is not as striking. Yet based on the value of housing in the two cities, it could be argued that both Negroes and Mexican-Americans in City A probably enjoy a higher standard of living; thus the argument that more police bias exists in City B appears convincing. (See Tables 17A and 17B.) The material from 1964 in City B (see Table 18) suggests that even with an assumed organizational bias against the apprehension and processing of middle- to upper-income families the number of such cases is high.

Shifting the argument slightly, notice that when age at time of last recorded offense (see Table 19) is broken down in terms of probable school level, more delinquency occurs in City B among high school students and decreases

Table 16

*Offenders by Housing Value Index
in Cities A and B (1960)*

Housing Value Index	City A		City B	
	N	Percent	N	Percent
Highest 0	27	9	16	6
1	23	7	25	9
2	36	12	13	5
3	33	11	19	7
4	26	8	14	5
5	25	8	27	10
6	39	13	40	15
7	28	9	24	9
8	35	11	36	13
Lowest 9	36	12	56	21
Totals	308[a]	100	270[b]	100

[a] The total number of cases which could not be included in the table is 138 and is based upon the fact that the addresses in question were outside of the 1960 city limits of City A. Many sections were annexed in both cities after 1960. The exceptions include two cases where there were insufficient addresses and twelve cases from a government-run institution.

[b] Except for four cases for which there was insufficient information, the missing cases were outside the city limits at the time of the 1960 Census.

rapidly as we move down to the junior high and elementary levels. While the same pattern is discernible in City A, the decrease is much slower. Table 20 for City B reports similar information from the 1964 material, with the figures higher for the fourteen- and fifteen-year-old groups, but decreasing in pretty much the same way revealed by the 1962 data. The discrepancy between the two cities could again be explained by reference to organizational policy differences between the two police departments whereby City B detectives are more likely to be concerned with older adolescents, whom they tend to treat as adults, thus screening applications for petition to be made by the Juvenile Bureau. Younger offenders in City B are more of a "nuisance" and political repercussions preclude their being handled as roughly as older juveniles.

But the argument of policy differences can be clarified by noting that the Juvenile Bureau in City B did not engage in investigations, but followed up reports by patrol and detectives, and there was less likelihood of official citations by officers in the juvenile section. Patrol officers and detectives are less likely to "bother" with younger juveniles. High school students in City B,

Table 17

*Offenders by Housing Value Index and Race
in Cities A and B (1960)*

Housing Value Index	City A			City B		
	White	Mex.-Amer.	Negro	White	Mex.-Amer.	Negro
	N %	N %	N %	N %	N %	N %
Highest 0	27	0	0	14	0	1
1	23	0	0	24	1	0
2	36	0	0	10	0	2
3	31	0	1	18	3	0
4	24	2	0	7	4	3
5	21	3	1	9	12	6
6	29	2	8	18	14	8
7	17	8	3	11	12	1
8	21	7	7	11	15	10
Lowest 9	13	16	7	23	24	9
Totals[a]	242	38	27	145	85	40

[a] Missing cases are due primarily to residence of offenders falling outside of city limits except for a few cases of insufficient address.

Table 17A

Housing Value Index Decile Data for City A (1960)

Decile	Number of Blocks	Number of Housing Units	Percent of Total Housing Units	Housing Value Index Range ($)
9	120	2560	9.9	3200-6400
8	117	2576	10.0	6417-8286
7	103	2549	9.9	8311-9620
6	89	2599	10.1	9642-10,711
5	82	2597	10.1	10,723-12,000
4	67	2591	10.1	12,120-13,239
3	65	2524	9.8	13,273-14,473
2	91	2712	10.5	14,500-16,000
1	85	2487	9.7	16,120-18,500
0	165	2543	9.9	18,665-40,000
Totals	984	25,738	100.0	

Table 17B
Housing Value Index Decile Data for City B (1960)

Decile	Number of Blocks	Number of Housing Units	Percent of Total Housing Units	Housing Value Index Range ($)
9	147	2932	9.9	2,300- 5,480
8	125	2938	10.0	5,500- 6,527
7	111	2975	10.1	6,565- 7,326
6	115	2944	10.0	7,333- 8,377
5	117	2940	10.0	8,393- 9,429
4	121	2889	9.8	9,433-10,465
3	147	2938	10.0	10,500-11,985
2	148	2996	10.2	12,000-13,091
1	157	3050	10.3	13,133-16,000
0	158	2875	9.7	16,165-42,000
Totals	1,346	29,477	100.0	

Table 18
Offenders in City B for 1964 by Housing Value Index (1960 Values)

		N	Percent
Highest	0	52	3.2
	1	73	4.5
	2	68	4.2
	3	64	4.0
	4	73	4.5
	5	97	6.0
	6	109	6.7
	7	60	3.7
	8	138	8.5
Lowest	9	143	8.9
No information	X	158	9.8
Outside city	—	580	36.0
Totals		1615	100

therefore, are of more interest to detectives and patrolmen because of the possibility that *any* suspected offense could lead to clearings of offenses they handle as adult cases that remain unsolved.

But the reader's attention should be directed to Table 21 where grade in school (by age) at the time of the offender's first offense is recorded for the two cities. While the information for City B is inadequate for lack of informa-

Table 19

School Grade and Age at Time of Last Recorded Offense (1962)

		City A		City B		
		N	%	N	%	
	17-18	66	14.8	113	22.7	
High	16-17	69	15.5	98	19.7	City A = 44.4
school	15-16	63	14.1	84	16.9	City B = 59.3
Junior	14-15	42	9.4	48	9.6	
high	13-14	46	10.3	21	4.2	City A = 27.3
school	12-13	34	7.6	27	5.4	City B = 19.2
	11-12	16	3.6	14	2.8	
Elementary	10-11	26	5.8	10	2.0	
school	9-10	10	2.2	10	2.0	
	8-9	11	2.5	8	1.6	
	7-8	11	2.5	3	0.6	
	6-7	15	3.4	2	0.4	
	5-6	4	0.9	2	0.4	
	4-5	7	1.6	2	0.4	
	3-4	2	0.4	2	0.4	
	2-3	2	0.4	3	0.6	
	1-2	2	0.4	—	—	
	0-1	1	0.2	—	—	
Totals[a]		427	95.6	447	89.7	

[a] There were 17 cases over the age of 18, while there was no information on 2 cases in City A. There were 50 cases over the age of 18, while there was no information on 1 case in City B.

tion, the material from City A points to the junior high level as the most important period for activities leading to police contact. Yet the number of offenders making first contact with the police in elementary school is not trivial in City A, suggesting, once again, that efficiency in police operations would reveal a more general problem of delinquency or juvenile "problems" as a *routine feature* of community life. Arguments about the correlation between "rebelliousness" (as a generic term including school "troubles" and community definitions of delinquency) and poor achievement or low expectation of success in school and in later occupational pursuits would have to show that the incidence of first and subsequent offenses began with the lack of school success and some image of later problems. I do not have such information for my two police samples. But the distribution of first offenses raises the question ɪf the time when children begin to think about school progress and some kind of occupational future, the nature of such thoughts

Table 20

School Grade and Age at Time of Recorded Offense for City B in 1964

	Age	N	Percent	
	17-18	378	20.2⎫	
High school	16-17	398	21.2⎬	60%
	15-16	350	18.7⎭	
	14-15	265	14.2⎫	
Junior high school	13-14	149	8.0⎬	27%
	12-13	91	4.9⎭	
	11-12	57	3.0⎫	
	10-11	25	1.3	
	9-10	15	0.8	
Elementary school	8-9	8	0.4⎬	7%
	7-8	6	0.3	
	6-7	19	1.0	
	5-6	6	0.3⎭	
	4-5	5	0.3	
	3-4	3	0.2	
	2-3	2	0.1	
	1-2	5	0.3	
Totals[a]		1782	95.1	

[a] No information on 70 cases, and 21 cases over age 18.

if and when they occur, and whether such notions are related to delinquency and social class differences.[11]

The standard argument linking delinquency with "stable" marital status of the parents can be examined in part by looking at Table 22. The table is not too helpful because of the number of "no information" cases, but this is not a severe problem because most of the "no information" cases fall outside of the city limits. The Table 22 data on City B lend some support to common conceptions public officials and sociologists impute to the delinquent's home situation. There are a large number of second marriages and separated, divorced (or, to a lesser extent, deceased) parents. But the material in Table 22 does not reveal an unusual connection between broken homes and delinquency. The material in Table 23 provides another breakdown of Table 22.[12] Table 23 reveals the incidence of intact marriages but high delinquency rates in City A. Tables 22 and 23 can be interpreted as saying that City B law-enforcement officials produce offenders fitting the popular and sociological stereotypes about delinquents with "unstable" families.

Delinquency and its seriousness take on somewhat different meaning and

Table 21

Grade in School at the Time of First Offense in City A and City B (1962)

Grade in School	City A		City B	
	N	Percent	N	Percent
12	1	0.2	6	1.2
11	25	5.6	16	3.2
10	31	7.0	26	5.2
9	52	11.7	35	7.0
8	50	11.2	24	4.8
7	47	10.5	20	4.0
6	33	7.4	16	3.2
5	40	9.0	7	1.4
4	38	8.5	7	1.4
3	21	4.7	8	1.6
2	18	4.0	6	1.2
Kindergarten or 1	28	6.3	3	0.6
Preschool	34	7.6	29	5.8
Totals[a]	418	93.7	203	40.6

[a] No information for 17 cases in City A, plus 11 cases attending special schools where the grades are not equivalent. No information on 283 cases in City B, plus 12 cases of dropouts.

Table 22

Marital Status of Offender's Parents in City A and City B (1962)

Marital Status	City A		City B	
	N	Percent	N	Percent
First marriage intact	216	48.4	189	38.0
Second or more marriage intact	23	5.1	36	7.2
Separated, divorced (or one or both dead)	76	17.3	142	28.7
Common-law marriage	1	0.2	12	2.4
No information	130[a]	29.1	119[a]	23.9
Totals	446	100.1	498	100.2

[a] No information on the families, but most of the cases fall outside of city limits for 1960 Census.

significance, however, if we take into account the distribution of reported offenses in the two cities. Note the difference in the number of felonies reported in Table 24 for both cities and the discrepancies between reported misdemeanors and "minor police contacts." Table 25, however, reveals a different distribution in City B for 1964, with a larger number of felonies and

Table 23

Offender's Home Environment by City A and City B (1962)

Home Environment	City A		City B	
	N	Percent	N	Percent
Lives with both parents	233	52	199	40
Mother and stepfather	21	5	33	7
Father and stepmother	1	—	2	—
Mother only	57	13	120	24
Father only	10	2	15	3
Both stepparents	—	—	1	—
Foster parents	10	2	5	1
Other relatives	14	3	20	4
Friends	3	1	5	1
Institution	13	3	2	—
Other	1	—	2	—
No information	83	19	94	19
Totals	446	100	498	99

Table 24

General Type of Offense Distribution in City A and City B (1962)

General Type of Offense	City A		City B	
	N	Percent	N	Percent
Felony	71	7	112	15
Misdemeanor	538	53	556	72
Minor police contact	392	38	95	12
No information	27	2	5	1
Totals	1028	100	768	100

minor police contacts reported. I have impressionistic information that the "ambiguous information" category is large in City B for 1964 because of a change in policy, whereby "raids" were made in areas where "wild parties" or possible "trouble" was anticipated. Tables 24, 25, and 26 raise the question of how the "seriousness" of juvenile offenses is to be decided. Studies of delinquency usually begin with the assumption that "the problem" is serious, particularly as it is tied to lay and police conceptions about its prevalence among lower income adolescents who are assumed to be candidates for adult criminality.[13] When mass media and annual state and FBI reports claim delinquency is increasing, it is not clear from formal breakdowns of felony, misdemeanor, and minor police contacts as to how we are to interpret their significance for different communities and the presumed menace to life and property. I am not denying the existence of juvenile activities I could label

Table 25
General Type of Offense in City B for 1964

	N	Percent
Felony	258	14
Misdemeanor	1326	71
Minor police contact	108	5
Ambiguous information		
(Minor contact likely)	181	10
Totals	1873	100

Table 26
General Type of Offense in City A for May, 1965

	N	Percent
Felony	58	7
Misdemeanor	539	68
Minor police contact	105	13
Prowler	69	9
Unclear	24	3
Totals	795	100

"serious," while I participated in the research, and I am also concerned as a member of a community, but I am asking how we decide the seriousness of juvenile activities vis-à-vis some ideal or practical state of affairs or in comparison with adult activity. If we assume there is a "serious" delinquency problem instead of viewing various juvenile activities as "normal" for adolescents and even many adults, then it becomes difficult to untangle the sociologist's pronouncements about community problems from ideal expectations and tolerance levels developed in the community. A closer look at the actual categories the police use under the gross labels of felony, misdemeanor, and minor contacts is necessary. The general problem we encounter is the lack of a theory to indicate how we can derive some conception of deviance based upon members' variable perspectives about activities that might be labeled delinquent, and how such views are held by law-enforcement officials in implementing organizational policy and practice. There are many cases where it is not clear that the term "felony" is warranted, or that something should be labeled "misdemeanor." There is no clear-cut procedure for determining that someone should be charged with "grand theft auto" as opposed to "joy-riding."[14] One case of murder involving juveniles is enough to exaggerate the "seriousness" of delinquent crimes, but it does not help us to understand the relevance of delinquency rates.

Tables 27, 28, and 29 underscore the significance of activities the police *variably* label "petty theft," "runaway," "malicious mischief," "truant," "drinking or possession of alcohol," "curfew," "incorrigible," "bothering," "family problem," and the like. A critical feature of any juvenile bureau is the policy adopted and its implementation: are officers to investigate "runaways" and "incorrigibles" because of the perspective (lay or law-enforcement view) that "family problems or disorganization" are the causes of delinquency? Or is the stress to be placed upon "hard" criminal activities like burglary, robbery, and assault with a deadly weapon? Another policy might be the investigation of *all* juvenile activities called to the attention of the police on the assumption that illegal practices are to be expected routinely, and that a little probing will uncover many activities that could be labeled "hard" crimes. A similar statement could be made about all police officers and their routine activities. On many occasions my participant observation required accompanying detectives or patrolmen on calls not involving juveniles. The amount of time devoted to activities having little or nothing to do with popular or sociological conceptions of crime is impressive. The police spend considerable time answering calls that prove to be "dead ends," or they are called in to settle family disputes, or the "counseling" or punishment of children for family problems, and the like. Sitting next to the operators who handle incoming calls revealed a similar pattern, as did sitting in the station observing the "walk-ins" to the department. This more general conception of police work as intruding or being called upon to resolve routine family and neighborhood problems provides support for the control model view for understanding everyday police work, irrespective of lay conceptions of crime and police work. What is so striking are the ways in which the police impinge upon large sectors of the community in which no crime or delinquency problem is involved or suspected. Members of the community rely upon the police for settling many routine problems of daily living, and families are likely to receive considerable unwanted intrusion (often because of neighbors) into their private activities without being able to do much about it. The abusive side is likely to become most acute in lower-income areas, but calling on the police for different types of domestic

Table 27

Specific Types of Juvenile (or Juvenile Connected)
Offenses in City A and City B (1962)

	City A	City B
Rape	2	5
Armed robbery	1	2
Assault with deadly weapon	1	4
Burglary	37	47
Arson	9	2
Grand theft	1	6
Grand theft auto	17	45
Hit-and-run	3	1
Intent to assault with deadly weapon	—	1
Petty theft	83	181
Runaway	119	114
Malicious mischief	81	39
Truancy	44	6
Curfew	27	79
Battery	3	10
Joy riding	7	2
Assault and battery	5	—
Resisting an officer	—	1
Carrying dangerous weapon	15	4
Drinking or possession	4	12
Drunk in public	7	8
Disturbing the peace	16	17
School loitering	1	2
Trespassing	13	11
Immoral life	1	—
Lewd and lascivious conduct	4	6
Incorrigible	15	14
False alarm fire	7	8
Fireworks	12	2
BB guns	12	6
Vehicle check	1	7
Liquor check	—	1
Miscellaneous traffic violation	8	10
Picked up for investigation	10	14
Family problem	38	1
Loitering in public place	6	5
Dependency	69	49
"Juvenile problems"	22	—
Victim	36	2

Table 27 (*Continued*)
Specific Types of Juvenile (or Juvenile Connected)
Offenses in City A and City B (1962)

	City A	City B
Cruising	—	2
Referred to court for further disposition	69	—
Acting suspiciously	18	12
Hitch-hiker check	1	1
Fighting	21	2
Bothering	61	—
Violation of probation	18	3
Violation of court order	1	—
Auto accident	2	—
Glue sniffing	—	2
Go-cart racing	2	—
Playing ball in street	5	—
Petting	—	1
Prank	6	—
Possession of stolen property	6	3
Suspended from school	12	—
Accomplice	4	—
Disorderly conduct	—	1
Playing with matches	13	3
Possession of or reading of pornography	1	—
Informant, witness	12	—
Unspecified county or penal code ordinances	20	2
Escapee	3	5
Paroled or released from institution	3	1
Soliciting without permit	1	2
Possession of narcotics	1	—
Vagrancy	1	1
No information	10	3
Totals	1028	768

and neighborhood "help" is prevalent in all areas of the city. The impressive feature of police work, therefore, is the extent to which they become involved, both because of invitation and "tips" or curiosity, with virtually every sector of the community. Thus, any discussion of juveniles and adults suspected of criminal activities must include the perspectives adopted by police officers in defining their duties.

The interpretation of crime and delinquency rates, therefore, derives from everyday law-enforcement practices. The classification of offenses like auto

Table 28

Specific Types of Juvenile (or Juvenile-Connected) Offenses in City B for 1964

	N	Percent
Rape	7	0.4
Robbery	6	0.3
Aggravated assault	10	0.5
Burglary	158	8.4
Homicide	2	0.1
Arson	12	0.6
Grand theft	8	0.4
Sex crimes	17	0.9
Grand theft auto	36	1.9
Petty theft	412	22.1
Battery	21	1.1
Taking car without consent	60	3.2
Assault	3	0.2
Drinking	115	6.1
Malicious mischief	25	1.3
Truant	13	0.7
Runaway	291	15.6
Curfew	276	14.7
Incorrigible	28	1.5
Disturbing the peace	58	3.1
Weapons	15	0.8
Hit-and-run	2	0.1
Dependent	108	5.8
Traffic	6	0.3
Narcotics	3	0.2
Ambiguous information		
(Minor contacts likely)	181	9.7
Totals	1873	100

theft, burglary, and assault is never clear because the descriptive information in the police files is ambiguous, unless the material is tied to a knowledge
of various practices, the changing nature of the offense category as the case
'oves through various administrative stages, and the fact that investigative
procedures (and hence possible alterations) continue after some preliminary
classification has occurred. In cases filed for lack of information, it is
difficult to know how the offense should be listed. Discrepancies in petty
theft and auto theft between cities A and B are good examples; the absolute
numerical differences reported are difficult to explain by reference to the
composition of the two cities. The question we must ask is the extent to which

categories like petty theft is unidimensional: How do the behavioral displays of different acts come to be classified under the same category or label? Does "malicious mischief" (see Table 27) in City A as opposed to City B mean the same thing? Why would City A report so much truancy? Both cities seem to report the same amount of bicycle thefts, incidents of disturbing the peace, incorrigibility, runaways, and false fire alarms; however, there are vast differences in what is reported as "curfew" cases, "family problems," "juvenile problems," mentioning the fact that a record is kept on "victims," "fighting," "bothering," "violation of probation," "playing with matches," and so forth. What is equally impressive in the materials on specific types of juvenile (or juvenile-connected) offenses are those cases reported in Table 29 for the month of May of 1965 in City A, where cases reported as "not cleared" are listed. Herein lies the most serious problem facing sociologists interested in developing rigorous measurement devices for gauging the amount of "real" delinquency in a community. City B does not have such information available even in crude form.[15] This might account for some of the differences between the two cities in annual reports of activities, and the striking differences between actual categories used by both departments. The sergeant in City A spent considerable time keeping records and prided himself on the volume of cases handled. The sergeant in City B had less freedom in investigation and was not encouraged by superiors to strengthen juvenile work. But the differences between reported cases contained in their files by name of offender cannot be explained by reference to reports for which there are no suspects. Tables 27 and 28 are based on offenders known to the police, while Table 29 is based on the daily log in City A of all problems handled by the Juvenile Bureau. Thus, Table 29 must be viewed as posing an almost insurmountable problem for those social scientists interested in the literal measurement of delinquency. The questionable content of the categories themselves and the discrepancies between the two cities provide the researcher with outcomes that require reference to ways in which the police decide to include certain events and objects, often under *ad hoc* categories. The negotiable character of what is going on must not be underestimated by the "solid" appearing nature of the categories and numbers. It would be extremely difficult (and probably fruitless) to follow the uncleared cases in order to determine how many individuals were involved and if the initial offense category is relevant.

Probation Statistics

When the police decide that a juvenile requires the attention of the probation department, there is an automatic implication the case is "serious." The reasons the police give when making a decision to file an application

Table 29

Specific Types of Juvenile (or Juvenile Connected)
Offenses in City A for May, 1965

Offense	Cleared	Not Cleared	Total
Rape	4	3	7
Armed robbery	1	—	1
Assault with deadly weapon	2	3	5
Burglary	17	21	38
Grand theft auto	3	—	3
Embezzlement	—	1	1
Suicide (or attempt)	3	—	3
Petty theft (primarily bicycles)	51	50	101
Runaway	56	4	60
Malicious mischief	29	39	68
Incorrigible	23	2	25
Truant	29	—	29
Prowler	6	63	69
Drinking, possession of alcohol	21	1	22
Curfew	20	—	20
Lewd, annoying calls	3	33	36
Juvenile problem	38	1	39
Bothering	25	2	27
Disturbing the peace	42	1	43
Abandoned (bicycle)	13	14	27
Missing adult	12	—	12
Trespassing	7	1	8
Fighting	5	—	5
Child neglect (or possible)	6	1	6
Shooting in the city limits	3	1	4
Battery	3	5	8
Indecent exposure	1	6	7
Family problem	3	1	4
Suspicious man	4	5	9
Suspicious car	3	2	5
Loitering around school (possible molesting)	3	2	5
Suspicious call	—	3	3
Lack of parental control	5	—	5
Playing in the street	4	—	4
Destitute	5	—	5
Joy riding	5	—	5
Man bothering	2	2	4

Table 29 (*Continued*)
Specific Types of Juvenile (or Juvenile Connected)
Offenses in City A for May, 1965

Offense	Cleared	Not Cleared	Total
Attempt to locate	1	1	2
Missing	10	1	11
Failure to provide	1	1	2
Unfit home	1	1	2
Suspicious juvenile	4	—	4
Threat fight	2	—	2
Lewd writing	—	4	4
Drag race	6	—	6
Lost	3	—	3
Suspicious	3	—	3
Miscellaneous traffic	2	—	2
Tampering with mail	1	2	3
Hit-and-run	1	—	1
Carrying concealed weapon	1	—	1
Dependency	1	—	1
Escapee	—	1	1
Preventing or dissuading witness from attending	1	—	1
Zoning ordinance	1	—	1
Disturbing letter	—	1	1
Dog run over by car	1	—	1
Contributing to delinquency of minor	1	—	1
Motor Vehicle Code, bike	1	—	1
Outraging public decency	—	2	2
Attempt petty theft	—	1	1
Possession hypo	1	—	1
Drink party	1	—	1
Fire	—	1	1
Conspiracy	1	—	1
Parole notice	1	—	1
Oral copulation	1	—	1
Forgery	1	—	1
Entering school	—	1	1
Annoying woman	—	1	1
Injured boy	1	—	1
Released on parole	2	—	2
Missing patient	1	—	1
Child abandonment	—	1	1

Table 29 (*Continued*)

Specific Types of Juvenile (or Juvenile Connected)
Offenses in City A for May, 1965

Offense	Cleared	Not Cleared	Total
Throw at car	—	1	1
Sick	1	—	1
Child beating	1	—	1
Children not sent to school by parents	1	—	1
Boulevard stop	1	—	1
Lewd conduct	—	1	1
Unclear designation	14	—	14
Totals	507	288	795

for petition may have little to do with the conditions under which the probation authorities decide to accept the petition application. In this section there will appear a few tables on cases handled by the police and on whom the probation department had records. A glance at Table 30 reveals the original police samples are reduced considerably. Thus the larger part of police contacts never develop into probation cases even though many petitions may have been filed. Aside from the fact the police are usually annoyed by this discrepancy between petition applications filed and their acceptance

Table 30

Offenders with Probation Records in City A and City B (1962)

Probation Record	City A		City B	
	N	%	N	%
Yes	75	16	164	33
No	371	84	334	67
Totals	446	100	498	100

by probation, most juvenile activities are not viewed as sufficiently serious by the police, probation, or the court to warrant further action. The earlier tables illustrated the enormous range of juvenile activities and stressed the notion that the police spend much of their time dealing with incidents that could be called "minor." Probation contacts support this idea. The differences between City A and City B in Table 30 are of interest because my observations suggest police officers in City A continuously complain that their petitions are frequently not accepted, in spite of the fact the juveniles in question are seen as in "constant trouble." In City B, on the other hand, juvenile officers (but not regular detectives) usually do not file an application for petition until they have consulted someone in the probation department, or they are fairly certain that the petition will be accepted because of past conversations with probation, or there is some indication that probation would be disposed to accept the application. Another organizational explanation is necessary here because of the practice in City A of informally carrying juveniles on what amounts to a quasi-probation system for months (and even several years) before filing applications for petition. Thus, even though an application is not accepted by probation, the police officer might

Table 31

Probation Cases by Number of Offenses at Time of
Probation Officer Contact in City A and City B (1962)

	City A		City B	
	N	Percent	N	Percent
No offense	2	3	33	20
One offense	28	37	63	39
Two offenses	20	27	40	25
Three offenses	8	11	17	10
Four offenses	4	5	4	2
Five offenses	6	8	4	2
Six offenses	3	4	—	—
Seven offenses	—	—	—	—
Eight or more offenses	1	1	—	—
No date of offense	3	4	3	2
Totals	75	100	164	100

still ask the juvenile and his parents to contact him periodically. Finally, in City B, investigations by juvenile officers were rare, and cases tended to fall roughly into two categories: (1) warning and release, and (2) probation referral via an application for petition. The reason why the probation department in City B accepted more applications for petition was suggested by one probation officer as an interest in spending more time with juveniles to make up for probation's imputation of an inadequate juvenile bureau to the police department.

Table 31 reveals the probation department sees juveniles before they are known to have committed offenses, and that most offenders do not have long records before being seen. Many of these cases include child neglect or family problems. This view appears to contradict the material presented in Chapter 2 where it was suggested that the police may carry a juvenile for some time before filing an application for petition. The interpretation of these data

can only be made, however, by reference to some knowledge of organizational policy and procedures. Probation files may not have an accurate account of police contacts, and the filtering of recidivists varies with police discretion. This was my impression of probation files, but I did not systematically sample probation files to document this point. The police in City A would record many juvenile acts or contacts as "delinquent" but the probation department may never receive a copy of the police report. Precisely how police filtering affects the volume of recidivists handled by the probation department cannot be determined for this study. What does seem clear, however, is that the probation department (particularly in City B) may handle a case due, for example, to direct contact by parents, the schools, and churches, because they are convinced that the police will not handle the problem, handle the case "inadequately," or because the "delinquent" status of the juvenile is not clear. The probation file on a juvenile may include contributions by a variety of persons and various selective record-keeping procedures, and the time at which it is searched for research purposes may prove misleading without further information as to how it is assembled.[16] Therefore, using cases appearing before a juvenile court hearing for the study of delinquency is a highly truncated operation. I do wish to underscore the point, however, that the cases of probation contact with no offense in City B (Table 31) and my observations in City B on probation views of the police are meaningful if we assume such cases reflect an attempt by City B probation officials to "make up" for the lack of an active and well-organized police juvenile bureau. My speculations about the significance of the counts in the tables are articulated directly with my impressionistic observations of the agency from which the materials are taken. Thus, comparing various communities or examining national delinquency rates becomes an even more speculative enterprise.

The material presented in Tables 32 and 33 merely show the similar breakdowns on Tables 5 and 10 on the distribution of offenders by sex and race. The significance of Table 34 might be described as showing that probation

Table 32

Probation Cases by Sex in City A and City B (1962)

| | City A | | City B | |
	N	Percent	N	Percent
Male	46	61	116	71
Female	29	39	48	29
Totals	75	100	164	100

officials, like the police, spend most of their time with juveniles who have not achieved high school age.

The information contained in Tables 35 and 36 suggests possible effects of police or probation filtering of middle- and upper-income families. The differences, though not great, are in line with the organizational explanations tentatively suggested earlier; middle- and upper-income families are more likely to muster the resources to avoid contact with probation officials, or these officials are not as likely to accept petitions in such cases.

The materials presented in Tables 37 and 38, in contrast to Table 22, are consistent with the pilot information reported in Chapter II and can be

Table 33
Probation Cases by Race in City A and City B (1962)

	City A		City B	
	N	Percent	N	Percent
White	60	81	90	54
Mexican-American	7	9	53	32
Negro	7	9	19	12
Indian	1	1	1	1
Other	—	—	1	1
Totals	75	100	164	100

Table 34
Probation Cases by High School Status in City A and City B (1962)

	City A		City B	
	N	Percent	N	Percent
Expelled	2	3	3	2
Quit	2	3	4	2
Completed high school	—	—	—	—
Still in high school	15	20	23	14
Not yet in high school	53	70	104	64
No information	3	4	30	18
Totals	75	100	164	100

interpreted in the same way; probation officials are more likely to decide that juveniles with broken or "difficult" homes should receive the attention of the department as a means of stopping a "bad" situation from becoming worse. Thus, cases where the marriage is the first for both parents (and still intact) might be explained by reference to Tables 39 and 40 where general

Table 35

Probation Cases by Father's Occupation in City A and City B (1962)

	City A		City B	
	N	Percent	N	Percent
Higher executives	3	4	2	1
Business managers	—	—	—	—
Administrative personnel, etc.	2	3	8	5
Clerical, etc.	6	8	11	7
Skilled manual workers	15	20	18	11
Machine operators, etc.	13	17	16	10
Unskilled	10	13	14	9
Not specified	—	—	9	5
Unemployed	2	3	5	3
Mother head of house	15	20	27	16
No information	2	3	37	23
Deceased, etc.	7	9	17	10
Totals	75	100	164	100

Table 36

Probation Cases by Monthly Income of Parents in City A and City B (1962)

	City A		City B	
	N	Percent	N	Percent
Welfare	7	5	32	20
0-$200	4	5	2	1
$201-$300	11	15	6	4
$301-$400	12	16	20	12
$401-$500	6	8	10	6
$501-$600	5	7	5	3
$601-$700	6	8	3	2
$701-$800	2	3	2	1
$801-$900	2	3	—	—
$901-$1000	1	1	1	1
$1001	1	1	—	—
"Poor"	3	4	4	2
"Average"	—	—	2	1
"Good"	4	5	1	1
No information	11	15	76	46
Totals	75	100	164	100

Table 37

Probation Cases by Marital Status of Offender's
Parents in City A and City B (1962)

	City A		City B	
	N	Percent	N	Percent
First marriage intact	30	40	50	31
Divorced (mother remarried)	13	17	23	14
Divorced (father remarried)	2	3	10	6
Divorced (both remarried)	—	—	—	—
Husband dead (wife remarried)	—	—	2	1
Wife dead (husband remarried)	—	—	2	1
Divorced (mother not remarried)	6	8	17	10
Divorced (father not remarried)	2	3	3	2
Husband dead (wife not married)	4	5	6	4
Wife dead (husband not married)	1	1	—	—
Divorced (neither remarried)	5	7	1	1
Separated	5	7	22	13
Common-law or unmarried mother	5	7	4	2
Both parents dead	1	1	2	1
Both stepparents	—	—	1	1
No information	1	1	21	13
Totals	75	100	164	100

Table 38

Probation Cases by Offender's Resident Status in City A and City B (1962)

	City A		City B	
	N	Percent	N	Percent
Both parents	30	41	51	30
Mother and stepfather	13	17	29	18
Father and stepmother	1	1	10	6
Mother only	18	25	43	25
Father only	8	11	3	2
Other relatives	3	4	6	4
Both stepparents	—	—	1	1
Foster parents	1	1	6	4
Friends	—	—	3	2
Other	—	—	1	1
No information	1	1	11	7
Totals	75	101	164	100

Table 39

*Probation Cases by General Family Problems
Vis-à-vis Minor in City A and City B (1962)*

	City A		City B	
	N	Percent	N	Percent
No problems mentioned	12	16	30	18
"Strains" with parents	25	33	14	9
"Strains" with siblings	—	—	4	2
"Strains" with mother only	3	4	13	8
"Strains" with father only	9	12	11	7
Minor "lacks supervision"	8	11	27	16
Not applicable (too young)	6	8	11	7
No information	12	16	54	33
Totals	75	100	164	100

family problems and specific problems, as noted by the probation officer, are listed. The reader will notice that the "problems" of Tables 39 and 40 do not always match because it is not clear from the probation officer's remarks how one would articulate comments about "general" problems with the more specific categories employed.[17]

The problems mentioned by the probation officers are "factors" typically cited by researchers as contributing to juvenile delinquency. The obscure causal nexus linking ambiguous notions of social disorganization, as defined by members of the community (and the sociologist), with conduct labeled "delinquent" has not changed in over one hundred years.[18] The question of whether these data are merely *ad hoc* or improvised categories that conform with long-standing tautologies about the "causes" of crime and delinquency requires further organizational analysis and will be discussed in the following chapters. *Here I assert that the ways in which such factors are identified and "known" by the researcher are similar to the ways in which they are invoked by the practitioner to justify his actions.* The reader may feel that those cases (in Tables 39 and 40) where "no problems [are] mentioned" remain something of a mystery. Such cases may include juveniles who are still under probation and a report for the court has not been completed by the probation officer, cases where the seriousness of the case is deemphasized because of a "good" response from the juvenile and his family, or cases which are not very old and little information is contained in the file. The perusal of probation records for information about "problems" influencing delinquency is not only an *ad hoc* or improvised search for "categories" that are usually counted as standing for meaningful social relationships, but

Table 40

Probation Cases by Family Problems Mentioned by Probation Officer in Original or Major Home (But Not Foster) in City A and City B (1962)

	City A		City B	
	N	Percent	N	Percent
No problems mentioned	13	17	26	15
Drinking by parents or siblings	—	—	7	4
Marital difficulties	2	3	3	2
Unemployment by head of household	—	—	3	2
Father personality problems mentioned	1	1	4	2
Mother personality problems	—	—	6	4
Home lacks a disciplinary figure	6	8	24	15
Both parents have personality problems	2	3	7	4
Drinking and both parents with personality problems	—	—	1	1
Siblings also delinquent	—	—	1	1
Mother personality problem and lack of disciplinary figure	4	5	6	4
Father has history of illness	1	1	—	—
Drinking and marital difficulties	3	4	3	2
Drinking and mother personality problems	—	—	2	1
Head of household in institution	1	1	2	1
Mother engaging in prostitution	2	3	1	1
Marital difficulties and lack of disciplinary figure	4	5	1	1
Mother and/or father drug addict	1	1	1	1
Incest and marital difficulties	1	1	—	—
Unemployed head of household and lack of disciplinary figure	2	3	—	—
Drinking and lack of disciplinary figure	2	3	—	—
Both parents deceased	1	1	—	—
Marital difficulties and father with history of illness	1	1	—	—
Three or more of the above problems	23	32	20	12
No information	5	7	46	27
Totals	75	100	164	100

is a construction by the researcher of the probation officer's construction. Both constructions remain obscure in the conventional analysis presented here.

Table 41 suggests the same argument mentioned earlier; also, probation officials primarily handle cases that might not be called "serious" crimes.

Table 41

Probation General Types of Offenses in City A and City B (1962)

	City A		City B	
	N	Percent	N	Percent
Felony	6	3	8	2
Misdemeanor	127	69	312	84
Minor police contact or none	51	28	48	13
No information	—	—	3	1
Totals	184	100	371	100

Thus, the general notions of imputed family or personal problems and "social disorganization" in gross terms—not the notion of serious crime—seem to orient the probation officer's definition of juvenile delinquency. In the total number of cases handled, the differences between the two cities are in line with earlier remarks about the probation department of City B becoming involved in more activities because they feel the police are not doing their job. The Juvenile Bureau of the police department in City B did not investigate cases falling under the "minor police contacts" category because it did not have the resources or authority to pursue such problems.

Several issues emerge from the materials available from police and probation records, and the possibility of obtaining precise measures of "delinquent" activities.

1. The police and probation materials are not adequate for precise measurements of "crimes" presumably known to the police. First of all, we must ask "what is crime known to police?" The entries on daily logs or investigation assignment sheets do not reveal or capture the fidelity of "what happened," but merely provide the researcher with some standard references to the Penal Code, the Welfare and Institutions Code (in the case of California), a few apparently clear remarks like "runaway," "petty theft—shoplifting," "petty theft—bike," and then many ambiguous categories such as "attempt to locate," "missing," "family problem," "bothering," "abandoned," "man bothering," "possible unfit [home]," "conspiracy," and "suspicious juvenile." It is difficult to classify the cases listed on a daily log into general

categories like "felony," "misdemeanor," and "minor police incident." At the time of recording, the nature of the incident is not clear.

2. In addition to cases never reported to the police, there exist a large number of uncleared cases for which there are no suspects. These latter cases are difficult because there is no way of knowing how many suspects might have been involved or how many of the incidents involved the same suspects. The "on-the-spot" decision-making required for accomplishing daily tasks necessarily includes decisions not to bother with some incidents "this time" because of more "pressing" matters, because of the ambiguity of the incident (a combination of incident, suspect, and neighborhood), the lateness of the hour, and a large number of other contingencies that are routine features of police work.

3. The ambiguity of police classification and the description and classification of social events and objects by researchers are crude operations. But then both police officers (and other officials in bureaucratic settings) and researchers are confronted with the practical task of "getting it done" so that a product is available that purportedly describes "what happened." Legal rules of evidence may appear to be meticulous, but they fall short of adequate description, for the problems of objectification and verification remain commonsense activities. The police officer may use legal rules of evidence as ideals, but such rules do not adequately restrict the recognition and classification of empirical displays, while the contingencies of "getting the job done" or the "case wrapped up" permeate all decision-making.

4. For the researcher seeking to code police and probation materials, the practical demands of "getting the job done" also impose frustrating difficulties. Multiple offenses that range from possible felonies to "minor police contacts" are often part of the same case. It is difficult to code each offense listed for each case so that machine tabulation remains manageable. Conflicting addresses are frequent and the task of assigning a housing value index for estimations of income level of the family is confounded. Conflicting dates of birth make cross-tabulations with other factors problematic. It is especially difficult to unravel, even when following an actual case from its inception, how the different offenses were decided, how subsequent investigation invalidated earlier charges, how contacts with the parents modified early action vis-à-vis a petition, and the like, for a careful examination of the juvenile's "rap sheet" would have to be checked against the original reports to provide the researcher with enough information for imputing some order as to how the police came to "know" what they presumably "know." Truncated official records "freeze" the temporal properties of emergent interaction, so that what is "managed" by the police and probation in making decisions—the negotiated and bargaining character of assigning

charges and making dispositions—are distorted by a conventional search for "objective" indicators of delinquency and official actions.

5. The coding operations are similar to members' "closing" of activities to form sets that permit counting, and the arbitrary (*ad hoc*) procedures underscore how the researcher utilizes some unstated mixture of common sense and social scientific knowledge to arrive at "appropriate" categories as basic to primitive measurement.

How Do We Believe What We Read or Code?

To what extent are conclusions based upon the above data negated by problems leading to the assembly of the materials, of abstracting the information, and then categorizing data into groupings not congruent with either what might have been intended by the generator of the message, its interpretation when abstracted by the researcher, or its subsequent classification and reduction into tables?

To begin with, each offense category in each table represents a necessary reification of what the police or clerks recorded as instances of "what happened." Virtually every instance of categorization requires decisions that transform a truncated behavioral description of "what happened" into some precoded, but almost never unidimensional, category that enables the police to invoke legal language. To each behavioral description, therefore, there are attached N contingencies to be "explained away" if the case is to be "fitted into" an existing legal category. A glance at Table 29 (based upon the daily log in City A for May 1965) reveals fourteen "unclear" cases. Many other cases are also not clear, for example, "suspicious," "missing," and the like. Notice that 36 percent of all cases are "not cleared"; there are no suspects, only victims. In assembling the classification, I found myself "filling in" what I thought to be relevant conditions for understanding the truncated police labels. Decisions the police make when they must submit "official statistics" to the state or federal government are confusing abstractions and forced classifications of unclarified materials. The "file" or "not cleared" cases make it difficult to know whether or not the label employed in the daily log corresponds with "what happened," because subsequent investigations are an integral part of clarifying the original charge. This is clear when observing a juvenile officer undertake an investigation. Invariably, the details, the suspects, the activities, the victims, all multiply, and radically different meanings are generated vis-à-vis "what happened." A "minor" incident often leads to the discovery or imputation of more "serious" activities. The police also attempt to link present charges to uncleared offenses in all of their routine investigations.

I want to underscore that the *fact* of categorization provides the *meaning* to the cross-tabulations that follow, but the use of categories and the cutoff points remain arbitrary or quite variable in most cases. Even a category such such as age is problematic for the police because some juveniles often lie about it, and their records are continually being changed accordingly. The tendency of the police to be fairly literal in writing up their reports makes the business of classifying offenses difficult and arbitrary. Detailed behavioral descriptions provide alternative interpretations even though the police must use language and labels that are subject to a "proper fit" under some existing statute or policy.

The general problem is complicated because the police tend to provide graphic accounts, but simultaneously oversimplify the official categorization of "what happened." Thus, many details may appear in the body of the report, but the rationales for the offense category, given to the event or sequence of events, are truncated and contain a kind of language that presumes complete understanding of "what happened." The volume of "business" makes it difficult to give much time to the problems of "adequate" or defensible categorization. The practical demands of the job require rapid decisions to keep the paperwork moving. Merely mentioning sources of errors is not enough; therefore, it is necessary to note how labels and categories employed serve two general practical purposes: (1) a police argot mixed with everyday language enables the work unit to communicate within itself easily and with a minimum of debate as to "what happened" or the kind of person being dealt with, and (2) there is the language of the Penal Code or Welfare and Institutions Code which orients the formal description of "what happened." The language the police use among themselves provides a simplified, readily understood collection of meanings, whereby the varied activities of the persons they come into contact with are easily classified. The police have many theories about neighborhoods, persons, race, sex, ethnic groups, the effects of social mobility, "good" and "bad" families, occupations, politics, and the like, that constitute ready-made recipes for interpreting and labeling their daily activities. But the business of fitting their knowledge of what is going on or "what happened" into abstract legal statutes includes both arbitrary decisions and the interpretation of contingencies, so that the "facts" of the case appear to fit the legal category. In adult cases, the police are more careful because they know the district attorney demands certain kinds of "evidence," and that certain defense attorneys can make virtually any testimony and "evidence" problematic. Both in City A and City B, the police have fairly well-defined ideas about what the district attorney demands, and which lawyers can make "trouble" in some or all cases.

The analysis of materials taken from police records is confusing because the records themselves are not entirely clear and the coder must engage in countless arbitrary decisions as to cutoff points and the classification of each datum. In preparing the information contained in the above tables for coding and subsequent categorization into preliminary tables, something of a conspiracy was undertaken. I resisted every attempt on the part of the research assistants in charge of coding data, punching data, and making runs with data-processing equipment to involve me in the decisions being made. I insisted that the coders follow the "standard" categories utilized by "other" researchers on delinquency and, each time, merely reiterated a kind of formal statement about "known" categories. My interest was in seeing the graduate research assistants "solve" the problems in whatever ways they felt were adequate. I knew that the head assistant was well trained in data-processing procedures and that he was aware of the ambiguities of the materials, for he had helped abstract the materials from City B. I was out of the country during the time the coding decisions were being made and the actual work of fitting data into categories was being done.

After the data were coded, punched, and tabulated, I asked the head assistant about the difficulties involved. He began to catalogue a long series of problems that occurred at every step of the data-processing procedures. He described how he and his wife and another graduate student, would have continual argumentative sessions wherein categories, raw data, and coding procedures were disputed. Many impasses occurred, and these were finally resolved by the head research assistant more or less by fiat in order to settle the matter and so that they could all get on with the work. The assistant remarked: "I decided that I was responsible for getting the work done and had to take the responsibility for having it make sense. So I would simply make an arbitrary decision that seemed to settle matters at that point." The head assistant made the remark that: "My approach was that since I didn't know what would be most important to you I was going to bleed everything out of those files that I could possibly get, even if it seemed a waste of time to even code it. I just tried to bleed everything I could out of it and let you do what you wanted with it. But you have no way of knowing what information we were bleeding out of it and what was fairly obvious from the data." But the notion of extracting everything possible assumes criteria exist for justifying what is coded. I want to stress the impossibility of articulating an explicit theory with such materials in the absence of the *additional* materials on how the day-to-day operations transform "what happened" into categories and collections that a coder must make sense of. The materials in the files are already disengaged from the occasions of assembly. The coder must invoke whatever "seems reasonable" to him in accomplishing his task, unless he could talk to all officers handling the cases and reconstruct each occasion. One consequence of this problem is that the assistants felt the task was "futile" and a "waste of time." The assistants later agreed the technical operations cannot be detached from some knowledge of the action scenes that are being coded. The coders presumed many things about the materials that became an integral part of their work: "Oh, and another thing is that it was obvious sometimes that the police officer could have cited the guy for three or four different things but sometimes he picked the least serious one and other times he picked the more serious one." This problem was detected because: "If there were a description of what actually happened, plus the offense which the petition was filed for, then you could see discrepancies." Many problems emerged accidentally: "Sometimes we'd just make jokes about something on the sheet that seemed funny and through discussing this thing we'd discovered that we were coding it differently. Sometimes things just came up very accidentally." The coders generated considerable conflict in pursuing their task:

T: "Yeah, sometimes we were just . . . [cut off]"

S: [The coders would tell each other:] "Oh, we'll do it our own way."

T: "A couple of good battles in one morning would reduce the conflict in the afternoon."

B: "After a while we would just avoid conflict."

S: "We would independently add our own new category and just tell everybody there's a new category."

The entire set of procedures *for coding police and probation records constituted a continuous improvised set of decisions, whose primary purpose was to achieve practical solutions to problems whose outcomes or resolutions could not be decided according to explicit criteria based upon an explicit theoretical position vis-à-vis the intended meaning of the data.*
Many readers would argue the arbitrary character of the coding decisions is not clear nor held in all studies, and that sociologists have developed many "checks" and criteria for devising categories and cutoff points. Structural arguments, built into behavioral referents elicited via survey techniques of an attitudinal type or use of organizational records, do not constitute an observed behavioral environment, but rather questions, answers, and categories that are truncated indicators of what the actor may do or may have done. The problem is not that organizational categories, questions, and answers are irrelevant, but that surveys and official records typically structure materials, so that the answer is decided by the form in which the question is posed or formal categories provided for classification. What is lacking is the actor's conception of the operative social structures and the observer's description of actual scenes. Official descriptions include theories of "what happened," but they are also oriented by a set of legal categories (the Penal

Code and Welfare and Institutions Code) that summarize and force more literal descriptions of the police interrogation and written reports into standardized but equivocal categories. The researcher, who must then take police descriptions and categories as data for constructing additional indices for different purposes, faces the task of imposing explanations derived from an improvised theory.

 Structural arguments usually assume that position in the social structure is the "best" predictor of the actor's behavior, where the actor's behavior is indexed by another structural indicator. I assume the occupancy of a position in the social structures is a continuously managed product of concerted work or action on the part of the actors involved according to rules that take on meaning (and hence properties) in the course of interaction. Questionnaires, interrogative procedures, and organizational materials "freeze" objects and events so that sets are created, and a metalanguage generated for "talking about" (but not checking out systematically) "what happened." Such "freezing" is important for the stability of social order qua actor, but the researcher must study the phenomena, not trade upon it. The different ways in which the police achieve the production of juvenile delinquents according to socially organized procedures constitute two of many sources of data: (1) there is the ethnomethodology of how juveniles come to be seen, interviewed, categorized, and acted upon organizationally by the police, so that a population is produced and labeled as juvenile delinquents, and (2) there is the set of records that community agencies (and sociologists) utilize for documenting the "juvenile" or "crime" problem. The materials from (2) are employed as the source of data for indexing (1). But even when there is a direct survey of the police, the research instrument bypasses the observational and linguistic data derivable from an ethnomethodological study. Instead, the "findings" obtainable from police records become the basis for posing questions about structural and attitudinal conditions that can be cross-tabulated conveniently, but the referents for such findings remain obscure.

Subsequent chapters will examine negotiated conversational material and especially official records in detail. Special attention will be given to members' use of language categories for depicting "what happened," and showing how language usage is pivotal to "closing" a set for purposes of "counting."

NOTES

1. Cf. Norton E. Long, "The Local Community as an Ecology of Games," *American Journal of Sociology* (November 1958) **54**, 251-261.
2. Michel Crozier, *The Bureaucratic Phenomenon* (Chicago: University of Chicago Press, 1964).
3. In addition to Long's paper, the reader should consult Nelson W. Polsby, "The Sociology of Community Power: A Reassessment," *Social Forces* (March 1959) **37**, 232-236; Polsby, "Three Problems in the Analysis of Community Power," *American Sociological Review* (Dec. 1959) **24**, 796-803; and Raymond E. Wolfinger, "Reputation and Reality in the Study of Community Power," *American Sociological Review* (Oct. 1960) **25**, 636-644.
4. The quotation marks around the term "game" is intended to signal that the activity is not structured whereby "secondary rules" of recognition in H.L.A. Hart's sense are implied, as in a game of chess, for example, but that the relationships between members is more "open" and dependent upon interest and sustained interaction, according to unstated "rules" or tacit understandings. My discussion here is similar to Durkheims's notion of noncontractual conditions of contracts. For a recent empirical discussion, see Stewart Macaulay, "Non-Contractual Relations in Business," *American Sociological Review* (February 1963) **28**, 55-67.
5. Cf. Edward C. Banfield and James Q. Wilson, *City Politics* (Cambridge, Mass.: The Joint Center for Urban Studies, 1963).
6. Cf. the reports stemming from the American Bar Foundation investigation of the administration of criminal justice in the United States (Chicago: The American Bar Foundation, 1955), mimeographed, and Jerome Skolnick, *Justice Without Trial* (New York: Wiley, 1966).
7. In large California cities, more attention is now given to the use of adult arrest and search and seizure procedures than was true during my study. But the practices are not always standardized.
8. The reader should note that it is difficult to show always how police and probation satisfaction or dissatisfaction with their occupational predicaments influence their day-to-day activities; daily actions vis-à-vis juveniles and parents are likely to include their occupational problems as tacit difficulties seldom revealed in their work routines. My impressionistic observations revealed the intrusion of such problems in the form of disinterest in pursuing cases that meant working overtime, simplifying cases that required extensive paper work, taking more time when making investigations in the field, or spending more time on outside work activities, and the like. I should not hazard any generalizations about such matters, however, because my feeling was that considerable variation occurred in officers' depictions of "gripes," interest in their work, concern with organizational changes, personal changes, and the like. I should hesitate to give even impressionistic accounts of situational variations I have observed.
9. The reader will notice I am ignoring Merton's work on social structure and anomie (Robert K. Merton, *Social Theory and Social Structure*, rev. ed. (New York: Free Press, 1957), Chapter 4. I am concerned with the social organization of law enforcement and legal procedures, while Merton is interested in an abstract accounting of deviant behavior. However, Merton does not specify sociological definitions of deviance, but suggests that the sociologist may have to collect and organize his own data rather than rely upon those produced by governmental agencies. How the social structures exert pressures and the ways in which actors respond in social situations to the extent that sociologists (among others) call it deviance is not clear in Merton's formulation. Variation in the rates of deviant behavior—rates that cannot be gleaned satisfactorily from official statistics—presupposes that the activities of law-enforcement agencies that lead to arrest and conviction are not problematic, nor is the phenomena of nonconforming behavior. Presumably, laymen, law-enforcement per-

sonnel, and social scientists are all agreed as to who should be labeled deviant. Merton's formulation lacks a conceptional and empirical clarification of the significance of (1) members' views about, and reaction to, deviance, (2) the sociologist's views and reaction, (3) the articulation, if any, between (1) and (2), while the criticisms of Kitsuse, Cicourel, and Lemert do not specify how environments of objects and events are labeled deviant by members and researchers, and how both objectify and verify the properties that generate identifiable forms of behavior that come to be labeled deviant. Cf. John I. Kitsuse and A. V. Cicourel, "A Note on the Uses of Official Statistics," *Social Problems* (Fall 1963) **11**, 131-39; and the pointed critique of Merton's theory of deviance contained in Edwin M. Lemert, "Social Structure, Social Control, and Deviation," in M. B. Clinard (ed.), *Anomie and Deviant Behavior* (New York: Free Press, 1964), pp. 57-97.

10. City B remained at three juvenile officers throughout the study.
11. Neither Merton (cf. "Anomie, Anomia, and Social Interaction: Contexts of Deviant Behavior," in Clinard, *op. cit.*) nor Arthur L. Stinchcombe's findings (*Rebellion in a High School*, Chicago: Quadrangle Books, 1964) deal with this problem. Stinchcombe's empirical study includes neither juveniles who have dropped out of high school nor juveniles with police records. The amount of police-reported delinquency in junior high schools suggests Stinchcombe should have explored his thesis much earlier.
12. The discrepancy between Tables 22 and 23 is due to the lack of precision of police records as to the family organization of the juvenile. It was often possible to find information about the existence of two parents, but not their marital history.
13. Cf. the special issue of *The Negro Journal of Education*, "Juvenile Delinquency among Negroes in the United States," **28** (Summer 1959).
14. When I sat and observed the juvenile sergeant in City A classify cases and asked him about the activities presupposed in different labels, he responded with elaborate explanations of a few cases. Each case has its own special history. Occasionally he would call over to another officer for additional information. The officer's remarks were matter-of-fact. He assumed that his remarks were "obvious" to me. He soon tired of explaining more than five cases, stating that "it's the same for the rest, but it would take us forever to go over them."
15. The recent work by T. Sellin and M. Wolfgang, *The Measurement of Delinquency* (New York: Wiley, 1964) does not seem to escape this problem.
16. My experience suggests that no orderly procedures exist for developing a particular case, but that new information is added or sought as "felt to be necessary" to account for emergent problems. Many juveniles have encounters with the police while their case is pending a court hearing. The lack of any orderly assembly means that the impression of the record on different temporal occasions can lead to different "readings" of the same material, objects, and events, over time, by agency officials and researchers. The record is not a clear, orderly account of what has happened to the juvenile.
17. Notice how the problems of objectification and verification can be ignored when using organizational materials, for example, the categories employed in Tables 39 and 40. The categories imply organized "answers" to known "problems" of delinquency, but how the referents are objectified and interpreted remains unknown to both reseacher and reader, while for the practitioner the referents are part of an "obvious" environment of objects that "anyone knows." This section has benefited from Harold Garfinkel's paper "Remarks on Ethnomethodology," American Sociological Association Annual Meetings, Chicago (1965).
18. Cf. Anthony Platt, *The Child Savers: The Emergence of the Juvenile Court in Chicago* (Berkeley: School of Criminology, unpublished doctoral dissertation, June 1966).

Chapter 4

CONVERSATIONAL DEPICTIONS OF SOCIAL ORGANIZATION

A theoretical statement about social organization must clarify the organization of social actions that produce phenomena viewed as "routine," "normal," or "common" instances of the events and objects handled by participating actors. The clarification of the commonsense features of organized social actions of the police and probation departments is presupposed in any attempt to demonstrate the sense in which the sociologist comes to decide that structural arrangements are identifiable; structural features that "stand for" a set of social actions not necessarily observed by the researcher, but taken for granted when utilizing some set of outcomes such as arrest reports, distributions of offenses, and rates per thousand members of the population, treated as objective indicators of "what happened."

The notion of the "definition of the situation" seeks to describe how actors see social scenes from "within." Such a characterization is too abstract. What is crucial is the *sense of social structure* contained in the actor's definition of the situation which provides him with grounds for further inference and action, but the sociologist is interested in specifying the sense of social structure, depicted in the actor's characterization of his environment, and the congruence between the actor's characterization and the sociologist's theory of the same structural conditions of everyday life assumed to be operative. The general argument can be summarized as follows:

1. How actors define situations as "real" suggests how they "prepare" the scene for further inference and action. The term "prepare" is used to communicate the idea that the actor's environment is a managed product of his judgmental, perceptual, and typifying "work" (the managing) that he must engage in if he is to make sense of his environment in order to prepare the scene for further inference and action.[1]

2. The task is to identify what is typical, normal, and routine for the actor in "preparing" the scene, that is, interpreting what is going on, what happened, as well as what appears as strange, unusual, crazy, and the like.

111

The previous chapter indicated the ways in which theoretical conceptions and practical coding procedures produce both members' and reseachers' categories. The improvised or *ad hoc* coding rules, categories, and theoretical conceptions employed are not based upon explicit theories at either the level of social process or social structure, but require for their successful use implicit commonsense or folk notions of what are routine, normal events and objects so that some general rules can be labeled and used to organize actual cases.[2] The identification of typical features in cases permits the actor and the researcher to treat the object or event as falling under a general practice or general knowledge concerning objects and events, thereby providing the necessary warrant to the decision made and action taken.

The structural argument assumes the formal conditions or general practices said to obtain in a society and can be linked directly to the particular cases falling under the general condition or practice,[3] even though the connection between abstract categories and objectifiable referents is not clear as to the kinds of observables being subsumed.

I am saying that private and public agencies that produce structural data and social scientific surveys employ improvised or *ad hoc* procedures for obtaining, labeling, categorizing, and presenting their information in tabular form; such procedures produce data containing not merely technical errors that can be estimated, for which allowances can be made when making inferences about findings, but the improvised procedures are integral features of arriving at and interpreting the end product and cannot be dismissed or "corrected" by estimates of error. The improvised or *ad hoc* procedures are necessary features of making sense out of the events or objects under consideration.

There is little information available on how the actor in everyday life employs particular gestures, body motions, voice intonation, grammatical structures, facial expressions, or relies upon certain ecological cues, spatial arrangements, and the like, in order to make sense of his environment. Nor is it clear how scientific observers of social settings accomplish the same activities, according to scientific rules of procedure, that *any man* can follow.

Process and Structure in Juvenile Justice

I have argued that police and probation officials "make the system work" despite many problems associated with classifying juveniles, events labeled "offenses," "family settings," and the like. How the day-to-day activities of the police, probation, and other officials associated with the court or detention facilities produce information that becomes part of an official file on the juvenile (as distinct from the ways in which the file may be interpreted after its assembly) is not understandable without reference to the improvised but "normal" rules and theories utilized by officials. The rules and theories, however, have their roots in common sense or folk typifications making up law-enforcement officials' stock of knowledge. Without some understanding of everyday categories—the "strange," "unusual," "wrong," and what is "routine," "normal," "harmless," "right,"—we cannot understand how improvisation necessarily enters into the picture in making the formal legal and clinical categories invoked by law-enforcement officials work.

The everyday language of reports and contacts between policemen, juveniles, probation officers, and parents (as articulated with or as abstract referents of nonverbal communication) provides the information. The crucial task is to specify how the content of messages contained in interviews and official reports provide the law-enforcement official and the juvenile, parent, or school official with the basis for deciding "what happened" and the next course of action. A detailed analysis of the language of conversations and the language of official reports has the methodological significance of not relying upon illustrative quotations examined only by implication and indirectly; the researcher must make explicit remarks as to the meaning of the communication exchanges. Thus, a particular case must reveal something of the structure of all social action, reflect the ways in which the actor's theories are combined with organizational rules and practices for "making sense" of "what happened" and "preparing" the scene for further inference and action. Therefore, references to communication content are not intended as anecdotes left for the reader to interpret.

The police must locate events and objects they investigate in some legal context, or characterize the situation in such a way that their presence or interference can be warranted now and later on if further justification is required. The police must map the event and social objects into socially and legally relevant categories as a condition for inference and action. The officer's tacit knowledge combines with information he has received, and his own observations of the action scene, to provide him with a preliminary mapping, but he invariably asks fairly standardized questions about "what happened" and who were the principal actors involved. The initial search procedures combine with prior assumptions and information to give the scene structure, but body motion, facial expressions, voice intonation, and the like, can make problematic the routine use of social and legal categories, and alter or "push" the interpretation of events and objects into categories calling for more or less "serious" action. "Normal" appearances are crucial here for routine action. Two general classes of encounters are common in juvenile cases: (1) patrol being called to the scene or they may be passing a situation that is viewed as suspicious, and (2) juvenile officers making telephone or personal inquiries in the field or at the station. In the first class of encounters, appearances are critical for invoking a presumption of guilt and deciding "what happened." Practical solutions are immediate, for readily available categories usually exist for subsuming the events described by the participants. For example, a street fight, a variety store clerk with a male or female juvenile accused of stealing candy or cosmetics, juveniles with "questionable" grounds for not being in school, and a juvenile unable to identify his ownership of a car or establish an appropriate link with the owner, are all viewed as routine objects and events easily categorized. The "game" is understandable because it is possible to map some general features of the objects and events involved, with categories and general practices "known" to fall within the policeman's proper domain of activities. When the patrol officer finds that the situation does not readily fit available categories for deciding "what happened," he may take down more than the routine kind of face sheet data and description and bring everyone involved down to the station for further interrogation or for detention, until a juvenile officer or detective (depending on the policy of the organization) can pursue the matter further. The imputed suspicions of the patrolman may be communicated in the official report as something like "they couldn't give a straight story as to what they were up to around the garage so I brought them in." Or the report may say "The same suspects have been known to break into houses in the X area so the undersigned decided it was best to have the juvenile bureau talk to them." The initial remarks, however, may be loaded or indirect, depending upon how much information the officer had prior to arrival or what was immediately observable as he pulled up, and, of course, the particular style the officer employs for such occasions: "What's up?" "What's going on around here?" "O.K., what are you guys up to?" "O.K., who did it?" "Which one of you started it?" "O.K., now, who are you? What are you doing here?" "In trouble again, huh?" "O.K., let's have it." "O.K., what else did you take?" If the patrolman is involved with a more complicated problem involving witnesses and several possible offenders, the initial question may be followed by more systematic attempts to establish the sequence and timing of "what happened." The critical feature of the initial remarks, coupled with any prior information related or observed, is that some attempt at mapping the objects and events into a readily understandable police situation is signaled by the language used and the categories therein. Thus the body motion, facial expressions, voice intonation, a known past record by the juveniles involved provide the officer with an initial basis for inferences, judgments, routinized evaluations as revealed in the language categories he employs. My field experiences, however, differ little from those reported elsewhere and I would not be adding much to repeat similar descriptions.[4]

The case of interrogations by juvenile officers in the field or at the station is another matter for several reasons.

1. The juvenile officer is skilled in his ability to interview suspects and has had considerable experience with virtually every "type" known to the police. There is little that is likely to surprise him and he will seldom lack appropriate categories with which to classify, evaluate, or summarize any concrete case.

2. The juvenile officer can pursue the case and contact different witnesses or others relevant to the case such as school officials, parents, neighbors, and victims. He can draw upon whatever information the police have on the suspect and supplement it by other contacts. Thus the "picture" can be fairly complete prior to the interrogation. The language of the interview is often more managed than those encounters experienced by patrolmen in the field.

3. The juvenile officer has had experience with a variety of offenders and possible dispositions, troublesome parents, probation, and a particular style of interviewing he follows, depending upon the initial assumptions he makes about the case at hand. The interrogation, therefore, is often based upon some fairly definite interpretations of "what happened" and a kind of plan of action for reaching a particular disposition. The alternatives that might emerge here are contingent upon the suspect's demeanor, the details he reveals about participation in activities under investigation, his past record, the kind of imputations the officer makes about his home situation, and the control the officer assumes can be exercised by the parents and police over his future conduct.

4. Because the juvenile officer has more information available and accessible, and because of his knowledge of probation-court procedures, he is able to manipulate the interview more than the patrolman. The juvenile officer, therefore, becomes a critical gatekeeper in the administration of juvenile justice because the same information can lead him to make quite different recommendations. Thus he is in a position to bargain with the juvenile and negotiate terms under which some disposition will be accomplished. The bargaining and negotiations reveal how members "close" activities, resolve contingencies, and arrive at seemingly "clear" accounts as to "what happened."

The juvenile officer interview is oriented by a variety of hunches, theories, rules of thumb, general procedures, and on the spot strategies for dealing with different juvenile suspects. The officer's past experience and the information available prior to the interview, lead him to make quick evaluations of his client as soon as there is a confrontation. The interrogation, therefore, is highly structured in the sense that the information revealed by the juvenile is evaluated quickly in terms of a set of categories which the officer invokes by means of questions posed for the suspect. The interrogation is designed to confirm the officer's suspicions or firm beliefs about "what happened" and how the particular suspect is implicated. The language used links the juvenile to particular activities, relations with peers, family, school officials, and the like, locates the suspect in a network of social relationships, and imputes routine motives and grounds to his action. For example:

POLICE OFFICER. Hi, you Jack Jones?

JUVENILE. Yaa, that's me.

OFF. Fine, sit down, Jack, I wanta ask ya a few questions about that dance out at the ———— Club last Saturday night. You were there, weren't you?

JUV. Yaa, I guess I was there. Why?

OFF. I wanta ask ya a few questions, that's all.

The officer may not reveal that the juvenile is the prime suspect in an incident involving an assault with a deadly weapon, that is, not until he can establish certain factors as to the youth's presence, for instance, his knowledge of what happened, his friends, his whereabouts at the time of the incident, his general manner of talking, the confidence he reveals about his affairs and their description. But the officer does seek to establish some immediate conditions for preparing the youth for a particular line of questioning. The initial gambit seeks to establish a nonthreatening setting if the officer assumes the juvenile's presence cannot be clearly established by witnesses. If this information is available to him (i.e., there are witnesses of the youth at the dance), then the opening line may include a "pleasant" or "neutral" tone of voice and seemingly a routine line of questioning without any apparent implications about the guilt or innocence of the youth. The meaning of the message and the particular line of questioning are constrained by the social context. Now it is possible that the officer has no prior information, the suspect is a kind of shot in the dark, and he intends to bluff his way while "playing it by ear." The officer may plunge into the following: "Why do you cheat, lie, and act this way?" The decision to "bluff" a "hard line" may be motivated by the fact that a serious offense was committed and there are few leads to follow. The many possibilities, however, are endless, but they are not all "independent" cases; some can be analyzed for routinized patterns. The officer engages in a preliminary mapping of events and objects into social categories to establish the relevance of prior knowledge, present assumptions, and what is "happening." The language employed, therefore, may or may not reflect the initial strategy of the policeman's intentions, but locates officer and juvenile in a preliminary network of relationships. The officer seeks to keep the suspect in a state of "informational imbalance." The sense of bargaining or fatality that is communicated can vary with the particular officer's style of interviewing, his estimation of who is guilty or implicated, the juvenile's demeanor, the juvenile's past record, and how much information the officer possesses that can be used to convey particular power conditions he has available. Now each of these conditions is not available to the officer as an explicit and obvious possibility he will or can utilize to "nail down" the case, but the conditions are revealed to the researcher in two ways. First, the interview itself, as it unfolds, reveals something of the officer's strategy. Second, in discussing cases with officers, general conditions of interrogation are described over and over again in distinct cases and cut across officers.

Some idea of police interrogation strategies can be obtained from reading the official policy of large metropolitan juvenile bureaus such as the following from a large city in southern California:

> *Interrogation.* Juveniles are to be interrogated, keeping in mind the same procedures and techniques used with adults, with one exception: the interrogation of a female under the age of eighteen years regarding sex matters shall be conducted by a policewoman, except if none is available and the situation demands immediate investigation.
>
> Many times a juvenile is anxious to tell the entire story about his suspected crimes immediately upon arrest. After a period of waiting in a police station without being interrogated, he may gain composure or he may think about the reaction of his parents when they learn of his arrest. This waiting period may afford him a good opportunity to think of an excuse or a story to cover his arrest. Many admissions have no doubt been lost by the fact that officers failed to interrogate juvenile suspects properly upon initial contact.
>
> Juveniles are more inclined to "cop-out" than an adult, and a good interrogation will result often in the admission of other crimes and the identification of accomplices.

Notice how the above general statement of policy and strategy stresses the importance of interrogation under conditions where the juvenile may not be "composed." The "suspect" appears to be viewed as "guilty," even though the language does not make the apparent presumption clear. The statement makes explicit reference to the possibility of obtaining information about "other crimes and the identification of accomplices." What remains unclear, of course, is how one "interrogate(s) juvenile(s) properly."

A caution is necessary at this point. I am not saying that it is typical for officers to follow the same line of questioning or strategy, given the different conditions of demeanor, past record, information available, and discretionary power to follow the same strategy. Various routinized procedures exist for the ways in which the juvenile is prepared for adjudication of his criminality or competency or illness vis-à-vis the event or events in question. The "preparation" leading to inferences and further action extends to the juvenile's future in that an estimation of projected future behavior can influence the present course of action. The initial categories used to describe the juvenile depend upon the information available to structure the "set" or "stance" assumed by the officer when he enters the action scene with the juvenile. The language employed in the course of the interview reveals the interplay between the conditions mentioned and provides the researcher with a basis for deciding "what happened" based upon a commitment to the manner in which the participants made sense of "what happened." The fact that the officer is not bound by explicit rules governing adversary settings with adults, such as right to council (particularly its effective use), and the fact that the juvenile is often aware that he is dealing with a unilateral arrangement, whereby he is at a disadvantage that can become considerably worse if he does not demean himself in a way that the officer considers "appropriate," invariably lead the officer to make fairly explicit statements about his evaluation of the juvenile, his disposition feelings, and what the juvenile can expect in future encounters. The generalization I propose is that irrespective of different types of officers as social types, of different interviewing strategies, of different conditions of information about the juvenile (seriousness of offense, past record, demeanor, etc.), the "preparation" of the juvenile's case, leading to decisions, follows consistent patterns of encoding information into language categories assumed to have "obvious" meaning.

Juvenile Problems and Their Social Settings

I should like to outline typical juvenile problems in order to orient the reader further about everyday police activities, but the price is that of reifying the empirically observable features of actual juveniles as they appear to the researcher in different encounters with the police. Any set of types must be an exaggerated depiction of those juveniles actually seen by the police, but I justify the use of such a set here because it will sensitize the reader to the implicit one the police utilize in making their decisions about the social object in question, "what happened," and taking further action. The seriousness of the offense from the point of view of the police and their interpretation of the penal code, does not reveal how much time the police spend with different classes of juveniles. The following typology suggests the order of decreasing time spent with different classes of juvenile cases.

1. *Dependency cases.* These cases seldom involve acts, regarded as criminal or delinquent, committed by juveniles. Information is supplied to the police by school or welfare authorities, neighbors, and even the juveniles themselves, to the effect that children are being neglected, the home is "unfit," the parents "beat" the children excessively, and the like. In such cases the police intervene into the everyday lives of the family and have considerable discretion over search and seizure procedures in deciding that immediate action is justified. Differences between the probation department, the welfare department and the police are not uncommon here, since the police seem to react more strongly than the former agencies in seeking to separate the children from parents and bringing charges against the parents. The probation officials may view the home as "adequate" for the "type of people" involved, while the welfare representative may feel the police are not informed sufficiently about the "real" problems of the case.

2. Family and juvenile problems. The police are frequently called in by the parents to intervene in problems where juvenile responses at home are viewed as excessive, abusive, or unwarranted; the youth doesn't "mind" or do "what he is told" and is abusive to the parents, siblings, friends, neighbors, or the like. Many cases of incorrigibility and runaways are included here. In some middle-class homes, this might include parental requests that the police interfere with the juvenile's "going around with the wrong crowd," or going out with members of the opposite sex viewed as "bad" types or "embarrassing," for example, middle-income families concerned with their girls dating lower-income or ethnic males. A frequent problem involves juveniles who wish to marry against their parents' wishes and continually run away. In these cases, police intervention is welcomed by the family, and controlling of the activities of juveniles viewed as "bad," "disrespectful," "wild," or "immature" becomes the issue.

3. "Minor" misdemeanors or "normal" juvenile "delinquency." In every city in the United States the weekend invariably includes any number of dances, parties, and gatherings at popular juvenile "hangouts" such as drive-in restaurants, ice-cream parlors, drug stores, and hot-dog stands. Most of these activities are known to the police, and calls to "break up" a crowd, "check out" a party, and so forth, are routine activities. The lateness of the gatherings is an immediate basis for interference by the police, and there is a tacit assumption that drinking, sexual activity, curfew, fighting, and the like, accompany such gatherings. From a routine investigation of a drunken party, the police may uncover clues or suspects involved in something more serious; such inquiries are not viewed as trivial. Juveniles considered "bad," or "punks," for reasons like prior petty theft, grand theft auto, burglaries, and malicious mischief may be recommended for serious disposition because of activities (otherwise viewed as trivial) in drunk parties, fighting, and so on.

4. "Normal" misdemeanors. This category represents activities for which persons in the community expect to hear juveniles are in trouble. A striking feature of juveniles picked up for such activities as petty theft, malicious mischief, joyriding, shooting in the city limits, battery, etc., is that the police report (but not always the "rap sheet" summarizing offenses) may mention many additional cases the juvenile admits to when questioned by the officer. Many juvenile officers routinely ask: "Now tell me about how many other times you did the same thing." Many parents register surprise when the officer tells them their child has been involved in many past incidents, thus challenging the parents' claim to an official "first offense." The confrontation, where the juvenile admits before the parent the information revealed to police during private interrogation, provides the officer with leverage for making threats about what will happen in the future and allows him to give the juvenile "another chance" even though a more severe disposition may be warranted. The important feature of this category is that, the juveniles in question are not merely engaged in occasional delinquent activity, but systematic criminal activities for which they are seldom apprehended. But inasmuch as it is difficult to link these reported acts with prior complaints from victims, the confessed acts do not become part of the official material from which official statistics are constructed. Such information provides the officer with routine grounds for recommending a court hearing and applying informal pressure on the probation officer even though the official record does not contain all of the details about past activities. The cards ("rap sheets") of all juveniles often include such statements as "this boy likes to rub cheeks with other boys," "this boy is a liar," "this boy is a mama's boy," or "this boy can't be trusted." Notice that many of the juveniles in this category may systematically engage in activities that the police and, presumably, a juvenile court consider to be misdemeanors, and juveniles confess to such activities freely (according to various interrogation procedures).

5. *"Serious" offenses and general felonies.* It is important to distinguish between those juveniles who routinely may be involved in one or more of the categories described above and those who are viewed as a kind of "hard core" type of criminal for whom the label "delinquent" is merely a euphemism for "gangster" or common thief. The former juveniles may routinely fall into categories 2 or 3 above, but on some particular occasion become involved in an offense considered serious. Depending upon the family situation, demeanor of the juvenile, and his official past record, such cases may not lead to a Youth Authority commitment but, at most, removal from the community to a boys ranch or a private school if the family can afford it. The "hard core" cases, however, will be sent to the Youth Authority, and may be parolees from state institutions. The police are convinced "hard core" cases are involved routinely in systematic criminality. This latter group of juveniles (a minority of the total "delinquency" population) will include the stereotypical ethnic group cases, school dropouts, those who come from "bad" homes, and candidates for adult criminality. To the police, this group of juveniles *are* criminal types.

The above five general types are not intended as equivalence classes to enable the researcher to subsume actual cases, nor are they in one-to-one correspondence with types employed by police and probation officers. The probation officer's clinical orientation tends to take the edge off the criminal categories the police use with "hard core" types. The five categories represent my efforts to identify agencies' organized attempts to generate data placed in official files, and from which stem official or community notions of delinquency. Thus, even though category 5 occupies the least part of the police officer's time, it tends to provide generic notions of delinquency, in both community and social science conceptions, viewed as typical.

The Generation of Delinquent Categories

Constructing rates of delinquency from police records provides *one* method for showing how law-enforcement activities generate data said to reflect "delinquent behavior." The socially organized ways in which juvenile activities are translated into types of "delinquents" by observing behavior during initial encounters with the police and, by subsequent interrogations and official reports, provide a *second* method for showing how notions of delinquency are generated. What the two methods have in common is that the same juvenile activities lead to different pictures of something called delinquency.

The two methods for generating delinquency provide a basis for understanding how process and structure are inferred by sociologists and enable the researcher to compare the formal or ideal conceptions of community-defined problems as handled by the legal system, and the practiced and enforced activities making up the routine character of everyday problems. The first method does not reveal the bargaining or negotiated character of all legal procedures. Through day-to-day encounters with the police, juvenile cases are filtered so that some cases assume typical "delinquent" features, that is, coming from broken homes, exhibiting "bad attitudes" toward authority, poor school performance, ethnic group membership, low-income families, and the like. The official records mask the filtering, particularly when the first method is used. When we merely abstract information from official records so that structural comparisons are possible (e.g., broken home, low income, ethnicity, negative social character), the contingencies of unfolding interaction, the typifications (theories of "good" and "bad" juveniles, families, etc.), are excluded from our understanding of how legal or other rules were invoked to justify a particular interpretation and course of action. We are forced to interpret the categories established in accordance with *ad hoc* or improvised theoretical or substantive rules. There is no articulation between procedural rules and observable referents, joined by a theory of action. The "logic-in-use" of the organizational actors (for example, policemen, probation officers) is obscured because the organizational records contain information reconstructed for various practical reasons. Knowledge of how reports are assembled is needed to transform the formal report descriptions into processual statements about the public and private ideologies of law-enforcement agencies.

If the routine procedures and ideologies of police and probation officials filter juveniles into various categories and courses of action, then the research-er's construction of tables based upon structural information must reflect the typifications employed by officials. The structural or so-called objective data extracted from official records are labels stripped of their contextual signifi-cance. The meanings, which the researcher assigns to "broken home," "bad attitute toward authority," "gang influence" and "bad neighborhood," are divorced from the social context in which the labeling and actor's routine activities occur. These labels provide meanings to the police and probation officers for making both evaluations and disposition decisions. Offense cate-gories, therefore, cannot be divorced from the typifications employed by the police and probation officials.

The initial police encounter produces typical "face-sheet" data about the juvenile and a few cryptic notes. The formal report is often literal in the lan-guage employed (for example, "he then urinated against the side of the build-ing," "as they drove past the girl, X put his bare bottom out the car window," "X said that Z told him to leave his house, but he refused, whereupon Z went up the stairs and X and Y followed him to his bedroom where Z bent over and came up with the rifle"), but the report can also be general (for example, "it is obvious to the undersigned that X is not about to listen to his mother and is headed for a lot of trouble with this department").

The descriptions I shall give in this and in subsequent chapters presuppose my acceptability to the police as trustworthy and able to simulate being a "policeman." The same assumption would have to be true of probation descrip-tions. Therefore, my accounts represent a view of how delinquent types are produced by assuming "inside" knowledge, the routine social meanings em-ployed by law-enforcement personnel in face-to-face encounters, and the more managed language of the official report. The tape-recorded accounts of inter-action sequences are not sufficient for the observer to derive his interpretation of the encounters merely by reference to actors' categories. The physical appearance of the juveniles, their facial expressions, affectual communication, and body motion are all integral features of the action scene. The officer's sense of the enterprise he is engaged in, namely, assisting juveniles who need "help," juveniles who are no different than adult criminals, juveniles who need a "good whipping" by their parents, juveniles who need to have the "shit kicked out of them," juveniles who could use different parents, and so forth, suggests the researcher must untangle the use of language categories reflecting everyday organizational theories and practices, together with the features of legality and justice or procedural due process.

Legal requirements often lead to a kind of window dressing necessary to making the sometimes nasty business of police work compatible with demands for legal safeguards. The police assume their violation of a person's civil rights will not occur "in the long run" if the accused is "really innocent." The assumption of guilt or innocence on intuitive, commonsense grounds, based on considerable experience in typing different persons suspected or labeled offenders, is the core of law enforcement. Legal rules and conceptions of justice or fairness, before arraignment, are not relevant when the police are engaged in pursuing an adversary who is already viewed as guilty or suspect, and for whom no advantages are viewed as warranted. The adversary legal system with procedural due process, is viewed as a hindrance by the police because of a belief in their own integrity and their devotion to the control of persons variously "known" as "bad," "criminal," or "punks." Practical theorizing, based on extensive day-to-day contacts with various types of juveniles and adults in the community, provides the police with the *only* basis with which they feel comfortable and knowledgeable for tacking legal rules onto their routine activities.

Verbal Depictions of Social Organization[5]

A detailed analysis of conversations will provide the reader with concrete material for understanding how the police and probation seek to interpret the juvenile's character and actions by means of interviews. The initial brief conversations represent my verbatim notes of what happened. It was impossible for me to write down all elements of the conversations, and attempts to tape-record these interviews were not successful or were simply refused, although I was able to obtain tapes of a few probation interviews that I did not witness.

In Case A, City B, the following interview took place between a male juvenile and a policewoman about an alleged theft.

POLICEWOMAN. What's your name?

JUVENILE. Fleece.

POL. What?

JUV. Fleece!

POL. [Looking at the files on juvenile offenders] You've never been here before have you? Come over here will ya please. I understand you had something to do with stealing some screwdrivers from . . .

JUV. Yah.

POL. When were you born? [The officer then begins filling out an arrest report with facesheet type of information.] Well, what about this?

JUV. What you mean what about it?

POL. Well, . . .

JUV. I took a tool case from a guy's place and put it in the bushes. [A quick exchange then occurred during which time the officer sought to establish the sequence of events that led to the theft.]

POL. Now he's out a tool kit, right?

JUV. Yah.

POL. Would you like to be out something like that?

JUV. No.

POL. Now right is right! If you do something wrong you ought to pay for it. I think that your folks should get $5.00 out of your hide one way or another. . . .

The establishment of the category "first offense" and the juvenile's appearance and general demeanor before the police officer are integral features of the conversation, even though I can only document the "first offense" part of the picture. I can only tell the reader that my impression of the youth was that of a neatly dressed person. The conversation itself, even when stripped of its paralinguistic properties, suggests a casual or "light" exchange. My impression of the conversation was that the police officer did not regard this offense as a "serious" matter; the parents would report to the Juvenile Bureau, and a "lecture" given to the juvenile would be repeated in the parents' presence in order to impress the juvenile and his parents with the future consequences of such conduct. The issue was not to establish guilt, but to deliver a "lecture" on the evils of criminal acts. Having observed this police officer at work on many occasions for over two years, I can describe her as "confident." The tone of her voice suggested to me that she did not regard the case as "serious." Her remark that "I understand you had something to do with stealing. . . ." was said in a "casual" way. The statement "Well, what about this" can be viewed as an invitation to the juvenile to engage in self-recrimination about his act, reveal his remorsefulness, and afford him the opportunity to indicate that he is "sorry" and will not "do it again." The officer continually tries to have the juvenile voluntarily express his remorse, his plans for reform, and the comment "Now he's out a tool kit, right" seeks to prod the juvenile into a remorseful statement. The response of "Yah" is not enough for the officer. She pushes the issue once more by asking: "Would you like to be out something like that?" She then seemed impatient with the juvenile and proceeded to spell out her concern without waiting for answers each time. During this part of the exchange, the juvenile sat with his head down, looking rather ashamed, while the officer indicated the terms of the disposition—repayment of the loss to the victim and (not quoted) a "talkin to" by his parents. The remark, "Now right is right," triggered off a very long "lecture" by the officer that I could not record. It was like a sermon on the importance of being honest and the sacredness of the property of others. This "sermon" was suggested in the earlier statements quoted: "Would you like to be out something like that?" and "If you do something wrong you ought to pay for it." The interrogation provides the officer with the opportunity to develop a trust relationship with the juvenile if the latter indicates remorse and a desire to "not do it again." The officer can then say she will "forget about this time" provided restitution is made and the juvenile "promises" to "stay out of trouble." The police continually make reference to notions about property, fairness to others, the dangers of unilateral action against others, and the like, and sociologists often label these vaguely stated conditions "middle-class values," but they appear to be empty abstract phrases for both juvenile and officer in cases not viewed as "serious." The abstract phrases are invoked as grounds for punishment if the offense is considered serious, the juvenile is a recidivist, and there is no trust relationship, or the relationship is viewed as violated.

The following excerpt from a very long interrogation of a thirteen-year-old juvenile in City A, suspected of breaking several windows at a school he previously attended, is a "first offense" case. The boy is the son of a physician and has not been in difficulty with the police, but he has had difficulty "getting along" with a particular teacher at a junior high school he formerly attended. He is now attending a Catholic school, and the interview occurred at the school. Before the interview began, it was my impression the juvenile was "nervous" about being called out of class by the police. The juvenile kept asking "What's the matter" and the officer kept saying "We just want to talk with you about something." Then the officer began asking circuitous questions about the juvenile's whereabouts on particular dates, seeking to establish his presence on the school grounds on two different weekends. The officer finally got around to the broken windows, but would not directly say he was trying to accuse the juvenile, but couched his questions and remarks in a kind of rhetoric that seemed designed to obtain information and also allow the juvenile to reveal spontaneously his own actions or connection with the broken windows. But when the boy denied knowing anything about "what happened" after admitting being in the area, the officer then stated ". . . the grapevine tells me . . . ," and he proceeded to suggest the juvenile was involved in the incident.

OFFICER. I'm afraid you're not telling the whole story, Mitch, and this is bugging me.

JUVENILE. Okay, okay, on the other side of the building I found a spoon and . . . [the juvenile then admits he threw the spoon at the windows several times, breaking one of them.]

[During the conversation the juvenile kept scratching the glass surface of the table we were all seated around, and the officer responded as follows:]

OFF. This shows a lack of respect, a lack of respect for property and other people. You don't show respect for other people or yourself when you do that.

JUV. Well, everybody breaks a window once in his life.

[A rapid exchange followed over the seriousness of the juvenile's behavior vis-à-vis the table and its implications for the breaking of windows.]

OFF. You didn't think did you . . . [when you broke the windows.]

JUV. [Shakes his head in agreement, but not looking up to the officer's face.]

OFF. More people get locked up for not telling the truth than for committing a crime.

[The juvenile now appeared to be rather unhappy and "remorseful."]

OFF. I appreciate your being honest, Mitch . . . [The juvenile is now only mumbling what seems to be an agreement to the officer's remarks.]

The strategy utilized by the above officer in "breaking down" the juvenile's "story" is not revealed entirely by the above conversation because the officer was able to employ information the juvenile could not check out independently. For example, the officer told the juvenile that "the grapevine tells me" and then mentioned the name of someone the boy knew, a boy apparently at the school grounds the day the windows were broken. Without saying the other boy had incriminated Mitch, the officer made it clear he was in possession of the "facts." Other information with which the officer finally confronted the boy after the initial admission of breaking one of the windows, but with a denial he had broken others, was the remark the boy had been enrolled at the school a few months ago, and the windows broken were those of a classroom occupied by the teacher with whom Mitch had the difficulty that led to his changing schools. By telling the boy that "you're not telling me the whole story" and implying he was in possession of information that implicated the juvenile, the police officer sought to convince the boy he would only "make it worse" if he did not relate what "really happened." After establishing guilt for the broken windows, the officer then used the technique of scratching the glass surface of the table to "lecture" the boy about how his behavior "showed a lack of respect" for both property and persons, as well as himself. The juvenile's remark that "everybody breaks a window once in his life" led to another "sermon" about the seriousness of the incident and its *being a sign of a general flaw in the boy's "attitude" toward life.* It is only after the boy indicated (by his facial expressions and tone of voice, neither of which I can objectify for the reader) his remorse and the realization of his error, that the officer tells him "you didn't think, did you." The officer seemed satisfied he had "gotten the message across" to the boy and then suggested that now that Mitch had seen the "light," "I appreciate your being honest, Mitch. . . ." What is not revealed is the impression I had that the officer did not feel the juvenile was "acting smart," although trying to withhold information. The boy's neat appearance and (I felt) polite tone of voice seemed to be crucial to what I took to be the officer's interest in providing the boy with a "lecture" about his activities and their consequences.

The following case, also from City A, reveals how background expectancies enter into police interrogations. The police report does not provide the reader with a clear sense of "what happened" because formal reports do not include information found in the conversational materials that follow. The case involves a sixteen-year-old Negro male with approximately seventeen contacts with the police as a result of many charges of petty theft, several burglaries, and a few miscellaneous contacts, including a child-molesting charge. The boy has had six applications for petition filed on him by the police, and he was still a ward of the court when I accompanied the juvenile officer to the school for the interrogation. The officer explained that the boy had been handled as a "psycho" case because his second contact with police involved the child-molesting charge mentioned above. The boy was described as a "perpetual liar" although the officer conceded that perhaps the juvenile did have some "problems." The presumption of psychological problems seemed to preclude sending this boy directly to the Youth Authority. The boy's appearance is that of a well-dressed, "clean-cut," and polite adolescent. The reason for the interview is a trumpet stolen from school; this juvenile is considered a suspect. The officer opens the conversation by saying that he is seeking "some information."

JUVENILE. [Starts talking about the day the trumpet was stolen by saying]
It was the day I went to the store for my mother.
OFFICER. I never told you what day it was stolen.
JUV. Well, you said it was about a week and a half ago.
OFF. We know a boy who saw you get the trumpet.
JUV. What! That can't be.
OFF. Look, this can't go on. "Talked to and released," "talked to and released." It can't go on. Even probation is going to get tired of this. I can't speak for probation, but they are not going to take it much longer. I know you got a problem and I want to help you with your problem.
JUV. Yeah, but people know about my problem and put the blame on me.
OFF. Now, I'd try and get you out of anything you didn't do.

[The conversation then covered several topics rapidly with the juvenile admitting that he was at school the day the trumpet was taken. The juvenile claimed that he was at school but didn't take anything. He said that he went directly home and then to the store for his mother. He was accompanied by another juvenile (with a long police record) and stated that they encountered another juvenile with a .22 rifle, and he claimed that he was going to shoot his companion. The officer listened and then seemed to be viewing the conversation as an evasion of the purpose of the interview.]

OFF. If you're involved in this, tell me. I won't place you in the Hall. If I find out you were involved, I'll place you in the Hall. I'll report it to probation anyway. I think I can prove you were involved.
JUV. You think I'm involved. You say you can prove it?
OFF. I can't prove it, but I have a boy who'll testify against you. I'd hate to place you in the Hall, because of your problem.

JUV. So you figure I'm the guy.

OFF. Well, I don't say I can do it beyond a shadow of a doubt, but there is one guy who says you did it.

JUV. Well, I wasn't even with Maurice that day; wait a minute, I was with him for a little bit, he had my dog, but I swear that yesterday was the first day I heard about it. I think it was some of these guys. I don't want to say they did it, but I think they did and they're blaming me. I don't want to go to Juvy.

[The conversation continued for another ten minutes but I was unable to record any more of it verbatim because both the officer and the juvenile began talking very rapidly. Apparently this juvenile had handled the trumpet somehow, but it was not clear how he came to have it for a period of time. The officer finally gave up, telling me it was "no use" talking to a "perpetual liar."] My impression was that the juvenile knew about the stolen trumpet. The officer seemed to have made the same assumption and spoke to this juvenile first because he felt the others involved were "even bigger liars." The officer's remark "I never told you what day it was stolen" seems to imply the juvenile was not merely being questioned, but was the guilty party, and his remark about the same "day I went to the store . . ." supports the officer's unstated presumption of guilt. The juvenile's response seems to be an attempt to neutralize the officer's remark, but the officer counters with a direct accusation, making it clear that the interview is not merely a matter of seeking "information." The officer is not impressed with the juvenile's response and launches into a complex statement, suggesting the juvenile is continually in difficulty with the police, that nothing comes of being "talked to and released" except further troubles, and that even probation is "not going to take it much longer." The implication here is that while the police (as represented by this officer) have now reached the end of their trust relationship with the boy and will not tolerate a disposition that merely involves talking to the boy about his actions and then releasing him to his parents, probation will undoubtedly reach the same conclusion even though they have supported the juvenile in the past. The officer does not say that he will or has contacted probation, and although he "can't speak for probation," he seems to be speaking for them nonetheless. This remark also carries the implication that the officer will see to it probation is apprised of his views. The officer then refers to the psychological "problem" and his presumed desire to "help" the juvenile. The juvenile's response seems to turn the officer's remark "on its head" by implying the "problem" generates accusations by others directed at him, rather than cause him to engage in delinquent activities. The officer's response that he would "try and get you out of anything you didn't do," implies the present situation has nothing to do with the possibility the boy could be justified in his claim that he is accused because others "know" he has a "problem." The officer seems to be saying there is some legitimacy to the "problem," and he would honor it if he personally knew of unwarranted accusations. The officer then allowed the juvenile to "have his say," and I vaguely felt the officer was perhaps responding to the possibility the "problem" gave the boy the right to voice his opinions and defend himself. After the boy's remarks, the officer shrugged his shoulders and seemed to adopt a mixed strategy of entertaining the possibility the juvenile was involved and, if he admitted his involvement immediately, he would not be placed in Juvenile Hall. Yet the officer served notice that if the juvenile denied involvement now, and the officer was later to find that he had lied, there would be automatic placement in Juvenile Hall, and probation would be given a negative report. The sequence "if I find out you were involved . . . I think I can prove you were involved," leads to a hard line, after initially "giving the kid a break" by saying an immediate confession would not result in serious consequences. The bargaining here is of interest because the officer seems to place considerable importance on his feeling the boy is always lying, and a quick confession would lead to nonplacement at Juvenile Hall as a kind of reward for admitting involvement. But the officer then shifts to the view that not only would later establishment of guilt lead to placement at Juvenile Hall and notification given to probation, but the officer is in fact convinced the juvenile is guilty after all. The juvenile's response seems to be one of testing the officer, seeking more information by repeating the officer's accusations and claims of possible proof. The officer then admits he cannot "prove it, but I have a boy who'll testify against you," implying that "proof" may be relative but effective. Thus, the absence of a confession will not convince the officer of the boy's innocence, yet he implies a reluctance to place the boy in Juvenile Hall "because of your problem." It would appear the officer is constrained by his knowledge the boy is viewed as someone "with a problem." But the juvenile continues the earlier stance of noncommitment when the officer attempts to elicit a confession by saying "So you figure I'm the guy." The officer then repeats explicitly what was revealed in his earlier remarks: "We know a boy who saw you get the trumpet," by now saying: "There is one guy who says you did it." The juvenile generates further conversation to allow for his presence with others presumably involved in the theft, but maintains a line which denies his participation. The attempt to implicate others—others who are seeking to "blame" him—ends with his concern about avoiding a trip to Juvenile Hall the officer had been proposing earlier. The officer has now completed his "bag of tricks," but has failed to elicit a confession. The officer's strategy seemed to hinge upon the assumption the boy would be very unhappy over the possibility of going to Juvenile Hall and the possibility of having the incident reported to probation, even though there was no confession or concrete "proof." ("I'll report it to probation anyway. I think I can prove you were involved.") The officer seemed to be allowing for the relevance of the "problem" while claiming "this can't go on." The boy attempted to use the "problem" as a means of placing the responsibility of the theft on others, who were aware of the "problem," and were using their knowledge to "blame" him.

The bargaining relationship between officer and juvenile is a routine feature of all the encounters I observed in Cities A and B, but where the written official report is a highly truncated interpretation of the exchange. In moving from the actual encounter to the official report, and then to a 5 x 7 card (in City A) listing the juvenile's police contacts, the reduction in information makes it impossible to identify the contextual conditions in which the officer decided the suspect was guilty, or the basis for writing a report with whatever "convincing" arguments it contains. Notice, therefore, how difficult it is to interpret a highly abstract entry on a card file used for quick reference when "checking out" a juvenile's past activities. The conversational material calls attention to hints, direct accusations, moral arguments, denials, defamation of character, threats, presumed or imputed lying, and the like, that invariably arise in the course of the exchange. Many of these characterizations, admissions, denials, etc., are occurrences that others and the suspect might claim "didn't happen," depending upon the actor(s) involved, but could be included in an official police report or viewed as evidence when given orally in other meetings, official or unofficial, where decisions are reached or discussed. Therefore, terse reports or documents necessarily require, for their understanding, unstated meaning structures, the "facts," imputations, admissions, denials, and the like, of the conversational exchanges that preceded or followed the construction or interpretation of the documents. Knowledge about such conversations, even when there exists no verbatim transcript nevertheless provides the observer with background knowledge for raising questions about a more abstract, truncated report or document. The conceptual play or imagination required to interpret a document, whose conversational antecedents are unknown, merely complicates the problem, but it does not preclude the observer's attempts to pose contrastive readings for the reader. The likelihood that members do their own reflecting on the problem complicates the analysis, but this too does not preclude contrastive readings.

Audrey

To illustrate further the problem of articulating conversational exchanges with truncated documentary accounts, the case of a fifteen-year-old Negro female will be used because of the availability of an almost complete transcription of a recorded interview between the girl and her probation officer, and the probation officer's informal notes based on the conversation placed in the juvenile's file.

The juvenile's first contacts with the police began at the end of sixth grade in elementary school when she was accused of several thefts. The following fall, while attending junior high school, the juvenile was suspended for taking another girl's purse. On her way home, the juvenile entered another student's home and took twenty dollars. The victim's parents discovered the juvenile's suspension slip on the floor of the bedroom from which the money was taken. The juvenile was placed on probation, with the probation officer noting that, although the parents earned a comfortable living (about $700.00 per month) and the house was in very good condition, the juvenile and her three siblings "have a lack of adult and parental supervision and control. Both parents are employed and either unable or uninterested in having Audrey properly supervised." The probation officer (hereafter: P.O.) stated: "It appears obvious that Audrey has quite a problem with her thievery and should have some type of professional help." After several other incidents following the above burglary in the spring of 1964 (including the discovery of various purses of fellow students in her school locker), and sexual intercourse with at least two boys, the juvenile was sent to a state mental hospital for ninety days of observation. The P.O. requested and obtained foster home placement after the hospital authorities reported Audrey was: "hyperactive and superficially well-behaved. They feel that she acts out her hostilities and anger by stealing, as she never loses her temper verbally. They feel that she has an extremely low self-esteem which she compensates by stealing." It is difficult to objectify what is meant by any of the P.O.'s remarks, either with reference to the juvenile's home situation, her "problem," or the hospital's account of what is wrong with the girl. The fact of many thefts leads to an examination of the juvenile's home life and the presumption that there must be a "deep" underlying "problem" causing the thefts. The following account (by the P.O.), contained in a foster home request, provides the "evidence" for the decision taken about placement outside of the home:

Audrey is a very appealing and attractive girl, who has not matured physically yet. She wants very much to be liked and relates in a friendly manner to all around her. She is not obviously disturbed, until you realize that her stealing and lying traits are deep, underlying symptoms. The doctors state that although she is emotionally disturbed, she is not antisocial or psychotic, and that she is capable of rehabilitation. Foster parents should be firm, understanding and realistic, without any sadistic tendencies for punishment, such as her father has used.

The amount of information possessed by the P.O. is obviously greater than what a reader can discern from an official report, but how such information has been interpreted by the P.O., much less how it was produced, does not provide unambiguous verification in a legal sense. If the girl was described as a "punk" or a "bitch" in conjunction with her stealing activities, the likely disposition is to send the juvenile to the Youth Authority. But a juvenile who is "appealing and attractive," and who "wants very much to be liked and relates in a friendly manner to all around her," is a prime candidate for clinical interpretations as opposed to criminal imputations. Finding "problems" in the home is not difficult, but there is no way for the observer to decide such matters independently if he relies solely upon documents. The transformation of the juvenile into a sick object permits all concerned to suspend the criminal imputations of her acts, even though the penal code sections are quoted each time the police report theft or burglary. The picture is clouded by the psychiatric information suggesting there is emotional disturbance but not psychosis. The juvenile's appearances, therefore, cannot be used to document the "underlying problem," except when there are thefts or some activity like sexual intercourse, for the juvenile is depicted as "appealing and attractive."

Having established the juvenile as "sick," the P.O. must sustain this depiction despite activities by the juvenile appearing to contradict this label. But having the label, it is easier to "explain" infractions by reference to aggravating conditions and the necessity of "more treatment." The interview quoted below between Audrey and her P.O. occurred because, after Audrey's placement in the foster home, she became involved in some difficulties at school that were considered possible violations of the terms of her probation. The interview was conducted at the juvenile's school.

PROBATION OFFICER. Audrey, do you know why I'm here?
JUVENILE. Yes.
P.O. Do you want to tell me about it?
JUV. I had trouble about that fighting?
P.O. That's part of it.
JUV. [response inaudible]
JUV. What you're going to make the notes for?
P.O. Well, just if you have anything to explain [cut off by juvenile].
JUV. You're going to take me to court?
P.O. No, darling, I just want to talk to you about it and see what we can do so it doesn't happen any more.
JUV. Well, I have to tell you the truth because you're my probation officer.
P.O. Right. And that's the way we work that, isn't it?—the truth from me and the truth from you.
JUV. Well, you know, . . . I'm just going to tell you how it works. First place I didn't know it had started because I was over there eating lunch with Bob; you probably don't know him . . . and then after I got through, you know, he, Penny, Candy and Jane were standing over there so I went over there, you know, I always fool around with them after I get through with my lunch, so I

went over there and they . . . so I was talking to 'em and Candy said—you know, I didn't know the girl so I asked him to show her to me—we were out in the field—I didn't know what the girl Iris was going to start fighting with them before. I didn't know that what kind of girls they were going to start a fight with. I don't know their names.

P.O. They're white girls?

JUV. Uh, one was big and one was short.

P.O. Are they sisters?

JUV. Yes.

P.O. And are they new here to the school?

JUV. Yes.

P.O. Are you saying now that you didn't know that the girls planned on starting a fight?

JUV. I didn't know that Candy and them had already planned it because you know, they walk home and I ride the bus.

P.O. But they had planned it that evening before.

JUV. I guess so, because they planned for Rose to beat her because Rose was small like she was. And then the next morning, you know, I was standing over there and I was talking to these two new, those girls, you know, the ones that got beat up yesterday, you know, but first the way it started Candy was talking about the girl's shoes, you know, her shoes [cut off by Probation Officer].

P.O. Making fun of them or what?

JUV. Yes, sure, like, girl where do you get your kicks from? You know, like that.

P.O. What kind of shoes were they?

JUV. They were black shoes and they were turned all over on the side and had a big hole in the middle of them.

P.O. Well, because they didn't have enough money to buy other kind of shoes.

JUV. Oh, she had some more because she wore them the next day. Anyway, anyway, well, the next day we just got in a fight.

P.O. Well, how did it start and how did you get into it?

JUV. See, uh, Jane told me to hold her wallet, you know, so I held her wallet. [Pause] Jane is [pause] Candy's sister. And so she went around the corner and I was standing up there waiting for her. She told me to wait for her. So I guess she went to her locker. She told me to hold her wallet and then I held it and when she come back she got her wallet, you know. So I said "Jane, we'd better hurry up so we can go on down and get our books because I gotta meet . . ." and so those girls were standing up in the corner, you know, down here by the boys' gym. Yeah. Well right there on the 7th grade—the girls are in the 7th grade—and so Jane said something and the girls said come up here and then, and so Jane she just grabbed one of them and started fighting. I would never got in it you see, but both of them starting jumping on Jane.

P.O. Both the white girls started jumping on your friend, Jane?

JUV. See, Jane was beating up her sister. See, I would never have jumped in, see, because it was just a fair fight between her and her sister, but both of them jumped in it.

P.O.   Didn't uh. Didn't Jane jump on the little one?

JUV.   Yes. The—the little one?

P.O.   Did you think that was fair?

JUV.   No.

P.O.   Anyway, you shouldn't have fights, but if you have a fight do you think it's fair for a 9th grade big girl to jump on a 7th grade little girl?

JUV.   No.

P.O.   So then what happened after Jane had the little girl down?

JUV.   I don't know whether she had the little girl down or not. I was, I was mostly trying to keep the other girl from jumping on Jane.

P.O.   Oh, you jumped on the big sister?

JUV.   Yeah, because she was trying to keep her from jumping on Jane and then Candy came in there and beat her up.

P.O.   And you hit the big girl?

JUV.   Yes.

P.O.   Audrey, what made you think it was any of your business anyway, for getting on this fight?

JUV.   But both of them shouldn't have been jumping on Jane.

P.O.   You should have gone and just gotten away from the situation all together. Jane started the fight, however it turned out was her own responsibility. It was up to the big sister to protect her little sister as far as I could see. They were the innocent ones. By you jumping in you were taking up for the wrong side regardless of whether Jane is your friend. Because when someone starts a fight they're to blame. You know that. Have you had any other fights there?

JUV.   No. This is my first time I ever got in trouble.

P.O.   I know.

The conversation shifts at this point. Before quoting the remainder of the conversation, I want to discuss briefly the material quoted above. The opening remarks suggest that both parties were aware of the conditions leading to the meeting, and the P.O. allows the juvenile to state the reason. The qualified response ("That's part of it") by the P.O. will be apparent when we return to the remainder of the conversation. The mention of fighting was enough to proceed. The juvenile's remark "What you're going to make notes for?" implies special significance is being assigned to the meeting, and the P.O. seems to be interested in cutting down on her notes. The juvenile's fears come out in her remark about taking "me to court." The P.O. again tries to mollify the girl, but does not state flatly how the matter will be resolved. The comment about telling "the truth because you're my probation officer," could be viewed as a "proper" response to the assurance the matter was not destined for court, but it also provides the P.O. with the opportunity to reestablish explicitly the idea that a trust relationship should exist. While I cannot objectify the referent, the voice intonation suggested to me the P.O. was attempting to reassure the girl this was a "routine" interview about a matter that cannot be overlooked, but not serious enough to warrant the girl's fears about court. The P.O. seemed interested in "getting the story" before giving the juvenile "advice." Notice how the juvenile's story of "what happened" suggests a fortuitous involvement and not a well-ordered causal chain of events. The juvenile suggests her participation began with routine contact with friends who described the situation ("so I was talking to 'em and Candy said") to her. The juvenile seems to suggest her innocence by the remark: "I didn't know the girl so I asked him to show her to me. . . . I don't know their names." But the P.O. is not interested in the fact that such descriptions may be inherently vague for the participant and impossible to objectify.

The officer must establish some causal sequence (terminate and "close" activities so they can be identified and counted) as a condition for evaluating and reaching a decision as to what the present circumstances "mean" vis-à-vis the juvenile's probationary status. The juvenile seems to be describing "life as usual," while claiming ignorance about the antecedent conditions of the fight. The P.O. then seeks to cut through the description by establishing the race of the victims and then saying "you didn't know that the girls planned on starting a fight?" The juvenile states "I didn't know that Candy and them had already planned it because you know, they walk home and I ride the bus," suggesting either the planning was done when they walked home or she knew they were making plans but did not hear the details because of going home on the bus; she was agreeing to the P.O.'s suggestion that it was planned but that she could not have known about it because of the difference in their ways of getting home. The juvenile seems to be saying perhaps she did hear of plans but, because of going home by bus, she was not privy to the actual strategies planned. The fight seemed planned; the P.O. first mentioned planning as a possibility. Yet the juvenile's account supports planning and a fortuitous entry on her part. The P.O. suggests the fight had been planned "that evening before." And the juvenile remarks "I guess so, because they planned for Rose to beat her . . . ," implying she did know Rose was to initiate the fight because of her size vis-à-vis the victim. As the juvenile begins to provide further details about how the fight started, the P.O. intrudes with an additional structured interpretation, "Making fun of them . . . ," and the juvenile seems to agree when she states "Yes, sure, like, girl where do you get your kicks from?" This remark suggests the shoes were the basis for triggering off the fight.

The P.O. seeks to standardize the event so that classification and a causal sequence can be constructed, and the juvenile seems to be "cooperating." But it is not clear how much of the juvenile's response is motivated by the kind of structuring provided by the P.O., or if the P.O. is merely making explicit what the juvenile is trying (but not able) to make clear. The P.O.'s suggestion that the white girls did not "have enough money to buy other kind of shoes," did not impress the delinquent as relevant, for she replies this could not be the case "because she had some more . . . she wore them the next day." The P.O.'s suggestion that the juvenile and her friends were being nasty by teasing the white girls because of their poverty seemed irrelevant to Audrey and her friends because they would not have known what shoes would be worn the next day to now retrospectively undercut the P.O.'s remark.

Thus, for the P.O., the teasing was a serious matter if it meant the white girl was unable to have better shoes, while for Audrey this was not an issue though she understood it retrospectively. The different shoes, seen the next day retrospectively, meant the teasing had nothing to do with shoes *per se*, but was merely a vehicle for making talk and provoking a fight. For the juvenile, the talk about the shoes seemed irrelevant for "anyway, anyway, well the next day we just got in a fight." It is difficult to say how much of what the juvenile stated could be considered "just talk" for the benefit of the P.O., where the juvenile's intention is to give some account, any account, that would satisfy the P.O. The P.O., meanwhile, is searching for a "rational" explanation of "what happened." The "search" leads to structured questions that seek to eliminate the contingencies of "what happened" so as to arrive at an orderly sequence leading up to the fight. Thus, both are agreed there was a fight, but the juvenile's explanation could be taken as an attempt to "play it cool," provide the P.O. with many details to allow the P.O. to propose an interpretation of "what happened," and thereby relieve the juvenile of having to commit herself to an interpretation that would not please the P.O. Or the juvenile's explanation could be taken as an attempt to provide all of the contingencies possible to emphasize that the fight unfolded in an ambiguous way, to underscore the view that it was not necessarily (as implied by the P.O.) well-ordered, and that she had nothing to do with it. Admitting that perhaps there was "planning" prior to the fight provides an explanation, but does not necessarily involve the juvenile. For the juvenile, the contingencies seem to be integral to "what happened," while for the P.O., they merely confuse the "central" issues, namely, that a fight occurred, that the juvenile (a ward of the court) was involved, and that a "reasonable" accounting was being demanded.

The P.O. again seeks to pinpoint "what happened" by asking "well, how did it start and how did you get into it?" The "well" suggests impatience and doubts about the juvenile's story. The juvenile's "answer" again begins by noting some of the detailed contingencies preceding the fight and could be construed as an attempt to show that everything leading up to the fight was "life as usual" until "so Jane said something and the girls said come up here and then, and so Jane she just grabbed one of them and started fighting." The phrase "Jane said something and the girls said come up here" presumably refers to some exchange wherein something was said that challenged or angered one party, and each or one party decided that the challenge or response to the initial comment required further action. The P.O.'s "both the white girls started jumping on your friend," ignores possible inadvertence in the way the fight started, and suggests a closed possibility with few relevant details. The P.O. seeks to "get to the heart of the matter" by suggesting "what happened," but the juvenile responds with "See, Jane was beating up her sister . . . it was just a fair fight between her and her sister, but both of them jumped in it." It appears that Audrey entered the fight after both sisters began fighting with her friend Jane, but this is never connected to the earlier description of some exchange of words leading to the fight. The P.O. ignores this apparent confusion and asks if the friend (Jane) jumped on the smaller white girl, a point the P.O. seems to have been informed about prior to the interview. The juvenile's response again seems to follow the P.O.'s lead in what appears to be a hesitating acknowledgment— the question about "the little one" who was the presumed object of attack by Jane. The P.O. shifts to the question "Did you think that was fair?" and thereby establishes the line of discussion she wishes to follow, moving it away from another attempt to specify more precisely how the juvenile became involved in the fight. The P.O. establishes her view that the juvenile had become associated with an "unfair" fight, while noting that although fights were "bad," they are especially "bad" when a discrepancy existed in the physical size of the parties involved. The P.O. then structures the fight situation by remarking "So then what happened after Jane had the little girl down?" The juvenile's answer is to question ("I don't know whether she had the little girl down or not") the P.O.'s interpretation, implying it was not at all clear to her that this had occurred since she "was mostly trying to keep the other girl from jumping on Jane." Notice, therefore, that from the earlier allusion to the notion that Rose, Jane's sister, would be the one who would take on the smaller white girl because of similarity in size, we have an ambiguous sequence leading up to a fight that suddenly has Jane and not Rose as the one who has "jumped" on the smaller white girl. The P.O. did not inquire as to how the alleged "plan" was altered or if there was the possibility that the turn in events could implicate the white girls. The P.O. then states "Oh, you jumped on the big sister?" and the juvenile suggests this was done to maintain a one-to-one relationship, ignoring the size differential noted by the P.O. But the juvenile then introduces another friend, Candy, who "came in there and beat her up." Candy, therefore, presumably "beat up" the larger white girl. The P.O., however, is interested in establishing the fact that the juvenile hit the larger white girl.

Having established that the juvenile actually hit someone, the P.O. then begins to criticize the juvenile's participation in the fight. The juvenile seeks to defend herself by referring to a different fact, that of the two white girls "jumping on Jane," her friend. The juvenile is not interested in the size differential noted by the P.O., and the P.O. does not feel the unclear sequence of events leading to the fight is relevant to the two facts of Jane, the larger Negro girl, beating up the smaller white girl, and Audrey's jumping on the larger white girl when she apparently came to the aid of her smaller sister. The P.O. states the juvenile should not have become involved, regardless of the circumstances, and proceeds to then structure the sequence as one where "Jane started the fight," and that it was "up to the big sister to protect her little sister" because "they were the innocent ones." The P.O. then notes how the juvenile was to blame for "jumping in" regardless of her friendship with Jane (and "because when someone starts a fight they're to blame") with the implication that there could be no mitigating circumstances in such instances. The P.O. then asks if the juvenile has had "any other fights there?" to which the juvenile replies "No." The P.O., however, seems to be saying that she was already aware of this ("I know") and appears to be testing the girl. The exchange continues as follows:

PROBATION OFFICER. I've been real pleased with you, Audrey. I've been keeping tabs on you. I talk to Mr. James sometimes, [pause] you know? I didn't know whether you knew that or not—

JUVENILE. [garbled response from Audrey here]

P.O. —and that is why I haven't found it necessary to come and talk with you because you've been doing real good. You've really been trying, haven't you?

JUV. Yes. I haven't got into any trouble by stealing.

P.O. That's very good [with emphasis], and I don't want you to start that.

JUV. I won't start that.

P.O. But at the same time, Audrey, because you haven't done one thing bad doesn't mean that you can do something else that's wrong. Fighting is wrong also. Fighting can trick you personally, it can get you suspended from school, can't it?

JUV. I think I did get suspended from school for a half day.

P.O. Was that your first suspension?

JUV. Yes. But I didn't get suspended, see, I just got suspended by 12 and he told, they were so excited he told me to come back Monday so I did.

P.O. Now if you're going to have problems because of the group you hang around with, you know, the girls you hang around with—if they are going to start getting in fights and trouble all the time, Audrey, I'm going to tell you that you cannot associate with them. [pause] If you get in trouble once more with these girls, I'm going to make it a probation directive that you will have to not be friends with them any more. So that is going to make it difficult. If you want to continue being friends and associating with them you're going to have to see that nobody do anything wrong or that you're not involved in it. Which would be easier, not to associate with them at all or to stay out of trouble even if they get in trouble? Do you understand what I mean exactly?

JUV. Yes.

P.O. This is the choice you're going to have to make, Audrey. Either to stay away from them and have some new friends, or to be sure you don't get in any trouble if they do.

JUV. I can . . . I don't get in no trouble.

P.O. What if they get involved in another fight? Can you say "count me out" and walk away?

JUV. Yes.

P.O. Can you?

JUV. Yes, I can say it.

P.O. And come in and report to Mr. James if somebody is going to have a fight to protect everybody, could you do that?

JUV. Yes, I can do it.

P.O. Tell me some of the other little things. You said there were a few little things.

JUV. Well, I had to write a 200 word essay for, you know, you know . . . it wouldn't have been so bad but Mr. G——, if he could, gives us . . .

P.O. You're talking about the time you swiped the boy's shoes and hit him?

JUV. Yes.

P.O. This was with the same group of girls, wasn't it?

JUV. Uh, huh [cut off]

P.O. Candy and Jane . . .

JUV. It was me and Emma, Cindy, and uh, Miriam.

P.O. Was this a joke?

JUV. Yes, we were just playing with him.

P.O. That's so?

JUV. We took their shoes, see, I gave my shoes back and they took my shoes but they gave them back. I have my shoes back. Some of the girls that had their shoes took their shoes in the gym, and hid them . . .

P.O. The boy's shoes?

JUV. Mr. James said that if we didn't . . . we had to write 10 words every minute or something; so anyway it ended up 200 words.

P.O. Until somebody showed him where the shoes were, right?

JUV. Uh, huh. So we found them . . . yesterday, you know, at lunch time, me and Sherri, you know, were, were out there riding in that laundry truck and the lady told us to get off.

P.O. Did you?

JUV. No, I got back on and then . . . Mr. James and he told me not to do it any more.

P.O. That's right, Audrey. You are to mind everybody that's in a position to tell you what or what not to do.

JUV. My mother said you're supposed to respect that uniform.

P.O. Right. You can't just make a choice you're going to obey some people like Mr. James and not other people. You have to obey everybody involved in directing, in the classroom, the teachers, on the grounds, whoever is in charge out there, Mr. James when you're in here, the bus driver when you are on the bus.

The P.O. now shifts to how she checks on the girl by reference to a general remark about the juvenile's apparent success, revealed to her by the school official. The second comment by the P.O. suggests that the fighting incident prompted her to set up a formal interview, but notice how the remark "You've really been trying, haven't you?" leads the juvenile to say "I haven't got into any trouble by stealing." The reference to "trying" seems to remind the juvenile about the stealing incidents of the past, and the P.O. follows through with the comment "I don't want you to start that." But the juvenile's further response "I won't start that" triggers off a shift in the argument that seems to undercut the comments about "doing real good," by bringing up the fighting again. The P.O. seems to be trying to give the juvenile some kind of support vis-à-vis past problems with stealing, but also seeking to make it clear that fighting can also create trouble with the court. The juvenile's admission of a suspension seems to be contradicted by her subsequent remark that "I didn't get suspended, see," because "they were so excited he told me to come back Monday so I did." The implication of the juvenile's remark about her suspension can be read as saying that there were contingencies surrounding her suspension because of the excitement created by the fight, and that the school official probably did not intend what he said, but that she, for unexplained reasons, decided to take it literally. But the P.O. seems intent on pursuing the original problem and abandons the laudatory line in favor of a more explicit indication of what will be the consequences of further "trouble once more with these girls," namely, "a probation directive that you will have to not be friends with them any more." The P.O. then provides the juvenile with the alternatives of "not to associate with them at all" or if association continues, to "stay out of trouble even when they get in trouble." The same set of alternatives is posed in the P.O.'s subsequent remark. The P.O. then pushes this argument by posing hypothetical situations as a test of what the juvenile would do, but in posing these situations, the P.O. provides the girl with the appropriate "answer," i.e., "Can you say 'count me out' and walk away?" The P.O. continues this line of argument when she suggests (by making it a question) that the juvenile "come in and report to Mr. James." The P.O. in effect tells the juvenile what is "wrong" about her actions and how she is to avoid "trouble" by pursuing what appears to be an explicit course of action. Any reference to the contingencies of the earlier fight or the possibility of such contingencies in the future are ruled out by the P.O., who views such situations as completely within the control of the juvenile, and thus the girl is to be held completely responsible for any violations thereof.

The P.O.'s remarks are consistent with interviews I witnessed between police and juveniles, and probation and juveniles. The juvenile is always asked to express "what happened" in his own words, then the officer provides a more explicit interpretation spelling out the consequences of the acts involved. The "right" course of action is then provided abstractly as if the "right" course was always available to the juvenile. The contingencies of collective behavior—peer group pressures, taunts, or provocation, and the like, or simply viewing the situation as a "lark" or "kicks"—are not seen as admissible excuses by the officer. The police or P.O.'s reference to courses of action presume that the rules governing such courses of action are explicit to all parties, particularly the juvenile, and the consequences are clear, so that a "rational" decision is always possible. Yet the P.O. insists that the juvenile agree to her characterization of how "trouble" occurs and how to avoid "trouble."

Notice that the incident of stealing that led to the court hearings, incarceration at the state mental hospital, and becoming a ward of the court are not easily equated with the fighting incident, or, for example, a subsequent laundry truck incident, unless the assumption is made that both types of conduct are products of the same "underlying pattern." But to describe the stealing and fighting as instances of the same "underlying pattern" is to assume that contingent features surrounding collective behavior, participation in routine peer group activities, and the like, are irrelevant to how adolescents "should" control their actions. The P.O., therefore, supplies a basis for classifying "what happened" into standard categories. The control expected appears to fit an ideal model of rational conduct. Yet other juveniles engaging in such incidents may be described as "just kids having fun," or "harmless pranks," and the like. Activities termed "serious" (for example, stealing) leads to a generalization of the "underlying causes," to include instances that might never be labeled as delinquent if they appeared as isolated events. The "typical" juvenile, therefore, is asked to maintain control over a range of activities that he, his friends, and his parents do not define as "trouble." But notice that the P.O., while taking this line, is also allowing herself to redefine the fighting and the shoe incident as not violating the terms of probation and thus not warranting another court hearing. But the P.O., at the same time, feels compelled to characterize the incidents as "serious" to the juvenile. The apparent paradox is not unusual if the trust notion is recalled. The P.O. must sustain some kind of trust relationship with the juvenile as a condition of obtaining compliance, and this relationship of trust implies that whatever actions led to the necessity of probation are not to be viewed as a manifestation of criminal (that is, purposely irresponsible) social character, but due to circumstances that the juvenile presumably cannot easily control, for example, a "bad" family situation, "underlying emotional problems," or "bad" friends. Yet the occurrence of still another incident calls into doubt the suspension of criminal-type motivations because the clinical stance is not effective when the same person (the P.O.) is responsible for controlling the day-to-day activities of the juvenile. The clinical perspective allows for the suspension of criminal-type imputations leading to incarceration in Youth Authority prisons, but breaks down in routine probation work because of the likelihood and occurrence of incidents by juveniles that could easily be construed as a violation of the conditions of probation. Like the presumed rationality of some forms of therapy, where the patient is expected to reflect on his acts and their consequences, the P.O. expects the juvenile to control himself by direct reflection at the time of potentially troublesome acts so as to avoid their occurrence in a systematic way. The recurrence of incidents leaves the P.O. in a dilemma: either she must acknowledge her failure at maintaining the trust relationship as a form of control, claim that the juvenile's conduct is motivated by uncontrollable "underlying emotions," or "deep-rooted" criminal or character formation. In either case the recommendation then becomes one of incarceration. Inasmuch as a clinical disposition would require additional professional support, it is easier to recommend placement in a Youth Authority facility. This same problem could be generalized easily to adult probation and parole cases in that the same kinds of circumstances surround the relationship between the offender and the probation or parole officer. The P.O. becomes a curious agent of the community in that he must pass judgment (classify activities unambiguously) over actions that are handled in ambiguous ways. Every act or event becomes subject to scrutiny and evaluation by others as trivial, situational, or acceptable. The fuzziness that surrounds acts considered "obviously" criminal (e.g., entering and breaking, armed robbery) is accentuated when probation or parole violation is the issue and forces ambiguous activities into seemingly explicit categories, so that a simple rule of thumb can be used for deciding violation. An ambiguous description of an event that unfolded situationally can now be used as evidence of "poor judgment," "lying," "evasion," and the like, for the practical circumstances of the investigating agent requires a two-valued logic for making sense of "what happened." The only way the officer can hedge is to state that while there are "problems," they are not "serious" and do not warrant further action for the present. But the retrospective-prospective character of the juvenile is such that some future time can lead to a rereading of a present series of "minor" acts, thereby providing a basis for questioning the judgment of a P.O. or police officer about the laxness in not taking action in what retrospectively is viewed as a "trend" or a "pattern" leading up to a "serious" act. The hedging, therefore, stems from the officer's seeking to protect himself against such contingencies by inserting a few remarks that would enable him to say that he "could see" the possibility of failure in earlier acts. The following chapter will provide some detailed material on this point.

Returning to the dialogue, the P.O. seems to shift again to "other little things" presumably affecting the juvenile's compliance with the conditions of probation. The juvenile begins talking about "a 200 word essay" and the dialogue is ambiguous in connection with an apparent attempt to register a complaint about the conditions for writing the essay. The P.O. seeks to connect the essay with an incident over hitting a boy and taking his shoes. Not only does the P.O. inform the girl that she is aware of everything she does, providing the juvenile with a description of "what happened," but then goes on to quickly connect the incident with the girls involved in the fight. Yet the juvenile begins to suggest other names. It is not clear if the same girls were involved, at least judging from the names the juvenile mentions. The P.O. supplies the juvenile with an apparent excuse for her behavior by asking if "this was a joke?" The juvenile quickly replied "yes" and added that "we were just playing with him." The next statement by the juvenile seems to indicate her initial participation first as perpetrator and then as victim, but it is difficult to know what background expectancies generated her remarks, and there is no answer to the P.O.'s question as to whether it was the boy's shoes that were hidden in the gym. Apparently the school official stated the conditions for returning the shoes as "10 words every minute or something; so anyway it ended up 200 words." The juvenile's remarks seem understandable *per se*, but the P.O.'s comments seem to ask for a more concise reason for the essay. The juvenile's "uh, huh," then becomes a pause for a shift in topic by launching into another incident—the laundry truck affair—but here again it is not at all clear what the sequence of events was that led to their "riding in that laundry truck." The P.O. does not question the sequence of events and, by not doing so, allows for the presumption that the fault is clear. The juvenile's response about whether she got off the truck, after being asked, suggests that the school official was called, and it was then that she got off. The juvenile's reference to the school official sets the P.O. off again on the general problem of minding "everybody that's in a position to tell you what or what not to do." The juvenile's response collaborates with the P.O. to drop the two incidents just discussed, by a shift in the conversation to an abstract reiteration of obeying anyone with authority. Notice the P.O.'s continual return to a general argument or rule with which to evaluate the juvenile's behavior, and to propose correct future action. The particulars described by the juvenile are ignored. Returning to the conversation:

PROBATION OFFICER. Now tell me about the bus.

JUVENILE. [Laughing] How do you know about the bus?

P.O. Oh, I have eyes in the back of my head.

JUV. Well, I think it was Monday the girl named Ginger, you know, you know Ginger?

P.O. I don't know her.

JUV. You probably don't know her. Anyway, I didn't like her noway from the first beginning. Ever since I've been here I never did like her. Because you know me and Kitty we used to be friends and every time Rita would kind of crack down on Cindy all of the time, and Ginger, she always had something to do and she wasn't even in it. I didn't like her for that one reason and then one night when [garbled name] called me up, you know, she got all mad just cause [garbled name] called me up. And she come talking about she wanted to fight me the last day of school. So I said you and who else? So she just walked away, you know, and she just gave me a dirty look after class and I've been hating her ever since. So then Monday, you know, on the bus I was mad, you know, and she was sitting up there, so I just hit her head with a ruler.

P.O. And then what happened?

JUV. She called me a name I didn't like, so I got mad and I started calling her a name, but I didn't curse.

P.O. So all this was after the other fight when Mr. James warned you, wasn't it?

JUV. Yes.

P.O. I call that a fight.

JUV. What fight.

P.O. You hit her with a ruler—that was fighting.

JUV. She hit me back.

P.O. So, it's not a fight until I hit you back, huh?

JUV. Uh, uh. [no, firmly]

P.O. Honey, but you started something that could have turned into a fight; shall we say it that way?

JUV. But she did say she gonna fight me the last day of school anyway.

P.O. You just better stay away from her. You just better stay away from her. Tell Mr. James if you think she ever is. [pause] Now the last day of school isn't for three months so maybe everything will smooth over by then. You just stay away from her.

JUV. If she hits me I'm supposed to hit her back, aren't I?

P.O. (With considerable emphasis) No, you are not! You come in and tell Mr. James. If you hit her back you're in trouble too.

JUV. But Mr. James said that if they start the fight they are the one they are going to suspend.

P.O. If you can get away and come and tell Mr. James you do that. If you have to protect yourself, you're being held or hurt, then get away from them even if you have to hit them, but you come and tell him and let *him* handle it. Otherwise he will probably say that you started it and nobody knows what happened and you both get punished. You see?

JUV. Yeah.

P.O. You have to think about what's going to happen afterwards, Audrey, when you start something. You understand that?

JUV. Yes.

P.O. Now I want you to promise me that there will be no more fights. If you have an argument with someone just walk away.

JUV. But somebody gets on the telephone that they're calling 'em up and telling 'em [cut off by Probation Officer]

P.O. Okay, someone wants you to get in a fight. If someone tries to start it you just stay away as much as you can if you feel you can't come in and tell Mr. James you're having a problem and you feel you're going to get in a fight if he doesn't take care of it. You see? You can, if you know something is going to happen; he can take care of it so nobody gets in trouble so that it doesn't happen. If you know the day before some girls are planning on a fight and you are afraid you are going to be mixed up in it, and get in trouble, come and tell Mr. James. He can fix it so it doesn't happen. You see? I'm not telling you [how] to think, honey, I'm telling you to protect yourself this way. Because you can't stand to get in trouble, honey. You're on probation now. If something, if you get in trouble you're going to have more consequences than someone else that isn't on probation. Do you see that?

JUV. Yes.

P.O. Because you've already come under the juvenile court. So therefore, there will be more punishment for you if you can't stay away from trouble. You see this is why you have to be more careful than some of the other girls. This is how you can tell how strong and how brave you are, is whether you can walk away. This takes real strength to say, "look, I'm not going to get myself in any more trouble, I'm leaving," and just walk away, from the girls who are trying to start by calling you names. Say "I'm bigger than you. I don't have to use names; I can walk away," you know? You don't make yourself bigger calling anybody names back even if they start it. Now you know, you know you've been studying a lot of things at church. Isn't this, is what Mrs. Wentworth [foster mother] would say also?

JUV. Yeah.

P.O. Sometimes it is harder to live up to what we believe, Audrey [pause], isn't it?

JUV. Yes.

P.O. Then, you know, cause sometimes other kids don't tease you or something, or you're a sissy or chicken or something. That's not true. You're showing strength and courage if you can walk away from something that will get you in trouble. You're pretty dumb just to walk into trouble, just to prove that you are not chicken. Do you understand what I'm talking about?

JUV.   Yes.

P.O.   If you know something is wrong, Audrey, what are you going to do?

JUV.   Walk away.

P.O.   You remember that. Tell Mrs. Wentworth or tell Mrs. —— . . . that someone needs to take care of it. You know I don't mean I want to see you get clobbered, you know, not like that; do what you have to to protect yourself but then tell someone who's in authority. Okay?

JUV.   Okay.

P.O.   And about laundry trucks, no more jumping or horsing around like that.

JUV.   Huh?

P.O.   That's a little thing, sure, but on top of these other things it's going to all add up. And no more trouble on the bus?

JUV.   No.

P.O.   Cause the bus is just like the school. You have to obey the rules there too, don't you?

JUV.   Yes.

P.O.   You wouldn't like to have to walk would you?

JUV.   No.

P.O.   That happens sometimes, you know, when somebody gets suspended from the bus service.

JUV.   Mmh?

Before continuing with the last section of the interview, which seems to represent another matter, I want to make a few remarks about the exchange just quoted.

The P.O.'s mention of the bus driver triggers off a question about the bus incident. The girl laughs, asking how the P.O. knew about the incident. The laughter appeared to me as "light-hearted" rather than "nervous," if I can again trade on the reader's imagination, and the P.O.'s response seems to support this inference by her remark about having "eyes in the back of my head." The P.O.'s remark is a standard way of informing someone you are "with it" or have the "upper hand" in dealing with him. Such remarks are subtle reminders that the surveillance is quite serious, even though it may be discussed in a "light-hearted" manner. The remark does not, therefore, absolve the other party from answering the original question of "what happened." The juvenile's laughter and the P.O.'s response could also be interpreted as a signal that the trust relationship prevails, even though it is the P.O. who must call attention to the incident.

The juvenile's account of "what happened" begins by reference to a "girl named Ginger," but the P.O. states she does not know the person. The juvenile then launches into "substandard" English again that presumes an "inside" view of "how-these-things-usually-happen," meaning the listener must assume the described sequence is "clear" even though its communicative content could be questioned. The fact that the P.O. does not appear to question the description does not mean she understood its content, but could mean she finds it irrelevant. Perhaps the juvenile's description could be described as incoherent unless the hearer was willing to fill in several truncated statements. The juvenile's remarks presuppose considerable unstated knowledge about relations with friends. If the P.O. assumes that adolescent girls "all talk like that" (that is, rambling, occasionally detailed, yet with vague referents expected and used), then the P.O., in searching for the "key" elements in the conversation, might assume that the truncated responses were irrelevant, and thus generates an undercutting remark such as, "and then what happened?" This response pointedly ignores any reference as to how the sequence leading up to the ruler incident follows "logically" from the initial reference to not liking "her noway from the first beginning." The juvenile's truncated remarks about how it "happened" suggest "good reasons" for being "mad" on the bus that Monday, and thus justify the decision to "hit her head with a ruler." It is not entirely obvious that it was "Ginger" who was hit with the ruler. The P.O. does not seem concerned with the victim, and her "then what happened?" leading to Audrey's remark, "She called me a name I didn't like, so I got mad . . . ," ignores the juvenile's attempt to justify her actions by referring to a set of contingencies that she views as "naturally" leading to hitting the unnamed girl with the ruler. The P.O. seems to be stressing, once again, a more general rule that she had elaborated earlier about "staying out of trouble." I assume this to be the case because of the P.O.'s remark: "So all this was after the other fight when Mr. James warned you. . . ." After Audrey's "yes" the P.O. states flatly "I call that a fight." The juvenile's response "What fight?" is clarified by the P.O.'s remark that "You hit her with a ruler—that was fighting." The juvenile's remark "She hit me back" could be interpreted to mean that if her earlier comments and action, which led to hitting the girl, were justified, the girl hitting her back presumably justifies her initial blow with the ruler. The P.O. then seizes upon this last remark by saying "So, it's not a fight until I hit you back, huh?" and undercuts the juvenile's reasoning by stressing not the girl's construction of "how it happened," but the fact that she hit the victim first and was attempting to justify this action by referring to the fact that her blow was returned by the victim. The juvenile's next response seems to indicate that she now "sees" the fallacy in her argument suggested by the P.O. By her voice intonation, it was my impression that the juvenile's response was firm (but not an admission of defeat) to a line of reasoning that assumed she was justified. The P.O.'s subsequent remark "Honey, but you started . . ." seems to avoid pushing the issue too far by suggesting the potential consequences of the incident were not to be taken lightly, but the P.O.'s sharp-appearing comments were not what they might have appeared, as expressed by the prefatory "honey," and the closing phrase "shall we say it that way?" The opening and closing parts of this last remark by the P.O. seem to be motivated by a desire to communicate to the juvenile that the P.O. is still a sympathetic "friend," even though she did pull the girl up short vis-à-vis her interpretation of the bus incident. The juvenile's rejoinder seems to cling to her original argument on how it all "happened," with its implication the action taken was justified under some vague allusions to how the victim told her "she gonna fight me the last day of school anyway." The reasoning offered by the juvenile refers to socially organized activities that have little to do with the perspective employed by the P.O. in determining how the juvenile's actions are to be justified. The P.O.'s following remark "You just better stay away from her . . ." or "Tell Mr. James" keeps stressing a general rule to avoid any situation that could lead to "trouble," or at least to "tell" the proper authorities if something develops that may be viewed as "trouble." But this general policy or rule, if I can call the P.O.'s line of reasoning a general policy or rule, is being imposed from "without" upon a set of unknown contingencies that emerge in the course of the juvenile's everyday life, so that anything the juvenile relates as "evidence" to support her argument is automatically null and void because any particular case (and its reasoning) could never fall within the general policy or rule laid down by the P.O., unless the P.O. permitted some kind of negotiation to take place whereby the juvenile's "excuses" could be transformed into legitimate "reasons." But then it could be argued that the P.O. is really allowing the juvenile's account to stand for something other than complete "blame," otherwise what could be the justification for not calling her actions a violation of probation? I would rather supplement this last remark with the proposal that the P.O.'s general policy or rule is a kind of rhetoric that law-enforcement agents continually invoke, regardless of their sympathy or annoyance with the contingencies of the occasion, because there is little else they could say about behavior they did not observe and that is situationally determined, but that is always being evaluated vis-à-vis a general policy or rule that cannot justify particular practices associated with more elusive "rules" we associate with emergent social interaction. The P.O. has apparently made her decision to view the incidents for which the interview was arranged not as a violation of probation, but as an occasion to elaborate a familiar rhetoric. I would argue that the P.O.'s earlier remarks about the apparent "success" of the juvenile to "stay out of trouble" have little to do with actual activities (e.g., the present difficulties), but are articulated in the girl's "good attitude," her willingness to accept the P.O.'s interpretation of "what happened," and what should be done in the future. The juvenile's reasoning remained intact; as she perceived the sequence of events leading to hitting the victim with a ruler, the action was justified. The P.O. was concerned with a more general policy, practice, or rule whereby the juvenile was "to stay away" or "tell Mr. James," and hope that everything "will smooth over" by the end of the semester. The general policy or rule appears to provide a simple and concise mandate: stay away from the sources of "trouble" or see the authority in charge. The contingencies of social interaction, the occasions of "special circumstances," "practical problems," and "good reasons," are all viewed as irrelevant as a general practice; the situational, contextual, or particular policies or rules, as a means of justifying a course of action for the juvenile, become documentary properties that lead to "trouble" as defined by the school authorities or the P.O.

The juvenile seems to propose a justifiable contingency when she states that "If she hits me I'm supposed to hit her back, aren't I?" The P.O.'s response, which sounded quite strong to me, was a direct "No, you are not!" and repeats the general rule to "come in and tell Mr. James." Practical circumstances, therefore, are irrelevant because "If you hit her back you're in trouble too." The juvenile's response does not mention her engaging in any "hitting," but calls attention to a presumed general policy or rule stated by Mr. James; "they" refers both to "others" who "start a fight," and the school authorities who will be suspending the "they" who "start a fight." The P.O.'s continual reference to a general policy or rule that negates the situational contingencies offered by the juvenile does not seem to register in the juvenile's voice intonation, nor in her attempts to justify her past actions and the possibility that such contingencies could arise in the future. The bargaining between the P.O. and the juvenile produces something of an impasse, but the P.O.'s subsequent remark seems to provide a partial break in the general policy or rule when she states: "If you can get away and come and tell Mr. James you do that," yet "If you have to protect yourself, you're being held or hurt, then get away from them even if you have to hit them, but you come and tell him and let *him* handle it." Notice that the subsequent part of this statement indicates the contingencies surrounding Mr. James' authority to decide "what happened" by the remark that "Otherwise he will probably say that you started it and nobody knows what happened and you both get punished." The P.O.'s position seems clear: avoid the "trouble" at all costs, but if you must "protect yourself," then report the event to someone with authority immediately so as to avoid being implicated. Yet the position seems to say that once there is involvement, the likelihood of being implicated is very high. Even though the juvenile seems to agree ("yeah"), the P.O. continues to speak as if the general policy or rule were still not clear to the girl, for example, "You have to think about what's going to happen afterwards . . ." The juvenile's "Yes" and the P.O.'s subsequent reiteration of a "promise" from the girl "that there will be no more fights," that she will "just walk away," seems undercut by the juvenile's return to contingencies: "But somebody gets on the telephone that they're . . ." The P.O.'s cutting off from this return to contingencies begins something of a monologue where the P.O. begins to reiterate all over again her previous remarks about staying out of "trouble" and the consequences of getting in "trouble" when on probation. But the P.O.'s remarks outlining a hypothetical case of potential "trouble" is highly simplified and contrasts sharply with earlier descriptions given by the juvenile. The juvenile's "Yes" is followed by another long statement that once again points out the consequences of having been to court. Notice that "there will be more punishment for you if you can't stay away from trouble." This remark flatly states that contingencies are irrelevant: if an act or sequence of activities is viewed as "trouble" by the school officials or the P.O., because of her own judgment or that of others (by calls or similar pressure), then the general policy or rule of the court prevails regardless of situational factors.

The monologue continues with the P.O. elaborating her previous remarks by noting: "Because you've already come under the juvenile court," it presumably follows "there will be more punishment for you if you can't stay away from trouble." The dialogue reiterates once again an abstract set of procedures for complying with the general policy or rule for staying out of "trouble," i.e., "walk away," "real strength to say . . . 'I'm leaving,' " " 'I can walk away,' you know. . . ." The P.O.'s remarks disregard the implications of the suggested procedures for staying out of "trouble": having to avoid past "friends" entirely or run the risk of being ridiculed by them, but learning to be "bigger" than they. The P.O.'s remarks are likely to make the juvenile an isolate or deviant in the eyes of her peers, but this consequence is not considered, nor the possibility of being victimized and thus producing more of the problems discussed earlier. The juvenile's initial "trouble" was viewed as having been caused by a "bad" home environment. Now the violation of probation and additional "serious trouble" is seen as emanating from peer relationships, but where the "blame" is irrelevant, and where no action is ever mentioned or contemplated against "others." Notice, therefore, the P.O. seems clearly to assert that any "trouble" will automatically be construed as "more serious," and could lead to "more punishment" because of the juvenile's probationary status. The juvenile's reference to the contingencies of encounters with peers is disregarded. Any sense of injustice on the part of the juvenile is defined automatically as indicative of a "bad attitude" toward the general policy or rule invoked by the P.O. for keeping the girl out of "trouble." The juvenile is being told how to reorient her thinking about "proper" courses of action. "The law" is being interpreted for the juvenile in general terms so as to condemn a range of particular types of situations, acts, or events, but where the juvenile's perspective is defined as "wrong" or irrelevant. Yet the juvenile does not seem to understand how the contingencies of the way "it happened" are being articulated with the general policy or rule. Thus the juvenile cannot understand the relevance of the general policy or rule being defined in terms of the presumed professional knowledge of the P.O. The P.O.'s categories are not meaningful for the juvenile because they are divorced from the day-to-day activities of the girl's environment. There is no attempt to understand the juvenile's environment "from within," but on the contrary, the P.O. seeks to have the girl implement a general policy or rule that is to apply "across the board," irrespective of the contingencies that can arise in the girl's everyday activities. The P.O. assumes the juvenile can detect in advance the kinds of "trouble" emerging, can inform the proper authorities in time to avoid being implicated, and if this latter strategy does not work, can simply "walk away," thereby revealing "how strong and how brave you are."

At the close of the last monologue, the P.O. suddenly shifts the thrust of her remarks by mentioning "things" studied "at church," and what the foster mother "would also say." The "shift" is an attempt to alter the basis for following the general policy or rules attributed to the juvenile court law as interpreted by the P.O., and now becomes an appeal to some vague referents at church and in the foster home. This line continues in the P.O.'s subsequent remarks; she begins to bring up the general problem of aligning beliefs with practice ("it is harder to live up to what we believe . . ."), and then reiterates once again the previous references to "showing strength and courage if you can walk away from something that will get you in trouble." There is a more pointed reference to this line vis-à-vis its relation to peer group activities when the P.O. states: "You're pretty dumb just to walk into trouble, just to prove that you are not chicken." The P.O.'s way of challenging the presumed attraction of the peer group is to call attention to this labeling of someone as "sissy or chicken," if they did precisely what the P.O. continually insists the juvenile should do. Calling the juvenile "dumb" could be viewed as the most pointed way in which the P.O. can neutralize the presumed peer group's influence over the girl. Notice the P.O.'s language appears to be less formal here. I think it is easy to infer the P.O. is trying to appeal to the juvenile on a level of trust that would replace, presumably, the attraction attributed to the peer group. But notice we have little information about this peer group, or that it is all that "organized" or influential. We do not know many of the details about how Audrey relates to the others she "hangs around with," but, instead, the P.O.

treats "other kids" as an organized force influencing or, at least, potentially influencing the activities of the juvenile in an area where this presumed influence would lead to negative results vis-à-vis the conditions of probation. I stress this point here because I want to note how easy it is for both the researcher and reader to lapse into a use of particular categories under the assumption the "groups" or "forces" are "real," but where we cannot objectify "what happens," much less verify some implicit theories about the relevance of such "groups" or "forces." But I also want to note that the use of such categories by members (probation officers, police, etc.) carries a double significance: they are used without the officials being able to objectify the referents, but it is also the case that the use of these categories has serious consequences for juveniles, and may also be binding upon the actions of others who view the use of these categories as products of professional competence that stand as "correct" depictions of the objects or events discussed. The juvenile is told to reject friendship relations and to accept those associated with church and (foster) family, while simultaneously adhering to the general policy or rule generated by the P.O.'s professional knowledge and interpretation of the juvenile court law. The use of colloquial terms by the P.O. appears to establish a relational affiliation that transcends the professional relationship by seeking a more intimate trust relationship with the juvenile.

In moving to the remainder of the dialogue, notice how the P.O. establishes the conditions of social organization for the juvenile by posing the question once again of "If you know something is wrong, Audrey, what are you going to do?" The juvenile now "knows" the "right" answer when she responds with "Walk away." The P.O. again reiterates the general policy or rule by taking the juvenile "through" the "proper" procedures for avoiding "trouble," thereby revealing "society's" view of what the "good" juvenile must do to preclude the development of unfavorable identities in his or her life. Yet there is included the reference to not getting "clobbered" so as "to protect yourself but then tell someone who's in authority." This last part of the quotation is a compromise of the earlier position because there is a recognition that some unknown amount of "self-protection" is necessary before it would be possible to register a complaint and avoid being in "trouble." But the P.O. does not reiterate her prior position that any involvement could lead to being labeled the "troublemaker" every time the juvenile became a participant. The previous advice was to avoid or "walk away" from anything that "looked like trouble." The laundry truck incident reminds the P.O. once more that "on top of these other things [being a ward of the court, fighting] it's going to all add up," so that a disproportionate punishment will come of even minor infractions. The juvenile seems to "know" what the P.O. wants and responds with the "appropriate" answers. The text shifts after the juvenile initiates a change in substance.

JUVENILE. Miss Wells, Miss Wells, did you hear about that boy that got restricted, uh, taken away from our home the other day?

PROBATION OFFICER. No. Did Ronald get taken away from your home?

JUV. 'Cause he was stealin'. He stole thirteen dollars from Mrs. Wentworth's room, and he admitted stealin' and broken houses, so mommie said she thought it was bad for us and especially me because I had already been in trouble for stealing. So she just got rid of him. 'Cause when she told him —— [cut off by P.O.]

P.O. Was he on probation?

JUV. I don't know. But I didn't like it.

P.O. How long was he there?

JUV. About, (pause) I would say four months, (pause) he was there about five or six months. A lot of kids stay, (pause) when they comin' out, come there, they have problems. But she say that in about six months they can be ready to overcome your problems.

P.O. Well, Audrey, you've overcome a lot of your problems, you really have. But now that we see maybe another problem is going to start getting you in trouble, this is the time to start handling that problem (pause) right? Not wait until it becomes so serious that it is difficult to tell other people that you're going to stop doing it. Now they'll still believe you like Mr. James. If you're not going to fight any more or not get mixed up in this stuff any more, he'll believe you. But if you went on doing it for a couple of months, you know, he'll find it difficult to believe you, wouldn't he?

JUV. Yes.

P.O. So you stick by what you've told him (pause), that you're not going to get in any more trouble, alright? [Cut off as "alright" uttered.]

JUV. You know, I could have went to juvie again, but Mr. James say uh [cut off by P.O.]

P.O. I know it. He helped you.

JUV. I know, 'cause he said I hadn't been in no trouble since I had been in.

P.O. See, (pause) so that good time helped you. If you had gotten in trouble right away he wouldn't have known if you could behave yourself. And he probably would have, you know, let you go to Juvenile Hall, but since you had all this—how many months?—six or seven months?

JUV. I figured eleven months.

P.O. Eleven months.

JUV. At the home.

P.O. Eleven months with no real difficulties either at home or at school, right?

JUV. Yeah.

P.O. So that's why he knew if you said you won't get in more trouble he knows you can if you stick by that.

JUV. You see I gotta [cut off by P.O.]

P.O. He trusts you, Audrey, so it is up to you to keep his trust. You got another what?

(The juvenile seems to be leading up to a change in the content of the interview.)

In calling the P.O.'s attention to an incident in the foster home, the juvenile shifts the conversation to someone else in "trouble." The "trouble" is "stealin'." I see no obvious interpretation of this apparent diversion by the juvenile to the account of the boy who was also a ward of the court. I suggest that by calling attention to another ward in the foster home, one sent away allegedly because of "stealing and broken houses," the contrast with the girl's not stealing is underscored. Perhaps the juvenile's remarks are to be viewed as an attempt to terminate the P.O.'s continual reference to the girl's predicament. I would prefer not to invent additional explanations of this apparent diversion, but note the juvenile's remark about the "kids" who come to the foster home, "they have problems." Notice the use of pronouns in the sentence: "she say that in about six months they can be ready to overcome your problems." I am not as interested in the substandard features of the utterance as in the shift from "they" to "your problems." The sentence presumably refers to the foster mother's commentary on the types of juveniles that pass through her home, particularly how they have "problems" when they arrive, but "they can be ready to overcome your problems" after six months. The use of "your" instead of "their" problems suggests more than an erroneous use of the pronoun, but calls attention to the girl's own "problems." The response by the P.O. returns the topic of conversation to the general policy or rule previously discussed. When the P.O. states that "you've overcome a lot of your problems, you really have," it appears to tie in with the juvenile's remark, "ready to overcome your problems." The P.O.'s remarks inform the juvenile that she is pleased with her "progress," "But now that we see maybe another problem is going to start getting you in trouble . . . ," something must be done. In returning the conversation to the general policy or rule for avoiding "trouble," the P.O. seems to add a slight variation on a previously discussed theme: "Not wait until it becomes so serious that it is difficult to tell other people that you're going to stop doing it." The P.O. seems to be telling the juvenile that others can easily reach a kind of tolerance level whereby the fact of further "trouble" will undercut or deny the relevance of "good intentions." Thus, continued fighting or "trouble" will neutralize the best explanations or expressions of sincerity, and in the case of the school official "he'll find it difficult to believe you. . . ." As the P.O. continues her exhortation about staying out of "trouble," the juvenile cuts in with a remark that seems to seek agreement with the P.O. by an apparent reference to how the school official helped her avoid going to Juvenile Hall. The collaboration that seems evident here (juv. "I know, 'cause he said I hadn't been in no trouble since . . ."), between the P.O. and the juvenile appears to be a deliberate attempt by the juvenile to cooperate with the P.O. in stressing the importance of a "long" period of time without "trouble." The P.O. notes "so that good time helped you," for "If you had gotten in trouble right away he wouldn't have known if you could behave yourself," and thus would have "let you go to Juvenile Hall." The P.O.'s remarks appear to be a detailed attempt to show the juvenile how "bad" timing of one's "trouble" can lead to serious consequences, implying that certain cutoff points exist before or after which, "good intentions" will no longer be honored. Notice how the P.O. asks "how many months" and suggests "six or seven months?" while the juvenile answers "eleven months." The P.O. accepts the figure and notes "that's why he knew if you said you won't get in more trouble he knows you can if you stick by that." The P.O.'s remark sort of caps off her continual reference to the earlier general policy or rule on how to avoid "trouble." I think the P.O.'s remarks are important because of the way the general policy or rule is "made operational" vis-à-vis the P.O.'s perspective. There is an attempt to specify the temporal dimensions of "trust" as seen by the P.O. ("He trusts you, Audrey, so it is up to you to keep his trust" by staying out of "trouble.") The temporal character of "trouble" is crucial to more general notions of "guilt" or "innocence," as well as in determining, from the perspective of both law-enforcement agents and laymen, the "good intentions" or sincerity or "trust" one will impute to or invest in others. The problem is that of determining how to read temporal occurrences of "trouble" so as to call them "isolated" incidents that are not to be viewed as "serious," or whether to see them as part of a "pattern" based upon "underlying deeper problems." The P.O.'s remarks provide us with a concrete case; incidents of "trouble" are described as temporal events that can be extended retrospectively and prospectively. The P.O. suggests an interpretive "program" on how others will "read" or interpret activities and, notice, independently of whether the "good intentions" were presumed to be there "all along." The P.O. seems to be saying that the school official requires some (unspecified) "trouble-free" period of time in order to develop "trust" to "know if you could behave yourself." Furthermore, having established some basis for "trust," the school official, as the P.O. has been demonstrating throughout the interview, suggests subsequent "trouble" will not be interpreted as serious. The "set" remains "open" if a relationship of trust existed prior to later "trouble." But the P.O. then returns each time to the problem that some limit exists over the number and types of incidents beyond which some kind of punitive action would have to be taken. In the next chapter this problem occurs in broader perspective when a few cases are examined in detail, and the reader can grasp the significance of how the temporal occurrence of acts deemed delinquent are interpreted vis-à-vis the officer's interpretation of whether the juvenile is "heading for more trouble," or whether a given event is to be viewed as an isolated incident and not part of a "larger pattern." Recall the shift apparent in the closing lines above, and now the juvenile's intentions seem to crystallize with the following exchange.

JUVENILE. Mrs. Wells I don't want to go home.

PROBATION OFFICER. Well, we don't have to worry about that now as long as you're doing fine there, you stay there.

JUV. Yeah, but I saw a dream, you know one thing?

P.O. A dream?

JUV. Yeah. You might think it's crazy, but it's real. My mother interpreted it for me. You see I was—it was me and those three girls were in a house, you know, the street that comes down—(pause) it's, uh, Carl Drive that comes down this way, and I saw it was the [snaky?] girls always [slinking?] on the side of the road and there was a wild beast [snake?] with a mouth like a person, and he was real big. Do you know what that was?

P.O. No.

JUV. That was a [one inaudible word]. You know when June comes I have to have a big, a big decision to make? That's going to be the decision. I know it is.

P.O. And you think you should stay longer with the Wentworths.

JUV. I'm going to stay there.

P.O. Well, maybe not permanently, but you can stay there longer. We didn't set any definite time for you to stay there. We said at least a year. If you want to stay longer and you feel that you are still getting help and still need help, fine.

JUV. If I go back home then I can . . . just like I am.

P.O. What does your mother think of this? Have you told her?

JUV. I haven't talked to her but I'm going to tell her when she comes the next time.

P.O. Does she come to see you very often?

JUV. Yes. She had the flu once.

P.O. How often does she come?

JUV. She hasn't been now in about a month. She usually comes about once every month. Is it okay if I go to the game tonight?

P.O. This is up to Mrs. Wentworth. What did she say?

JUV. She said I could if my father was going.

P.O. Your father's going? You mean Mr. Wentworth?

JUV. Uh huh.

P.O. Good. And he'll be there—will he take you?

JUV. Yeah, he's taking [name] too.

P.O. Well, that's fine, why not? Just don't get in any fights there (laughter). If she said ya could. But if she put ya on restriction or anything, then I'm not going to change your restriction.

JUV. I know when she puts me on restriction she's trying to keep me out of trouble.

P.O. Right. Will you tell her hello for me when you get home this evening?

JUV. Yes.

P.O. And tell her that you promised me that there wouldn't be any more of this, because (pause) I'd have to do something. It's my responsibility, you know, ta . . . [cut off by juvenile]

JUV. Would you have ta . . . [inaudible]

P.O. I, I would have to figure out what would be best for you, Audrey. I don't know what it would be best, but if you don't stop having these problems that you just started having, I'd have to think up something.

JUV. Oh, I can stop having problems.

P.O. Well, then you'd better. You show me that you can and then I won't have to make any decisions. Right? I'm coming out here today mainly just to warn you about what can happen if you do any more of this. Do you understand that?

JUV. Uh, hmm.

P.O. You have anything you want to talk about? If you want to stay there, well this is fine with me. I go along with that. I think it's a real good idea. I'm not saying forever. I can't promise you forever either. Right?

JUV. Yeah.

P.O. But I think you should talk it over with your mother when you feel it is a good time to tell your mother, to explain it to your mother.

(The conversation shifts again.)

The juvenile seems to shift the conversation ("Mrs. Wells I don't want to go home.") by reference to a dream that was difficult to follow from the tape. With this shift in conversation, more of the juvenile's views about a variety of problems connected with her foster and former home are revealed. The reference to a dream is linked by the juvenile to a forthcoming decision about whether she will remain in the foster home. The comment that "My mother interpreted it for me" suggests there was a calculated connection by the mother, but it is not clear which "mother" the juvenile intends. Judging from the juvenile's comment "I'm going to stay there" [at the foster home], the "mother" could have been the foster mother. But on the other hand, the "mother" could have been the biological mother if we want to imagine some unstated conversation that precipitated a discussion of the June "deadline." I do not feel much can be made of the exchange over the renewal or nonrenewal of the foster home arrangement, because it is not clear how the dream notion emerged: as a device created by the juvenile to call attention to possible termination of the foster home arrangement she desired, or as a dream that was reported as an independent event to "mother," and interpreted as a "sign of" the pending "deadline" over the foster home arrangement because of the (foster?) "mother's" interest in seeing that the child remain or be returned to the original home. The P.O. does not seem to read any special meaning into the dream or the story given by the juvenile indicating that the girl is "really" bothered by the possibility of returning to the original home, yet the P.O. begins a line of questioning that first asks about the biological mother's response to the possibility of remaining in the foster home, and then shifts to "Does she come to see you very often?" The shift appears to be a direct attempt to assess the biological mother's relationship with the juvenile as revealed by her visits. The juvenile's responses are not entirely clear, but they suggest a degree of regularity in the visits. The juvenile then seems to introduce a shift by asking "Is it okay if I go to the game tonight?" The P.O. invokes the proprieties of the juvenile's subordination to the wishes of the foster mother, and then asks "What did she say?" as if first to reaffirm the authority of the foster mother, and then to inquire about the response, where the presumption may be made that the juvenile had been turned down initially by the foster mother. This last assumption seems clear from the following statement by the juvenile: "She said I could if my father was going." The juvenile was apparently trying to pull the P.O. into foster home problems, and the P.O. seemed to be aware of this. The P.O. and the juvenile then seem to "cooperate" in first making it clear that the foster mother's authority takes primacy as far as outings are concerned, and then providing the juvenile with the invitation to note, rather "properly," "when she puts me on restriction she's trying to keep me out of trouble."

When the P.O. tells the juvenile "that you promised me that there wouldn't be any more of this, because (pause) I'd have to do something" and because "It's my responsibility, you know," there is a return to the general policy or rule that is concerned with the presumed fact of probation violation, and a disinterest in contingencies the juvenile or others might have considered relevant. The juvenile's response was not entirely audible, but seems to have addressed or proposed some consequence that might follow further "trouble." The P.O.'s response, however, seems noncommittal (as was seen on several earlier occasions); yet there is an obvious threat, but the nature of the punishment is not clear. Nor is it clear "how much" further "trouble" would lead to doing "something." The juvenile's response of "I can stop having problems" implies that whatever behavior was being labeled as "problems" can be terminated easily. The P.O. then seems to make clear that her present visit was "mainly just to warn you about what can happen if you do any more of this." I think it is safe to venture that the P.O. would probably tolerate several more incidents as long as the juvenile was "cooperative" and displayed the "right attitude."

Returning to the dialogue, the juvenile states:

JUVENILE. I can talk to my mother but I can't talk to my father 'cause I don't like him.

PROBATION OFFICER. Well, you explain to your mother as much as possible, and why don't you like your father?

JUV. Because he's not right.

P.O. In what?

JUV. He's just not right. He's a boss man, that's what he is.

P.O. He's a father, maybe father is the boss.

JUV. But they're not supposed to be boss man.

P.O. What do you mean by that?

JUV. They have ta, (pause) why most men marry really is to be boss men. That's why women get married to men, 'cause the men want these ladies for their real purposes, and for them to do work, housework they do. That's right. If you look into it you'll see.

P.O. Sometimes our marriages work both ways. You know, the man is sort of the head of the household and makes the basis of some of the decisions, but the wife makes some of them too, and they both get [cut off by juvenile].

JUV. But the man ain't going ta take care of you. Most of the time you have to work, (pause) you take care of yourself, and in the house cleaning you be taking care of yourself. He don't be taking care of you most of the time. 'Cause if he was able to take care of you then he'd hire help.

P.O. Yeah, but not all men are able to afford it. But if they give you, cherish and love you enough, sometimes you don't care if you have to work. Do you?

JUV. I don't know, but I know I not going to get married.

P.O. Well, Mr. Wentworth is nice, isn't he?

JUV. Yeah.

P.O. Don't you think he and Mrs. Wentworth get along?

JUV. He's not no boss man.

P.O. Well, you see there are men like that though. Right? Considerate [Yes?—juvenile]—Well, honey, this isn't a decision we have to make now whether or not you're going to get married. Right?

JUV. [Short inaudible response]

P.O. So you try real hard to stay out of any difficulties and promise me if you have a feeling you are going to get mixed up in something and you know it's wrong, come talk to Mr. James if it's at school, (pause) or go talk to Mrs. Wentworth if it's home. Will you? Promise?

JUV. Okay, I will.

P.O. Fine, so you tell her 'hi' and I'm, uh, have been pleased with you up til this last week, and now I'll give you another chance to show me you can get right back on the same track you were, Audrey. How are you doing in school?

JUV. Fine.

P.O. Real good. I'm real pleased in this too.

JUV. You want to see something pretty?

P.O. Oh, isn't that lovely.

JUV. . . . it was a . . . from my father . . .

P.O. Your real father?

JUV. Yes.

P.O. See, that boss man has some good points, doesn't he?

JUV.   [inaudible response] Are we supposed to sign in?

P.O.   I think they sign in at the office. Right out there, honey. So you let me know any time you want me to come in and talk to you again. I can either do it here or at the foster home. Okay? Bye-bye.

In suggesting that the juvenile "talk it over with your mother" vis-à-vis staying at the foster home, the girl responds that she can talk to her biological mother, but not her biological father "because I don't like him." This last remark opens up a different line of discussion that the P.O. picks up immediately: "and why don't you like your father?" When the P.O. seeks further information here, the girl merely responds with "Because he's not right." The P.O. then pushes the girl further by asking "In what?" The juvenile's response repeats the phrase "He's just not right," and then adds: "He's a boss man, that's what he is." The juvenile suggests the father as a social type she designates as "boss man," while the P.O. seems to invoke a conventional reference to "father is the boss." Yet the girl responds with "But they're not supposed to be boss man," and the P.O. acknowledges that some discrepancy exists between their uses of "boss" here. The juvenile has suggested that "fathers" are not "supposed to be boss man." The girl then seeks to clarify her usage of the term "boss man" by reference to men as types who seek to exploit women, i.e., "the men want these ladies for their real purposes, and for them to do work, housework they do." The P.O.'s response provides an ideal normative general policy or rule that refers to "expected" divisions of labor in a marriage relationship, but the juvenile cuts her off and returns to the juvenile's perspective on men by providing the P.O. with particulars that are intended to pinpoint her argument. The girl states that "the man ain't going to take care of you," and that "Most of the time you have to work, (pause) you take care of yourself," for if the man was really interested in you "he'd hire help." Notice the juvenile is stating a generalization about men and family life as general practice, but the P.O. responds first by reference to what is presumably a factual observation that "not all men are able to afford it," and then follows through with a general policy or rule that seeks to neutralize the girl's generalization by reference to terms like "cherish and love you," in an effort to convince the girl that her particulars are not necessarily relevant "as long as" there is emotional support from the man. The juvenile seems to reject the P.O.'s view entirely when she states that "I don't know, but I know I not going to get married." The P.O. then seeks to undercut the girl's view by reference to a particular case, that of her foster father. The juvenile's response is "yeah," and in response to the P.O.'s remark that "Don't you think he and Mrs. Wentworth get along?" the girl seems to acknowledge that this particular case does not fit her generalization on the grounds that "He's not no boss man." The P.O. seeks first to continue this line long enough to obtain some sort of agreement from the juvenile that her generalization requires qualification ("you see there are men like that though"), but the girl's responses are not clear. My impression of the tape leads me to infer that the girl was not convinced, but merely wanted to go along with the P.O. to terminate this particular discussion and, perhaps, to shorten the interview. The P.O. also seems to want to cut off the discussion when she notes that "this isn't a decision we have to make now . . ." I want to pursue this juvenile's view of marriage and family life further, but only after a few other remarks about the remainder of the dialogue.

Notice that the P.O. shifts the discussion back to the now familiar theme of staying "out of any difficulties" and the implementation of the general policy or rule by reference to particulars mentioned earlier, "if you have a feeling you are going to get mixed up in something and you know it's wrong, come talk to Mr. James if it's at school, (pause) or go talk to Mrs. Wentworth if it's home." The remainder of the interview seems to be a cooperative effort on the part of both participants to terminate the dialogue pleasantly. The reference to "something pretty" provides a "nice" ending to the exchange and the P.O. once again seeks to turn the girl's remarks into a justification (using the gift as the particular case that fits the general rule) of her earlier efforts to convince the juvenile that her (the P.O.'s) perspective is the "correct" or "more accurate" one. The reference to the biological father ("that boss man has some good points . . .") is, however, ignored by the juvenile, for she seems merely to have sort of grunted a response I list as inaudible, but which I think could be taken as a weak affirmative.

The reader should note it was seldom possible to find juveniles making statements about their perspective of "what happened" except in truncated form. In the present case, the juvenile made her views clear to the P.O. on several occasions, but soon learned to agree with the P.O.'s interpretation of "what happened" or "what should happen." It is difficult to say that the observer elicits the juvenile's perspective independent of the police or P.O.'s "educating" influence. We do not know if the interview with the police or P.O. is enough in itself to preclude the juvenile from expressing his own views. But then there is the problem of disentangling the extent to which the juvenile assumes the officers expect a particular line or rhetoric from him, as opposed to what he might express to peers. Finally, it is difficult to know how much of the rhetoric the juvenile begins to accept or believe. I feel the organized character of law-enforcement agencies renders the juvenile's "real" views or motives almost irrelevant for the present study. The juvenile's views are not treated as possible sources of innovation and legitimate complaints or dissent, but as deviations from some presumed (community) general policy or rules to which others adhere. Therefore, the juvenile's rights are few; they do not include the right to have different views about the nature of social organization, community or family values, and what fathers and mothers, teachers, policemen, and probation officers should be like, because his delinquent status undercuts the right to such views. The occasions on which the juvenile is asked his views vis-à-vis parents, or perhaps a teacher or a neighbor, are when law-enforcement agents have permitted such persons to be viewed as suspect in their dealings with the juvenile. Thus, in child neglect or child custody cases, the legal authorities may request the juvenile's opinion and abide by his or her wishes. What I want to stress is that the juvenile's perspective is seldom relevant and often cut off by law enforcement agents after it is determined that a "bad attitude" exists, and delinquent imputations have already been made toward the youth. It is a way of saying the delinquent features of the juvenile do not warrant his right to evaluate or criticize persons and social arrangements that include adults.

The affirmative responses, which the juvenile gave above, are not clear-cut "agreements" to what the P.O. was advocating, but acknowledgments that, after all, she (the juvenile) can "now see" the "correctness" of the P.O.'s remarks. Thus the present case reflects routine and consistent practice by both police and probation officers when interviewing a juvenile. There is invariably a monologue between juvenile and officer, whereby the latter seeks to first ascertain the "facts" and then, depending upon the juvenile's "attitude," begins to provide the juvenile with the moral stuff with which to interpret his (the juvenile's) acts, and the moral perspective that is required to stay out of "trouble." The morality seems very clear: walk away when you "see" that there may be "trouble," protect yourself if necessary but proceed immediately to persons in authority so that you can indicate your innocence or, even better, choose your friends so that the possibility of "trouble" is precluded. The P.O.'s remarks can be read as a literal account of what sociologists often loosely call "middle-class values."

Before concluding this chapter, I want to call attention to the P.O.'s resumé as written up and included in the juvenile's file. I attach considerable significance to this summary statement because it is present in all encounters between juveniles and police and probation officers. Such encounters occur every day, but they are not always recorded in writing. Recorded or not, such encounters inform all subsequent exchanges between law-enforcement agents and the juvenile if there are later incidents. If the encounter is recorded and entered in the juvenile's file, then there are additional problems such as how will the report be read at some future date given the circumstances of a new incident? *Notice how such reports provide its author, on subsequent occasions, the opportunity to review "what happened," reinterpret the past incident in light of present activities, bring to light elements of past incidents that were not included in the report, and "see" how a "pattern" that is now "evident" was actually begun "back then."* Officers who do not "know" the juvenile (and have not spoken with those officers who have had prior contacts with him) must now utilize the report to "see" its significance for the present incident. The establishment of identities for juveniles is to be found in the characterization of the juvenile in the report, what the officer supplies from his experience with other juveniles, and his present reaction. Such practical decision-making involves "drawing the line" so that some "pattern" or "type" is produced that allows for a course of action consistent with general policies or rules laid down by penal, welfare, and institution code statutes, and the everyday practices of the agencies involved. Thus the particulars—the contingencies of the case— are always being interpreted vis-à-vis past reports or encounters, present depictions of the youth, and the general policies or rules to be found in statutes and departmental activities. The officers must somehow articulate the particulars or contingencies of present cases with general policies, rules, or typologies they utilize for "making sense" of emergent social interaction over time. Before summarizing this point of view, the reader should be exposed to the P.O.'s remarks about her interview with Audrey.

> Talked to Mr. J. at Jr. Hi. re Audrey—he says Audrey jumped into the fight to pull white girl off Jane Johnson—(negro) who was beating up the girl's younger sister. Audrey hit the oldest Penn girl a couple of times & then Candy Noland took over & Audrey withdrew. Audrey was suspended the rest of that day. A couple of minor incidents since—yesterday she & some other girls jumped on a laundry truck at school & Audrey didn't obey bus driver on bus. However, Mr. J. reports that Audrey's attitude was good—admitted everything & promised she wouldn't any more.
>
> Talked to Audrey at school—lectured her re any fighting or disobedience. Told her if she hadn't done so well up to now, she would be in serious trouble. Audrey promised not to get involved in anything & "to walk away" if trouble started around her.
>
> Says she wants to stay at Wentworths forever—doesn't like father. Advised her we want her to stay as long as progressing; suggested she tell mo. how she feels so mo. will understand.

The first half of the P.O.'s remarks deal with a conversation between her and the school official and is reported without any of the details obtained in the subsequent conversation with the juvenile. The P.O.'s remarks, however, constitute the "facts" of the case. The P.O. labels the laundry truck and bus incidents as "minor," and then notes that the school official "reports that Audrey's attitude was good—admitted everything & promised she wouldn't any more." What is critical about the P.O.'s remarks is her reference to the school official's comment that "Audrey's attitude was good," for such a remark neutralizes the incidents, at least for the *here* and *now* of this report. It is easily argued that the P.O.'s interview with the juvenile was structured entirely by the school official's remarks that the girl's "attitude was good." Thus the P.O. was able to enter the interview with the tacit assumption that nothing serious was involved, and that her "trouble" was not to be viewed as a critical violation of probation. The P.O. seems to make this same point when she relates that "Told her if she hadn't done so well up to now, she would be in serious trouble." Her task was viewed as that of "lecturing" and "educating" the girl as to how the P.O. was viewing the "trouble" and what was expected of her in the future. The general policy or rule of "walking away" from "trouble" is included in the remarks, as well as the reference to remaining in the foster home. Notice, however, that the P.O.'s report only includes a truncated version of her (often) monologue with the girl, and there is no way for the reader of such remarks to deduce the juvenile's perspective. The P.O. was interested in having the juvenile "accept" the interpretation provided by the P.O., irrespective of the girl's point of view. The girl's point of view was irrelevant as long as it did not agree with the P.O., for having a "good attitude" meant agreeing with the P.O., not talking back and thus coming to "see" things as they "should" be seen. The conversation reveals how the P.O. informs the juvenile about that which the P.O. sees as important, and how the girl is expected to respond when general policies or rules are offered as guides to future conduct. Further, the P.O. informs the girl how present incidents are to be interpreted vis-à-vis the "explanations" and general policies or rules governing past "trouble." Thus the general policies or rules have both prospective and retrospective significance. Such rules enable the officer to categorize or classify the particular case—a variety of particulars provided by the juvenile—into the general policies or rules that define the significance of legal statutes and organizational practices.

Notice how the problem of measurement can be seen as directly relevant if we ask how the researcher is to establish some basis for counting types of delinquents or violations of probation. When the police or probation officers initially (or subsequently) encounter a juvenile, the problems to be resolved are how acts or sequences of events require action leading to an arrest, a court hearing, further interrogation, and the like. The day-to-day procedures of the police and probation officers amount to producing "lay indicators" of "what happened." Such indicators become the researcher's grounds for revealing how both he and members decide inclusion and exclusion in categories or sets, according to lay and scientific theories. In cases where the police officer "eye-balled" (personally witnessed) an incident, and the event is viewed as a clear violation of some legal statute, subsequent action on the part of the officer, or by others, is not an automatic implementation of procedures leading to the imputation of a delinquent identity and a firm basis for counting. The particulars of the situation are always evaluated against a backdrop of background expectancies, and the juvenile's behavior before the officer. The problem may be outlined as follows:

1. The articulation of a general policy or rule with particular situations requires attention to the selection of contingencies, which the actor will utilize for deciding a particular case or event falls under the general rule. The actor's decisions become the basis for the researcher's decisions, although the researcher may choose to reassemble the actor's products according to different theoretical reasoning.

2. The researcher's scientific reasoning presumably adheres to an explicit articulation between a theoretical conception, available to colleagues, and materials labeled data, obtained by procedures open to inspection and replication. But the utilization of information generated by the actions of members of organized social activities, such as police or probation departments, requires that the researcher seek an explicit account of how such members accomplish the practical reasoning leading to the establishment of categories or labels counted "as standing for" or "as signs of" "delinquent" activity, a "bad attitude," an "uncooperative," attitude and so on. Chapter 3 revealed a variety of problems involved in understanding and coding the information that can be obtained from police and probation records, and the chapters following the present one will provide considerable detail on the difficulties of deciding how to interpret the day-by-day activities of police and probation officers during the course of their work. In each type of activity the members' decisions are negotiated.

3. The negotiated character of members' activities underscores the arbitrariness of practical decision-making. I am not arguing, however, that there are no "good reasons" for the actions taken, but that the "push" required to "tip the scales," so an act, event, or person is now viewed as "delinquent," is not the product of a carefully reasoned sequence of analysis. The reasoning contains many "jumps" or "leaps," imaginative "filling in" of "what could have happened" when there are gaps and, above all, continual retrospective interpretive readings, justifications of how it "could have happened" or "probably happened," so the member can settle the business at hand and move on to something else. Nor am I arguing that there is *nothing* "final" about everyday decisions for members (as opposed to researchers); the final character of practical decision-making for members always depends upon "further notice." The statistical information forwarded to governmental agencies or retained in the files will "stand" for some span of time to indicate the "nature of delinquency" in a community or some part of the community, but *"circumstances," "events,"* can mean that in any particular case, the characterization of the

object may be open to some future contingency, and so can tables depicting some clock-time interval.

4. It is not so much a problem of "can we count," but how does the member count, and what does counting signify vis-à-vis what can be demonstrated when viewed from the day-to-day social organization of police and probation activities?[6] The sociologist may seek to justify his counting procedures by reference to his theoretical reasoning, but the counting is not to be disengaged from the day-to-day activities and practical reasoning of the members engaged in accomplishing their tasks. The different conditions under which counting may be possible is not to be confused with the notion that some counting procedures are "more scientific" than others. We may not want to call the member's counting procedures "scientific," but that is not the important issue; the issue is, rather, how does the member decide to "terminate" an activity, or decide that some cut-off point has been reached, the juvenile "rehabilitated," a petition warranted, and the like. What is relevant to the member is taking practical action, and how such reasoning determines—by fiat or otherwise—the conditions under which some kind of counting operation becomes possible.

Concluding Remarks

I call the reader's attention to the discrepancy that always exists between the unfolding dialogue between two or more persons and how the exchange is written up as a report of "what happened." In the materials presented in the next chapters, it will not be possible to show always how a particular conversation led to a specific report. I nevertheless take the position that the interview and brief report presented earlier is an adequate general reflection of *all* encounters between the police and probation officials and juveniles. My assertion is not based upon a sampling device that can be demonstrated to the reader; my participation with police and probation officials was based upon several years of accompanying officers on their daily round of activities. I can only tell the reader that I was able to witness hundreds of interviews, and then check the official or unofficial report soon after it was written. Not being able to tape-record the interviews between police and probation officers and juveniles in different settings in the two cities precludes the presentation of additional cases. But it should be fairly clear to the reader that even if the researcher were armed with two hundred tape-recorded encounters, and the official or unofficial reports of them, it would not be possible to contrast many of the two versions of the interviews because of space limitations.

The actual exchange between officer and juvenile is an occasion for "lecturing," "fact" finding, character assessment, threats of possible subsequent action, and the like, and is seldom a guarded activity, but usually wide-ranging both in content and styles of behavior. The officer may resort to a "buddy-

buddy" line to communicate "sympathy," equality, "intimacy," a threatening line to "scare" the juvenile or elicit information, or some combination of several tacks from a general repertoire. The juvenile may be cajoled, pleaded with, lied to, his rights violated continuously and systematically, and his social character maligned or praised, but the official or unofficial report may be quite truncated, and may never reveal how the information was elicited, or what kinds of conversational exchanges preceded the disclosure of information that is then recorded as if it were volunteered, or recorded as an obvious part of the exchange. The ways in which the conversation unfolded may have little or nothing to do with the information intended by the official or unofficial report, or *read into the report* by others unfamiliar with the original exchange, or how such encounters are assembled. An important result of contrasting actual encounters with the ways in which they are written up in reports or documents is how others decide their meaning, and take action with binding consequences and then, of course, what the researcher makes of such reports in his attempts to measure "what happened." The researcher, like others who must read the document without benefit of the actual dialogue that led to the report, must make inferences about the meaning of the remarks in view of perhaps quite different experiences with the juvenile or officer connected with the incident. In the present study, I was able to witness a wide range of encounters over several years; therefore, my interpretation of reports and documents is informed by a broad stock of knowledge gained through my participation in the two communities as an officer. The reader, however, does not have access to an objectified account of my experiences and, therefore, cannot control the kinds of questions I "ask" of the documents because of my participation. In the chapters that follow I have tried to utilize the document itself as a generator of questions about "what happened" so the reader can follow my reasoning. Further, I have tried to signal those occasions when my tacit knowledge is being used to explicate the text. The reader should view the present chapter as a reference when in doubt about the kinds of conversational material that could have preceded the assembling of documents presented in subsequent chapters. *The dialogue presented above is an integral part of all of the materials that follow.*

Before closing this chapter, I should like to suggest that the study of different conversational procedures that occur in natural settings in everyday life is not only a rich source of information about how members communicate with (understand) each other, how the researcher can gain insight into members' practical reasoning or decision-making, how members communicate the significance of rules, social identities, and the like, but also provides the basis for understanding something about how history is created. In moving from conversations in natural settings *to accounts by members who participated* in the conversations or were told about the encounters, a general problem emerges, having to do with how researchers will decide the significance of reports and documents in developing scholarly accounts of "what happened." I am suggesting that the routine problems, which law-enforcement agents encounter in accomplishing their daily activities, provide excellent sources of information for understanding how researchers come to characterize objects and events in particular and general formulations over time. The document can be viewed as a disengaged version of "what happened," so that the researcher's interpretation of it is integral to the particulars or contingencies subsumed under more abstract terms or phrases that pretend to depict "what happened." The ways in which the unfolding situation or action scene is perceived and interpreted by the members and depicted with language categories that locate "what happened" in some socially organized context, provide the basis for understanding how members "measure," by means of the cutoff points of "I know," "I see," "let it pass," "of course," "that's enough," "fine," "that will do," "a little more," and the like, thus creating the activities we label "the social structures." Notice that members of the community or society are themselves constantly engaged in the use of language categories that "make history." The fact that members' accounts are accepted by other members and researchers provides the warrant for labeling some set of activities or objects or events as "data." When documents are written, there are inevitable "negotiations" by the writer with himself and the materials with which he deals, leading to general and particular ways of depicting "what happened," and thereby structuring the ways in which a given reader will then make sense of the document or report. How the researcher decides "cutoff" points cannot ignore how members, who constructed the documents he utilizes, also arrived at "cutoff" points. Thus, if the researcher is not to impose some system of measurement by fiat upon the materials, he must seek ways of accounting for the members' use of categories and cutoff points; otherwise the negotiated document or report is then treated as a literal depiction of "what happened." Notice that both conversational and documentary materials are assembled according to members' use of language categories and cutoff points that presupposes some knowledge of the routine grounds of everyday decision-making. To argue that natural language contains "natural" cut-off points and thus a "logic" of its own is not to say this "logic" is in correspondence with the logical properties contained in conventional mathematical systems.

The major point of the theoretical and empirical materials contained in this book is that natural language is governed, for example, by the properties of vagueness, taken-for-granted properties of objects and events, and standardizing occurrences until "further notice," described earlier. A question like "What 'forces' motivate or structure the entrance into delinquent activity?"

misses the general relevance of the problem of practical reasoning that juveniles engage in when pursuing daily activities, how the police and probation officials are drawn into contact with juveniles, and how the police or probation officers decide that particular events fall under general policies or rules deemed relevant. A simple reference to "forces" or "social structure" or "values" imposes an order instead of seeking to discover the nature of socially organized activities. Before we first assume and then directly assign motives, assume the existence of values and norms, institutional pressures, and the like, the study of everyday life or history requires careful attention to the ways in which social interaction unfolds over time so that members "make sense" of "what happened" (by means of their physical, verbal, and "silent" behavior), and recount their experiences to one another and in written or some other behavioral or symbolic form. The study of practical activities provides the sociologist with a fundamental point of departure in the study of social organization, and also becomes a basis for developing a theory of data when seeking higher order or more complicated forms of social life.

NOTES

1. The notion of typicality, perceivedly normal, and similar usage is taken from the works of Alfred Schutz and Harold Garfinkel cited throughout earlier chapters.
2. Cf. Harold Garfinkel, "Remarks on Ethnomethodology," paper presented at the American Sociological Association Annual Meeting, Chicago, September 1965; and Garfinkel, *Studies in Ethnomethodology* (Englewood Cliffs, N.J.: Prentice-Hall, 1967).
3. Cf. John Rawls, "Two Concepts of Rules," *Philosophical Review,* **LXIV,** 3-32 (January 1955).
4. Cf. Carl Werthman, *Delinquency and Authority,* unpublished M.A. thesis (Berkeley: Department of Sociology, 1964) ; I. Piliavin and Scott Briar, "Police Encounters with Juveniles," *American Journal of Sociology,* (September 1964) **LXX,** 206-214.
   Werthman's thesis contains some of the best material I have seen on the details of police encounters with Negro juvenile males and how the juvenile perceives and interprets police activities.
5. The reader should be advised that throughout Chapters 4, 5, 6, and 7, there are numerous quotations containing various kinds of errors. These quotations are verbatim accounts taken from the original documents or conversations I recorded during my field work. The same errors are repeated whenever I make use of the quoted material in my analysis. I have not tried to correct the errors in order to preserve the context within which the materials were generated.
6. Cf. Lindsey Churchill, "On Everyday Quantitative Practices," unpublished manuscript, for similar arguments. Problems associated with members' counting procedures and how members can be said to "index" their everyday environments are discussed at length in unpublished work by Harold Garfinkel. I am indebted to Garfinkel for allowing me to examine his materials in rough-draft form.

Chapter 5

ROUTINE PRACTICES OF
LAW-ENFORCEMENT AGENCIES

The initial plans of the study were to follow a cohort of juveniles in each county from their first police contact through their disposition by probation officials or the juvenile court. I had hoped to observe and tape-record the various encounters over the course of each contact between juvenile and law-enforcement personnel. It was not possible for me to do either activity as planned. The use of a tape recorder bothered the officers; they did not respond to the idea at all. Further, it was not possible to follow the same cohort of juveniles from initial contact to final disposition without an incredible amount of time lost. Even when a case emerged that seemed destined for probation review and probable juvenile court hearing, it was not always possible to be at every subsequent encounter because I had to be on call virtually twenty-four hours a day for many months. Even when only one case was picked up at a time, the scheduling proved too difficult. When more than one case was being followed, conflicting interviews, meetings, or hearings occurred.

During the last year of the study, I participated rather intensely with the various departments and followed many cases from different points of entry into the system. I was able to follow a few cases from beginning to end or final disposition. While the ideal procedures were not followed, I was able to observe the social organization of the police and probation activities at every step, during each day of the week, month, and year. I was made a probation officer without pay in one of the counties, and this enabled me to participate as a police officer and probation officer whenever I went with a member of a department. I was able to follow, therefore, all aspects of police and probation work and court hearings in both counties, including night work by the police and the juvenile hall operations of the probation department. Considerable time was necessary to gain the confidence of officers (two years in City B and three years in City A) to learn about irregular activities, internal organizational problems, and political power struggles. I attribute my access to the fact that I participated socially with many officers in circumstances that had little or nothing to do with the study or the work of law enforcement; such situations always produced a more relaxed atmosphere when the study context was resumed. In City A, the informal social encounters did not occur until very late in the study and it was not until that time I felt "close" to the "inside" details of day-to-day activities, jealousies, power conflicts, dissatisfactions with the job, the promotion system, and the like.

Without considerable social contact, "friendly" exchanges, attempts to know the officers informally so that the researcher is on a first-name basis with all he works with closely, I doubt if the detailed operations of day-to-day police and probation work could be observed in anything approaching what could be termed their "normal" work environment. The fact of being present in an office day-in, day-out, busy with "paper work," but privy to every conceivable kind of case, interaction, annoyances, "inside" discussions, being drawn into one's "confidence," and the like, provides the researcher with an invaluable perspective on the everyday character of law enforcement. But it also exposes him to the danger of taking it all for granted in the same way as the officers do. I would occasionally pose interview-type questions to officers about different routines, procedures, conceptions about work, about juveniles, parents, politicians, and so forth, to call my attention to the possibility of taking too much for granted. I found it impossible to continue to take notes after each day of participation or observation because the repetition was boring, and it was not possible to record all of the innumerable details of action scenes. The scene moved too quickly for me to utilize something like Birdwhistell's kinesic methods, even if I felt confident enough in their use. But verbatim written reports, notes, or transcripts of conversations are used below so that the interpretation of moods and social performances is attempted, despite the fact I must often urge them upon the reader.

The materials presented are intended as routine and characteristic instances of all day-to-day communication, decision-making activity of the organizations studied, or "what goes on all of the time." The analyses and raw materials could have been improved; I have given some indication of the discrepancy between what I had hoped to do and was able to accomplish. In recommending the materials, I want to stress that reducing them to a set of cross-tabulated counts for presentation in tabular form is not warranted because the counts would not represent how the action unfolded over time, and how decisions were being made on the basis of gestures, voice intonation, body motion, dissatisfaction with answers to hypothetical questions, imputations about family organization, imputations about personal character, and so on. It is difficult to measure how officials become incensed, visibly angry, and proceed to treat a case in terms that I can only describe as the "last straw" of outrage concerning the extent to which some juvenile or group of them have flaunted the law, community morality, and the like, and where every attempt is then made to obtain prompt action I would describe as punitive. Let me note, however, that seen from the vantage point of the officer's experiences with the case his reaction is understandable even though one can say that "cooler heads" should have prevailed, the juvenile "deserved it" and "any man" would agree.

The Community Setting

In this section I provide the reader with additional substantive details about the two cities with some repetition of remarks given in Chapter 3. The immediate contrast between City A and City B was the direct intervention by the mayor of City B into the day-to-day activities of the police department, while in City A the Mayor and City Manager would not enter directly into such activities, nor would the Chief in City A tolerate direct interference. The Chief of City B changed during the study and, for a short time, there was a regular Chief rather than an acting one. The Chief of City A came closest to advocating the kind of professional orientation that has been changing police departments all over the country into administratively oriented organizations that stress efficiency in controlling crime and delinquency. In City B the mayor, a former detective, was known to have a direct influence on policy and would intervene in cases involving the children of known "dignitaries" in the city. Several cases (not discussed below) involved children of prominent lawyers and a contractor in a "wild party," and the mayor came over to the juvenile bureau to make inquiries about "what happened?" The Captain of Detectives was especially prone to intervene in cases involving higher-income or politically influential families. The juvenile bureau in City A was under the direct control of the detective bureau, but maintained autonomous operations. The Sergeant in charge was very active and well-known locally and in the state for his work with the juvenile officers association, having been elected to important offices many times. The Chief relied upon him for many speeches in the community on problems relating to juvenile delinquency.

The superior court judges in both counties usually rotate on a yearly basis. Relations between the Chief Probation Officers and Juvenile Court Judges were close in both counties. In County A the judges varied considerably in the extent to which they became involved in probation activities. One judge in City A underscored the gravity of juveniles' court appearances, and commitment to the youth authority always jumped markedly during this particular judge's time on the juvenile court bench. Several probation officers in County A reported that they often felt compelled to alter their case histories radically when the "hard" judge was on the bench. They attempted to manipulate the report to minimize the present offense and the past record, so the "hard" judge would not be as strict in his disposition of the case. The referee in County B appeared to spend more time going over cases, and seemed more acquainted with probation interests and policy. The presiding juvenile court judge in County B was only called in (or asked to be called in) when the case received publicity in the local papers or involved a "serious" offense. In County B, therefore, there was considerable consultation between probation officer and referee before the hearing, and before and after the probation report and disposition recommendation were made.

While I did not devote any special block of time to the study of judges and their relationship to the political networks in the two counties, their names were mentioned frequently when respondents were asked to explain political appointments and local politics. The police characteristically imputed biases in handling juveniles to probation-officer control over judges. The police felt that if the judge "knew" what was "going on," he would probably alter his adjudication procedures vis-à-vis juveniles. Probation officers, on the other hand, because of closer contact with the judge for both routine and special cases, are likely to be more cynical of judges they feel do not carry their "load," suggesting the judge is neither motivated nor informed about the nature of the problem at hand. The police in juvenile cases are somewhat removed from the activities of the juvenile court, except on those occasions when they are called in as witnesses to establish allegations. The probation officer, on the other hand, must, as a condition of successfully accomplishing his daily activities, depict each judge or referee in terms that would enable him to anticipate reactions to prepared reports and recommended dispositions. In either case, therefore, the police and probation officers are confronted with tasks requiring the creation of reports substantiating a particular depiction of the offender, so that the judge or referee will not view the allegations as questionable or problematic. Most cases have the appearance of "typical juvenile crimes or offenses," seen as routine, with classes of persons of similar social characteristics, typical circumstances, "attitudes," and so forth, that both police and probation view as "natural" or the "same old stuff." Operationally, therefore, certain males are always watched at football games or dances, or questioned in connection with certain offenses, or picked up immediately when particular patterns of crime or "bothering" are referred to a department.

In the communities studied, size facilitates contacts between judges, top-level probation and police officers, businessmen, professionals, and city and county officials, so that fraternal orders, country clubs, social affairs, and community political and civic functions provide many occasions whereby direct and indirect pressures can be exerted on law-enforcement officials. The specific cases of political pressure I was able to hear about or observe directly usually involved upper-middle income to upper-income families. A local judge cannot avoid compromises in the community before he takes office, and he continues to be involved politically and socially in local affairs.

In County A, the probation department works closely with the superior court judge in charge, but most of the judges assume a passive role in routine cases. County B, on the other hand, relies upon a referee who has almost complete control over routine cases; the referee consults with the presiding judge but is more responsive to the Chief Probation Officer. The routine treatment accorded typical cases is decided by the probation officer, his or her supervisor, and the referee. Whereas the police in City A tried to apply pressure upon the judge and probation officer, in City B the police department had little or nothing to do with the disposition of court cases. The police in City A took active interest in the outcomes of their recommendations, while in City B the Juvenile Bureau was almost a kind of subdivision of the probation department.

Both Chief Probation Officers maintain considerable political (but not necessarily partisan) contact with wide segments of the city and county. The contacts include everything from belonging to fraternal orders and civic clubs to church and personal relationships with persons who can provide a kind of general protection for the probation department's activities. In City A the police sustained cordial relations (and informal monthly luncheons) with the probation people, even though there is very little real communication over basically different formal conceptions of delinquency, over who the offenders are, and over what should be done with them. In actual practice, as noted earlier, they may reach the same conclusions but never communicate their agreement. The Chief Probation Officer and the former Assistant Chief of Police (now Chief) in City A are old friends who see each other socially, and this relationship minimizes many areas of potential and actual friction between probation and police. In City B the Chief Probation Officer and Chief of Police were seldom on friendly terms. Except for the juvenile officers in City B, the police department regarded the probation department as a protector of juveniles "who should be in jail" and welfare cases that should be given "their due" (not helped by public monies) and placed in jail if not able to find their own means of support.

In City A, the day-to-day routine of the police involves considerable paper work, frequent telephone conversations, and field trips. Field investigations provide the officer with some freedom from the administrative orientation of the office, enable him to take a coffee break, occasionally run a few errands for himself, or simply follow up some vague leads in a case that he is annoyed about or would like to terminate. Coffee breaks and personal affairs are part of police routines but, in City A, there are too many administrative controls for any prolonged neglect of duties. Each officer is assigned cases on a regular basis, keeps a personal log of his activities, turns in a report to the Sergeant, and signs in and out on a location control sheet. His whereabouts and time are generally accounted for each day. The Sergeant turns in a monthly report showing how many cases each officer handled and how many reports were written—in short, how each man's time was spent. The volume of work in City A is large and routinizes enthusiasm generated from time to time in particular cases. When particularly annoying offenders or family types are encountered, or "soft" treatment by the probation department or court occurs, the juvenile officers engage in a "gripe" session over the specific case in question and other cases they have had or are now dealing with that involve similar problems. Most of the daily activities, however, are treated as routine, and the interrogation is fairly standardized for each officer, but each officer develops his own interviewing procedures or "line" that usually includes a repertoire of stock phrases, depending upon their interpretation of the case and the particular juvenile(s) and families involved. The officer's stock of knowledge at hand, in the form of typified conceptions of juvenile types, offense-juvenile types, is invoked in routine questioning.

In City B, the administrative model of police organization is bureaucratic in orientation, as opposed to efficiency interests of City A. The atmosphere of the police station is less formal, the routine arrangements for "protecting" high-ranking personnel (as in the military) is not operative, the control over each man's work is loose, and there is a considerable amount of general talk and "horseplay" that takes place every day. The officers are not controlled tightly as to their time and the reports they write up. The sign-out procedure consists of a large blackboard; the officers chalk in their destination and approximate time of return or call in changes in destination to the police radio. It is difficult to account for each officer's whereabouts retrospectively, since a written record does not exist.

The amount of "moonlighting" is striking in City B. Whereas in City A much of the routine extra-duty work such as policing a dance or a football game is organized by the department itself, few officers have exceptionally time-consuming outside jobs (even though many have become involved in minor activities over the years), while in City B some officers have elaborate business operations. In City B, therefore, an officer might engage in personal business in the police station, use police cars when going out for business and personal errands, and rely upon contacts made as a police officer to further his business.

The response to criminal and delinquent activities in City B tends to be quite variable, often depending upon the publicity given the case by the local paper, or the pressure generated by the mayor or chief or Captain of Detectives. The police in City B spend considerable time discussing politics in the station, and their views are for the most part quite conservative. The majority were for Goldwater in the 1964 election, and several were supposed to be active members of the John Birch Society. Politics were seldom discussed in City A, although most of the officers seemed to comment favorably on conservative views whenever they did utter occasional remarks about political issues.

The Juvenile Bureau is subservient to the Detective Bureau in City B. Detectives employ considerable discretion when dealing with juveniles, and may never refer a case they choose to handle alone because the juvenile is involved with adults they seek to prosecute. They make separate "deals" with juveniles to obtain their cooperation in the adult case. Detectives and patrolmen cooperate in dealing with juveniles suspected of repeated robberies or burglaries. With the cooperation of a small group of junior high school teachers, I was able to interview a group of juveniles who claimed that they had been beaten up by detectives or patrolmen. The juvenile officers knew of beatings and tried to obtain a release or stop the action, but their knowledge of such events was uneven. Most of the beatings took place at night, either in the field or in the police station when the juvenile officers were off duty. One patrolman on night duty was known by both the juveniles and juvenile officers as a "brutal guy." But little could be done about this matter as far as the Juvenile Bureau was concerned. The Juvenile Bureau's work consisted primarily of maintaining a record system on the cases brought to their attention for disposition. The two male juvenile officers in City B were registered and active Democrats. They were continually ridiculed for their political activities by the other policemen, including the Captain of Detectives. These juvenile officers were known in the Negro and Mexican-American neighborhoods as "good guys" who could be counted on for fair treatment. Both juvenile officers were members of ethnic groups and this seemed to influence their sympathies. Disaffection with the way in which the police department was run, the low possibilities for promotion and change, discouraged juvenile and several other officers known to the writer. Catholics were particularly affected. Juvenile officers in City B wrote few reports based upon interrogation of the suspected offender, and had little or no control over the decision to arrest and detain. Their job was primarily that of deciding when to release the offender and whether to file an application for petition. Their view of the suspect was obtained from the arresting officer, and little was done to investigate the circumstances of arrest and detention. Thus the records of the Juvenile Bureau in City B do not represent a very clear picture of juvenile delinquency as known and handled by the police. The patrolmen and detectives were always utilizing the considerable discretion at their disposal and could settle for a beating or a night in the City Jail rather than a referral to the Juvenile Bureau, particularly when the patrolman or detective viewed the Juvenile Bureau's work as a "waste of time" and ineffective. Furthermore, the detectives, and particularly the Captain of Detectives, made it their business to check for juveniles from "important families" so that the possibility of political advantage could be exploited with the family itself or the chief or mayor. I was able to observe a few such instances and to notice that such youths did not have a file started on them. The Captain of Detectives would call their parents directly, and the entire matter was forgotten. In City A, a direct release to the parents always resulted in a written report and the opening of a file card on the youth.

One direct contrast I was able to follow between the two cities involved two different evening parties, at different times, with different juveniles, in both cases involving city officials and their children. In City A the occasion was a gathering "crashed" by middle-income juveniles who stole items belonging to the City Manager. In City B, there was a "rough" party where a juvenile girl from a middle-income family submitted to sexual intercourse with approximately ten males; the children of a councilman were in attendance (but the police report did not mention who all of the suspected males were). In the case of City A, nothing was done by the City Manager to bring pressure on the police, and I did not observe any special attention given to the case. The situation in City B contrasted sharply in that the mayor came over to the Juvenile Bureau the next morning inquiring into the case, wanting to know what was being done, and asking against whom were charges being filed.

In both cities ethnic and religious issues seem to affect police activities, but the issues were considerably sharper in City B than in City A. City B has a Negro–Mexican-American ghetto that is ecologically removed from middle and higher-income areas of the city. The ethnic area in City A is not as isolated as in City B and is contiguous with one of the highest-income areas of City A. Intergroup relations in City A are relatively mild by comparison with those of City B, where more explicit hatred is expressed by the police and other groups in the city. City A appears more integrated, more concerned with avoiding conflict, and is regarded as a more benign community. Yet my impressions led me to feel that when relations between ethnics and "anglos" are established in City B, these appear to include social interaction in the home and in business, while in City A the "good relations" seem confined to "daytime" contacts and formal occasions. The "rules" of conflict seem clearer in City B, but so do the social relationships established. In City A, there is strain to avoid anything that might prove embarrassing and an interest in keeping up appearances.

The religious issue is primarily one of Catholic versus Protestant groups and could be characterized in terms similar to that used in discussing ethnic relations. Catholics in both cities are well-organized vis-à-vis their own social, educational, and religious activities, but there is more apparent outside contact in City A than in City B. The situation in City B seems to be more sharply focused; Catholics seem to view themselves as a minority group. Thus there is more open discussion of the "infiltration" of Catholic judges, city officials, and religious groups into the everyday life of the city. My informants in City B would tell stories about promotion policies they felt discriminated against Catholics in city and county government and how, within the police department, Protestant officers would seek ways of embarrassing Catholic officers, for example, parading arrested priests accused of being drunken or homosexual before them and offering them dispositional authority in their "own problems." In City A, nothing so blatant ever reached my ears, but there were occasional offhand remarks about apparent coincidence between the appointment of a particular judge and the fact that the governor was Catholic, or the handling of a case where the juvenile defendant, judge, and defending attorney were Catholic. But the reader should note that my information can be described only as impressionistic. I have no way of demonstrating its representativeness.

In providing ethnographic material for understanding the everyday activities of law-enforcement agencies in Cities A and B, I want to comment briefly on the nature of employment and advancement possibilities. Both probation and police departments (in all counties in California) have a tendency to offer little opportunity for advancement to the officer, even when the department is expanding rapidly. The ratio of supervisory personnel to the rank and file is considerable, and the civil service-merit system nature of the organizations makes it difficult for anyone to leave after several years of steady employment. Probation officers seem to have the greatest opportunity to leave, but few can really move up by leaving unless they change their work. The system of promotion in City B is politically controlled even though the tests for different ranks within the police department, for example, are open to all and have an objective part to them. It is in the oral part of the examination that officers claim that discrimination occurs. In City A, the complaints take a somewhat different form in that discretion by superiors is said to occur when several eligible candidates are available and no objective criteria exist for making the selection. But this situation is hardly news. What is of interest is the fatalistic way officers describe their future prospects through various subtle (if invented) obstacles that are impossible to objectify or about which it is impossible to accumulate evidence. The fatalism seems to rigidify what can be described as the matter-of-fact or mundane perspective that the officers adopt toward their clients. There are relatively few "unusual" or "exciting" cases, but many annoying cases, and these remain as instances of what is wrong with "kids," parents, probation, etc.

There are opportunities for changing counties but not for moving up in the probation department, and one quickly reaches a salary plateau. Probation officers seemed to be more active in church and community affairs. Their education and semiprofessional occupation are similar to that of a teacher. The probation officer is also plagued by paper work and the necessity of turning out hurried reports. Thus he is likely to routinize the character of the cases he handles and view them as falling within some general (but not explicit) principles about human nature, youth, and delinquency. Whereas the policeman is likely to have a less formal education and to obtain anything he does have beyond high school during off-duty hours after he is employed, the probation officer is likely to have had his formal education before obtaining his job, and may continue to take courses at night because of additional aspirations within and even beyond his present job. There were no noticeable differences between the educational backgrounds of the two sets of police and probation departments, although in City A, a few of the higher-ranking police officers have more additional education than their counterparts in City B. I do not feel educational differences at the top could account for all of the differences in everyday working behavior, but I do not have information to argue either way. One could argue that professionally oriented departments have better educated officers but, in City B, there were several officers, with considerable higher education, who resigned because they could not "break" existing political conditions over promotions.

I have traced out an impressionistic account of the departments studied to suggest the social context within which police and probation do their work. In the next section, I shall spell out how such differences affect the day-to-day administration of juvenile justice.

Jorge

The first case is that of a 15-year-old Mexican-American juvenile from City B. I shall begin with this case because it involves a murder charge. I did not want the reader to think that serious offenses do not occur despite data on their infrequence. The case is important because it reveals a source of considerable ethnic "trouble" with the police; gang fights often connected with social activities. I will not present the case in detail because the City B juvenile files are not complete, do not reveal juvenile investigation and interpretation, and the probation record is based only on the recent charge of murder. For probation the case is "typical" of a minority group member from a "poor environment." The juvenile's arrest record is as follows:

3/23/55 Petty theft (bike)	Action suspended
3/20/55 Petty theft (chickens)	Action suspended
3/15/55 Petty theft (two bikes)	Action suspended
5/ 9/55 Petty theft (bike)	Placed in Juvenile Hall— no petition
5/21/55 Dependency (petition filed)	Petition dismissed
4/25/63 Petty theft (bike)	Action suspended
8/ 4/63 Petty theft (gum, book)	Placed in Hall of Justice [city jail] Released—action suspended
10/25/64 Assault with deadly weapon (murder)	Placed in Juvenile Hall— petition Youth Authority placement

After the first three petty thefts noted above, the juvenile (then age seven) was tested by the city schools. The guidance report stated that the boy was "intellectually retarded," and gave the following details:

Special Strengths—Cooperative Attitude.
Special Weaknesses—Limited mental capacity and emotional immaturity.
Behavior—Jorge cooperated satisfactorily throughout the testing program.
Emotional—Jorge is disturbed emotionally.
Personality—Jorge is a likeable child. He wants to be loved and shows it by
    meek and humble cooperation.

Jorge's greatest weakness was found in the verbal area. He functioned typically within the borderline classification. He is weak in informational background and maturity that is so vital to making a positive social adjustment. This little boy projected much of himself in the answers he gave, especially in matters of comprehension. For example, he seemed to feel that the solution to all problems was to "call the cops." At least he felt that such an answer would be acceptable to an adult!—(the psychologist). This child is disturbed emotionally. He is confused and his sense of values is strongly colored by his negative childhood experiences. In his present state of immaturity and limited mental abilities, he cannot evaluate cause and effect sufficiently well to change his behavior pattern. He needs firm but kind guidance and limits. Jorge's parents also need help. Sharing these test findings may help them to understand their son better. Placement in a primary Special Education class now would help. He needs the comfort and sense of well-being of such a class. The normal classroom would probably cause him to feel more rebellion.

The guidance report was placed in the juvenile's police file, and I was told that subsequent encounters with the police led to "action suspended" after it became known that the boy was "mentally retarded." The guidance report did not state the juvenile's parents were having "trouble," nor was there any description of his home life.

The many police descriptions of the murder charge all agreed that Jorge shot two other juveniles, killing one, and Jorge acknowledged firing the weapon the police say hit the victims. The probation department accepted the police accounts, but rejected the label of "murder," insisting the victims had provoked the suspect after a "heated argument." The following excerpt from the police reports summarizes "what happened."

In reference to the above crime the undersigned interviewed JORGE SALA-ZAR (male, Mexican, Juvenile, 15 years of age with DOB: 11-8-48) who resides at [residence given]. After the suspect was advised of his rights according to the California Supreme Court Decision on Durado, he related the following: He stated he had been a member of the Martians' Club, and was elected a guard in this club. He stated he became inactive in the club approximately two weeks ago. On the evening in question he and some of his friends went to the party at [streets given], but did not enter the house, and stayed on the sidewalk.

He went on to relate that several fights broke out at the party, and that the police and the people at the house disbanded the party.

The suspect stated he knew several people were after him and his brother Ronald. He also stated that beside the Martians Club the other two clubs present at the party were the "Targets" and the "Big Riders." He stated after the party was broken up that Stan Nunez handed him a gun, and from there the suspect and the subject with him, Albert Norberto, walked around the street until they arrived at [streets given], where they met the victims and the subjects with the victims.

Jorge stated that an argument began, and that the people he was arguing with attempted to attack him and Albert with chains. Jorge stated he pulled the gun from his waistband of his trousers and began shooting. He stated that the subject who was coming at him had a chain in his hand and that Jorge aimed at a leg, and shot, but at this time the subject ducked and Jorge shot him in the stomach.

From this time on he related that he went "wild" and just kept on shooting until the gun was empty, and that he and Albert then fled the area and hid in the back yard of [address given], along with Angel Herrera, who had stayed in the back yard of that address. Jorge stated he had been drinking some beer, but did not think he was drunk.

For the police the case was "routine" in the sense that Mexican-Americans in City B are "always raising hell." The police report stresses advising the juvenile "of his rights" and, as noted in previous chapters, this procedure was seldom followed except in "serious" cases that might involve legal technicalities. The police were aware of Jorge's history of "mental retardation," but did not question the meaning of advising someone of his "rights" if doubt existed as to the suspect's competence to understand such advice. The report notes the "typical" elements of gang fights: a party, opposing "clubs," pending "trouble," someone "after" the juvenile and his brother, various weapons, and so forth. But for the police it was a case of "murder," regardless of provocation and a "heated argument." The report also revealed the gun given to the juvenile had come from an older (age 22) male who was described as an unemployed ex-convict and the "leader" of the club to which Jorge belonged. The reference to the older male appears to be similar to activities reported by others.[1]

The probation officer's report provides further "typical" information about the "background" of gang members. For example:

> The minor's parents, Ralph and Victoria Salazar, nee Ramirez, were married December 10, 1945 in [city given]; and, in June of 1955, they were separated as the father deserted the family. The father's whereabouts have remained unknown since the desertion. To the above union eight children were born, and the minor is the second oldest child. Subsequently the mother had four illegitimate children. Presently residing in the home are Ella, born December 10, 1947; Ronald, born December 11, 1949; Daniel, born March 2, 1951; Donna, born May 10, 1952; Ellen, birth date unknown; Vina, born April 17, 1954; Cuyo, born May 11, 1955; Vera, born July 21, 1956 (due to illegitimate union with a Mr. Ronald Sweeny, whom the mother had known for approximately two weeks); Romulo, born February 13, 1959; and Ellena, born December 17, 1961. Both Ellena and Romulo are products of an illegitimate union with a Mr. Walter Printer, who was married at the time. Another child Jane, born January 11, 1963, who now lives with the grandmother [address given], was the product of an illegitimate union with a Mr. Velez. . . .
>
> Mrs. Salazar explained she quit school in order to support herself and also explains that her husband left her because they argued constantly over his affairs with other women. . . . They have resided at this residence for approx. the last five years. The home is a stucco type tract home, located in a high delinquency area. The home is sparsely furnished and the furnishings show extensive use.

The probation officer's remarks begin with a reference to the husband's desertion, eight closely spaced children, and the existence of four additional children of illegitimate birth. The names of the fathers of the illegitimate children are also given, and the probation officer notes that the mother knew one father for "approximately two weeks." The remarks appear calculated, stressing the probation officer's interest in giving the reader a quick "understanding" of the case. Mentioning eight children in nine and one-half years and four illegitimate ones in eight years does not leave much to the imagination, but adding the remark about how long one father was known provides immediate reinforcement. The comment that "her husband left her because they argued constantly over his affairs with other women" does not provide "new" information about the case, but does remove any "doubts" the reader might have about "home." The probation officer also notes that the home is "located in a high delinquency area," and "the [sparse] furnishings show extensive use."

I shall begin the analysis of particular cases by discussing "Jorge" because there is little disagreement between police and probation as to "what happens" in such cases, even though probation may "gloss" the disposition, and it will do this by minimizing the criminal nature of the incident and stressing the "need for treatment." The description of the home, the juvenile being labeled as "mentally retarded," and the seriousness of the charge did not lead to a recommendation of a foster home because pressure was generated in the community to "get rid of the boy." Different groups spoke to both probation and police officials about the case, suggesting "something has gotta be done about the Mexican gangs." The case of Jorge "fits" the conceptions members of the community have about "conventional" delinquency. There are no surprises. The police and probation officials view the case as "the same old story." The police in City B spent most of their time attempting to document the details of how the incident occurred. They were not concerned with the juvenile's background, personal problems, and future possibilities. Probation officials viewed the case as typical of "kids who never had a chance." The extensive interviews conducted by the police, probation, and myself, suggest the incident as contingent upon a series of routine activities between the gangs involved. The issues described are those of territoriality, the beating of a lone member of one gang by several members of another gang, and social activities with girls.

The case of Jorge, therefore, seems to reflect the kind of juvenile activities and social environment sociological theories of delinquency have stressed. But as was indicated by the tabulated material in Chapter 5, the "serious" juvenile activities do not make up the majority or even a noticeable amount of incidents known to the police. I have, therefore, reduced my discussion of such cases because the problems of juvenile delinquency and the social organization of juvenile justice take on significance when examined in the context of other cases generated by day-to-day practical decision-making of agencies of social control.

Mark

One afternoon I accompanied a juvenile officer to one of the local high schools in City A to investigate a series of robberies in a neighborhood near the school. The officer had the names of several juveniles believed to be involved in the theft of $80.00 from a house on the same block on which they all lived. The officer had obtained information from neighbors that one of the boys seemed to have an unusual amount of money in his possession. We used the vice-principal's office to interview the juveniles. The officer's plan was to bring in first those he felt were "weakest," in the hope of having them place the blame on the one he felt was guilty and reported to have all of the money. The dialogue consisted of a direct accusation that the juvenile was the recipient of stolen money, and that the officer was in possession of the evidence for demonstrating this charge. The officer told the boy he was "basically a good kid," and he would consider being lenient if the boy made it easy on all concerned and told how the money was stolen. The style of interviewing was one of a "friendly," joking relationship, mixed with remarks that even though he was a "tough cop," the officer could still be lenient with the boy if the latter spoke up immediately. But the questions were posed rapidly and immediate answers were demanded as a way—or so it seemed to me—of confusing the boy so that he would blurt out an admission of guilt or participation. With each boy the officer would state that he had such and such information as to the juvenile's involvement in the incident, even though there was no such information. Then he would urge the boy to "cop out" and thereby receive leniency in the disposition of his case. If the boy admitted receiving some of the stolen money, the officer would seek to pinpoint what was done with the funds. The next boy would be told that the previous boy had "confessed" and implicated him. One boy kept denying this and only after the officer said "O.K., make it harder on yourself if you want. I hate to throw the book at you when I know you was only partly involved, but you don't leave me much choice if you won't come clean." The direct statement by the officer was intended to convince the boy it was only his obstinacy preventing the officer from helping him "get a break," and (a) it was obvious to the officer the boy was involved and therefore guilty, (b) a direct confession would mitigate his involvement, and (c) it was foolish for the boy to be charged with something he was only partly to blame for, implying he was a naive party to the offense and not a central figure. As each of the boys provided the officer with more concrete details of how they obtained some of the money and their participation in other delinquent activities in the neighborhood, the case against Mark seemed assured.

Mark was called in and directly accused of stealing the $80.00 and sharing it with his buddies. Mark denied it, saying, "I don't know what you're talking about." When told that all of the other boys had confessed and implicated him, Mark stated: "Oh yah, I just saw a couple of them and they told me you didn't know who did it." The officer now appeared very serious and in measured tones said: "Look, Mark, I'm through playing around with you. If you don't cop out right this very instant we're going to take a little trip to the [Juvenile] Hall. If you cop out then we'll go right home and I'll be easy on ya. I'm tough, Mark, but I'm always fair too. You play it straight with me and I'll give you a break too." Mark immediately denied any involvement. The officer then, with an attempt to be dramatic, opened the door leading to the office staff and called out that he was taking Mark to the Hall. We all walked out of the building in the direction of the police car. On the way the officer said there was still time for Mark to "re-think" his earlier proposition about going home instead of the Hall. The boy insisted he didn't steal the money. We entered the car and the officer started the motor. We remained in the parked car while the officer once more encouraged Mark to confess, reiterating the negative consequences of going to the Hall, and the possibility of being sent away from home for a long time. Suddenly the boy began crying and blurted out that he had stolen the money. We drove the boy home.

The officer would give a rapid rundown of his thoughts about each boy and his family during the course of the interrogation. His feelings about a particular boy seemed to be independent of the way the officer would distort the conversation to convince the juvenile he knew all about the incident. He felt that this particular group was all weak-character types always in trouble in the neighborhood, and it was simply a matter of "breaking them down" to clear many reported offenses for the area in which they resided. The officer was convinced Mark would "break down" at some point; it was a matter of timing and the "right" remarks. The imputation of a particular character type, as revealed by the use of a category like "wise guy," is routine when the boy is assumed to be mocking the officer's authority. The term "punk" is used by some, while other officers use "troublemaker," something general like "the kind of guy who's always playing around," or direct profanity.

The boys involved in the above case were from middle-income families. For the police they are bothersome to the neighborhood, but this was the first time Mark had been apprehended for something considered quite "serious." The conversation can be depicted as unilateral, with the police officer imputing a set of descriptive features that are unwarranted or warranted (as seen by others) within the context of the social scene. Viewed from the standpoint of the penal code, procedural due process, or the treatment-oriented juvenile court law, the conversation does not represent the model of impartial legal procedures oriented toward the dignity of the actor. I am suggesting, however, that both the police officer and the juvenile shared a system of relevances or meaning structures that could be described as "normal" for both. Therefore, the exchange for police officer and juvenile is part of a larger game that they participate in periodically and may expect to continue for the remainder of the age period that organizationally defines the official grounds for contact. The episode, therefore, was "life as usual" for all of the participants. The officer had been in contact with Mark on a previous occasion and had informally asked Mark to provide information on juvenile activities. In the station the information immediately relevant to the officer consisted of a 5 × 7 card (a "rap sheet") with the following information about past police contacts:

6/16/60	Possible neglect [victim]	Released (Patrol)
2/ 1/61	Neighborhood problem, mentioned as involved	
9/16/61	Bothering (removed manhole cover)	Released (Patrol)
2/15/62	Mischief (X high school)	Warned & Released, restitution
3/18/62	Child neglect (victim), unfounded	
8/ 2/62	Attempted arson	Warned & Released to parents
11/ 9/63	Threat to fight (victim)	Released
11/23/63	Mischief	Warned & Released, restitution
11/24/63	Trespass on construction	Released, restitution
8/ 3/64	Petty theft (wood) neighborhood problem	Warned & Released
9/21/64	Burglary	Petition
9/21/64	(also suspect on 2 burg, 1 P.T., 1 mal misch)	Warned & Released
10/23/64	Probation Dept., informal probation (6 mos) till 4/23/65, 9:30 p.m. [curfew]	
12/14/64	Battery (X assaulted by Y [both friends of Mark]) witness	
5/12/65	Incorrigible female, companion of	No contact
6/ 7/65	Petty theft cab fare (with Y and Z)	Petition

The above information can be clarified by reference to remarks contained in the official police reports. The line after the 9/21/64 entry indicates the point at which I no longer had contact with the case. The following quotations from official reports will indicate the content from which the above entries were made. [The original investigation began as a malicious mischief case involving Mark's younger sister L.]

6/16/60 Contacted informant, who stated that Mrs. F had returned some torn up mail to him a few minutes earlier. She told him she had found his mail plus a few other families mail in her back yard this afternoon. . . . Her next door neighbor, Mrs. C [Mark's mother] had no idea who had been taking the mail.

Writer then contacted Mrs. C. She stated that her daughter, L, had admitted taking the mail last Sat. However, L told her mother that she hadn't bothered the mail this date. Mrs. C stated she would keep a closer watch on L in the future. Possible that older children took the mail this date as the M's [victim] mail box is approx. 5 ft. above their porch & it would take at least a grammar school aged child to reach same. [Patrol Officer]

A follow-up report was made by the Juvenile Bureau after a neighbor called and (reactivated) the case. The following is taken from the follow-up report:

ATT. RECORDS: NOTE CHANGE OF HEADING TO POSSIBLE CHILD NEGLECT— 702, W & I Code. In regard to this investigation concerning the family at [Mark's home address], this writer was contacted by B. S. [girl B. S.'s address a few doors down the street], who identified herself as a part-time baby sitter for Mrs. C. The informant was aware of the report wherein Mrs. C's daughter, L. C. (4 years) had taken mail belonging to several neighbors on several occasions. Contrary to the information in this report, L had admitted taking the mail on May 16th. This admission was made to Mrs. S [baby sitter]. The neighbors' prime concern is for the welfare of this child L and a boy, Mark C. Mrs. S states that Mr. C is a plasterer and is usually gone from 7:00 a.m. until 5:00 p.m. Mrs. C is quite active in the [fraternal lodge], bowling, and other activities. These children are allowed to run the streets and are out at all hours of the day and many times until 10:00 o'clock at night. On Sunday, May 1st, Mrs. C left her daughter, L, with Mrs. S, stating she would be back at 6:30 p.m. for the child. However, Mrs. C never returned until 11:30 p.m. Mrs. C bowls three or four times a week. The house, according to Mrs. S, is a mess. As stated, she baby-sits quite often and she states the house is filthy. She believes, also, that most of the money goes for Mrs. C's entertainment, as the children quite often go to the neighbors for something to eat. The other day, B [Mrs. S] went to the house at 9:30 a.m. and the woman was still in bed. The child, L, was out on the streets, playing. When B [Mrs. S] woke Mrs. C., she asked B where L was and asked if she was wearing that blue dress. B looked for the child, found her, and brought her to her mother. The mother gave the child a spanking and made her remove the blue dress, as she did not want her to wear it. Apparently, the child dressed herself as usual, and this time took a dress her mother did not want her to wear. This was the situation, instead of the woman being up to take care of this duty herself. B wishes to remain anonymous, if possible but she does feel that the children are being neglected. She adds that a good scare might wake this woman up to her responsibilities. She will advise the outcome, after our talk with the woman. [Juvenile officer]

The obvious point to be made initially is that what started as a routine complaint about small children engaged in mail-tampering was transformed after the Juvenile Bureau received a copy of the patrol officer's report and then a telephone call from the baby-sitter neighbor. The acts by the children were displaced in importance by the clear suggestion that the case was really one of child neglect. The Juvenile Bureau now becomes interested in intruding because of a neighbor's complaint. The officer quickly identifies the neighbor's interests as the "welfare of this child L and a boy" and, thereby, the Juvenile Bureau's interest. The neighbor provides the officer with a description that he interprets as a kind of behaviorized version of what happened by an interested but objective third party. The phrases "run the streets," "all hours of the day and many times until 10:00 o'clock at night," instead of being "back at 6:30 p.m . . . never returned until 11:30 p.m.," "house . . . is a mess," "money goes for Mrs. C's entertainment," while the children "go to the neighbors for something to eat," and the mother is irresponsible in caring for the girl and punishes her because "this time [the girl] took a dress her mother did not want her to wear," and the like, all provide the officer with relevant activities for deciding the case warrants further investigation. Notice how the officer begins to use the informant's first name toward the end of the report, suggesting how both the informant and officer now "see" the situation identically, that a reciprocity of perspectives exists, presuming the existence of similar relevance or meaning structures about "what is going on." The neighbor also provides the remedy; "a good scare might wake this woman up to her responsibilities." The category "mother" is being called into doubt, and the report provides behavioral referents for questioning structural notions of status and role, and specifies the kind of activities "third parties" and law-enforcement officials respond to as deviant. The evidence that the mother is falling short of "community expectations" as seen by the neighbor and police officer is provided in the charges of mail tampering, "filthy" house, uncontrolled children's activities, alleged misuse of money, etc. The picture is not complete as yet because we do not have the additional follow-up report made by the juvenile officer after interviewing Mrs. C.

When this officer arrived at the C residence it was after 10.00 a.m. Milk bottles were on the front steps, and children's toys and clothing were littering the front yard. Mrs. C came to the door in her nightgown, and she had been in bed. After being admitted into the house, it was observed to be strewn with papers, clothing, blankets, dirty dishes on the floor and on the furniture. Mrs. C excused herself to tend to the baby, who was crying. She also dressed and returned. Mrs. C was asked where L was, and she said "outside, playing." Shortly after, L entered the house, where she was asked if she had eaten breakfat. She said "no." Mrs. C interrupted, saying, "she never eats breakfast, even when I cook it." L was asked if she dressed herself. She said "yes." Mrs. C said, "she always dresses herself." L was asked if her mother goes out often at night. L said that she goes out almost every night. She said that her father baby-sits, but when he goes to bed, they get up and go outside.

Mrs. C was asked about L going outdoors at night, and she said, "one time, L went over to a neighbor's house at 9:30 p.m. Can you imagine the neighbor letting her stay that late. I was bowling that night, and wasn't home." Mrs. C was asked if she is still bowling; she said, "no, just the winter league." She stated that she was at home all the time, and when she goes anywhere, she takes her children with her, or gets a babysitter. She went on to say that she arises at 5:45-6:00 a.m. to fix her husband's breakfast, and then goes back to bed. Mrs. C was asked if Mark fixed his own breakfast. She said that he always does, even when she is up to fix it.

Mrs. C was warned about what would happen to L if she were found wandering around the streets again late at night. She was advised that her daughter would be taken to Juv. Hall. The neighbors were all advised to call the [City A] P.D. if L were out late again. An inter-office memo will be sent to the Watch Commander of the third watch, requesting that the Patrolman in the area keep a lookout for L. [Signed by a different juvenile officer than the one who spoke to the neighbor.]

When I visited the C home four years later in connection with the burglary Mark was charged with, the home appeared as described by the second juvenile officer, and there was now another baby in Mrs. C's arms as she walked out of her bedroom at about 10:30 a.m. when we arrived with Mark from school. The descriptions of the home, therefore, are not being challenged, but the use being made of such descriptions at the time of the interrogation, and how such information is passed along to other officers investigating future incidents. Notice how each element (dirty house, feeding the children, bowling, the girl staying out late) of the first follow-up report is mentioned by the officer who interviewed Mrs. C.

What is significant about the second investigating officer's interrogation of Mrs. C is that his report suggested that grounds for calling the matter child neglect were substantiated to *his* satisfaction, based upon questions that corresponded closely to issues raised by the neighbor. But the evidence was not viewed as "adequate" for officially charging Mrs. C with child neglect; however, the family became known to other officers, particularly in the juvenile bureau, as one where a "bad" family situation existed. The officer continually assumed there was child neglect ("asked if she had eaten breakfast, . . ." "if she dressed herself," "if her mother goes out often at night," "Mrs. C was asked about L going outdoors at night,") throughout his interrogation, and left little doubt of his negative view of the mother and his intention to keep careful watch for future infractions. Subsequent trouble in the neighborhood always led the police to Mark, and future encounters with the police must be negotiated within the context of the police characterization of the home as "bad." I want to stress that Mark and his family fit the police conception of "normal" causes of delinquency, and officers will thereafter "expect" Mark to be in trouble. But I am not saying that the police created Mark's trouble, or that Mark did not engage in activities considered delinquent by the community. Many juvenile activities that might go unnoticed or regarded as "minor" pranks will not be so viewed by the juvenile officers vis-à-vis Mark, because he now fits their conception of the potential delinquent, and they will seek him out whenever there is reported "trouble" in his neighborhood. Routine juvenile activities, therefore, can be turned into serious "delinquent acts."

The next incident reported on the file card states "Neighborhood problem, mentioned as involved." The report reads as follows:

> Mrs. A states quite a problem has developed in her neighborhood mainly with a family named C. She states the children in that family are allowed to run the neighborhood at all hours and are constantly making nuisances of themselves. . . . Mrs. A states L came to another neighbors door with some of Mrs. A mail yesterday this was 1-31-61 and Mrs. A does not know what to do about the situation as she states she and her husband both receive checks through the mail and they never know when one of these is going to turn up missing. Mrs. A was advised the juv. div. would get a copy of this report to determine if further contacts were needed also Mrs. A was advised a mail slot through the door is a very good preventitive of the above since all the mail then falls into the house. [Patrol Officer]

The report was received and acknowledged by the Juvenile Bureau, but no further action taken. The entry, however, implicates the boy, even though it was the girl who was said to have taken the mail; all of the children "run the neighborhood." The report does not allow the Juvenile Bureau to follow through on child neglect charges. Depending on how busy the officers are at the time the patrol report crosses the Sergeant's desk, he could make the entry on the card file and forget the matter until further notice, or assign an officer to make a routine investigation.

Several months later, another entry appears on the card as "Bothering, removed manhole cover." The report states the following:

> To prevent further incidents of this nature [Mark and juvenile neighbor removed manhole cover leaving the opening exposed] where someone might be hurt by falling into the opening the writer contacted the above named boys and their mothers. Mrs. O [mother of juvenile neighbor involved] stated that she has four sons and has to work at the local newspaper to support the family. The juveniles have been causing the lady some trouble of late and the lady appreciated the writer's talk with her son. Mrs. C was also appreciative of this department's interest in the matter before someone was injured and a law suit resulted against her family. . . . Since there was no actual damage done and since it is felt that the juveniles will learn a lesson from the writer's contact and their

parents discipline no further action appears necessary in this matter." [Patrol officer who has never had contact with the families in question.]

There was no juvenile bureau follow-up investigation of the patrol officer's report.

The following entry states "Mischief (X high school)." Mark's name is mentioned on the juvenile officer's report, and the officer notes that it is not clear who actually started breaking open lockers. The officer notes that Mark denies participating in the incident. Mark's name does not figure in the report at any other place or in the officer's description of the principal suspects. The entry on the card, however, does not mention Mark's denial of participation, nor the fact that his name does not figure as a principal suspect. For any officer examining the card (for it is unlikely that the original report will be consulted in the record room), Mark was a regular participant in the incident. The report stated Mark was one of the "smaller boys" involved. The report stated that "B and K [two older boys] were called to the office and they also admitted that they had broken open lockers, but maintained that they saw smaller boys doing it first." There is no indication in the report, therefore, that Mark was viewed as a critical participant, and no special mention of his name was made.

The following month, patrol was called to investigate the possibility of child neglect at the C residence. The officer decided that Mark, now thirteen, was old enough to care for the smaller children he was left with for two hours. The officer did remark that "other than the house being somewhat untidy, a little more than usual, the children did not seem to be sick or improperly cared for. . . ." There was no follow-up report by the Juvenile Bureau and the card file entry reads "Child Neglect (victim), unfounded." Mrs. C was using Mark as a baby sitter, and the neighbors were still interested enough to call the police.

Several months later during the summer, there was a call by neighbors that some boys were making fire bombs, like Molotov cocktails, and were tossing them into a storm drain. Mark's name did not figure significantly in the episode, but the police report listed him as one of the group involved. One "bomb" was placed in the garage of one of the boys, but it was not set off. It was never determined by the police who was "lying" about the incident. Everyone refused to implicate others, and the officer merely reported the incident with no follow-up. Mark's card file now contained the entry "Attempted Arson."

The next entry did not appear for over a year and stated "Threat to Fight (victim)." The actual report listed the incident as "Suspicious juveniles—X theatre." The report reads as follows:

Received a call to contact a Mr. S the Asst. Mgr at the theater regarding some business selling illegal knives to juveniles. S stated a male juvenile ID as Mark C, age 12, told him that another male juvenile was going to cut his balls off when he was in the rest room. S rounded up the juveniles and found a pocket knife belonging to one B. H., age 12 [address follows] (poss ficticious name and number) accompanied by M. S., age 12, [address follows]. S stated that H told him he bought the knife at the Greyhound and paid $1.30 for it. S took the knife from H and let him go. He then attempted to call the boys phone number so as to advise his parents, but found the number belonging to someone else. H may have gave the informant a ficticious name and phone number. . . . The knife was legal and a check at the Greyhound found that the knives are sold there. S stated that no attempt was made to castrate C [Mark], just a threat was made. S felt that such a large knife shouldn't be legal (5 in) and sold to youngster. [Patrol]

Mark's involvement as a victim was not a focal point of the police report, but, as shown in the follow-up report below, the potential suspect was of interest. The follow-up report by the juvenile sergeant points to a recurrent problem the police complain about vis-à-vis the probation department: that warnings about juveniles go unheeded and result in worse incidents later, because probation is too lenient with cases referred to them by the police.

The fact that the subject of this report who had the knife and made the threat is on probation a copy of this report was sent to that dept regarding the boy: B.E.H., [address and date of birth follows]. This boy was originally made a ward of Ct on 3/16/61 as a result of our Inv. . . . On 10/3/63 an additional petition request was sent down to the probation dept regarding this boy under our Inv. . . . but that request was handled by his Probation Officer and never reached juvenile court of the judge, but was handled by his P.O. Copy of this report to Probation Dept.

For the police, the incident leads to another entry for Mark (even though he is the presumed victim in the case) and calls attention to an irritating problem that juveniles have with probation officials. The police report assumes that their previous action on B.E.H. is *clearly* documented by the present behavior of the youth. The logic of police reasoning is: their judgments are accurate; and an adversary is unnecessary for recommending controls because of taking for granted the "obvious" character of what had happened previously. In view of the preoccupation of police with social control, their analysis is supported by their action, so that original estimates are "documented" by subsequent actions, enabling officers to fit new events to past interpretations. Once the pattern has been indicated, usually in general form but with vague or, at least, inconclusive evidence, all subsequent readings are likely to preclude the relevance of fortuitous elements, independent causality, or the possibility of change in the juvenile's future actions.

Returning to Mark, we see that the next entry is called "Mischief." The official report by the patrol officer sent to investigate states the following:

> Received a call to contact the informant, Mrs. Osburn about some suspicious juveniles. Mrs. Osburn stated that about six teen age juveniles were getting up and hanging on the street signs at the corner of S and S, causing the signs to bend down. The signs had been bent before but Mrs. O stated her husband had straightened the signs. The juveniles also had taken some Plumes from Pampus grass and set fire to them. While the plumes were burning they poked them at each other. . . . [The juveniles were gone by the time the officer arrived.]

The supplementary report written after the juvenile officer investigated the incident states the following:

> Through a tip regarding one boy in this group (S.O., R., J.N.J., M.C.) all of [same street, where M.C. is Mark], and H.Z. of [address of latter given] and through questioning him and others connected with him, writer was able to determine that the subjects listed above were responsible for this act and for many other miscellaneous acts of rowdyism in their neighborhood and in [shopping center named]. These boys all admit to this, although they claim that O who did most of the physical damage, and with all the rest doing some. Also, through this investigation, we were able to clear our Inv. . . . (headed "suspicious circumstances") and Inv. . . . (headed Petty Theft and Malicious Mischief), wherein they were stealing gas caps and leaving them in the seats of people's cars. This was done by R. and O. [Note that this juvenile officer was also the same one who did the interrogating that was reported at the beginning of the case on Mark. This brief report summarizes several hours of intensive interviewing of the same type described above.]
>
> In addition to these offenses, these boys have been plaguing the merchants in [shopping center named] by ringing the delivery bells at the rear of their places of business; and when the people come to the door, they make smart remarks and laugh at the persons who answered the bell. Usually, it is O who opens his mouth with smart remarks, but the other boys think this is just great. We had a long discussion, with the parents concurring in all ways, as to what will happen to them if their conduct continues along this line. They have all been forbidden to associate or to communicate with each other in any way until Monday, December 2nd. If these rules are broken in any particular, the parents will call this officer and we will place him (or them) in Juvenile Hall under this heading: Malicious Mischief, plus 601, W & I Code. Undoubtedly, this is not the last we have heard of this group, or least some of the individuals involved." [Note that R was one of the "older" boys involved in school locker incident mentioned above. The O boy is well known to juvenile bureau and viewed as a chronic "trouble-maker."]

Notice how "through questioning" that remains unclear, the officer "was able to determine that the subjects listed above were responsible for this act and for many other. . . ." The reader must supply the sequences of interaction that would render the officer's remarks "obvious." The officer's language leaves little doubt as to his including the juveniles in a "delinquent set." The officer's language is fairly graphic in depicting the kind of "rowdyism" considered to be an integral feature of delinquency. The "smart remarks" and bell ringing and "laughs" indicate not having the "right attitude" toward adults. The threat of being sent to Juvenile Hall as punishment is a routine part of police interrogation, even though it is unlikely the juveniles would be accepted or detained by probation for such charges. It is difficult to portray the parental reactions suggested by the officer independently of his statements. The report is more a blanket basis for future police action, than a clear indication of parental support for police interpretations of juvenile problems. In City B, patrol officers are less likely to settle for the same threats or attempt to send the juveniles to Juvenile Hall; instead, they are placed in the city jail overnight or over the weekend if possible as a means of punishment. The juveniles O and R are cases the police have indicated to me they disliked rather intensely and were always looking for ways of punishing them. Both boys are viewed as "leaders" who exploit younger boys as accomplices in getting their stealing accomplished, and the police feel the use of the younger boys for this purpose often neutralizes the legal measures they can take against O and R when filing an application for petition.

The following entry states "Trespass on Construction" and adds "Released, restitution." The patrol officer sent to investigate mentioned the names of R, Z, O, and Mark, the same boys involved in the last incident. The official report lists the incident as "Juveniles Bothering." The report follows:

> Arrived and learned that the above 4 juveniles were playing in the basement of the above location. Informant, worker (writer failed to get his name) stated that these kids are a big problem, that numerous small thefts have taken place, along with numerous acts of malicious mischief. . . . Might note that the boys were just playing in the basement (hide and seek) and no damage found by this officer. [No other investigation made by the juvenile bureau.]

Notice that the file card entry implies that some kind of restitution was made, presumably because of damage incurred by the juveniles; yet the patrol officer states on the official report that no damage was evident to him and that it appeared to be a case of "boys just playing in the basement (hide and seek)." Recall that the juvenile officer does not refer back to the original report but only to the entry on the file card. Therefore, according to the file card, Mark would be viewed as having been involved in damaging the construction area.

About nine months later Mark's file card reveals the following entry: "Petty Theft (wood), neighborhood problem—warned and released." Mark and

J.N.J. were apparently involved in stealing wood from a neighbor and were seen by another neighbor named Mrs. D. The patrol officer reports that:

> . . . Mrs. D. stated that she became alarmed over the size of the fire stating the flames were going approx. 10′ to 15′ in the air, that she was hesitant about calling the police as there is usually a large amount of juvenile boys and girls holding parties in the rear yard and that her husband is stationed in Korea and she is afraid that the youths may cause damage to her or her home.
>
> Writer proceeded to [Mark's home address given] and knocked several times on the door which was finally answered by a small girl, approx. 7 yrs of age who stated that her mother was in bed sleeping and that her brother was sleeping in the yard. Writer proceeded to rear of yard, the condition of said yard deplorable. Mark and J. were sleeping in sleeping bags on canvas cots. Writer noticed a large amount of wood stacked in the barbecue pit and along side the pit in a cardboard box. The boys were awakened but stated they did not take the wood. Further questioning was done whereupon J. admitted taking the wood and that Mark had told him it was okay as the lady was a friend of theirs and that she wouldn't object. Writer talked with the young girl again and asked to speak with the mother. Mrs. C., [first name of mother and father given here] came to rear door where writer explained his presence and circumstances. Mrs. C. said the woman was a friend but that she sure wasn't acting like one now. Both the boys were informed to pile the wood up and return it to the owner and that an apology was in order. This was done by the boys.

From the file card and the official report it seems clear that an offense had been committed. The statement that "further questioning was done whereupon J. admitted taking the wood and that Mark had told him it was okay" does not reveal, as usual, the kinds of interrogation that preceded the admission of guilt. Mark and his mother independently commented that the woman from whose house the wood was taken is "a friend." This negation of offense on the grounds that the woman is a friend is also revealed in the following statement by the juvenile officer's follow-up report:

> Contacted the mothers of the two suspects, C. and J., and found that [the neighbor] has let children in the neighborhood have scrap lumber in the past. This lumber is obtained by Mr. [neighbor] at construction sites where he works. Restitution for the burned lumber will be made and the lumber that was not burned was returned.
>
> This matter handled on the warned and released basis with restrictions being imposed by the parents.

The supplementary report is not clear as to how the neighbor felt about the wood being removed, but merely sustains the possibility that both the neighbor and local juveniles might have had some kind of agreement about its justified removal. The event was not handled as a serious case.

The following entry, "Burglary—Petition," brings us to the point at which we entered above. The juvenile officer (the same one who handled the trespass on construction incident) received a tip from another juvenile that Mark was overheard "this morning talking with group of children about splitting up money; several other houses supposed to have been hit, but people don't want to get involved." (From the officer's informal notes.) The interrogation of Mark and his friends at the high school I described earlier followed. The following report represents a highly truncated version of the actual interviews conducted. It reveals how the juvenile officer (along with an interpretation of the file card entries that was pointedly revealed to the researcher as an example of "a kid whose been in trouble all the time") now "sees" the past activities in light of the present offense of residential burglary. What is instructive about the report is not the fact of guilt or innocence— Mark admitted this after the long interview and after threats about spending time in Juvenile Hall—but the way each juvenile is characterized in terms of the routine background expectancies employed by juvenile officers:

> Through neighborhood checks, listening to rumors, questioning various people, the main suspect, who later admitted the charge, Mark C. was determined. Also this investigation incorporates the investigating of [file number] Burglary—not cleared, [file number], Burglary, not cleared [file number], Mal Misch, not cleared, [file number] Mal Misch, cleared, P.T. Gas caps, [file number], [file number], not cleared entirely. Mark admits to this burglary and partial restitution has been made. The other two burglaries [file number] and [file number] which it would appear that he is responsible for, he refuses to admit; and it is quiet possible that I.R. is the responsible person, but not provable. In this burglary Mark did not use the same M.O. that was used in the other two burglaries. Through neighbors and other type of info it was understood that Mark had more money than usual in his possession. Also through the neighborhood they complained of Mark, J.R., and J. of stealing gas caps, malicious mischief and just tearing up the neighborhood in general. All of these things discussed with these boys as they were interviewed.
>
> J.N.J.—Denied that he had been involved in this burglary. He did say that he had ditched school with Mark the day after it happened and that Mark had paid him a dollar he owed him. J. also admitted that he has been stealing gas caps for kicks and was made to pay back the money for one to a person that he could remember specifically stealing. He was warned about this and further activity and told that next time he would be referred to court. His mother also made aware of this.
>
> J.R.—Admitted the Mark had told him that he had committed burglary and that Mark had given him $20.00 of the money taken from the burglary. He also admitted being along when some of the trouble in the neighborhood developed. He claims that J. is the one that steals the gas caps, but he and his friends don't do anything about it when J. does these things. J.R. was warned against

his friends, malicious mischief, his Petty Thefts that this officer is sure that he and his friends pull; and he was made to return the $20.00 to this officer and that money returned to the victim.

Mark—Mark admitted the burglary, but denies the others. He outlined how he had spend some of the money and given some to J.R. He as well as J.R. admitted that they had made up a story that Mark had found the money by [shopping center], but that J.R. knew all along where he had gotten it. Mark also puts most of the stealing of the gas caps on N.J., but admits that he and J.R. have in the past have taken a couple of them. He was warned about this, his friends and informed as well as his mother, that a petition for Burglary would be filed. Mark returned to this Officer $30.00 that he still had left from the original $80.00 that he had stolen. The total returned to the victim comes to $50.00. Mark should, by the Probation Dept., be made to give the victim the other $30.00.

Mark said that O. told him that L. R. had told him that it was he that stole the money from his mother.

O.—Was questioned about everything. He said that he had heard and figured that it was Mark that pulled this burglary, but denies that L. R. told him that he had stole the money from his mother. O. also said that he doubted that he would tell me the truth if he knew that it was L. R. He was also warned and released.

L.R.—Was not questioned if he stole the money from his mother. We are still working on that angle. As of this writing it is felt that it should not be mentioned to him yet. L.R. did help with info that pinned this on Mark, but at the time it was strange how he did it, so it is possible that he did steal the money from his mother and see's a chance to pin it on Mark. This case at this time has been carried as far as possible. The $50.00 returned to the victim and it was suggested to him that he contact the Probation Dept. for restitution. Also it was suggested to Mrs. C. that she and her boy contact the victim and make arrangements for this, she said she would, but knowing them it is doubtful."

An important feature of the above report is its similarity to the way adult criminal investigation proceeds: the use of informants, whatever interrogation procedures the suspect will become party to, the attempt to link the case with other cases not cleared, the continual use of threats (but with room for negotiation). In all of the interviews, the officer sought to bargain with the juveniles if they would "come clean, and cop out." Both the actual interview exchanges and the official report reveal a language that leaves little doubt as to the officer's belief in the guilt of the suspects; he states flatly to them and in the report that he is sure of their guilt in many offenses that he cannot "prove." There is no suggestion in this report that we are dealing with "wayward youth" who need a "helping hand," but, instead, with juveniles who engage in continuous criminal activity ("it was Mark that pulled this burglary") throughout the area ("stealing gas caps, malicious mischief and just tearing up the neighborhood in general"). The previous indications that the home situation was "bad" merely confirm the "fact" of the existence of a basic delinquent type who is running around with worse types. The file card information was shown to me as a confirmation of gradual criminal development. The present burglary was viewed as the "break" leading to some concrete action (a petition filing) to punish the youth for continual delinquent activities. The additional entry for 9/21/64 on the file card states "also suspect on 2 burg—1 P.T.—1 mal misch," and is intended to document the fact of further involvement that cannot be "proved" at the time of the writing. Notice how the officer continually tells the juveniles that he "is sure that he and his friends pull" petty thefts or engage in malicious mischief. The officer's reference to the possibility of L.R. stealing money from his mother and attempting "to pin it on Mark" is not clarified by the officer. The officer has concluded a causal chain to his present satisfaction based upon his background expectancies. But the expectancies are not explicit elements for revealing a determination of "the facts." The officer's final remark to Mrs. C that restitution be made to the victim ended with "but knowing them it is doubtful" that they will in fact make restitution, makes it clear how the kinds of negative remarks he revealed in the actual interview are telescoped into the report and how the report would be informed by his observations and evaluations during the interview.

In an earlier chapter, I suggested the police sought to establish a "trust" relationship with the juvenile during early delinquent encounters that amounted to a preliminary probation arrangement. When the "trust" is viewed as broken by the police then they invoke criminal categories and relevances to explain the juvenile's actions and to construct and seek to justify a disposition. The "trust" relationship, however, assumes the juvenile is able to convey some kind of sincerity to the officers involved so that "treatment" as opposed to a "punishment oriented" disposition is discussed and prescribed. The case of Mark does not always reveal direct criminal imputations because all of the juvenile officers (the file card record reveals that he has seen several of them) viewed him as a "fresh punk," considered to be basically "weak and scared," who follows the leadership of two peers and will not "wise up." The police feel Mark seeks to impress them and his buddies with the idea that he is a "tough guy," and does not have the "right attitude" toward them and other authority figures. One of Mark's friends, noted above, comes from a family where both parents are college-educated and have professional occupations. There is a penciled notation by the police report on the burglary case that states one of Mark's peers is a "real problem—Psychotic." Without denying the involvement of the juveniles mentioned above, present circumstances lead the police to reread the past entries as a causal sequence leading to more serious crimes and to disregard legal issues when handling particular cases they "know" are "guilty."

Mark received informal probation for the burglary because there was no probation record other than the burglary report. The police viewed this as another example of how "soft" the probation department was on "kids" they viewed as "punks" and had known for a long time. The file card shows three more entries that should be mentioned briefly. The entry for 12/14/64 states that Mark was a witness to a fight between J.R. and J.N.J. The police report does not implicate Mark. The entry for 5/12/65 suggests that Mark was a companion of an incorrigible female. According to the official report, the girl is a neighbor of Mark's and went across the street to visit him when she noticed his light was still on. The girl's mother reported her missing to the police. The girl was crossing the street heading back for her home when the police arrived. The mother did not request an investigation. The officer stated that ". . . anything that happens in the future, she will notify this dept. & make an appointment. No contact was made with Mark C." The final entry states that Mark, along with J.N.J. and O., were picked up for petty theft of a cab driver's fare. According to the patrol officer's report, three boys entered a cab in a remote section of the city and told the driver they had had an accident with their car and had no money. The driver was asked to cash a check and agreed to do so if proof or identity could be established. The driver was told that either a check or the money could be obtained from the suspect's uncle and the driver agreed to take them there. While driving near the juvenile's home they told the driver that the uncle was probably visiting at an address nearby (their own neighborhood). The driver pulled into the driveway of the designated house and the three youths fled. The police could not find the abandoned vehicle. The Juvenile Bureau then investigated the case and reported the following:

> Writer checked at the address where the three suspects had gotten the ride in the cab [address follows] and found that the three boys had walked up to the house and had asked to use the phone to call a cab as they had run off the road in their car in the [name of area given] and disabled the car. The occupant of the house stated that he could identify the three youths if need be. Writer and Det [name] then checked out the [name of area] and on one of the dirt roads found where a: [description of vehicle and registered owner's name given—owner listed as J.N.J.'s mother] Had run off the road and was still sitting there. It appeared that the car had lost control and upon going off the road ran over a boulder and caused the gas tank to come loose and apparently hang up on the soft shoulder of the road.
>
> Contacted Mrs. J. [states place of employment] and found that her son had permission to use the car on Monday evening to drive up to the hills to go snake hunting. She was not sure who else was with her son J. but he had told of running off the road and getting stuck. She knew that a tow truck was neces-

sary to tow the car home. She was advised of the cab incident and that three boys had run off without paying the fare. An appointment was made for J. to come in and see writer this a.m.

J.J. came to the Juv Bur at 9 AM date and admitted to writer that he had been with Mark C. and S.O. that evening. After running off the roadway they walked the several (approx 3 or 4) miles to the address on [street name given]. They used the phone there and called for a cab. J. stated S.O. gave the cab driver the statements that his uncle would give them money for the fare, and that he directed the cab driver to the [address where they fled]. He felt all three of them were responsible for not paying. Arrangements were made with Mrs. J. to pay the fare which amounted to $4.80. ($1.60 for each boy). (She will be paid back by the other two boys). A receipt is to be brought in to writer by J. at 9 AM on 6/10/65 to show where [name] Cab Company has been paid. Found that neither O. nor C. were attending school this date. Went by the C. residence and talked to Mark and his mother. Mark lied at first about what they did and he had to be told that writer knew of them taking a cab back to the area of [street] and then running off without paying the fare. He then admitted to writer and his mother that this happened. He stated that O. got out of the cab and stated "shag ass" and they took off running down the midblock walkway to a field located at the rear of the residences. They later went on home by the back streets. In talking to Mrs. C. she related that she had been told by Mark that he was going snake hunting with S.O. and that Mrs. O. was driving them to the hills. She stated that she has forbid her son with associating with the J. boy. She will see that Mrs. J. is refunded for the portion of the cab fare that she was to pay for Mark's behalf. Mark's attitude was not to good at first and he was suppose to be home with the stomach flu. He did not appear to be sick. When writer first walked in the house he was observed to be sitting down and talking to someone on the phone. He was smoking a cigarette.

Writer was able to contact the O. boy and his mother by phone. S. admitted his part in the failure to pay for the cab fare. In questioning Mrs. O. about her son not being in school on the date of this incident (monday) she stated that he had the stomach flu and was at home. He got better and let him go out that evening. She did not actually know who he was with while he was gone. She is not on speaking terms with the J's so she would not have expected her son to be with J.J. She also stated she does not approve of the way J. drives. She will also see that $1.00 is paid to Mrs. J. for her sons part of the cab fare.

Disposition: J.J. is presently on formal probation with his PO being Mr. S. This matter was talked over with him and it was decided that this report concerning J. will be handled on a referral basis with him with action to be taken by the Probation Officer. Mark C. was on informal probation for a 6 month period and was recently excused from this program. During those 6 months he pretty well stayed out of trouble and was not contacted for any violations of the law by this dept. A petition will be filed on his behalf and a disposition as to possibly putting the boy back on probation will be made by the Prob. Dept.

S.O. has a court hearing on 6/11/65 regarding a prior Petition. Mr. S. of the Prob. Dept was talked to regarding this matter and a Petition regarding this theft will also be submitted to the Prob. Dept.

The above material was written by a different police officer than the one who handled the burglary case. While the officers inform each other on the same youths being handled continuously, differences in the ways in which they typify juveniles, interrogate, and reach a decision on disposition varies with the "mesh" between the social types they employ. The organizational procedures, suggested earlier, whereby a progressive and reified transformation of the juvenile object occurs over time, leading to categorical statements about the youth's social character (e.g., "he is a punk") are not always well-ordered, sequential operations.

The cab incident is, for the police, a clear-cut case of delinquency, and the first half of the report establishes the causal sequence of the incident and fixes the blame on all three boys. It does not reveal how the police officer obtained the information or conversed with Mrs. J. or her son. Finding the car and contacting the party from whose house the telephone call for a cab had been made provided the police with a solid case. Little urging was required by the police officer. The additional information about O.'s and Mark's absence from school and the recovery that permitted them to accompany J. provides clues as to the officer's reasoning about the juveniles' "bad" intentions. The remark that "Mark lied at first" further implicated Mark as an untrustworthy object. Mark's statement that it was O. who said "shag ass" could be read as an indication of O.'s leadership in directing the incident, since it was his uncle they were supposed to contact for the money. The officer's account suggests the signal to "shag ass" was planned in advance; the possibility of O. deciding to take such a course of action and creating pressure on the others to follow him is not provided in the description rendered in the report. Mark's presence in the area where the car was found is partially documented by Mrs. C. when she states he was to go snake-hunting with S.O., and Mrs. O. was to do the driving. The relationship of the three mothers of the juveniles is brought out when both Mrs. C. and Mrs. O. comment on Mrs. J., stating the boys should not have been together. The officer's remark that "Mark's attitude was not too good at first" is not clarified, but there are presumed "hints" in the remark on the "stomach flu" absence, followed by the officer's comment about the boy being on the phone when he arrived and smoking a cigarette. The remarks suggest the officer intended a causal relationship between Mark's "bad attitude," his lying, his questionable "illness," and his smoking. Later in the report the officer states Mark had been on probation and seemed to have stayed out of trouble, but felt that the boy should be placed back on probation and was filing a petition "on his behalf." The remark about Mark's probation, "he pretty well stayed out of trouble," suggests the absence of police contact and makes it difficult to recommend more than the resumption of probation. The report does not reveal the dialogue leading to the recommended disposition. The bargaining, whereby the police seek to elicit remorse from the juvenile and some indication of reform (or where they flatly tell the youth he is being watched constantly and any deviation, no matter how slight, will lead to a petition and recommendation that he be sent to the Youth Authority), is masked effectively by the formal report, even though some clues are revealed by the style and actual language of the remarks. There are differences in the language employed, but language differences do not always discriminate between different officers, unless some of the paralinguistic properties of voice intonation and gestures could be objectified. Differences in education background and the officers' ability to write reports mask the kinds of remarks they make during actual encounters with juveniles. Therefore, a juvenile's fate is contingent upon how a particular officer (at a given *here* and *now*) interprets his past activities as revealed on the summary file card, whom he asks for advice or information about the youth from other officers, the kind of behavioral performance enacted by the juvenile during the interrogation procedures, and the parental responsiveness or lack of interest as evaluated by the officer. The fact that the juvenile's organizational record is subject to differential evaluations (and can be reevaluated on any given occasion) means that transformations of the juvenile object always remain unwritten in part, since the formal reports reflect truncated views of actual encounters, and vary by type of officer on the case.

The organizational characterizations of the juvenile, however, become reified social structures because commitments are made to the nature of social relationships between officer and juvenile as well as juvenile and juvenile, or the lack of comment may lead to the presumption that no problems exist with the parents, or that the parents are "adequate" in some unstated sense. The police officer is convinced that what he "knows" about the juvenile is accurate and stands as adequate evidence for his official and unofficial characterizations. The police, even in adult cases where they are aware of the legal problems involved, do not feel that legal rules of evidence are adequate guides for supporting their characterizations. The police "know" what they "know," and the problem of legal evidence becomes unnecessarily problematic for their routine procedures.

Providing accurate descriptions of actual encounters is difficult. Even a video-tape transcription is not convincing for the showing of the objective character of the meanings intended and understood by the participants. The researcher's theory is a necessary part of explicating "what happened." Yet video tapes and transcriptions must provide the raw materials for showing the meaning structures of conversations as integral to an analysis of documents, such as organizational reports, where the managed character of social meanings is more difficult to disentangle. Notice, however, that my participation and observational experiences constitute a nonobjectified source of information when describing the significance of the materials presented. The police must then find ways of incorporating their conceptions into legal terminology. The language of the law, like printouts from a computer, does not contain precise behavioral properties of the objects and events being described and evaluated. The police materials on "Mark" suggest how depictions of social character, family life, and prognosis are generated as practical activities and not legal rules of procedure. The following case provides additional materials from probation and school officials.

Smithfield

In presenting material on Smithfield Elston, I stress more than another "case study." The excerpts cited below represent the comments of many people about the same actor over time. There is more than a police view (but contrasts within school and probation views) to reveal elements in the production of a juvenile career.

Smithfield's delinquent career began officially a few months after his parents were separated in County A, in a city not far from City A. As a Negro (from a broken home) on welfare, Smithfield's case seems to fit existing theories about how delinquency is produced. When compared to Mark, however, Smithfield's career is more dramatic and accelerated vis-à-vis contact with law-enforcement authorities. His summary card file reads as follows:

3/ 9/61	Juvenile Court Order (Petition)	—Ward of court (burglary-school) released to parents
12/19/61	Burglary (receation center)	Refer to probation officer
1/15/62	Burglary—junior high school	—To Juv. Hall—petition filed
2/ 8/62	Juv. court order declared in violation of probation	—Released to parents
3/12/62	Petty theft, defiance of authority at school	—Suspended, refer to probation
4/ 5/62	Juv. court order: continued ward of court	—Placed in suitable foster home
9/ 5/63	Burglary [city near A]	—To the Youth Authority
3/18/64	IOD (burglary)—[city near to A]	—Released to officer from other city
6/ 8/64	Petty theft (tires and wheels)	—To Juv. Hall, petition
7/ 9/64	Juv. Court Order—California Youth Authority warrant received	—To be released to the Youth Authority

A crucial feature of organizational activities is the differential accounting of events. Selective factors influence the information kept in a file system. Juvenile careers are partially the product of fortuitous circumstances surrounding the reporting of incidents, the extent to which agencies communicate to one another, and whether particular agencies enter the picture and are charged with obtaining general information about the juvenile. Because Mark was only on informal probation, there was virtually no probation file on him. Thus, little official information was available on his family and school performance. I was told by school officials that Mark was a "C" student and was not excessively "bad" in school. Smithfield's probation file was extensive because he was a ward of the court. Smithfield's parents separated in August 1960, and the school reports obtained after his first contact with the police in February 1961 show that the boy was considered a troublemaker (May 1960) in school prior to the time of the separation. I am not trying to argue that in Smithfield's case it was the divorce that precipitated all of the trouble. I have no way of checking out this juxtaposition of events. Smithfield possessed all of the "classical" sociological attributes for being defined as delinquent, and he fits the standard categories employed in the community and law-enforcement agencies for labeling someone a "typical" delinquent.

A more important contrast between Mark and Smithfield is the application for a petition submitted for Smithfield after his first encounter with the police, while for Mark it did not occur until after several encounters. But the petition came to both after burglaries. For Mark it was $80.00 from a neighbor's house, while for Smithfield it was a first offense with another youth and the amount stolen from school was $6.97. Mark was placed on informal probation and thus did not appear before the juvenile court, while Smithfield was made a ward of the court after the first hearing and while he was a sixth grade pupil.

Because of the burglary and petition, Smithfield's prior school performance was investigated by the Probation Officer and revealed the following information:

PSYCHOLOGICAL TESTING REPORT. SIXTH GRADE

TEST BEHAVIOR. Smithfield was courteous and helpful, almost to the point of overdoing it. He quickly offered a pencil when my pencil was lost, jumped to his feet when it was necessary to answer the door. He worked especially hard for a bit of praise and recognition.

SUMMARY AND CONCLUSIONS. Smithfield is mentally retarded, or at least appears that way. He would profit from placement in the special class. Smithfield responds well to praise and recognition, and these methods should probably be used in teaching self control and acceptable school behavior.

The testing report is rather equivocal and the remark "Smithfield is mentally retarded, or at least appears that way," raises more doubts about the juvenile's depiction than clarifies his predicament. Suggesting "praise and recognition" for the boy "in teaching self-control and acceptable school behavior" does not diminish the equivocality of the report. But after being placed in the special class the teacher reported the following:

> November 18, 1960. He became very belligerent and violent on the school playground and had to be restrained from beating a smaller boy who reported Smithfield's aggressiveness toward him. He refused to listen or maintain any self-control or respect as an effort was made to probe into the cause of the conflict. He used profane language, calling those on the scene very dirty names. One word was one defaming the word mother.
>
> Another conference, the fourth such conference since September of this school year, was held with his mother. As a result, Smithfield's conduct was somewhat improved for approximately two weeks. He was cooperative in class and attempted to do his classwork. He participated in classroom activities. Two weeks before the Christmas vacation he was asked to surrender a three-inch switch blade knife. He was seen flashing the knife in front of the class. I happened to be at the rear of the class working with a group of pupils. He was asked questions concerning the knife, and he stated that he obtained it from his brother. This made a second such knife taken from him. He merely grinned when an attempt was made to point out the great possibility of him getting into trouble if he carried knives. The incident reported to his mother and Principal. December 4, 1960. Smithfield again had to be restrained from fighting in class. It was the result of a pupil bumping his seat. It was an accident and the entire class witnessed the incident. In spite of the pupil's apologies and the classes attempt to appeal to Smithfield, Smithfield was boisterous and made moves toward the pupil.
>
> No respect was shown towards teacher or pupils of the class. There have been frequent outbursts of disturbances by Smithfield. He yells out in class, walks around at will, refuses to do any work, regardless of how simple the task, is inattentive, and annoys other pupils who are attempting to do their work.
>
> I often hear him relating experiences he has had outside of school and there have been occasions when I have had to discourage him at the moment.
>
> Various efforts have been made in trying to find out just what his interests are. He had been praised for the things he had done in class and I have taken him aside in many conferences and lengthy sessions have been held. Special tasks have been assigned him. As of this date, he has not completed a single assignment. Instead, he continues to run around the classroom displaying an overly aggressive attitude—bullying boys (often many times his size) and using vile language, the type one would hear around the most sordid places.

The school report provided the probation officer with considerable material for justifying the acceptance of the petition after the first offense, but the fact that Smithfield was detained in Juvenile Hall until the court hearing suggests the school material was communicated informally very shortly after the arrest.

Some informal contact with the probation officer probably preceded the offense, so an unofficial file probably existed on the boy prior to official proceedings. The school report does not leave much to the imagination; it mentions physical violence, the use of profanity, possession of knives, and continual disruption of classroom activities. The categories employed for describing offensive behavior do not require extensive interpretation, but the depictions of attempts to "help" the boy are less convincing and behaviorally ambiguous, particularly when we have no idea of how the juvenile communicated with the teacher and vice versa. What seems clear about the teacher's description is that there is no doubt in *his* mind as to Smithfield's social character, but we have no way of detecting how the boy viewed the situation, or the nature of the exchanges when the teacher sought to "help" the juvenile.

The first paragraph is graphically described by the teacher, while the reference to "improved" conduct is ambiguous. The description of the knife incident appears clear, but it is not obvious that the encounter was a "bad" one, although the remark that Smithfield "merely grinned when an attempt was made to point out the great possibility of him getting into trouble if he carried knives" appears intended as a documentation of the youth's mean character or bizarre orientation to what the teacher regarded as an "obviously" serious matter. The "bumping" incident seems clear as written, but we are forced again to take activity for granted if the teacher's remarks are to be honored as a literal portrayal of Smithfield's presumably negative character. Yet the outcome is not clear because the statement that Smithfield "made moves toward the pupil" is not clear behaviorally, although the intended implication seems clear; Smithfield insisted on inflicting harm on another pupil even though for the teacher it was a clear case of "accidental bumping." The teacher makes it clear in subsequent lines that Smithfield is a thorough nuisance to him and the class and is not interested in his school work, despite his attempts to help the boy. Without denying the clear communication of an apparently "wild" juvenile, such a report does not permit the researcher to determine the extent to which the social object in question has been reified or transformed by the use of language, or the ways in which one could justify the boy's actions (or some part of them) by reference to behavioral or ideological elements not mentioned by the teacher. There are many comments that I could add of an impressionistic nature about the small community in which the school is located, or the imputations of discrimination informants related to me about Negro-white relations in the comunity. But my remarks would not differ from those of the teacher.

After being made a ward of the court the boy was allowed to live with his mother who moved to City A. The following remarks are from Smithfield's teacher at the junior high school in City A.

.

7th grade teacher. During the time Smithfield has been in the room his adjustment has been very ineffective. His social values seem to be functioning at a different level than the rest of the class. He appears to have no personal goals and does not appear to recognize significant problems which face him. The antagonistic attitude with which he meets both students and teachers aggravates all of his social situations. This deviation from the rest of his classmates tends to put the classroom under unnecessary strains and restricts the type and amount of learning of the class.

The above statement reveals an abstract standard language with which various types of organizations (schools, social work agencies, probation departments, psychiatric clinics) characterize their clients. The teacher states that "his adjustment has been very ineffective," the boy's "social values" are different from others in his class, there is an absence of "personal goals," and there is no recognition of "significant problems which face him." The boy is said to have an "antagonistic attitude" toward students and teachers and all "social situations." For the teacher there is no doubt as to Smithfield's "deviation from the rest of his classmates," and the extent to which everyone in class is disrupted by his presence. It would not be difficult to substitute some of the referents employed previously by the special class instructor from the other school (for example, possession of knives, use of profanity, etc.) in order to supply the reader with concrete imagery for interpreting the formal language of the 7th grade teacher. Further, I am not trying to refute the "correctness" of the formal remarks made by either teacher. The teachers' language cannot be disputed on behavioral grounds because there is no way of objectifying either report. But what is perhaps "clear" to readers (knowing Smithfield is a Negro male) is that the formal descriptions offered by the teachers leave little room for explanatory remarks based on information that the boy's parents had recently separated, the absence of prior reports about his being a "behavior problem," and the fact that he demonstrated "proper" behavior at times even though it did not last long. A clinical view would perhaps take the latter information into account, and presumably the intent of the juvenile court law is to maximize the use of such information. But a clinical view requires that the client not "resist" the authority of the therapist, that he recognize his "problem," and that he cooperate in helping to resolve difficulties. But it is difficult for white, middle-income teachers, probation officers, policemen, therapists, students, and the like, to view social objects like Smithfield in clinical terms, and make clinical imputations about the cause of his "deviant" behavior, because the appearance of the object is itself a frightening experience for all of them, since there is no way for them to envisage a procedure for predicting behavior and controlling the boy. We ordinarily are forced to take for granted that in their dealings with the boy, the teacher, students, administrators, and so on, are able to suspend the appearance of this male Negro as a potentially violent object in their midst, so as to provide us with objective descriptions of how the relevant parties interact. The formal characterizations assume the factual nature of the boy's apparent wildness, almost random generation of hatred, physical violence, and complete rejection of "acceptable" goals. Merton's typology seems appropriate here, but, like the abstract remarks of the teachers, does not provide a basis for conceptualizing much less objectifying participants' preconceptions and negative typifications as contextual elements for generating reactions to appearances. Merton's typology does not make variable the interaction itself, much less what the participants regard as relevant in deciding what is "proper" or "deviant" or "acceptable." Finally, the use of information about family problems, the boy's reaction to them, and the like, cannot sustain a clinical picture if the appearance of the object and the implied behavioral features neutralize an illness category because of activities viewed as deliberately "belligerent and violent."

I want to digress for a moment and compare Smithfield's predicament with a potential suicide or a prisoner returning to the community after a period of incarceration. All three cases ("hard core" delinquent, suicidal person, parolee) are similar because the present or past behavior of the objects warrant, presumably, some kind of remedial activity, not only by a therapist, but also by some network of social organization that includes the family and the "community." The "community" refers to others the object encounters in the course of routine living, presumably teachers, students, employers, husbands, wives, brothers, sisters, mothers, fathers, neighbors, friends, salesmen, bank officials, and the like. In all three cases ("hard core" delinquent, suicidal person, parolee) each has defined his predicament in such a way that "there is no one to turn to."[2] There are presumably others willing to "help," but the problem is the extent to which the helpers extend themselves and are able to "communicate" or "touch base" with the objects in trouble. Professional remedial agents find it difficult to help suicidal persons and parolees, because they have little control over life circumstances once the client leaves the office. The most "favorable" clinical atmosphere remains something of an illusion when the client must face an environment defined as unfamiliar with "his problem." The persons close to the deviant object, while presumably informed about the "problem," find it difficult to divorce the appearances and behavior observed from the abstract characterizations they might imagine or that are provided by remedial agents. Those further away may suspend the relevance of the "problem" entirely. The central point with all three deviant types, therefore, is that the task of transforming them into competent objects remains formidable because someone must assume direct operational procedures in seeking the change; the operations required demand that the participants involve themselves with the deviant object extensively so that almost total support and control can be achieved for an indeterminate period of time. The demands are great and require an almost total change on the part of the "helpers," but few are willing or, from their point of view, able to make the effort. Consequently both the family and "community" rely upon formal agencies precisely because the commitment they would have to make is viewed as beyond their ability, interest, or means to achieve. The involvement of formal agencies of control and remedial activities becomes a datum for the deviant object in that "help" is couched in procedures and relationships that are removed from those sociologists define as "primary." A relationship of trust is sought to simulate intimacy in the relationship. Therefore "others" can be viewed as not removed from the general "problem" but perhaps unsympathetic to the juvenile's particular "problems." I would stretch the point further by stating that "successful" clients achieve "success" because their problems do not demand "total involvement" from others, and there is little interest in becoming involved. The rationality presupposed by formal therapy is that the client recognizes a "problem," wishes to discuss it discretely, and, above all, seeks to "stay on top" of the matter at all times. Those persons considered to be deviant objects and then incarcerated have, in effect, given up their claims to rational control over their acts (though not willingly) by the total commitment and supervision imposed upon them. To have arrived at the point of total control presupposes a series of encounters with others whereby an inability (variably defined by the participants) to "communicate" or "touch base" occurred. It is assumed that the object with "problems" was at fault, but from the object's point of view he is not being "understood" even by those to whom he is presumably bound by kinship or other close ties. I am assuming that Smithfield, like psychopaths and parolees, is viewed as "hopeless," making a clinical view unlikely.

Formal organizations of control and remedial activities relieve others from responsibilities vis-à-vis deviant objects, including members considered "close" to the object. Yet these agencies are incapable of controlling and reconstructing the everyday life of the deviant "lost cause" in the community. The best hope for the deviant who is given "another chance" is sympathy from law-enforcement officials for his "failure" if it occurs, but the researcher's task is to clarify contingencies surrounding the "failure" and to determine how contingencies come to be viewed as "exemptive" mechanisms (with "good reasons" for the "apparent" failure) or as documentary evidence of the "hopelessness" of the case. The practice by police (but especially probation and parole officers) of accommodating to "failures" after the juvenile "explains" the contingencies of "what happened" signifies a relationship of "trust" still exists between the juvenile and the agent of control. It is this "trust" relationship that reflects the rehabilitative side of the law. When it is dissolved, only the punitive side remains.

The teachers' descriptions of Smithfield's activities are behavioral referents that are taken for granted, and we have no behavioral indication of how Smithfield viewed the teachers and students. The picture is truncated, although the part about the possession of knives, use of profanity, and seemingly random physical activity (both violent and harmless) conveys concrete referents in the case of the first description. The question is what sorts of behavioral referents would any or different readers impute to the second description where concrete referents about knives, profanity, and violence are missing? The following verbatim report by the probation officer suggests a "trust relationship" is presupposed between the officer and Smithfield. My *post facto* reasons for inferring the "trust relationship" are based upon the following comments by the probation officer and noted below.[3]

FAMILY HISTORY

Smithfield is one of six children born to the marriage of S. Elston nee Flint, age 36 and L. Elston, Sr., age 40. This couple was married on December 24, 1944 in Texas and separated on August 1, 1960 in Sycamore, California. Mrs. Elston states when she files for divorce, she will allege mental cruelty and jealousy. The mother states her husband is living at [address], Los Angeles, California. The father works as an upholsterer when employed. Mrs. Elston and her young family recently moved to City A and now live on the east side of the city. She is renting adequate quarters for her family. This family is a recipient of Welfare aid and the mother states she does not plan on working until school is out this summer.

PAST HISTORY

A check of the Central Juvenile Index files revealed no prior contacts for Smithfield.

CAUSE OF COURT HEARING

On February 21, 1961, a petition was filed in behalf of Smithfield Elston by John Jones, Intake Deputy, alleging the said minor came within the provisions of Subdivision M, Section 700 of the Welfare and Institutions Code, for violating Section 459 of the California Penal Code (burglary).

CIRCUMSTANCES SURROUNDING THE OFFENSE

In reference to the arresting officer's report, on or about February 18, 1961, the principal of the Sycamore Elementary School, Mr. B., notified the police department that an office at the school had been burglarized; a desk drawer had been pried open and $6.97 was taken. The principal had reason to believe the two suspects were Smithfield Elston and J.R.P. Following this lead, the officers contacted Elston and P. The subjects admitted to the act and the money was recovered. In discussing the offense with the minors, it was related each had gone to the school separately, with the intentions of meeting companions. Smithfield stated he was to meet a cousin and to play basketball and J.P. related he and some companions had planned on going for a hike. Both boys admitted entering the school office by going through a bathroom window and using a pair of scissors to pry open the desk drawer. Each had hidden his portion of the money after the burglary, with the intent of using it at a later time. The Court will note J.P. appeared on this matter on March 2, 1961. Although this is Smithfield's first appearance in Juvenile Court for a law violation, the Probation Officer was aware of the minor's emotional problems, as the school in Sycamore had discussed this child on several occasions. They were of the opinion that possibly Smithfield was influenced by his older brother, Lawrence, who is presently a ward of the Juvenile Court and is now residing in a foster home placement. The County School Administration Office had contacted this writer and discussed the possibility of filing on Smithfield as an incorrigible, but withdrew the suggestion once Lawrence had been removed from the home. A typical classroom evaluation was given by Mr. [name], his 7th grade teacher: "During the time Smithfield has been in the room, his adjustment has been very ineffective; his social values seem to be functioning at a different level than the rest of the class. The antagonistic attitude with which he meets both students and teachers aggravates all of his social situations."

This writer contacted the Child Welfare and Attendance Office of the City A Schools and discussed Smithfield's case with them. They are well aware of his school problems and knowing the circumstances would be in a position to work with the minor.

Mrs. Elston is handicapped in coping with her son's problems, primarily because of her inability to be firm. She does realize, after firm counselling that it is her responsibility as a parent to work with agencies that are attempting to assist her. It is encouraging to note the mother figure has taken a firmer attitude in the matter of her delinquent son and will attempt to be more realistic in the future.

There is little the Probation Officer can add to the above remarks and at this point, it would appear a change of environment as well as schools, possibly will assist those concerned in rehabilitating this child.

RECOMMENDATION

It is respectfully recommended to the Court that if the Allegations contained in the petition filed in behalf of Smithfield Elston are found to be true that he be declared a ward of the Juvenile Court of County A, his care, custody and control to be placed with [name], the Probation Officer, who is authorized and directed to release the minor to the direct custody of his mother under the following terms and conditions of probation:

1. That he violate no law or ordinance;
2. That he obey the reasonable directives of his mother and the Probation Officer at all times;

3. That he attend school regularly and obey all school rules and regulations;
4. That he not be out after dark unless accompanied by his mother or some adult person approved by her;
5. That he report once each month to the Probation Officer, either in Person or in writing. [March 9, 1961]

The Probation Officer's report reveals a family on welfare, in the process of filing for divorce, a father who has moved away and presumably unemployed, an older brother who is a ward of the court and considered a "bad" influence, and a mother who "is handicapped in coping with her son's problems, primarily because of her inability to be firm." Notice that Smithfield had no prior police contacts and the probation officer seems to justify the court appearance after the first violation (highly unusual in County A) by the remark that he had already been contacted about the boy as an "emotional" problem at school, and informal contact with the school almost led to a petition being filed on the boy as an "incorrigible." The removal of his older brother is given as the reason for not following through with the earlier petition. Therefore, the police had little to do with Smithfield's court hearing; the rapidity with which he was given a hearing seems to be based upon unofficial action between the school authorities and the probation officer. The probation officer's concern with rehabilitation is expressed by his reference to a change in residence and school. But the report implies the probation officer, through discussions with the Child Welfare and Attendance Office in City A, has worked out some kind of special program the school will follow in attempting to rehabilitate the boy. The "special" part, however, would be confined to the school classroom setting. Any additional control or "help" would presumably come from contacts with the probation officer and the boy's mother. To say the school "would be in a position to work with the minor" does not reveal that the junior high school in question is located in the Negro–Mexican-American section of City A, where juveniles like Smithfield are feared by teachers, and not viewed as candidates for "rehabilitation," but "trouble-makers." On the occasions I visited the junior high school, once when Smithfield was considered a suspect, but not the principal one, the police-teacher-administrator contacts appeared to exhibit agreement on the need for cooperation in controlling the "bad" elements always "causing trouble." Smithfield was considered one of the serious problems, and the language used to describe him could not, in my opinion, be described as "rehabilitative." Note, also, how the probation officer states Mrs. Elston "is handicapped in coping with her son's problems" because of not being "firm," and then remarks she was apparently told to be more "firm" and to assume more responsibility in controlling the boy and helping Probation. The probation officer noted his pleasure in the apparent way "the mother figure has taken a firmer attitude" in her conception of the boy. My observations of probation officer-parent-juvenile interviews revealed that such remarks are only made when the officer has encouraged or voluntarily received statements from the parents and juvenile that a "sincere" effort will be made to correct acknowledged irresponsibility. The interview described in Chapter 4 stressed this point repeatedly. Parental acknowledgments of needed "help" on their part provide the officer with a basis for establishing some kind of trust relationship with the parents and juvenile, and for convincing the judge that the boy deserves "another chance." The estimation of a "proper attitude" on the parent's part and by the boy is based upon the officer's background expectancies and revealed by the language and paralinguistic behavior of parent and juvenile during interviews with the officer. When the probation officer is convinced of this trust, and the number of offenses and their severity is considered within "reason," the judge almost always goes along with the officer's recommendations. Important exceptions occur and will be described below. The report, therefore, must justify the court appearance and also justify the disposition recommended. The later justification must somehow characterize the object in question as "salvageable" or "beyond control" and in need of the "services" an agency of total control (the California Youth Authority) can "provide." In either case clinical-type grounds officially may be given for making the decision, although in the case of prison incarceration there is a tacit agreement among all parties that the youth really needs punishment.

On December 19, 1961, Smithfield was involved in another incident with the police: breaking into a local recreation office and taking 80 cents from a purse. Smithfield and another boy were interrogated after a Negro detective of the City A police department received information from an informant suggesting that they were the offenders. The report continues:

> After the theft both boys rec'd 40¢ apiece out of the 80¢ total that was actually in the purse at the time of the theft. The boys intended to return the purse to the room after removing it's money contents but were unable to do so. The T. boy in this case is a ward of Court under Mr. [name] of the Probation Dept and the Elston boy altho new to this city moved here from Sycamore this past summer where he had been picked up for Burglary and as a consequence he is also an active ward of Ct from that area. This writer talked with Mrs. Elston and advised her of the case and on demand she came to the station to claim both boys. Mrs. T. was not available but word was left at her place of employment to contact this writer at 3 PM this date. Both boys were released to Mrs. Elston with instructions to make restitution to the victim for 80¢ offer their apologies, and contact Mr. [name] at the probation Dept on Tuesday 12/26/61 to make an appointment with him for disposition. This T. boy in particular definitely lacks parental supervision and is very easily led as in this case.

The police report does not reveal the school difficulties described earlier, and the officer did not file an application for petition, although it was known to the officer that Smithfield had been picked up for burglary in Sycamore and was a ward of the court. The officer's remark about the T. boy ("definitely lacks parental supervision and is very easily led as in this case") suggests the Elston boy may have been the "leader," but stresses the T. boy as the one lacking parental supervision. I am assuming the theft was not viewed as serious enough to warrant filing an application for petition, and that the officer presumed Probation would not respond favorably to a petition given the existence of probationary status for the juveniles. There is no way of explaining the selective remarks about the one juvenile, but not Smithfield's participation.

The next entry on the summary file card is for 1/15/62, and is listed as a burglary at Smithfield's junior high school. The police report indicates the following:

> Received call to contact the Principal at the [name] Jr. Hi, on [address] arrived there and he stated that one of the school teachers a Mr. R. had caught two young subjects hiding inside of the Cafeteria, the suspects had been caught hiding behind some counters. Mr. [Principal] stated that they have been having a lot of break ins in the Cafeteria and that the suspects always just take either Ice Cream or Food from the Refrigerators. Mr. [Principal] stated that they have been trying to catch the suspects for a long time but had been unable too until today when Mr. R. caught the two above name juveniles. Mr. [Principal] stated that he had already called this office and had talked Juv. Officer [name], and that [Juv. Off.] had advised him [Principal] that the suspects could be released today and taken home by this officer [the patrol officer making out this report], and that he [Juv. Off.] would contact the suspects and their parents tomorrow 1/16/62 and take care of the matter. This officer then took the suspects home and turned them over to their mothers, both mothers took the case very serious and did not belittle the incident at all. They also appreciated the fact that the suspects were brought home, as they were beginning to worry about them since they had not arrived home from school yet. Both of these suspects have been in trouble before and are on probation at the present time.

With this incident, the police were told about Smithfield's general behavior at school by the school officials. This is common practice and I have observed such "briefings" many times, including an incident where Smithfield was considered to be a suspect, but not questioned because I was told that he was a "pathological liar" and that questioning him was futile. The patrol officer's report indicates the boys were considered suspects vis-à-vis illegal entries into the cafeteria on previous occasions, even though the boys had not actually stolen anything at the time they were picked up by the teacher. The patrol officer's remarks appear to be routine; the officer seemed impressed with the mothers' responses, and the remark that both boys had "been in trouble before" appears "typical." The juvenile officer's report provides more information:

> Upon releasing the boys to Officer [patrol officer's name] the previous evening the boys had been instructed not to return to school this date regardless. Both boys were brought to the office and they both continued to deny that they had done this type thing before, K. denied ever hearing of any one else doing it and both stated that they just happened to be walking by and walked down to look around, K. was the first to admit that they intended to steal some ice cream but was caught by Mr. R. before it could be effected. Elston finally also admitted the same and finally stated that he had heard an unknown Mex boy known only as Ralph mention that some boys hid out behind and above the stage in the auditorium until about 10 PM at night and then would get ice cream and other eats. He would not admit knowing this Ralph. Further Inv will be made along these lines. K. is a Parolee under Mr. [name] who requested that the boy be placed in custody. . . .
>
> Elston was again contacted at the Hall and he denied any knowledge of knowing the other subjects responsible for past thefts. His probation officer was later contacted and he advised that no doubt the boys mother could get the truth out of him, it appears that the mother is the only one who has any control over the boys telling the truth, he will have the mother question the boy and advise this officer.

The juvenile officer sought without success to link the two boys to prior thefts from the cafeteria and his report suggests others were involved, but he felt Smithfield was not telling him the truth about what he presumably knew. The remark that further investigation will be made and the statement on the subsequent interview with Smithfield at Juvenile Hall suggest the officer was still convinced of the two juveniles' implication in the other thefts. The "truth" would come from the mother.

Notice that a police officer's interrogation of someone like Smithfield presumes that a male Negro is a basic source of trouble in the community, a generic source of trouble for all agencies of social control, an offender who cannot be trusted, and someone viewed as a prime suspect whenever there are crimes without suspects. Interviews I have observed between officers and lower-income Negro males typically involve direct accusations about the youth's dishonesty, his general style of life, and his defiance and disrespect of authority, as revealed by his posture, speech mannerisms, demeanor, dress patterns, lack of remorse, seemingly unconcerned view about the consequences of his acts, what could happen to him, and so on. Whether or not police action is viewed as a degradation ceremony for the youth cannot be demonstrated with the present material, but my impression was that the police made little effort to conceal their contempt for the male Negro whom they felt was a "pathological liar," constantly violating the law, unconcerned about property and person, and a continual "danger" to the "decent people" of the community. For the police, much less the probation officer, it is difficult to establish much of a trust relationship with Negro males like Smithfield because there is little to which either can really become committed so as to enable both to respect and trust each other. The same problem exists with school teachers and Negro and Mexican-American juveniles. Therefore, it is difficult to imagine how the spirit, much less the practice of the juvenile court law, could be implemented by agencies of social control when juveniles like Smithfield are handled. The police or probation officer's report, therefore, is not the objective reporting of a detached interview where the object's social standing in the community, his physical appearance, and immediate behavior (in an extra-legal sense) are suspended so that the "facts" of the case can be discerned and reported.

The probation officer handling the case sought additional school reports before submitting his recommendation to the court. The following comments are taken from each of Smithfield's eighth grade teachers' reports to the Probation Department:

Wood Shop

ACADEMIC PROGRESS. Gets a lot done in shop, but can't do anything that requires math or problem solving. Can't follow directions too well. The things he gets done are on a step to step basis.

SOCIAL ADJUSTMENT. Not too good as far as working with others in respect to sharing tools and shop obligations. Habitually tardy to class.

SUGGESTIONS OR RECOMMENDATIONS. Needs very close supervision.

English

ACADEMIC PROGRESS. He does absolutely nothing. If he *does* feel called upon for effort, he cheats.

SOCIAL ADJUSTMENT. He causes confusion in class when he is not watched every minute.

[No suggestions or recommendations.]

Science

ACADEMIC PROGRESS. Very poor work. Little ability, does not do assignments.

SOCIAL ADJUSTMENT. Smithfield is sullen most of the time when corrected. His conduct is not good, but he is not a serious problem.

SUGGESTIONS OR RECOMMENDATIONS. His lack of interest in class is probably caused by his limited ability. No suggestions.

Physical Education

SOCIAL ADJUSTMENT. This boy is very lazy and difficult to motivate. He has P.E. first period and on two occasions he came directly to class from home. It seems he has no one at home to get him up and see that he gets to school let alone see that he is properly supervised during the fifteen hours he is out of school. He dresses everyday for me and participates very well, however, I keep after him constantly letting him know what I expect. With a lot of "pushing" he does very well for me. He will try on any chance to hang around the locker room after everyone leaves. These have been occasions that money was missing during the first P.E. class. It was never proven who took the money, however, it has never happened since I have kept a close watch on him and made him report to class with the rest of the group. He was a member of my football team and we never had problems of money missing there. Was very cooperative but not what you would call a "ball of fire."

SUGGESTIONS OR RECOMMENDATIONS. Mine would probably be impossible to carry out. That is simply, put this boy in a home where fairness, love and *vigilance* prevail.

Mathematics

ACADEMIC PROGRESS. Smithfield does nothing academically in class. Most of the time he refuses to even hand in any work. Any work he does hand in has been copied.

SOCIAL ADJUSTMENT. He will not sit in his seat. He does anything he can to disrupt the class and create a disturbance. Anytime he is corrected he gets very mad and will sit and pout. [No suggestions or recommendations.]

Homeroom

ACADEMIC PROGRESS. Does very little toward the unit. Never volunteers.

SOCIAL ADJUSTMENT. Poor attitude—late often—does not obey when told to do anything—is a real problem in home room (and the only one who is)

SUGGESTIONS OR RECOMMENDATIONS. Needs firm hand.

Social Studies

ACADEMIC PROGRESS. Very poor student. Although an 8th grader, can barely read simple text books. Wastes time and gets into trouble. Once when he created a disturbance, I sent him out of the room into the hall. A few minutes later, I caught him *lighting matches* in the hall.

SOCIAL ADJUSTMENT. Would rather tell a *lie* than tell the truth. A typical sentence: "I didn't do it. Besides you did not catch me." Has a hard time keeping his hands off other peoples property. I have changed his seat in class several times, hoping he would improve, to no avail.

SUGGESTIONS OR RECOMMENDATIONS. What suggestions can one make for a boy who is dishonest, a chronic liar, a very poor student and a constant trouble maker???

The picture that the school provides seems clear. Smithfield was described as a "poor" student who does not do his work and cheats when he does decide to work. His "social adjustment" was described as primarily "disruptive," a "chronic liar," "constant trouble maker," and the like; yet there is some variation, although hardly enough to convince any reader about the fine qualities of Smithfield's character as seen by his teachers. The one area in

which Smithfield seems to excel is physical education, and here the teacher recommends a "home where fairness, love, and *vigilance* prevail," viewed as an
impossibility, for who would provide him with such a home? It would take
little urging to convince the reader that from the point of view of the agencies
of social control, Smithfield is a serious problem because he is viewed as
"beyond reach" and cannot be controlled by "normal" forms of authority.
He simply does not behave as an adolescent "should," and his lack of respect
for "authority" (his apparent refusal to try to adopt the definition of classroom behavior and work implied by his teachers) leaves them all quite annoyed. There is almost no hope given for change. I have no information on
teacher-teacher exchanges on Smithfield, but differences among them are not
likely to be discerned by a reader who "knows" the juvenile. There is no
suggestion for breaking the vicious circle (except for the physical education
teacher's remarks which he viewed as unrealistic) because most of the persons involved appear exasperated and do not attribute the notion of "vicious
circle" to Smithfield's daily round of activities.

The problem of control (the maintenance of authority) is paramount for
the police, probation, and the schools. Smithfield epitomizes the "worst type"
juvenile these agencies deal with. Carl Werthman's work illustrates the other
side of this picture: how the juvenile sees these same agencies as "messing
up" his life because of preconceptions that keep the "vicious circle" going
until adulthood concretizes the syndrome.[4] The hard core delinquent, therefore, cannot avoid appearing continuously in official statistics. The problem
of objective data here remains pretty much untouched, however, because it
is difficult to break out of the commonsense typifications that lay and professional social scientists use to depict the way authority is "defied." Werthman's materials, however, are quite informative on how the "hard core"
Negro male delinquent type perceives and interprets various areas of his
daily environment. Werthman's characterization of the problem of authority
is consistent with the kinds of actual encounters that I witnessed over a four-
year period, even though there are several variations that would have to
be added when juveniles from different income levels are included.

The picture revealed by a stay at Juvenile Hall indicates similar problems
although there are a few possible exceptions. The teacher states:

Smithfield is moody and his attitude towards school varies. On some days he
completes his assignments willingly, while on others he makes only a token attempt to do so. When told to perform a task that he doesn't wish to do he sits
and pouts. He is capable of average work but his performance as a whole is below
average. He cooperates at physical education and appears to enjoy it.

[Statement by the Superintendent of Juvenile Hall:]

Smithfield appears to be an emotionally disturbed boy who has considerable
difficulty relating with his peers. He is loud and aggressive, and has a tendency

to pick fights with the smaller and less physically adept group members. He refuses to accept authority of any nature. When counselled, concerning his negative conduct and attitude, he becomes emotionally upset using crying tactics as a means of getting sympathy instead of admonishment. Smithfield is reluctant to participate in work assignments, but does take part actively in sports program, revealing above average ability for his size. He manages his personal affairs well, and presents a neat appearance. Smithfield tends to identify with the negative element, being a follower rather than a leader. He is not considered a security risk at this time.

The Hall teacher suggests Smithfield can complete work assignments and is at his best when engaged in sports. The Hall teacher suggests Smithfield *can* do the work even though his actual performance is below average. The junior high school teachers all felt he could not do the work and did not try. The superintendent's remarks begin by characterizing Smithfield as "emotionally disturbed" and unable to get along with others. A key phrase is that Smithfield "refuses to accept authority of any nature." The focus upon problems of "authority" continually arise in the juvenile's relations with the police, the teachers, and probation officers. The description following the remark on authority (crying when counselled about "negative conduct") is not that of defiance expressed by the teachers in junior high school, but seemingly quite the opposite. It is clear that between the science teacher, the physical education teacher, and the counsellors at Juvenile Hall, Smithfield presumably *was* able to establish some kind of social relationship that was not viewed as entirely negative (for example, in "defiance" of authority). Finally, note that the superintendent states Smithfield "presents a neat appearance" and "is not considered a security risk at this time." The significance of the variations in the characterization of Smithfield lies in the interpretations made by different officials making decisions about Smithfield's moral character and how to dispose of him. The officials can easily find all of the "documentary" evidence necessary for building the most negative case imaginable. The appearances the juvenile presents before some official, therefore, provide contingent elements for ignoring or suspending the relevance of the various documents portraying Smithfield to "whosoever" is officially capable of utilizing such information to pass judgment over his past activities and to decide his future fate.

Before proceeding to the probation officer's report triggered by the burglary incident noted above, I want to quote a letter by Smithfield's father to the probation officer. The letter is important because I feel it contributes to the officer's decisions about "what to do" with Smithfield. The only remark about the father in the probation officer's report states that "Mr. Elston is reportedly presently unemployed." The father would be a logical possible choice for placement, but it is not clear from the remark about his unemployed condition that the only reason for not allowing Smithfield to remain with the father is employment.

the other day I was in your offices, I promise to furnish you with My living quater Setup which if Very Poor, in this case, Of couse I am am trying to improve them, So If at anytime the Court See fit to Grant Me Custom over Smithfield, I will be able to exsept him, of course, I am willing Now but as I just Stated living condation are poor. I feel that Smithfield can be help, but the kind of help he really Need and that is Spiritual help teaching him the way of Christ, in his condation he need that kind help to over come his hibits. As you Said on Several complain on him as pearce snaching. I did not know that he was doing Such things as that, he has a Demon Spirit which at times he has no control over, which Many Many peoples has those problems, adults as well, ad yet they are Normal, Officer [name]. I am praying that Someway Smithfield case can be work out without destroying his life future.

Yours very truly,

While much could be said about Smithfield's father based upon the above letter, I am interested in how the father's predicament is evaluated and influences the probation officer's disposition. If the probation officer decides the father is not a source of help for the juvenile, then the possibility of averting a juvenile prison record is not available. The probation officer must decide whether the juvenile's home (or part of it) is "adequate" for keeping the juvenile "out of trouble." It is doubtful if the father would be seen as a source of "help." Being sent to the Youth Authority prison is an expedient solution for continued "trouble." If the juvenile is sent to a foster home, it can be viewed as an indication that the probation officer was willing to extend the trust relationship despite the recent encounter with the police.

The probation officer submitted the following report: (*Note:* Most of the first part is identical to that reported earlier in this case. I shall only quote material not included above.)

Smithfield's matter was discussed with the Welfare and Attendance office of [City A] City Schools and they acknowledged a willingness to attempt to work with the minor in the [City A] City Schools. After re-evaluating the situation it was decided that Smithfield should not be put in special education but was put in a modified program at [name] Junior High School. Smithfield did fair in school for the remainder of the school year, however, he has more difficulty during the current school year. Although not actually caught, he was suspected of thefts at the school and as aforementioned, was involved in the theft of a purse at [name] Recreation Center. It is the observation of the Probation Officer that at the time Smithfield moved to City A and started in attendance at the city school his general attitude was good. He appeared to be motivated and further appeared to make an honest effort to conform. It appears that after a period of time Smithfield was influenced by undesirable companions and his general attitude regressed. As at the time he was counselled regarding the offense of theft in December, 1961, seemed to mouth the "I don't want to have anyone telling me what to do" attitude of his companion. It was the opinion of the Probation Officer who initially handled Smithfield's matter that Mrs. Elston was handicapped in coping with Smithfield's problems because of her inability to be firm. She was advised to take a more firm and realistic attitude in the future.

It appeared to this writer that Mrs. Elston was able to control Smithfield's activities and companions for a long period of time but that during the current year Smithfield acquired undesirable companions without the knowledge of his mother. Consequently, his general attitude regressed. The School personnel have acknowledged that they are willing to continue working with Smithfield and the minor's mother has acknowledged a desire to continue working with him and further acknowledges that she will contact the Probation Officer if the minor does not conform, therefore, the Probation Officer is recommending that Smithfield be continued on probation and allowed to remain in the custody of his mother, but it is further recommended that the Court structure the minor and his mother regarding their responsibilities and inform them that if they are not able to meet them the Court will find it necessary to remove the minor from his home and place him elsewhere.

The remainder of the report repeats the conditions of probation as quoted above. The probation officer states the "Welfare and Attendance office" sought to "work with" Smithfield and he was placed in something called a "modified program." The report gives the impression something is "done" for juveniles like Smithfield. My own impressionistic observation revealed that what is "done" is to "talk with" Smithfield on a few occasions about "staying out of trouble." The probation officer suggests that Smithfield initially "did fair" but then began to have "difficulty." The offense is not mentioned as something "serious," but as "suspected," while simultaneously reminding the judge there had been a theft incident earlier. The officer states there was a "good" attitude initially and an "honest effort to conform." But after some unspecified time and unstated conditions, Smithfield then "was influenced by undesirable companions and his general attitude regressed." Previously the brother was mentioned as the "bad" influence, with the mother unable to "control" Smithfield. Now the "undesirable" influence of companions is "seen" as "obvious" by reference to the following observation: Smithfield "seemed to mouth the 'I don't want to have anyone telling me what to do' attitude of his companion." Notice how the problem of the "attitude" is central to every characterization of juveniles, but the reports do not clarify what the probation officer or police officer or teacher perceives as referents for the language employed. The teachers state Smithfield is simply an impossible person and the locus of "fault" is the juvenile himself. The police reports take for granted the juvenile is a "liar," and generally assume the law is always being violated by this type of juvenile. The juvenile is simply a "no good punk," and not someone to help and support. The probation officer stresses the distinctive features of the juvenile's social environment, moving from one "social fact" (the mother is "handicapped" in controlling her child) to another (the juvenile's brother is a "bad influence"), to still another (the juvenile's companions are an "undesirable influence"). Yet the mother was "able to control Smithfield's activities and companions for a long period of time," and it is only during the current school year that the "undesirable companions" have exercised their effect. But there is Smithfield's "general attitude" which "regressed" because of associating with undesirable companions against his mother's wishes and knowledge. Thus, the "attitude" is affected by negative social conditions (the companions) despite other presumed positive social conditions (the mother, the school personnel presumably "working with him"). But the fact that the school personnel have said "they are willing to continue working with Smithfield and the minor's mother has acknowledged a desire to continue working with him" and will contact the probation officer when the boy doesn't "conform," all lead to the recommendation that probation be continued. The warning is stated fairly directly that if "their responsibilities" are not met, then the juvenile will be removed from the home. What is missing from the report are the many conversations between the probation officer and Smithfield's mother, Smithfield and the probation officer, persons in the Welfare and Attendance office and the probation officer, where exchanges on Smithfield focus on some interest in "doing something" for the juvenile, the juvenile indicating remorse, a willingness to "try harder," "be careful," let the probation officer know when "things get rough," and the like. The probation officer's report becomes an unclear synthesis of the encounters so that activities and "feelings" are "closed" to create sets in which the probation officer "sizes up" the situation so he can apply abstract or general rules allowing the trust relationship to operate and can thus assume the juvenile is worth supporting. The juvenile must convince the probation officer that he will follow the general policies or rules suggested by: "obey" your mother, "work hard in school," stay away from "undesirable" friends, and, most important, maintain a "good attitude" toward persons with some kind of official authority. Notice how the interview in Chapter 4 is integral to an understanding of all cases. Virtually everything pivots on behavior regarded as reflecting a "good attitude." And the determination that a "good attitude" exists is based upon the use of background expectancies. Actual crimes, from the point of view of the police, do not become aggravated cases unless they are considered "serious" and accompanied by a "bad attitude." Such characterizations are not simply a function of rule violations. But notice that very little actually changes in Smithfield's life. The school situation remains the same; he will be unwelcomed by his teachers; the school personnel from Attendance and Welfare will ask if he is "adjusting" well; the police will continue to question him about any incidents occurring at his school or neighborhood under the assumption he is "probably involved"; his mother will remind him "bad things" are in store for him if he "messes up" again; and his probation officer will either speak with him by phone, occasionally see him in his office, or merely receive a monthly form filled out by the juvenile stating he is "staying out of trouble" and meeting the conditions of his probation.

The digression is intended to underscore the conditions under which any change in the juvenile or the family's daily activities could occur. I am arguing that in cases like Smithfield there is virtually no change because no one is prepared to pay the price of altering their own daily existence as a condition for influencing or altering the juvenile's daily round of activities. While the general policies or rules laid down are recognized by all as important (curfew, association with "bad" friends, etc.), the implementation is difficult because it presumes careful attention to particular problems that can arise and concerted action by others. It is much easier and convenient to assume that verbal discussions will somehow accomplish the same objective, that is, "it will only lead to more trouble," "you've got to change your attitude," and the like. The law-enforcement agencies seem to rely primarily upon sporadic verbal exchanges until such time as they feel it no longer "does any good." At this point families with resources can obtain counsel or send their children out of the community, while those not so disposed or without resources must go along with county and state remedies.

Two months after the burglary episode Smithfield became involved in another matter with the police and the incident was listed on the police report as Petty Theft from the junior high school he was attending. The report states:

> While at [name] Jr. Hi on another matter the informant reported that the above three boys have been involved in and suspect in many thefts in the past. On the above date a young girl reported her coin purse missing while in class, the purse contained 70 cents. Investigation revealed that C [juvenile] reportedly found the purse and laid it on the desk of M who stated, Are you giving it to me, C reported he was at which time Elston took the purse and contents. Later M asked Elston if he was going to give it back and Elston said no and gave M half of the money, all lied when first questioned about the matter. Mr. [teacher] stated that Elston had since been suspended and thrown off the school grounds for theft, open defiance of authority etc. He was going to

recommend to the boys P.O. [Probation Officer] that he be excluded from the school. C was also suspended and the matter referred to his P.O. Writer talked to M about this theft, the theft of a jacket sometime ago and advised him that further theft would result in formal action. His parents advised by the school. Copy of Report to the probation office Re: Elston and C.

Notice that the officer was at the junior high school "on another matter" and obtained information about Smithfield from an informant. The phrase "investigation revealed" again truncates considerable conversation. There is a reference to "open defiance of authority" and the sense of dealing with routine troublemakers. The officer's remark that "all lied when first questioned" suggests the kind of dialogue upon which the report was drafted, but masks the unstated information the officer regarded as "lies." The officer's assertion that the juveniles all lied cannot be taken for granted, but we have no way of specifying the conditions under which it would be accepted or rejected. It can be speculated, however, that if the probation officer also states the juvenile is a "liar," then the judge is likely to accept such an allegation. Many judges whom I observed made remarks like "you have lied to us too often" when denying a lenient final disposition. Probation officers are initially sympathetic to the juvenile despite police insistence upon punitive action, yet allegations about the juvenile's social or moral character constitute "evidence" of guilt, innocence, incorrigibility, dangerousness, "bad attitude toward authority," and the like, providing others with information for nontrivial decisions affecting immediate and long-range life chances of the juvenile. The juvenile initially is evaluated, therefore, within a context of contingent scenes of interaction by persons who have the authority to influence his present and future life chances, but where the ambiguous character of their referents (the things to which they allude, point, describe) must be taken for granted in written reports as clear, cogent, "obvious," and objective properties.

Remarks about the juvenile's activities are "conclusive" for the police qua police, and they expect others will recognize and honor their intentions. For the officer to say he "talked to M about this theft, the theft of a jacket sometime ago and advised him that further theft would result in formal action," assumes the officer is convinced M is definitely guilty, even though formal action was not being taken against him. The officer does not always make it clear that his action (filing or not filing an application for petition) is justified by some body of evidence, or his feeling that the boy is a "good kid," although such reflections often are intended by the officer. The juvenile may tell the officer "you got nothing on me," and the officer may reply that if there is any way to "get" the juvenile on some later occasion, it will be done. If the juvenile has the "right attitude," then the officer may tell him he will not take any action because the juvenile is a "good kid," although the officer may privately feel the evidence or his "case" against the juvenile did not warrant arrest or a petition, or will not be acceptable to others like his superiors, the probation department, the judge, etc. When dealing with juveniles like Smithfield, officers usually feel that the issue is clear regardless of the legality of their actions; they feel morally "right," and convinced the "community" is behind them.

Smithfield was placed in Juvenile Hall following this latest encounter with the police, and his probation officer began collecting additional information from the school officials to include in his next report to the juvenile court. The school report stated that Smithfield's I.Q. was 86 with low scores in various other tests given to him. Attendance at school was given as satisfactory with no truancies. The following information was given as evidence of academic and nonacademic progress:

Has good work habits	Failure
Gets along well with others	Below average
Accepts responsibility	Failure
Uses his abilities	Below average
Has good manual coordination	Superior
Has good health habits	Below average
Is obedient and cooperative	Failure
Brings work material regularly	Below average

Grade 7 From 4/10/61 to 6/16/61		Grade 8 from 9/11/61 to present	
English	D	English	D
Social Studies	D	Social Studies	D
Math	C	Math	F
Music, vocal	C	Science	D
Woodworking	B	Woodworking	B
Homeroom	D	Homeroom	D
P.E.	B	P.E.	B

SOCIAL STUDIES—MR. [NAME]—ACADEMIC PROGRESS. Smithfield is barely getting by with D or D— grades. When here, if he would spend more energy on subject matter instead of fooling around, goofing off, etc., he might do better. The first week he returned from Juvenile hall he did fairly good, but soon he reverted to the old ways. He cannot read.

SOCIAL ADJUSTMENT. Is dishonest, will cheat, copy, and do most everything except do his work.

ENGLISH—MRS. [NAME]—ACADEMIC PROGRESS. Very poor, but he has very low ability. He does not put forth any effort.

SOCIAL ADJUSTMENT. He has a sense of humor in the classroom. He has to be watched constantly, however.

MATH—MRS. [NAME]—ACADEMIC PROGRESS. Recently Smithfield seems to be trying in class. He is very limited as to ability—but acts as though he wants to do some work for a change. I don't know how long this change will be effective though.

SOCIAL ADJUSTMENT. Since he started trying in class he has caused very little trouble. For a long time he was one of the ones who created most of the class disturbance.

SCIENCE—MRS. [NAME]—ACADEMIC PROGRESS. Very poor science student— ranging from D to F. I believe he could do better if he could develop a better listening approach and applied himself. Smithfield does have slight reading difficulty.

SOCIAL ADJUSTMENT. Smithfield seems to be most unhappy with school. He has a rather belligerent attitude toward anyone in authority but seems to be fairly well adjusted with his peer group.

ART—MR. [NAME]—ACADEMIC PROGRESS. Doing next to failing work. Partly because of absence but has little desire to achieve.

SOCIAL ADJUSTMENT. Listless attitude—not a trouble maker but has no positive desire to work.

P.E.—MR. [NAME]—ACADEMIC PROGRESS. I have written reports on this boy at least three times. His problems have not lessened visibly since these other reports.

SOCIAL ADJUSTMENT. He has never been a discipline problem in my class. He is not a trustworthy person and bears watching all the time. I would say this boy has problems at home which are deep rooted and of long duration. If given an opportunity to excel he seems to do his best work. He is likeable, and not a trouble maker for me.

HOMEROOM—MRS. [NAME]—ACADEMIC PROGRESS. Since he has come back this last time he has done better—has made some progress in doing written work. I do not expect this to last, however.

SOCIAL ADJUSTMENT. Behaves somewhat better.

Notice that except for science and art, the teachers remain the same persons who submitted reports quoted earlier. The science teacher states that he is a poor student, but Smithfield "could do better" if he "applied himself." That Smithfield has a "slight reading difficulty" and is "most unhappy with school." After noting a "belligerent attitude toward anyone in authority," this teacher concludes that Smithfield is "fairly well adjusted with his peer group." The art teacher, however, does not mention the "authority" problem and states Smithfield is "not a trouble maker," but he does say the work is failing only because there is "no positive desire to work." The social studies teacher seems to hold the same views expressed in the earlier report, while the English teacher now states that Smithfield "has very low ability," and although he must "be watched constantly," there is the remark that "he has a sense of humor in the classroom." The math teacher acknowledges that Smithfield "seems to be trying in class" and that "he wants to do some work for a change." But he then adds that "I don't know how long this change will be effective though." The math teacher also acknowledges that his "social adjustment" has improved. The P.E. teacher continues to feel that Smithfield is not "trustworthy," but can do better, and that he is not "a troublemaker for me." Finally, the homeroom teacher notes an improvement in work and adjustment, but states that she does "not expect this to last."

The teachers are not very optimistic about Smithfield changing his "bad" ways, but would, of course, welcome a change. Their remarks suggest that he is a "hopeless" case. The teachers cannot believe their own acknowledged observations that he has improved or changed, but expect him to return to his "old ways." At this stage of Smithfield's career, the juvenile officers of City A were telling me that there was no "hope" in this case, suggesting the probation department was obstructing police efforts to send the boy away. The exchanges I witnessed between juvenile officers and Smithfield's junior high school teachers and administrators suggested Smithfield should be sent away, preferably to a Youth Authority prison. My impression was that school officials were cooperating with the police to find the grounds for convincing the probation officials Smithfield should be sent away. Notice, however, the probation officer must view any new problems at school, or with the police, as a violation of trust between the probation officer and Smithfield. The "proof" of change rests with Smithfield, and even his teachers acknowledged, although often disbelievingly, that there was a change, but that it would not "last."

The probation officer also obtained the customary reports from Juvenile Hall about Smithfield's latest stay there. The teacher reports the following:

> Smithfield does not appear to be interested in improving his educational status. He constantly expresses his dislike for school. He does not complete his assignments because he wastes his time. Smithfield enjoys participating in disturbances, whenever anyone else starts one. He also enjoys starting disturbances. Smithfield has no respect for authority. When asked to do something he often is recalcitrant and sits and pouts. He does not get along well with his peers.

The superintendent of Juvenile Hall submitted the following report which is based primarily upon information provided by counselors and supervisors who work with the juveniles on a day-to-day basis:

> Smithfield has displayed an inconsistent behavior pattern during his detention, revealing both friendly and argumentative attitudes towards his peers

and supervisors. These attitudes have manifested themselves in both the work and recreational phases of our group activities. He has demonstrated an ability to think and act for himself and does not appear to be easily influenced. Comparing his present detention with those previous, he has shown improvement in some areas.

Smithfield needs constant supervision in managing his personal affairs, though his grooming and hygiene habits are favorable. He is not considered a security risk at this time.

Both the teacher and superintendent are the same persons who wrote the previously quoted reports (see pp. 218-9), and a change is noticeable in both. The teacher has apparently decided that Smithfield is a total failure; "when asked to do something he often is recalcitrant and sits and pouts," and he "has no respect for authority." The junior high school teachers' remarks about Smithfield's lack of "respect toward authority" does not clarify the use of "pouting" as part of the behavior pattern, for it is not clear if the "pouting" means a total disregard for the teacher's authority. The "pouting" remark, along with the superintendent's more favorable remarks, do not suggest someone (using the language quoted as evidence) who is completely unconcerned with something called "authority." The various utterances complicate a simple interpretation of "no respect for authority." The superintendent's remarks seem to support the "disbelieving" or "temporary" improvement noted by the junior high school teachers.

Now I turn to the probation officer's interpretation of the above-cited statements presented in his official report to the court. The key question is: how does the probation officer seek to utilize the materials for recommending a particular course of action to the judge? Much of the report repeats prior accounts given by the probation officer, but some repetition is unavoidable if the sequence as told by the officer is to be quoted verbatim. The theft reported by the police does not appear to be the central issue, but the "defiance of authority" charge from the school officials is underscored.

On or about March 14, 1962, while attending [name] Jr. High School, Smithfield Elston was running in an area of the school grounds, contrary to the directives of the school authorities, and was observed by a "safety." This writer is advised that a "safety" is a person appointed by official school personnel to attempt to police the campus. The "safety" reportedly asked Smithfield to stop running; Smithfield ignored the "safety" and the "safety" reported this incident to Mr. [name], Vice-Principal at [name] Jr. High. Mr. [vice-prin.] saw Smithfield near a basketball court at the school and told him to sit on a specific bench until the end of the period. Mr. [vice-prin.] then walked to an area which was out of Smithfield's vision and Smithfield, believing Mr. [vice-prin.] to have left the area, left the bench, sought out the aforementioned safety and attempted to assault the said student and was pushing the student around in an effort to get him to fight when stopped by Mr. [vice-prin.] Smithfield was immediately suspended from school, sent home and Mr. [vice-prin.] has advised the Probation Officer that the school authorities intend to take exclusion proceedings, because of the minor's history of school difficulty. . . .

It appeared to this writer, when Smithfield last appeared in Juvenile Court in February, 1962, that, although Mrs. Elston had been unable to control Smithfield's activities and companions for a long period of time, it was felt that she was making progress in that area. Consequently, the Probation Officer recommended that the minor be returned home on continued probation. It now appears to the Probation Officer that the minor's actions in themselves show a general attitude and behavior regression. This, coupled with the fact that the minor is having continued difficulty at his present school, indicates that the boy should be removed from the home and program worked out outside of the community. Although many of Smithfield's attitudes indicate that he might be in need of professional help, as could be rendered by the California Youth Authority, it would appear realistic to attempt an adjustment in a foster home before considering Commitment. Therefore, foster home placement is being recommended. The minor is eligible to receive Aid to Needy Children Funds. [dated April 5, 1962]

The probation officer states that Smithfield's mother had been unable to control the boy's behavior and companions even though he felt she made "progress." The school incident is viewed as ["bad"] "actions in themselves" and "show a general attitude and behavior regression." The mention of a "program . . . outside of the community" and that Smithfield's "attitudes indicate that he might be in need of professional help, as could be rendered by the California Youth Authority," and then the suggestion of a foster home, suggest the boy has been warned that his present conduct will lead to Youth Authority imprisonment, but will be spared the latter and sent to a foster home if he "shapes up." Few probation officers ever wish to recommend Youth Authority commitment because it signifies they were unsuccessful in working with the juvenile. But such a recommendation is sometimes used as a threat to obtain compliance, or some kind of commitment to the trust relationship previously established. For the probation officer to recommend a foster home placement, he must convince himself and the judge that the juvenile is "really a good kid" even though his behavior is making it difficult to keep him home. The officer can, in effect, "side with the kid," but cannot convince the school or the judge if there are continual incidents. To say that the juvenile "might be in need for professional help" at the Youth Authority might appear to mean there are better psychiatric and social work services available. But the Youth Authority is viewed by probation officers as the last resource available because it is known to be a prison for juveniles regardless of what other label is attached. Notice that no professional help was given Smithfield in the school or community.

On May 3, 1962 Smithfield was placed in a foster home in a small town near City A. There are no remarks in the record to indicate the nature of the home. On May 24, 1962, the new school in the city of Forest wrote the foster parents that Smithfield "failed to dress regularly for Physical Education." Yet physical education was his "best" school activity in City A. No other difficulties are reported until the following September when Smithfield was tardy to class five times and a letter was sent to his foster home. The school record reveals the following entries:

9/25/62 Disrespectful in an unserious manner. A sort of "Hey Man" attitude.	Conference & discussed seriousness of such an attitude. Agreed it would not happen again.
10/ 3/62 Talking, not obeying his teacher and disrespectful to the teacher.	Conduct report sent to his guardian, Mrs. [name], and probation officer, Mr. [name].
11/16/62 Running on campus.	Detention 11/20/62.
11/20/62 7 unexcused tardies to classes.	Detention 11/11/62.
12/11/62 Suspension—cheating and lying.	Suspended until Jan. 2, 1963.

Another form from the school states that Smithfield was in "open and persistent defiance of the authority of the teacher."

1/ 4/63 Parent (guardian) conference.	Guardian conf.—should improve since conf. Guardian very cooperative.
1/16/63 Belligerent to another student.	Conduct report home—Talked with Mrs. [foster mother] about the incident on the phone. I will call the incident to the attention of Mr. [probation officer].
1/17/63 Marking up the floors with his shoes.	Detention on 1/24/63 to clean the floors in Mr. [teacher] room.
2/ 8/63 Too many tardies to classes.	Detention 2/14/63.
2/18/63 Disobeys his teacher constantly. ("When he is told to stop talking and singing in the classroom he just ignores her as if he didn't even hear her.")	Sent to the office and is quite anti-school. Conduct report sent home to Mrs. [foster mother].

The probation officer's record contains a note dated 2/21/63, stating: "Made call to [name] Jr. Hi—talked with [ass't prin., prin., teachers] and Smithfield. Smithfield desirous of return home. Consequently was encouraged to set this as goal and give P.O. ammunition to ask for an order to allow this at completion of present school year." The school record continues:

3/ 5/63 Using vulgar language in the classroom.	Conduct report sent home.
3/ 6/63 Shooting beans from a beanshooter.	Smithfield admits shooting beans at other students with a beanshooter. One boy has been hit in the face this a.m. with a bean covered with saliva. The bean shooter was confiscated.
3/27/63 Misbehaving in the classroom.	One swat administered in the Principals Office by [ass't prin.] in the presence of [principal].
5/ 1/63 Insubordinate—refused to quit talking. Smithfield, according to other students, has been stealing food from the Cafeteria.	Letter sent home and copy to probation off.

(The probation officer's notes here reveal that he received the report and "Went to [school], counselled with Smithfield 5/10/63.")

5/14/63 He insists on talking in class even after he was told not to. He was told to write 50 punishment sentences and he boldly refused.	Mr. [prob. off.] was contacted and interviewed Smithfield at school. Smithfield's general attitude is poor.
5/27/63 Noon time disturbance.	Letter attached.

I suggest the small town in which Smithfield was sent for foster home placement is not geared to handle juveniles already labeled "troublemakers." The presence of a "troublemaker" is widely disseminated to all teachers and students in a small school at the outset, but the fact of dissemination of information is not included in the various remarks made about Smithfield's "adjustment" to his new environment. I assume it is clear from the probation officer's remarks that he still had hopes of having Smithfield return to his home in City A: "Smithfield is desirous of return home. Consequently was encouraged to set this as goal and give P.O. ammunition to ask for an order to allow this at completion of present school year." I am not denying the significance for the school of the statements that Smithfield did engage in activities considered "bad," but wish to note the absence of any reference to the juvenile's views on the matter; they were never considered relevant and included as some kind of defense. Nor were there remarks suggesting Smithfield did not like his foster home, or was disturbed by the move, or found the teachers and students to be negative towards him. It is difficult to document my impressionistic observations suggesting the school officials and students found Smithfield "dangerous" and "frightening," regardless of what he did, viewing his presence as grounds for suspicion. The school report is clearly negative and provides ample justification for the subsequent action of placing Smithfield back in Juvenile Hall, as do the following two letters, which include the school's final statement.

REGARDING SMITHFIELD ELSTON   May 27, 1963

At 12:30 p.m., during lunch hour, Smithfield refused to obey the requests and orders of Mr. [name], noontime supervisor. Mr. [name] had asked Smithfield 2 or 3 times to refrain from "cutting" into the lunch line. Smithfield replied he didn't have to do what Mr. [name] had told him to do. He said to Mr. [name] he [Smithfield] would do what he wanted to do regardless of what the teacher said.

After these remarks, Mr. [name] referred Smithfield to the office. I talked with Smithfield at some length about what I felt the probation department was attempting to do with him (get him back to his mother in City A after his school year) and how we had tried to help him in spite of his many referrals. While talking with Smithfield about his problems, I also felt the situation was serious enough to warrant suspension.

Knowing how close Mr. [name], Smithfield's Probation Officer, was working with the boy, I felt I should call him and ask his advice. Mr. [name] suggested I suspend the boy for a rather short period until he could come out and talk with him. Mr. [name] implied that it would possibly be Wednesday [2 days away]. I then attempted to call Mrs. [name], Smithfield's foster mother or guardian. I called her number at least 3 times at different intervals but received no answer. At this time, with Mr. [principal] advice, we suspended Smithfield for three days. The reasoning was along the lines of Mr. [prob. off.] recommendation.

Smithfield was then informed he was suspended for three school days verbally. At the same time I asked him to sign the suspension letters and put one of them in an envelope along with a note to Mrs. [foster mother] explaining what we were trying to do. Smithfield ripped open the envelope and read the contents of the note even though I told him what was in the letter. As it was then 2:40, I assumed Smithfield was leaving to get on the bus. He left my office muttering to himself.

Later after the episode with Mr. [teacher] a second time, as he was standing in the office, he told me he was not going to wait for Mr. [prob. off.] but was going home with his brother. Mr. [prob. off.] arrived shortly after the remark. Later in the office with Mr. [teacher] and Mr. [prob. off.], Smithfield admitted most of the allegations against him. He only differed with the number of times

Mr. [teacher] had asked him to refrain from cutting and with the statement of Mr. [teacher] that he [Smithfield] had said he did not have to obey Mr. [teacher].

Mrs. [foster mother] also came into the school Tuesday May 28, 1963, and covered most of the events in which she was involved with Smithfield and the Probation Department. She said she felt the school had been very patient and understanding with Smithfield and that actually we had waited too long in suspending him (in her opinion). She said he was one of the "worst" boys she had ever had in her home. He violated her curfew and seem to have money when, in her opinion, he should not have had it. He also contributed to a great deal of the household damage during his stay.

[name], ASSISTANT PRINCIPAL.

(The actual incidents are described in some detail by the teacher involved in the following report:)

REGARDING SMITHFIELD ELSTON   May 31, 1963

At approximately 12:20 p.m., May 27, 1963, Mr. [teacher] took Smithfield Elston out of the lunch line for cutting in front of other students. A few minutes later, I observed Smithfield away from the table where Mr. [teacher] had placed him. I told him to sit down again, but he told me he didn't have to do what I said since Mr. [teacher] had sent him to the table. After repeating my order several times, he finally sat down, but not without arguing all this time about not doing what I told him to do. Later, Mr. [teacher] released him to go to lunch.

Some time later I observed Smithfield near the front of the line again, but he was *not in* line. I asked him to move away, but a while later was again at the front of the line. When I asked him to move, he again argued, and told me I couldn't stop him from talking to a friend, which he claims he was doing. After a while of arguing I sent him to the office. He didn't seem to want to move, so I took him by the elbow, and attempted to lead him to the office. He jerked away, and did not head toward the office. Finally, when he got to the office, he told me he didn't have to stay there.

Later, after Mr. [ass't prin.] spoke with Smithfield, he was sent to the bus to go home. Rather than going home, he came down to my room. The time was between 6th and 7th periods, and I was at the back of the room. Smithfield came to the door and when I realized it, I told him to get away from the door, and out of the room. After the third time I told him to leave he pushed the door closed, and started down the hall. As he left he said, "kiss my ass." I went after him and by holding his arm, stopped him, since he refused to stop when I told him to stop. We talked, but he kept trying to get away. I sent him to the office, but decided to escort him. He refused to move in the direction I sent him in, and was very slow, so I took him to the office by pulling him by the arm. All the way up to the office he held back, grabbed posts to hold on to, etc. He had his fist clenched all the way as if to hit me. His remarks on the way to the office were that I had no right to hold on to him, and that he didn't have to go to the office.

[name], Instructor

The seriousness of Smithfield's conduct to the school officials seems clear, although the encounters described by the assistant principal and the instructors do not include the juvenile's perspective. The instructor's remarks about "cutting in front of other students," arguing, refusing to obey an order, having to force Smithfield to the office, returning to harass the teacher in his class, telling the teacher to "kiss my ass," having to be forced to the office again, and having "his fist clenched all the way as if to hit me," leave little doubt as to the school's interpretation of Smithfield's conduct. The assistant principal notes that he told Smithfield "how we had tried to help him in spite of his many referrals" and that the suspension would have been for a short period (following the probation officer's suggestion). But then Smithfield "ripped open the envelope" and had the second encounter with the instructor. The foster mother's remarks were included as an apparent final documentation of the seriousness of Smithfield's conduct. A reader of such documents could only conclude that Smithfield is "bad," as the remarks suggest. For the participants, Smithfield was a menace; yet notice the kind of vicious circle that develops in which the kind of "rehabilitation" presumably intended by the juvenile court law presumes we "know" the obvious nature of the juvenile's conduct, and can agree as to what would be "acceptable" behavior, supposedly based on identical meaning structures for the participants. In depicting the juvenile, only negative, or at best, guarded positive features are emphasized or reported. The judgments of each participant are honored as "just" and "accurate," but the juvenile's view is missing. The probation officer must decide between the pressures the police, school officials, and the neighborhood exert for sending the juvenile away, and his own feelings that the juvenile is "basically a good kid," or the police have "got it in for the kid," or the juvenile is "not trying hard enough." The official reports never reveal the reservations directly and, even when revealed indirectly, can only be documented with verbatim offhand remarks that indicate the doubts. As observers, we are forced to suspend, because of a lack of documentation, what the consequences are of assuming the participants at school view Smithfield as the "worse kind of Negro," as opposed to viewing his behavior as "remarkable," given the environment he must negotiate. When Smithfield states "they" all "pick on" him, it is difficult to specify the significance of his remarks because we are not privy to the complicated network of communications that would lend credence to such utterances. Nor is it possible to determine the relevance of the foster home or the views of some probation officers who claim foster homes are attempts to "make money" and not to help juveniles. But the probation officer appears to be motivated by a desire to delay commitment to the Youth Authority.

I want to note further information before closing my discussion of Smithfield. His school report of June 4, 1963 revealed four C's, one D, and one F. His "citizenship" is listed as "unsatisfactory" in two of the six courses. The report also reveals the following:

Description of behavior

Truancy—No. Days	0	Fighting	
Tardies—No. Times	8	Gambling	
Disobedient	8	Smoking	
Insolent	3	Destruction of School	
Cursing	1	Property	1
Poor School Work		Other	
Persistent defiance of school rules and regulations			X

Expulsion is recommended   Yes   X   No

Summary of case:

Smithfield went out of his way to show lack of respect for authority. He openly swore at the teacher, in front of other students, and also defied Mr. [teacher]. This type of behavior cannot be tolerated.

Summary prepared by [principal]

I do not want to belabor the point that Smithfield actually improved as a student during the year in the foster home, but based strictly on his school record and the lack of police contacts for the year, there is much that could be said of a positive nature given the same "facts." Although viewed by officials as a "hard core" delinquent type, Smithfield's behavior does not include activities such as truancy, fighting, gambling, smoking, and official violations of the penal code. The remorse and "promise" shown the probation officer, an essential element for maintaining the trust relationship, is not readily demonstrated to the judge unless the probation officer manipulates the school letters and reports of the type quoted above. On June 12, 1963, the Juvenile Court in City A decided to allow Smithfield to return to his mother's home in City A. Most of the probation officer's report repeats earlier material, including remarks taken from the statements by the assistant principal and the instructor. A few of the probation officer's remarks are worth quoting here, however:

Smithfield then was placed in the home of Mrs. [name] and according to Mrs. [name], made a fair adjustment in the home but as reflected in the circumstances, has not adjusted in a school program and as had been set as a pattern while living in City A, was attracted to the least desirable companions in the school setting.

Smithfield is sullen, full of hostility, uncooperative, antagonistic, will not accept the fact that many of his difficulties are of his own making and constantly blames all others for his troubles and seems to feel that he is being picked on. Smithfield's open defiance of authority and attitude indicate that stronger placement than foster home is needed, however, this same attitude and behavior indicate that a program such as [name] Boys' Ranch would not be strong enough to control him. It would appear that in respect to placement, the facility of the California Youth Authority would more closely meet this minor's needs. However, due to the fact that Smithfield has been out of his home for over a year, combined with the fact that his brother, [name], who is a much more stable person and is looked up to by Smithfield is being returned home at the end of the current school year, that there is a possibility of Smithfield working with [brother] during the summer vacation and because of the fact that he will be starting a new school, [name] High School, and the Juvenile Hall comment that Smithfield has shown some progress since his previous detention, the Probation Officer is recommending that Smithfield be returned home. This recommendation is being made, however, with the intention of recommending to the Juvenile Court that the minor be committed to the Youth Authority if he fails to adjust at home, becomes involved in difficulty with the law or begins having the same difficulty with the law or begins having the same difficulty at [name] High School next fall as he has in his last three schools.

The Probation Officer states Smithfield "made a fair adjustment in the home" contrary to what was reported in the principal's report about the foster mother's negative statement. The behavior at school is viewed as a "pattern," but there is no mention of the variation from teacher to teacher in each school, nor any mention of the students' and teachers' conceptions of Smithfield personally, or the causes of Smithfield's "sullen, full of hostility, uncooperative, antagonistic" behavior. The probation officer is the only one mentioning "least desirable companions." The emphasis is on Smithfield's inability to control himself, not on his environment as a problematic issue, because according to the probation officer, Smithfield "constantly blames all others for his troubles and seems to feel that he is being picked on." The continual reference to Smithfield's "open defiance of authority and attitude" is viewed as ruling out the possibility of placement in a boys' ranch, where he is likely to receive the personalized and sympathetic treatment he did not, in my opinion, obtain at school. The boys' ranch is a closely supervised environment, in pleasant, nonpunitive surroundings, with personnel not threatened nor as concerned with "trouble-making" Negro males. The fear that Smithfield will "mess up" at the boys' ranch and "spoil" the record of those who "successfully" complete the program there, is this writer's impressionistic opinion of why Smithfield would not be recommended for such a placement. The probation officer must take a calculated risk and then construct a biography of the juvenile in order to convince local probation and ranch authorities that Smithfield is a "good" risk. The fact that Youth Authority placement is not recommended but mentioned as the next logical placement (euphemistically referred to as the place to "meet this minor's needs") suggests the probation officer was wavering in his decision about what to do with Smithfield. A suggestion of placement at home requires some justification, for the latter as opposed to the boys' ranch offers far less control. Yet the probation officer covers himself by simultaneously mentioning the Youth Authority as the next logical choice. Mentioning the older brother seems quite unusual here, since an earlier probation report flatly stated that the juvenile was not to be returned home if this brother was in the home. In the earlier report the probation officer finally allowed Smithfield to return home because the older brother (a Youth Authority ward) *was not to be home.* To now call the older brother "a much more stable person" is a complete switch in the evaluation of the home environment. My conjecture is that the probation officer seemed to be sympathetic to the juvenile and felt Smithfield was not "bad enough" to be sent directly to the Youth Authority, but was not willing to take the risk of recommending someone to the boys' ranch who might "fail" and reflect badly on his judgment and the "good" record of the ranch. To justify sending the boy back home, the probation officer was forced to mention the older brother and the idea of a new school environment. Mentioning the Youth Authority provides the probation officer with the necessary justification for the next placement "if he fails to adjust at home, becomes involved in difficulty with the law, or begins having the same difficulty at" the new high school "as he has in his last three schools."

I want to mention the Juvenile Hall Superintendent's report dated June 13, 1963 (the Juvenile Hall school report is almost identical to past reports), because of the language used to describe Smithfield, by now a well-known visitor.

> Smithfield has shown some progress since his previous detention in Juvenile Hall. He associates freely with all elements and does not appear to be influenced by any particular members in the group. The youngster enters the recreational program with enthusiasm, possessing better than average ability. Smithfield accepts authority and appears to be sincere in his efforts to conform, however, he requires close supervision due to his "cocky" attitude and impatience with younger group members. He does not volunteer, however, assigned tasks are accomplished satisfactorily. Although Smithfield possesses leadership potential, he is not mature enough to utilize this ability. He manages his personal affairs well, displaying average hygiene and grooming habits. Smithfield is an individualist who requires positive recognition and stern parental type guidance. During this detention period, he has received no visitors.

The probation officer's sympathetic view of Smithfield may have been reinforced by the Juvenile Hall report. The suggestion that Smithfield "has
shown some progress" is underscored by the superintendent's remarks that
the boy "appears to be sincere in his efforts to conform," even though "he
requires close supervision due to his 'cocky' attitude." The use of the term
"individualist" is equivocal because the boy "requires positive recognition
and stern parental type guidance." Notice how properties one or more
"others" may label "open defiance of authority" or a "bad attitude," may
also be called "cocky" or the manifestation of an "individualist" who must
be "guided" closely. It is, of course, possible that the behavioral properties
are different for the different audiences and that they are responding differentially to different activities. But admitting the possibility of differential
performance before different audiences assumes the juvenile behaves differently because he perceives and interprets the others as "different," or
others "see" the object differently, or both possibilities. The school officials
and probation officers seldom provide the reader with information about
Smithfield's "point of view," but only with the "evidence" for negative sanctions. Even "positive" attributes imputed to Smithfield cannot be contrasted
with the many occasions of "trouble" perceived as negative activities.

On August 13, 1963, Smithfield and another juvenile were picked up for
a burglary involving the theft of a man's wrist watch, and a "piggy bank"
with $2.00 in dimes. Smithfield was placed in Juvenile Hall again, and the
teacher wrote another negative report, but the superintendent's report was
different from the one dated June 13, 1963.

> Since his previous detention period, Smithfield has shown some improvement
> in his general attitude. However, his peer relationships have suffered due to his
> aggressive and bully-like behavior toward weaker peers. The youngster is very
> active, and displays better than average ability. . . . Smithfield appears to be
> suspicious of authority figures. He requires maximum supervision. . . .
> Smithfield appears to have some leadership potential, but chooses not to use
> it, at least not in a positive manner. He is slovenly about his appearance, and
> his hygiene habits are poor. His table manners reflect a previous undesirable
> environment. . . . His general demeanor is swaggering and cocky, sometimes
> openly hostile. Smithfield is an individualist who requires positive recogni-
> tion. . . .

The last report from Juvenile Hall stated that Smithfield "accepts authority
and appears sincere in his efforts to conform," but that now he "appears to
be suspicious of authority figures." The previous report stated that he displays "average hygiene and grooming habits," but that now he "is slovenly
about his appearance, and his hygiene habits are poor." The superintendent's
report does not link the reported changes in Smithfield's behavior to such

possibilities as the juvenile seeing his predicament as hopeless, or the probation officer telling Juvenile Hall personnel that Smithfield has "had it," or telling the juvenile he has had his "last chance." There is now more of a blurring between "defiance of authority" and being an "individualist."

A discussion of how bureaucratically organized activities depict social objects must clarify how various officials perceive and interpret the object over time, how past and recent negative activities become documentary evidence for justifying the object's present predicament, and how such documents are then utilized and interpreted by others as "correct" depictions of events and the object in question.

A probation officer's report dated September 5, 1963 recommended, and the court concurred, that Smithfield be committed to the California Youth Authority. The probation officer's report was an almost exact duplication of prior reports. The boy was released from the Youth Authority on March 18, 1964 and returned to City A. On May 18, 1964, he was apprehended for burglary and placed in Juvenile Hall. On June 1, 1964, Smithfield was released from Juvenile Hall to the custody of his mother by order of the parole officer. On June 8, 1964, he was apprehended for theft and placed in Juvenile Hall again. On June 13, 1964, the boy was released to the Youth Authority. A few months later he was released again and then apprehended for another burglary and returned to the Youth Authority.

Smithfield is a "lost cause" and the probation officers recognize unofficially they have perhaps "failed" from the standpoint of their ability to "do something" for him. But the official record will always reveal that the juvenile did not or was not capable of "controlling his actions" and "conforming to the law." The probation officers recognize there is little they can do to alter the juvenile's everyday environment, for they have little control over his day-to-day activities inside and outside of the home. The juvenile's career as some ideal sequence of "what might have been," as opposed to the various interpretations of "what happened," cannot be understood without attention to the multiple perspectives of the different actors involved and how actual encounters are transformed into formal accounts.

The contrast between "Mark" and "Smithfield" is of interest because the problem of actual crime known to the police was never a significant issue as far as probation officials were concerned, whereas, for the police, both juveniles were considered Youth Authority "material." Mark was given informal probation and did not appear in court, and although initially "defiant" to the police, would then "break down" and not be considered a serious "troublemaker" (for instance, continue to question police authority) behaviorally. Smithfield's demeanor was viewed as "serious" because even though initially there were no criminal acts viewed as "serious," the behavior he displayed was considered to be indicative of "undesirable" future conduct. Both youngsters were about the same age, and both homes were described as "inadequate." But Mark's home was "intact" (despite allegations of child neglect), while there was a divorce in Smithfield's family, even though the home was always described as "neat and clean," and the mother as a "good" person. The school system seems to tolerate infractions of rules (school or legal statutes), but not demeanor labeled "defiance of authority." The latter is obviously more of a threat to the school personnel for the maintenance of order than the violation of legal statutes outside of school. But law-enforcement personnel view "defiance of authority" as a "sign" of "bad" things to come, and as an important threat to their ability to maintain control over persons. While different personnel in the juvenile bureau, probation office, or school system may recognize there are environmental conditions that are "unfortunate" and impinging upon the juvenile, the trust relationship each develops is contingent upon the juvenile conforming to abstract general policies or rules that have little articulation with the day-to-day particulars of getting along with peers at home and at school. Officials have limited control over the object in question; no one is willing to "stick their neck out" because each has very limited time and energy to devote to the kind of supervision felt necessary to insure a given program of action. The "objective" conditions labeled by law-enforcement officials hinge on behavioral depictions, divorced from objectified accounts the sociologist could use for revealing how the "same" or "similar" activities are perceived and interpreted by different personnel with different interests and different language usages, in order to convey their evaluations of the objects in question. The motivations of each juvenile are not relevant in the sense in which conventional theories of delinquency seek to explain the motivated character of "delinquent acts" because such motives are not relevant to the decisions of school, police, and probation officials, except as exhibited by an "attitude" in "defiance of authority." Nor do conventional theories of criminal law provide theoretical categories for explaining the interpretations and imputations that hinge on differences in the "right" or "wrong" attitude, or the "proper" kind of "attitude toward authority" that is expected and enforced. Yet a courtroom scene always includes such behavior implicitly. Such concerns do become expressed when parole is an issue. Conventional theories do not recognize the importance of the phenomena each party is responding to, making evaluations of, depicting in moral terms, and the like. Therefore, there is no objectifiable common set of referents from which the different perspectival views are generated in the different community agencies and the juvenile's family or neighbors.

Recall the information that could be inferred from the tables in Chapter 3. There is no way for a researcher to assign unequivocal quantitative significance to the juvenile's behavior before different officials who might define his moral character as "bad"; yet the actual violations of the law as decided by the police do not reveal that notions like "in defiance of authority" or having the "wrong attitude" are central to the decision for placement outside of the home, or the type of outside placement. The obvious evaluation of the "home situation," the parents, the juvenile's "attitude," the juvenile's "companions," his "habits," and his expression of "sorrow" or "remorse," are all integral features of deciding the "delinquent" character of the social object in question. To simply cross-tabulate presumably "objective" factors like broken home, school success as determined by grades, income level of the family (or occupation of the father or neighborhood), and the like, leads to "hard" but false findings, and to misleading conclusions about the behavioral features of delinquent activity considered relevant by law-enforcement agencies. The "leap" from police records, as produced by commonsense coding procedures, to sociological analysis of the motivational, ecological, and organizational properties of delinquency completely ignores direct study of phenomena variously labeled "delinquency," or "bad attitude," or "immature character." In each case the decision to arrest, or filing an application for petition, informal probation, court hearing, foster home placement, boys' ranch placement, or Youth Authority placement, revolves around various contingencies that are "closed" by decisions to include juveniles in reified categories. The idea of transforming the juvenile into a relevant social type permitting placement in a category that allows for a concrete course of action, as opposed to continuance of no arrest, no petition, no court hearing, no placement, or a particular kind of placement, requires that the contingencies either be dropped as relevant data, or interpreted as evidence for a particular characterization of the object, and thus leading to a subsequent concrete decision or avoidance of a decision. The alternative ways in which the object can be transformed is dependent upon the social scenes that develop and how the social context and object are described in later written reports, or in oral testimony before an official charged with concretizing (validating the transformation of) the object's character. The following chapters will reveal middle-class variations of the general argument.

NOTES

1. Cf. Lewis Yablonsky, *The Violent Gang* (New York: Free Press, 1962).
2. Cf. Harvey Sacks, *The Search for Help: No One to Turn To.* Unpublished doctoral dissertation (Berkeley: Department of Sociology, 1966).
3. Notice that the school reports, like all professional evaluations (particularly clinical ones), lack an adversary element. The writer always presumes that his description is the credible one and accurately portrays the social scene attended. The general and abstract character of the language used makes it difficult to speak precisely about such evaluations as "societal reactions" to deviance. In both lay and professional

evaluations the same problem of the environment of objects attended, according to stated and unstated rules, become obstacles to a more precise usage of the notion of "societal reaction." The term as now used is often a convenient gloss, but a gloss, nevertheless.

4. Carl Werthman, *Delinquency and Authority*, unpublished M.A. thesis (Berkeley: Department of Sociology, 1964).

Chapter 6

LAW-ENFORCEMENT PRACTICES AND
MIDDLE-INCOME FAMILIES

The first three cases of "Jorge," "Mark," and "Smithfield" were similar; the families involved would not "close ranks" and mobilize all possible resources "to protect" their child from law-enforcement officials, but often felt that the police and probation officials should "help" them in controlling the juvenile. All three juveniles routinely engaged in what police term "serious" juvenile offenses. In the two cases that follow we have dissimilar offense types, but higher-income families and direct attempts by the parents to block removal of the juvenile from the home.

The first case (that of "Drew") is of interest because the father is a police officer with a little rank, living in his own home and, from all outward appearances, his family would be described as "respectable" members of the community. The second case, that of "Donald" reflects a family that sociologists would describe as "upwardly mobile," living in a large home, in one of the "better" neighborhoods of City A, with both parents fairly active in civic groups and "society-column" type of activities. The cases demonstrate how both law-enforcement and family members, despite doubts, seek to preserve ideal images of the family unit and individual members. When parents challenge police and probation imputations of deviance, when parents can mobilize favorable occupational and household appearances, and when parents directly question law-enforcement evaluations and dispositions, law-enforcement personnel find it difficult (because of their own commitments to appearances—lack of a broken home, "reasonable" parents, "nice" neighborhoods, etc.) to make a case for criminality in direct confrontation with family resources and a "rosy" projected future. Imputations of illness replace those of criminality, or the incidents are viewed as "bad" but products of "things" done by "kids" today.

Drew

The case of Drew Timmons documents how the parents, police, and probation "cooperate" to transform the juvenile from a "delinquent" to a "sick" character and avoid placement outside of the home. Drew's police record follows: (Date of birth: 11/8/49)

4/27/60 Juvenile Bothering	Warned and released by patrol
12/ 6/61 Shoot B.B. Gun in city	Witness only
1/26/63 P. T. Shoplifting	Warned & Rel to parent
1/21/63 P. T. (purse & money)	Restitution—Rel to Dad, Pet. Filed
2/14/63 Prob. Office—Informal Prob., till 3/14/63	
5/28/63 Juvenile Fight	Contacted & Rel by patrol
6/ 1/63 P. T. Stepping Stones (Susp. only) not contacted.	
7/22/63 Burglary	Rel to Parents, Pet. filed
8/ 9/63 Burglary (susp.)	Cleared
9/ 1/63 Burglary	Ref. on above
9/21/63 Burglary	Rel to par, Pet. filed to include above
10/ 7/63 Burglary	Included on above
10/13/63 Susp. Juv.	Talked to—Warn & Rel
12/26/63 Juv. Court order: Declar. ward; rel to parents; curfew: 8:00 p.m. weekdays; 10:00 weekends; Restitution; am't. decided by P.O.	
4/24/64 P. T. Purse Burglary	(Suspect only) Dad will check out
10/ 6/64 P. T. Purse from Vehicle	Application for Pet. filed
10/ 8/64 Prob. Dept. above not filed yet pending Psycho. evaluation	
11/23/64 Battery (Teacher at [name of Jr. Hi.]) ; Loiter at Sch. Pet. filed	
12/28/64 Juv. Ct. Order	Cont. Ward; Rel to parents. Curfew: 8 p.m. (10 p.m. weekends)

The infractions listed on the police record are significant because one of the juvenile officers used it to illustrate how the probation department allows a juvenile with Drew's record to remain home and continually make "trouble" for everyone. Many of the entries actually refer to several different burglaries uncovered while investigation was proceeding on one of them. In order to avoid repeated lengthy quotations from the many police reports, I shall present several excerpts so the reader can follow my commentary.

4/27/60 The above listed juveniles were observed playing in the newly, and partially constructed homes, near the intersecting streets of [name] and [name], and one youth was observed by this officer, to be playing on top of one of the houses, running about on it's roof top.

1/26/63 [Witness saw Drew and a friend, John] take a yo yo each and remove it from their wrappers and place them inside their waiste bands. John had no money and when informant checked Drew he found that he had $24.73 (one ten, two fives, two ones and $2.73 in miscl. change). Drew stated at first that his parents were in [city 100 miles away] for the day and could not be contacted. Further questioning brought up the fact that his father was a [police—other jurisdiction] officer and that his mother was at home. When asked about the money he stated that he had found a wallet two days ago [address given] and it had contained a ten dollar bill and some change. He removed the money and threw the wallet over a building at [name] school. The rest of the money he stated belonged to him as he has saved it from his birthday money. (Check for wallet in area produced no results.) Drew was then taken home. His father was home for lunch so he was contacted along with his wife. They too stated that their son has been no problem and has not been in any trouble. The incident of the shoplifting was discussed with them and also the finding of the wallet. . . . The father of the Timmons boy was contacted and brought his son to this office, as directed. At that time, the boy was questioned as to where he got the money he had in his possession at the time of his apprehension. He continued to maintain that he had found the wallet on [name] Avenue, removed approximately $25.00. and later threw the wallet (empty) on the [name] School grounds. Then he changed his story to the effect that the wallet MIGHT have landed on the school roof and this writer got the impression that this was not the truth, but no amount of reasoning would entice the boy to change his story. [The juvenile officer and Drew's father established some restrictions for the boy and the officer added that Drew] was to submit a 1500 word essay to this writer on the subject of "LAW."

[The juvenile officer telephoned John's mother] and requested permission to contact her son at school, so that he might be questioned as to his knowledge of the money. Permission was readily given and she reported that the Timmons boy was telling the neighborhood children that he took the wallet out of a car. It was also learned at this time that this boy was in a habit of lying to his parents, who believe him without question. She advised that this is a continual source of trouble for the entire neighborhood. A later check with [name] School revealed that they had also had problems with the Timmons', in that Mrs. Timmons was continually accusing them of unfair treatment concerning her children. This finally resulted in the Timmons children being removed from [name] School. The School reported it is their feeling that the Timmons children were only slightly more mischievious than the average youngster, but the children had learned that their lies would be accepted by their parents; and this would lead to difficulties. [John's brother told officer that the wallet came from the car of a neighbor of the Timmons.]

An attempt was made to contact the Timmons boy at school, but it was found that he had been sent home previously by the school nurse. A check was made at the home, and while it was apparent that people were present, no one would answer the door bell. After that [neighbor's name] was contacted and he stated that his mother had lost her purse while her car was parked in his driveway, on 1-21-63; and further, that the matter was reported to our department under the heading 'LOST PURSE,' which was found to be our Inv. [number given]. Mr. C stated that he was almost confident at the time that the wallet had been taken by one of the children, but due to many past problems of this nature (with this family) he did not mention them as suspects. He pointed out that any action taken would be the result of this officer's feelings and NOT from his suggestion. By reading between the lines, it is apparent that a great deal of ill-feeling exists between all the other neighbors and the Timmons. They all did state that there have never been any incidents in the past wherein the parents were able to be made to believe that their children could do anything wrong. A telephone call was then placed to the Timmons' home and their housekeeper answered. Arrangements were made for Mr. Timmons to call this office on his arrival home. The neighbors had all indicated that Mrs. Timmons is a very sick woman and either has had or is on the verge of having a break-down; and that this has a direct bearing on the existing situation. Mr. Timmons later called as directed and was informed only that this writer had obtained proof that his son was lying and it was this writer's feeling that the boy should admit this to him in person. He was advised of the amount of money stolen ($35) and that part of the money had been given by his son to another youngster. Mr. Timmons was requested to question his son and to contact this writer at a later time. As of this writing, he has not returned the call. . . . No further action in this particular case—cleared.

Beginning with the investigation of a petty theft charge, the officer routinely asked the boys to empty their pockets and discovered Drew had $24.73 in his possession. The comment that "further questioning brought up the fact . . ." conceals continued questioning by the officer because he "felt the kid was lying," and how he then decided he was on to something more serious. Having the money triggered off the suspicion, but the way in which Drew spoke provided the officer with confirmatory "evidence." The parents defended the boy by stating that "their son has been no problem and has not been in any trouble." The officer decided it was best to continue the investigation at the police station. Another officer (with more experience—the first officer was fairly new as a juvenile officer) took over the case and then got the boy to admit there was $25.00 in the wallet rather than "a ten dollar bill and some change." There was the further assumption that the boy had probably thrown the wallet on the school roof. The second officer then states, "This writer got the impression that this was not the truth, but no amount of reasoning would entice the boy to change his story" during this interview with the father present. The juvenile officer could not employ the same tactics with the father present, so he settled for parental restrictions and an essay on "law." This procedure, along with informal reporting to juvenile officers, is not uncommon when a trust relationship is established with the juvenile, but here it appears that the officer did not feel he had any other recourse. But the officer continued the investigation by calling the mother of Drew's companion (John) in the shoplifting incident. In addition to learning about the possibility that the wallet had been taken from a neighbor's car, the officer sought and obtained information about Drew's "habit of lying to his parents, who believe him without question." Notice it appears the information was perhaps spontaneously given to the officer. Instead, the officer asked direct questions about the "kind of family" in question. Similar questioning was done at the school and the officer notes he was told "that the Timmons children were only slightly more mischievious than the the average youngster, but the children had learned that their lies would be accepted by their parents." After going to the Timmons home and deciding that "while it was apparent that people were present, no one would answer the door bell," the officer contacted the neighbor mentioned by John's brother. The officer concludes that "by reading between the lines, it is apparent that a great deal of ill-feeling exists between Mr. C. and the Timmons; and as far as this writer can determine, between all the other neighbors and the Timmons." The officer states that "they [the neighbors] did state that there have never been any incidents in the past wherein the parents were able to be made to believe that their children could do anything wrong." No mention is made of Mr. Timmons being an officer. The juvenile officer seems to have generalized his depiction of the Timmonses from two families on the block and speaking with an official from the elementary school the children formerly attended. The officer had asked if "everyone else" in the neighborhood "feels the same way" and was told "yes."

The officer then states, "The neighbors had all indicated that Mrs. Timmons is a very sick woman and either has had or is on the verge of having a breakdown; and that this has a direct bearing on the existing situation." This last statement provides the officer with the final bit of confirmatory material for "understanding" the case. When Mr. Timmons called, the juvenile officer's "proof" was not revealed, but some of the "facts" straightened out. Yet the officer decided to call the case "cleared" for the present. My impression is that if this had been any other family, the juvenile officer would have filed a petition immediately. A supplementary report and petition were filed after Mr. Timmons finally returned the juvenile officer's call. This supplementary report included the following:

> After the subjects father was advised [again] that the boy was lying he confirmed that the lad admitted the truth but reported that they didn't question the boy but allowed him to tell the truth on his own. Writer then advised the father that maybe the boy knew writer came to the house and had the necessary information to prove the story, to this the father reported that he doubted that anyone was home when writer called at the house. This pattern goes along with everything all of the neighbors have to say about the parents being protective. On one

occasion a neighbor is reported to have come home and found oil spilled on his garage floor, he found the Timmons boys with oil all down the front of their jeans and so he took them home and Mrs. Timmons asked the boys if they were in the garage and when they stated that they were not she excused their having oil on their clothing by saying that it must have been picked up from the street. From all information it appears that the neighbors are at the end of their rope. Mr. Timmons was agreeable that something should be done about the boys lying and was most cooperative throughout the investigation. Mr. Timmons made restitution for the amount of $36 . . . .

The juvenile officer suggested the lying went beyond the particular burglary, but also included the house call incident. The juvenile's father would not go along with this interpretation. The officer concludes that "this pattern goes along with everything all of the neighbors have to say about the parents being protective." For the police, it is one thing to have a juvenile whom they feel lies consistently, it is even more discouraging for them to deal with parents who are "over-protective." The spilled-oil incident is given as one more definitive bit of documentation. The following remark "caps off" the report by saying, "From all information it appears that the neighbors are at the end of their rope." The police, armed with information about what "all the neighbors" report about the family, feel they "really" have the evidence "to know" what kind of action is necessary in the case. Yet the officer concludes that "Mr. Timmons was agreeable that something should be done about the boys' lying and was most cooperative throughout the investigation." The fact the juvenile officer was dealing with another peace officer makes this final remark about the father's understanding and cooperation equivocal. Other parts of the reports continually suggest the juvenile officer feels both parents are integral parties to the "lying." An evaluation of the Timmons family was communicated in harsher terms during several informal discussions at the Juvenile Bureau office in my presence. At least two of the juvenile officers blamed the mother, and speculated the father would be harsh on the boy by "kicking the hell out of him." The Probation Department handled the case informally, so no attempt was made to obtain further information on the home situation or on the boy. Informal probation reports seldom record the probation officer's (hereafter P.O.) evaluation of the case because no court action occurs and the petition is rejected officially. Notice how the "rap sheet" summarizing Drew's contacts with the police, information used for constructing tables about rates of juvenile delinquency, or the "causes" of delinquency contains huge gaps about "what happened" or "how does it happen." Official or even unofficial rates do not reveal the day-to-day activities of agencies when officials react, evaluate, and decide the fate of juveniles, nor do referents reveal the behavioral environment which generates labels of delinquency.

The next two entries on Drew's file did not lead to Juvenile Bureau investigations, but notice how the patrol officer reports the information:

[A neighbor of the Timmons reported that someone stole his cement stepping stones to irritate him. The neighbor told the officer he] Doesn't actually have any idea who took these stones but stated that in past he's had a lot of trouble with the three Timmons sons, who live across the street from victim. Feels that they are only subjects in this neighborhood who would pull a stunt like this.

The Timmons family is implicated by the neighbor (but not contacted by the police), and this leads to an entry on the juvenile's card that he was under suspicion for the theft of the stones. Such entries assume increased significance for the police at each subsequent contact, as will be shown below. The next entry reveals the following:

[Burglary from a house down the street from the Timmons residence] Subject admitted that he entered to use female clothing to excite his sexual desires and while in the house took 2 one dollar bills. The victim later contacted and she stated that they were missing the 2 dollars but thought that it was on a later date, it appears possible that either the same boy was in the house twice or the money wasn't missed until later. . . . The subject later contacted and reported that he was in this house on three separate occasions.

This last report was filed by a juvenile officer but did not involve extensive interrogation; the officer told the juvenile he had the "proof" to show Drew was only possible suspect. The reference to entering the house "to use female clothing to excite his sexual desires" was of special interest to the police, and left me with the impression the police began searching for motives other than the usual criminal depiction of social character. My impression was triggered by offhand remarks by the officer several months later, particularly the reference to the "use of female clothing to excite his sexual desires." This latter remark was considered more important than the two dollars taken because, despite three separate occasions of entry, nothing else was reported missing.

The official police entry of 8/9/63 reports a burglary on the same street as that of the Timmons family, stating two containers full of pennies were stolen and a plastic bank, but the report does not state the Timmons boy was involved or even suspected. The entry states that the juvenile's suspect status was "cleared," yet the brief statement remains. I call attention to this type of entry because it is not atypical, but quite routine. It is routine for a juvenile officer to glance at the card and tell the juvenile (as I observed on many occasions) that he was not considered involved officially, that the case was not solved, and that this "could mean you did it but we never caught you."

The following entry of 9/1/63 reports another burglary and the official police report states various papers and a strong box were taken. The report does not mention Drew but the residence reporting the burglary is located in Drew's neighborhood. The brief remark "Ref. on above" does not clarify that Drew was either a suspect or had been "cleared." The next two entries also referred to burglaries (dated 9/21/63 and 10/7/63), yet the actual reports do not include reference to Drew, but merely mention the many stolen items. The investigating officer did state: "It appears to the writer that this was done by Juveniles and entry was made at either the front door or the patio door and after going through everything in the house they left the same way."

The significance of entering the above burglary incidents on Drew's juvenile record card may be inferred from the following police report, based upon a neighbor calling to say he had seen Drew enter the back of another house. The neighbor questioned Drew about his presence and received a "nasty answer," whereupon he called the police after obtaining Drew's name. The patrol officer contacted Mrs. Timmons and she stated the boy told her he went into the back yard of the house "to pet a cat, that he likes cats."

> A check was made with records and was advised that the boy had been involved in a theft of a purse in the past and other miscellaneous entries. Drew's mother verified the fact that Drew was very fond of cats, but also agreed with this officer, that Drew has no business going onto someone elses property. Drew and his mother were informed that should a like incident occur in the future—there was a good possibility that the disposition would be handled in a different manner.

The patrol officer checked with the Juvenile Bureau and received information about the purse incident and other "miscellaneous entries." The mother's response suggesting "cat petting" motives governing her son's behavior provides the police with documentary evidence of parental overprotection. Of interest here is the officer's remark about future incidents possibly being "handled in a different manner." The neighbor is not quoted as suspecting the Timmons boy for other things, nor does the officer make clear why the entrance of a juvenile into a neighbor's backyard should be subject to "different" handling, unless the officer made it known during the conversation with the mother that this incident was not unconnected with "other things" Drew has done. The entry is "Susp. Juv." or suspicious juvenile. Abstracting information from the "objective" features of the report would not reveal the conversational imputations (and hence inference) made by a neighbor or those made by the officer. Nor would "objective" accounts indicate how the juvenile record card lends itself to different or similar "readings" by police officers, particularly when the neighbors' remarks are taken seriously or literally and the juvenile record card is being interpreted by a juvenile officer who "knows" the case. A summary statistical account of the juvenile's activities (such as an official "rap-sheet") would not reveal what the police "know," nor how they "close" vague and dogmatic descriptions by informants to create classificatory sets.

A supplementary report dated 10/16/63, filed by a juvenile officer who knew Drew well, describes another burglary in detail in the next entry, and states: "It appears definite that the subject is a teenager, who would be interested in models and possibly is acquainted with the victim and knew where the various stolen articles were kept." The police were confronted with several thefts in the neighborhood and I was told by one of the officers that informal discussion at the Juvenile Bureau continually implicated the Timmons boy. For the police it was a matter of waiting for the "right break." The report upon which the next entry is based reveals further details:

On 10/13/63 the above subject came to the attention of this office for a Suspicious Juvenile, at that time this office was of the opinion that the youngster probably had problems but due to parents protective attitude in the past the boy was not questioned about this case, the informant even called and stated that it was their opinion that the boy was the responsible person and writer only suggested that she notify this office if she should learn anything of value.

On 11/26/63 the informant again called and reported that a neighbor boy was in the Timmons house and recognized some of the stolen items and returned one electric car which he obtained from the youngest Timmons boy who reported that he had bought the car from some other boy, having no past contacts with the younger Timmons boy writer and Det [name] contacted the above suspect [Drew] at school this date, as soon as the boy walked in it was apparent that he was scared, he tried to lie about the stolen items but finally admitted taking them from the victims back yard and for a long time wouldn't admit being in the house, he finally did admit that he entered through an unlocked door, the entry was affected to satisfy his sexual desires to fondle womens clothing while masterbating, he took the stolen items to throw suspicion away from the real reason for the entry. After the lad started to talk he also admitted entering two other houses for the same reason and that while in the home he stole money, refer to Inv [number] & [number] for information regarding these cases. In the former the boy admitted taking about 2 dollar bills, in the latter he stated he took a box of pennies which he believed contained about $3. He later gave this writer $2. in pennies which he stated came from this house. The boy was transported to his home where he produced a few of the remaining stolen items taken in this case, he also produced several school books which he had stolen from the school library, the boys mother couldn't believe the boy would do such a thing, at that time she was not told about the sexual end of the problem, she tried to excuse the boys acts by passing the blame to her husband by the excuse that he was never home and not a father to the boys. At the mothers request the boy was transported to the school, the mother and father later called at the office and writer explained in no uncertain terms that they would do some soul searching to determine where the responsibility for the problem might lie, each tried to blame the other and writer pointed out several places where both were wrong, it was still apparent that the mother was, is and will continue to be overly protective, from talking to the boy he gave the impression that he could overcome the parental problems if given the proper counselling.

The parents were concerned about what they should do but at the same time didn't want to accept reality, the mother didn't want the victims to even know the name of the family of the responsible persons and writer tried to convince them that the boy will never change until they let him grow up and be responsible for his own actions and it was suggested that the best thing for the boy would be for him to contact the victims and not only apologize to them but pay for the losses. The parents didn't give any indication that they would do this. Unless all members of this family make some drastic changes it appears that problems will continue to exist.

The parents were advised that the boy would be released to them and a Pet request filed in his behalf with the recommendation that the matter not be handled informally, this boy is in dire need of immediate help and will become progressively worse if not straightened out at once.

Victim will be advised and the recovered items released. A total of items listed as being about $16.55 were recovered which would leave a total of about $10. The boy denies drinking the beer but it appeared this was just one more thing he didn't want to talk about.

Copy to probation.   Clear.

This youngster has a total of 7 past contacts and on 1/21/63 was arrested for stealing, 2 cts, this matter referred to the Probation by pet request and handled on a 30 day probation and then dismissed.

The officer explicitly links the previous imputation "that the youngster probably had problems" to the present burglary charges, suggesting that the fault lies in the "parents' protective attitude," but did not question the boy even though an informant named Drew as the "responsible person." When the police "know" the juvenile is guilty they are unlikely to wait, as they did in the case of Drew, unless the parents are viewed as a "problem," and they feel detailed evidence is necessary. The officers would expect intensive questioning or circumstantial evidence of informants to be sufficient for filing an application for petition. As was seen in the case of Smithfield, suspicion of theft was viewed as serious enough to refer the matter to the probation officer. Therefore, when the officer states that a neighbor boy "recognized some of the stolen items," it suggests many persons in the neighborhood were alerted to Drew's possible guilt. In both cases (Smithfield and Drew), the police were operating with "common knowledge" not made explicit in their reports. In one case (Smithfield), such "knowledge" led to immediate action, while in the second case (Drew), it led to a search for more definitive evidence. A key statement occurs when the officer remarks, "As soon as the boy walked in it was apparent that he was scared; he tried to lie about the stolen items but finally admitted taking them from the victims back yard. . . ." The statement does not describe the boy's "scaredness," nor does it indicate the kind of questioning that produced the remark that Drew "tried to lie about the stolen items," and then "admitted taking them. . . ."

I want to separate the problem of "bottling" such terms as "he was scared" or "he tried to lie," as well as general police imputations, from the problem of tactics (such as telling the juvenile they have "proof," witnesses, trying to catch the subject contradicting himself, etc.) that renders information obtained legally inadmissible. Descriptions about "lying" or being "scared" are dependent upon implicit background expectancies, and not seen as legally problematic in juvenile cases. Yet they are not sharply distinguishable as "fact" or in impact from tactics deemed a violation of a person's legal rights.

The remark the boy entered "to satisfy his sexual desires," and "took the stolen items to throw suspicion away from the real reason for the entry" is not revealed as a spontaneous product nor as the possible result of posing leading questions, even telling the boy that his admitting the sexual motives might make it "easier" on him "later on." I would argue it is the latter kind of questioning that was crucial, although I cannot document my position with a verbatim transcript of the exchange. It is difficult to know if the police were now "closing the set," suggested in earlier reports about the mother being "sick," and posed the "sexual motives" to enable the boy to seize upon an "out" to his predicament. When the officer states "he finally did admit . . . the entry was affected to satisfy his sexual desire to fondle womens clothing while masterbating," there is the implication the exchange was directed by officers to the sexual theme. The remark "several school books which he had stolen from the school library" suggests the officers routinely asked Drew about other delinquent acts, perhaps telling the youth it is "better to tell us about these things now cause it'll be harder on you later if we found out more." My experience suggests the police are correct in assuming that most of their suspects have engaged and "gotten away with" many other delinquent acts. The police use such admissions on the part of the juvenile to "show" the parents their child is not being investigated for some rare event or temporary or accidental occurrence. The comment that "the boys mother couldn't believe the boy would do such a thing" is quite calculated, and is standard practice for juvenile officers, especially when dealing with "protective" or "stubborn" parents. The commentary on the behavior of the mother and father at the station obscures a lengthy conversation, but expresses the police view clearly by noting the parents should "do some soul-searching to determine where the responsibility for the problem might lie." Consequently, several combinations of possibilities are suggested by the police: (1) both parents are not "realistic" about their child's conduct; (2) the mother is "sick" and is "overprotective"; and there-fore (3) the boy is a "punk"; or (4) the boy has a "problem" of his own (but linked to his mother's) that can be "seen" in the "sexual desire" remarks quoted above. The officer states that "it was still apparent that the mother was, is, and will continue to be overly protective." Yet he notes the juvenile "gave the impression that he could overcome the parental problems if given the proper counselling." It is not clear what would be "proper counselling," that is, professional psychiatric help or a "good talking to" by the police, but the remark suggests the police were favorably impressed with the boy's response. The statement that the parents "didn't want to accept reality," even though admitting they were concerned, and the remark about the mother not wanting to let the neighbors know what was going on reveals a general police solution of "facing the music" by admitting the infractions, having the boy contact the neighbors and offer to make restitution for what was taken, and apologize for his actions. The officer states he is not optimistic about the possibility of "some drastic change" occurring, and notes his asking the Probation Department not to handle the matter informally. By saying "this boy is in dire need of imme-diate help and will become progressively worse if not straightened out at once," the officer could be saying the juvenile's actions are not peculiar to the boy, but linked to the parents, or that perhaps the boy can be helped despite the parents' reluctance to "accept reality." The remark about "drinking the beer" returns again to the police view about the juvenile always lying; inclusion of this remark suggests "obvious" guilt. Finally, note the officer mentions "7 past contacts" and the stealing incident, but it is not clear which of the various entries on the juvenile record card are the referents here, nor is there any mention of what meaning "contacts" is intended to convey to the reader. The police were quite lenient in this case. For a juvenile with the "wrong attitude" and passive parents, the same record would have led to placing the boy in Juvenile Hall.

The probation officer's report of December 1963 reveals the family earns approximately $950.00 per month and live in a three-bedroom home that "is adequate and well-furnished." The mother does not work outside of the home, the children attend church regularly, but the parents are "not affiliated with any particular church." The report is routine (and similar to those quoted in Chapter 7), but a few statements will be quoted directly to give some picture of how the P.O. viewed the case.

> According to the Timmons minor, on about July 22, 1963, he was walking in the afternoon in the neighborhood of his home when he decided to enter a residence at [address] in order to see what he could find. The minor rang the doorbell and hid nearby until he was certain none of the residents were home. He then entered the home through an unlocked door. . . .

The minor has admitted to the Probation Officer that he entered all three (3) of the residences as alleged in the petition. He also indicated that he entered one (1) of the residences a second time. According to the minor, he used female garments for masturbation purposes on only one occasion. . . .

The minor is a Ninth Grade student at [name] Junior High School. He has not been in any serious difficulty. On his last report card, he reportedly received five (5) C's and two (2) B's. . . .

Drew appears to be of about average intelligence. His responses and interests seem commensurate with his age. However, he appears somewhat immature and insecure. He has not been a problem at home and usually has met his parents' desires and demands without hesitation. The minor has apparently been closely supervised by his parents and his activities outside the family quite limited. According to the parents, the older and younger brothers are making a completely satisfactory adjustment. According to Mrs. Timmons, the minor was quite ill because of bronchial asthma until he was about six (6) years old. His condition brought the family to Southern California. It would appear to the Probation Officer that the close protectiveness of the parents as a young child has been carried over into recent years. It now appears that the minor is quite dependent upon his mother. Mr. Timmons, being out of the house because of service in the [military reserve] and [police officer], has not established a close relationship with the boys.

It appears to the Probation Officer that the minor is properly remorseful for his misdeeds and concerned about his proper development. He seems to accept counseling and indicates a willingness to cooperate with the Probation Officer. It would appear that there are several problems that may have precipitated the present matter. The Probation Officer believes that the minor should be declared a ward of the Court in order to provide him with probationary supervision and in order to assist his parents as well. Even though the minor's mother is especially defensive and over-protective, she is willing to listen to suggestions and has pledged her cooperation. Mr. Timmons has also indicated a willingness to cooperate toward a satisfactory solution to the problems existing.

Because of the nature of the matter before the Court and the seeming rather deep-seated problems, the Probation Officer feels that Juvenile Court jurisdiction may need to be continued over a rather lengthy period of time. It appears also that restitution should be required in this case and used as a therapeutic measure.

The P. O. suggests Drew did not become involved in his burglary escapades accidentally, but planned his entrance. The P. O. does not stress the "sexual desires" interpretation of the police, stating Drew "used female garments for masturbation purposes on only one occasion." There is an abstract reference to being "immature and insecure." The officer then notes there are no apparent difficulties at school or in the home, thereby minimizing two standard types of grounds for imputing delinquency and defective character traits. By linking the earlier asthma condition to "close protectiveness of the parents as a young child" (with a carry-over "into recent years"), the P. O. suggests that the "minor is quite dependent upon his mother," particularly since the father is usually "out of the house," and "has not established a close relationship with the boys." Though remarks made earlier by the juvenile officer stated the mother accuses the father of not spending time with the children and "not a father to the boys," the P. O.'s remarks do not reveal how he arrived at his conclusions—speaking with one or both parents, or using the police report. The reference to the asthma condition suggests the use of the parents' information for some of the report, but neither the researcher nor the reader can determine how the P. O. decided what will be described as his official view.

The P.O.'s depiction of the juvenile's home, his behavior at school, his social character, and the like, is always subject to additional reification by others. All such interpretations require some mention of the tacit knowledge the reader should take into account, and the background expectancies of the persons producing the reports.

My earlier remarks about the trust relationship which the P. O. seeks to establish, as well as his attempt to justify his recommendations by reference to some vague notion of the juvenile delinquent capable of being "helped," are revealed in remarks suggesting Drew "is properly remorseful for his misdeeds and concerned about his proper development." The remark that Drew "seems to accept counseling and indicates a willingness to cooperate with the P. O." suggests the juvenile's behavior satisfied the officer a trust relationship was possible. But the officer does not elaborate on the "several problems that may have precipitated the present matter," even though he states again that "the minor's mother is especially defensive and over-protective." The P. O.'s report reveals a more abstract, diplomatic, and clinical language than that of the police. He tries to balance the fact of delinquent acts with the juvenile's "problems" and "remorsefulness," along with the parental problems but a "willingness to cooperate," and tells the judge how his recommendation fits the "facts."

The trust relationship involves a bargaining process whereby the P. O. acts as the juvenile's broker for securing concessions from the judge in return for compliance with the P. O.'s demands. The P. O. may enter into several bargaining agreements, for example, with the juvenile, with the police, with the parents, with the school and, of course, with the judge.

The P. O. states there are "seeming rather deep-seated problems," but does not advise additional professional help. The officer does suggest a "lengthy period" of court jurisdiction and "restitution" as "a therapeutic measure." The P. O. guides the juvenile's case through the hearing, and may "coach" him on how to behave before the judge. The official report is written to justify formally the course of action he recommends to all interested parties. The

P. O.'s remarks about the juvenile's "respect for authority," his "remorseful-ness and willingness to cooperate," his ability to "get along" at home and at school appear as "clear" rules of appropriate conduct, yet refer to unclear contingencies of action that the officer utilizes for evaluating the juvenile, and then constructing a particular recommendation.

The next entry states Drew was a suspect in the burglary of tools and rifle shells. His name does not appear on the police report, but the officer remarks that "The boy listed as suspect, according to victim, has been involved in past" burglaries, and the "suspect had been at his house playing with victim's son but when he began picking on victim's son victim sent him home." The report was written by a patrol officer and the burglary occurred on the street where Drew lives. The neighbor, therefore, informed the patrol officer about Drew's past activities, and the report went to the Juvenile Bureau because of the neighbor's remarks. The Juvenile Bureau assumed Drew to be the juvenile involved. The Bureau did not, however, make a separate investigation of the incident. The boy's father was contacted informally, but there is no other written report on the matter. I was told that the father was "hard" on the boy, and would probably give the juvenile "hell," and that such a procedure was probably more effective than referring the case to probation.

A few months later Drew was implicated in another incident described in part in the following excerpts from a report by a patrol officer:

> While inside Mrs. L. home, she observed the suspect walk by her car and look thru the window. Mrs. B. remarked to Mrs. L that she thought the suspect was going to try and take her purse. The suspect walked on past the car, then walked back and reached into the car and picked up Mrs. B. purse from the seat. Mrs. B. then stepped out the door and called to the suspect and he dropped the purse. . . .
>
> The suspect was evasive in his answers as to where he lived and his name . . . Mrs. B. attempted to get the suspect to go with her to his home . . . and the suspect wouldn't. . . .
>
> . . . Mrs. L. told her that the suspect attended the [name of church]. Mrs. L. called the wife of the Pastor . . . it was suspected that [it] could very possibly be Timmons. . . .
>
> Mrs. B. identified Timmons as the boy . . . Mrs. Timmons felt that Mrs. B. shouldn't have called the police. Apparently Timmons is on probation at this time. . . .

The police report does not reveal discussion between the two friends and the patrol officer about the incident, but the victim was apparently concerned about a confrontation with Mrs. Timmons, and the report stated that she "felt she should be accompanied by a policeman." The victim did not want to settle the matter informally. In view of the previous remarks about the neighbors, it is easy to suggest the victim was perhaps encouraged by her friend, a neighbor of the Timmons family, to bring the police into the matter. It is curious the neighbor did not state she knew Drew immediately. The patrol officer declared the "suspect was evasive" and uncooperative. The juvenile officer's follow-up report contains the following information:

> Drew was questioned by writer in the presence of his mother—and admitted stealing the purse from the vehicle.
>
> Drew Timmons is presently a Ward of the Court, and still on Formal Probation as a result of thefts.
>
> During the questioning of Drew—he indicated that he has been getting away with other crimes (some of which he has been suspected of being responsible for in the past) and although he didn't wish to go into details at this time, Drew indicated that he would confide in his mother (regarding past crimes) and Mrs. Timmons said that she would furnish to this dept. anything learned from her son that could possibly either clear up cases or be of help to her son.
>
> Mrs. Timmons was informed that an Application for Petition Request was being filed on Drew, regarding this last incident—and that she and Drew could expect to be hearing from the Probation Dept. in the near future.
>
> Drew was then released to his mother.

The above report is based upon about one and one-half hours of interrogation by the juvenile officer first with the boy and then with the mother, and finally with both of them present. I attended all of the interviews. The officer first attempted to establish that Drew had engaged in many other offenses not known officially to the police. This was done to "convince" the mother the boy was "a hell of a lot worse than she ever wants to admit," as the officer suggested to me. The officer told me the boy's father was very severe when he learned of such incidents, while the mother was always trying to protect the boy by seeking to apologize for his actions, and making immediate restitution. The mother was quite angry, according to my impressions, because she felt the victim should never have gone to the police over the incident but merely reported it to her. The mother stated that the neighbor (the victim's friend) was trying to be "nasty" because she "knew" it was Drew, with the implication Drew was not liked by this neighbor. The officer told me no further action would be taken by the Juvenile Bureau unless the parents came in with details about the other offenses. For this officer it was more important to impress upon the mother that her boy was far worse than she could ever imagine, and of secondary importance at this time to investigate the other offenses and clear them for their files. The officer seemed interested in stressing to the mother the juvenile was "sick" and not criminal; "this was a problem" that went beyond the immediate petty theft of the purse. I recorded the following remarks:

MOTHER. Well, what do you mean?

OFFICER. Well, it could just be a problem [and then indicated he didn't want to elaborate].

MO. Well do you mean some kind of personal problem?

OFF. Yes, it could be a personal problem.

MO. Well, what is that supposed to mean?

OFF. Well, maybe he needs some kind of help.

MO. Well, what do you mean, therapy?

OFF. Yes, maybe he needs some kind of therapy.

MO. Well, I don't know why, and I don't see that that's the case.

OFF. Well, I'm not saying that it is, I'm only indicating that in some cases we've had, the boy needs some kind of help, that maybe it's something that he can't help himself from doing.

MO. [The woman seemed to frown in disagreement while shaking her head as if to say "no" and then said:] You mean something he'd get at the school?

OFF. That's right, the school would help by contact with mental hygiene.

The above excerpt from the interview crystallizes informal conversation among the officers at the Juvenile Bureau. Two of the officers felt the boy "had a problem," while another argued he "just needs a boot in the ass." My participant observation revealed many cases where the police officer made a similar suggestion to the juvenile or his parents and where, on subsequent encounters, the incident was discussed in terms of the juvenile's (clinical) "problem" rather than imputations of defective social and moral character. In such cases the police demanded some evidence of formal participation in a therapeutic activity when filing an application for petition. Notice that the police officer went so far as to suggest there was perhaps a "problem," but he indicated to me he would not have pursued the matter if the mother had simply cut him off and refused to participate in the conversation. But the mother seems to have been interested in pursuing the matter and did not totally reject the suggestion, although neither was willing to "push" the point. The terms "problem" and "help," then "therapy," and finally "mental hygiene" appear to represent an attempt to formalize gradually the initial suggestion of the officer. The mother was told by the P. O. the boy needed "help," had probably given some thought to the idea of "help" or therapy for the boy, but did not want to make it obvious. Perhaps the idea appealed to her because such an interpretation of her boy's actions would provide a basis for neutralizing negative imputations about his social and moral character. When the mother stated "Well, I don't know why, and I don't see that that's the case," she did not sound as if she wanted to cut off the discussion, and when the officer sought to soften his earlier remarks by saying "Well, I'm not saying that it is . . . in some cases we've had, the boy needs some kind of help . . . [because] he can't help himself from doing," the mother is provided with an "out" or possibly a more acceptable solution to a hardening situation where her boy is continually in "trouble." After her last remark about "something he'd get at the school," she mumbled something and seemed to indicate, with a shift of her head, that she preferred not to discuss the matter any further. The officer then called Drew into the room. The remark "I don't know why, and I don't see that that's the case" appears to be a denial of the "problem" both participants seem to have tacitly accepted all along. But, as with all of her previous remarks, the mother seems to be using a construction that simultaneously includes both denial and tacit acceptance of the officer's increasingly direct imputation of mental illness. Neither party is forced or wants to admit unequivocally that the boy is mentally ill and needs professional therapy, yet both the mother and officer appear to be invoking the same kinds of tacit knowledge or background expectancies in order to continue the conversation.

This brief conversation is not an isolated but a routine example of what happens in police interviews with juveniles or parents. There is a continual attempt on the part of both parties to suggest an "explanation" or elicit one from the persons involved. In the case of contacts with juveniles, the directness of the remarks will revolve around the officer's imputations about "lying" and "attitude toward authority," and how much he feels he "knows" about the situation. The direct suggestion of motives, causes, defective social and moral character, and the like, are integral features of the police officer's attempt to find out "what happened." It would be easy to examine the above conversation as if it were a manifestation of the officer's "guess" as to "what is wrong" with the juvenile based upon the latest incident, but knowing the case has received considerable attention by the Juvenile Bureau and the neighbors provides additional information for interpreting the officer's and mother's possible intentions. The denial-acceptance duality enables both parties to continue a conversation about something they prefer to keep in vague terms, which neither wishes to accept responsibility for advocating unequivocally, yet each party tacitly reveals an understanding of "what is going on." Notice how the materials on Smithfield based on reports from school personnel, juvenile hall officials, and the probation officer could have led to a similar imputation of "deep problems" rather than negative characterological readings. Drew was placed in a group-counseling program, but Smithfield was not.

In addition to the earlier remarks by the juvenile officer about Drew's mother needing "help," information the P. O. possessed, the latter's informal notes reveal more ambiguous material similar to the probation report quoted earlier.

Dec. 1963	. . . Boy still pretty careful about opening up. Adjustment O.K.
Jan. 23, 1964	. . . Discussed home adjustment, seems O.K.
Feb. 6, 1964	. . . Adjustment continues. Mother is still over-protective and defensive of his shortcomings. . . .
March 1964	Adjustment continues good. It seems that things are opening

up for him slowly, but any independence for him is going to come slowly because of mother. I had hoped to have more contact with father but so far none except at first.

April 2, 1964   . . . Is still progressing satisfactorily. . . .

April 30, 1964   Minor involved this date in group counseling session. He didn't have anything to add but listened to what others had to say. He really would like to be a part of the "group," I think, but doesn't know just how to go about it. This group would probably be especially good for him.

June 1964   Mother called to inform me that minor is doing satisfactorily. . . .

July 2, 1964   . . . Received B— average in school this year. . . . Minor hasn't opened up much during the time that he has been on probation but I doubt that he really will until he is older and more mature, still quite dependent. However, no real problems as far as I can tell.

Oct. 10, 1964   About this date conference with minor, mother and father regarding referral from [City A] PD regarding stolen purse. Minor admits theft and can offer no proper explanation. Requested permission from parents to request testing through the schools to determine need for counseling program and they agreed. Contacted [name of school official] at [name of high school] and he agreed to provide test if possible. Indicated that we would wait until test available before deciding what to do about the offense. Parents agreed to watch minor rather closely while we wait for report. Minor seemed remorseful enough to keep anything from happening again soon.

The P. O.'s notes reiterate the idea that it is the mother's "over-protectiveness" that is keeping the boy "from opening up." The P. O., however, does not perceive any "real problems," suggesting that the juvenile will improve as he gets "older and more mature." The P. O. reveals the boy's brief exploration of a group counseling experience. The P. O.'s informal comments leading up to the October 10, 1964 entry suggest everything was "still progressing satisfactorily." The purse incident contradicted this "satisfactory" interpretation. The suggestion that the boy be tested "through the schools to determine need for counseling program" follows the remark that the "minor admits theft and can offer no proper explanation." What would amount to a "proper explanation" here is not clear. The parents could hardly object to the testing idea, since "group counseling" was explored only for a short time. The police interview, in suggesting a clinical "problem," provided both the police and the parents with a "solution" to the juvenile's admission to continual infractions. The alternative would be a criminal imputation. The P. O. had already "diagnosed" the case as one where the boy needed "counseling" because of the mother, but no one directly tells the mother it is she who should receive the counseling. The P. O. states "we would wait until test available before deciding what to do about the offense." The test results would then provide him with a basis for documenting a more explicit follow-through on the counseling idea mentioned in his informal notes. Notice, however, that the P. O. felt the "minor seemed remorseful enough to keep anything from happening again soon," and therefore allowed the boy to return home. Drew was not viewed as in "defiance of authority" and never placed in Juvenile Hall. Smithfield's delinquent activities were not as frequent as Drew's, but Smithfield's "attitude" was considered "bad," and he was always placed in Juvenile Hall. What is not tolerable is a "bad attitude" or a "defiant attitude," or "defiance of authority." The "push" toward a clinical or criminal imputation, or some oscillation between the two, revolves around the actual encounters different officials have with the juvenile. The interpretation of the juvenile's behavior will then be related by these officials to other types of information about the "home," the boy's school "adjustment," and his expressed willingness to "conform."

On November 23, 1964, Drew was tested by a psychologist at the City A schools. But the report was not written up until December 15, 1964. After school on November 23, 1964, Drew became involved in an incident with a junior high school teacher on the school parking lot. The patrol officer who initially investigated the incident gives the following account:

> Received assignment of a suspicious juvenile at [name of junior high]. Upon arrival contacted Mr. [name], vice principal. Timmons was with [vice principal] in his office. [Vice principal] states that the Timmons [boy] had been observed in the parking lot holding a girl by the arm and apparently trying to get her to go with him. This was seen by [name], a teacher, he stated that he did not recognize the boy as a student and the girl was trying to pull away from him. [Teacher's name] went over to the boy and asked him who he was and what he was doing. The boy told him it was none of his business and continued to try and walk away with the girl. [Teacher's name] stated that he grabbed the boy by the arm and the boy turned and hit him knocking him to the ground. [Teacher's name] thought the boy might have hit him with a large book that the boy was carrying.
>
> Miss [name], also a teacher was a witness to this and she stated that it looked like the boy used the book. [Teacher's name] then got up and managed to get the boy to go into the office with him. There Mr. [vice principal] tried to get the boy to say who he was and what he was doing in the school grounds and with the girl. The boy refused and [vice principal] reached for the book hoping to find a name in it. The boy became belligerent and combative. It took three teachers to subdue him and take him to the room where he was at when writer arrived. Once writer began talking to the boy he became cooperative and identified himself as Timmons. He stated that he came to [name of school] to talk to his girl a [name and address of girl given]. This is the girl he was with in the

parking lot. They were having an argument and she did not want to talk to him. Timmons admits to hitting [teacher's name] not with the book but with his fist and only after [teacher's name] grabbed him.

Writer took Timmons home and talked with his parents. They were advised to contact the Juvenile Division on 11-24-64 for an appointment.

Timmons is on probation for petty theft.

The patrol officer's report is followed by an extensive Juvenile Bureau investigation, including a lengthy statement from the teacher who was hit by Drew. I shall only quote a few brief excerpts where new or contradictory information was indicated.

On 11-24-64 in the AM was contacted by the father of the suspect [name, date of birth, address, and school given]. Mr. Timmons wanted to know why his son was being held liable for this action and that the teacher wasn't, as his son had told him that the teacher had grabbed him before he (young Timmons) hit the teacher. It was tried by this Officer and others present to impress on Mr. Timmons that the teacher had the right to question people on the school ground. Mr. Timmons did not agree with us and after about a 1-1/2 hour conversation left the office with the understanding that the investigation was continuing and that if necessary, a petition would be requested by this department. . . .

. . . she [female teacher witness] saw Mr. [teacher hit] take the boy by the arm and told him that he should come to the office with him. She said that she saw the boy swing, but can't say if he hit Mr. [teacher hit] with his fist or his book that he was carrying in his hand. . . .

[back in the school office] Since the boy was un-cooperative and was loud and other kids were in the office they thought it best to move him back to a private office so that the other students couldn't see this scene or be involved. They asked the boy to the back room and he refused to come. They started to take the boy by the arm and take him back there awaiting the arrival of the police and the boy began to struggle. Mr. [vice principal] said that [he] obtained an arm lock on the boy and that they as easily as possible moved the boy to the back office although he struggled all of the time. The boy promised that he would not struggle any more and they immediately released the boy. Mr. [vice principal] said that he then to a degree settled down and when the police arrived became most co-operative with the Policeman. . . .

In her statement, [name of sister of Drew's girl friend] said Mr. [teacher] came up, asked the boy what he was doing there and he refused to answer Mr. [teacher hit]. He did tell Mr. [teacher hit] that he went to [name of high] School, but according to [name of girl also witness] he would not answer any other questions and that there was no excuse for this attitude of his not answering questions. She said that Mr. [teacher] then took Timmons by the shirt and that was when Timmons hit him. . . .

When Mr. [teacher] arrived, Drew maintained that it was he (Mr. [teacher]) who was the agresser; that he, himself, was polite at all times until Mr. [teacher hit] grabbed him by the shirt. Then, he admitted he hit Mr. [teacher] and after hitting him, he went with him to the office. Drew was asked pointedly if he knew Mr. [teacher] was a teacher at all times—and not just a stranger on the school grounds—and he stated, "I figured he was a teacher." He stated when he went to the office, he was a little sullen, but the others were the agressors and for no reason, they grabbed a hammer-lock on him and pushed him around.

The various reports seem to disagree over the interpretation of two features of the episode: the sequence of movements when the teacher was hit, and the occasion when Drew was moved from one office to another. The teacher who was hit was not clear about what he was hit with, nor was the female teacher witness certain, but the girls (including the girl friend) all stated it was with the fist, while the two teachers stated the victim grabbed the boy by the arm and was hit. The girls stated the teacher grabbed Drew by the shirt and, in a second statement to the juvenile officer, the victim stated he first grabbed Drew by the arm and, after Drew broke away, grabbed him by the shirt, and he was then hit. The later occasion when Drew claims the teachers "grabbed a hammer-lock on him and pushed him around" differs from the patrol officer who reports the vice principal as saying the boy became combative after the vice principal "reached for the book hoping to find a name in it," while the Juvenile Officer's report has the school officials saying that it was their attempt to move him out of the sight of other students to another office that precipitated the armlock. The police seek to establish a causal sequence and establish responsibility for rule violations. Note that the juvenile officer's report states the father was told that "the teacher had the right to question people on the school ground." The remark that "Mr. Timmons did not agree with us" does not state what the nature of the disagreement was, nor does the report discuss the possibility that the teacher began to touch Drew physically without sufficient cause. But the police officer states the girls felt that the victim "was polite from the beginning and that Drew was not out of line in the beginning, but was the first to get out of line." The officer paraphrases another girl witness as stating "there was no excuse for [Drew's] attitude of his not answering questions." Further, the officer underscores the admission on the part of Drew that he "figured he was a teacher." The report appears to be written in such a way as to document the school officials interpretation of "what happened." The informal remarks made to me about the incident by the police suggested they felt Drew was completely at fault, and the parents "as usual" were trying to "cover up" for the boy. Finally, the Juvenile Officer also stated, "Timmons was loitering on the school grounds . . . where he had no right to be, but that particular charge will not be listed." The officer appears to push Drew's guilt, but is not interested in following through with the legal technicalities of additional charges.

The P. O.'s informal notes for December 18, 1964 reveal that

> Before the above testing was completed and brought to my attention, minor involved himself in another offense requiring the filing of a petition. Matter being assigned to [initials of other probation officer] for investigation and supervision.

Because the teacher incident occurred the day of the testing, the psychologist learned of the latest incident before writing up his report. Meanwhile, the psychologist's report (which lists "suspicion of kleptomania" as reason for referral) was received a few days later, and contained the following information:

> Drew is an overly anxious and quite depressed young man. It seems that his defenses are very inadequate and he is rapidly losing the control that he does have. There was a great deal of manic behavior indicated on the tests even though he seems to be controlling this somewhat. He has a strong inclination to withdraw from the world about him, perhaps as a defense against having to deal with his world. His overmeticulousness seems more in the line with compulsive behavior than with the desire to be perfectionistic. Drew has a very poorly developed heterosexual relationship and there are strong attractions toward members of his own sex. However, this does not mean that there has been any involvement that may be considered perverse. There are several indications that Drew could well be a compulsive thief and not that the thefts would amount to any great involvement but would be such that cautions should be taken with certain items in which he may have an interest. It appears that a great deal of his activity is compensitory action to resolve some of his sexual conflicts.

> SUMMARY AND SUGGESTIONS
> All indications are that Drew is very much in need of psychiatric help. There are strong suicidal tendencies indicated on the several tests, strong indications that he is rapidly withdrawing any semblance of stability. A conference should be requested with the parents at the earliest time convenient for them and they should be apprised of Drew's needs, but with this they should also be apprised of the need for understanding. It may be that there is some strictness on the part of the father and a rather poor identification with him. At that time, it might be pointed out that his strong guilt feelings have probably brought out other behavior that has been unacceptable. Also, the unacceptable behavior will be likely to continue. It should be noted that Drew would likely be rather smooth in any operation that he has regarding thefts and that he would likely deny any such involvement unless caught in the act directly. Again, it should be mentioned that Drew has some very strong feelings of persecution. He is highly suspicious of others and this is, no doubt, adding to his anxiety.

The psychologist's report might be described as follows:

1. Drew is "overly anxious and quite depressed."
2. He seeks to "withdraw from the world . . . as a defense against having to deal with his world."
3. He is "compulsive."
4. He has homosexual tendencies but they should not be "considered perverse."
5. He could be a "compulsive thief" and a "great deal of his activity" could be viewed as "compensitory action to resolve some of his sexual conflicts."
6. "There are strong suicidal tendencies."
7. "It may be that there is some strictness on the part of the father and a rather poor identification with him."
8. Drew is likely to be "smooth" when stealing and probably "deny any such involvement unless caught in the act directly."
9. The boy has "very strong feelings of persecution" and is "highly suspicious of others," and all of this probably adds "to his anxiety."

I have listed some of the points made by the psychologist because the categories he uses should be examined independently of the verbatim report that tends to run everything together. The categories are difficult to document or justify vis-à-vis the test material. We are left with several possibilities to account for the referral label of "suspicion of kleptomania." What is perhaps surprising is that the psychologist did not recommend immediate incarceration. The clinical imputation is rather complete. A conference was held on December 15, 1964 (the day the report was completed) with the psychologist, the mother, and a high school counselor. The summary of the conference contains the following information:

> This conference was held as the result of tests administered recently where it was indicated that Drew needed some psychiatric help. The mother was very defensive from the beginning. It appeared that she had a chip on her shoulder. It was pointed out that the problems certainly existed and that it seemed that Drew had been into some difficulty since the tests were given. The mother defended this by, "We've taught our boys not to fight unless it was necessary to defend themselves and if the teacher hadn't attacked Drew he wouldn't have hit him." It was pointed out that this was not the important thing, the important thing was that the tests had already indicated that Drew lacked control and that there were other problems. It seemed that this was a useless attempt to get her to accept the fact that some problems exist, even though she did admit to some of them. She did ask about the kind of service available and

it was suggested that she might talk with Mental Hygiene Clinic or someone in private practice. It seems unlikely that too much will be done with Drew.

The psychologist states the tests "indicated that Drew needed some psychiatric help," and everyone involved officially agreed. But how do we decide the seriousness of the psychologist's report as an estimation of the juvenile's mental health? Is it a *post factum* explanation based upon extensive knowledge about delinquent conduct? What is not clear is how the police and probation officials decide the boy is disturbed, as opposed to saying the mother is the cause of it all. I raise this question because a juvenile with a record of thefts, "defiance of authority," continual fights, and the like, might never see a psychologist. The psychologist's prior knowledge suggests the test was tailored to fit official common knowledge. The juvenile's behavioral acts are not unequivocal; therefore, all juveniles subject to a clinical examination might automatically qualify as "disturbed." Why not argue the psychologist seeks to justify the referral by reference to abstract general explanations, ambiguously tied to police and probation materials? My observations suggest this is the case, but I cannot document this implication precisely. The psychologist's report neatly fits all of the general observations made by the police and probation officials (including his remarks about the conference with Mrs. Timmons), where the comment "the mother was very defensive from the beginning" calls attention to an interpretation quoted earlier by other officials. The psychologist seems to shift his language and professional stance when he states that "it appeared that she had a chip on her shoulder." The locus of the "problem" resides in the boy as "the important thing was that the tests had already indicated that Drew lacked control and that there were other problems." The psychologist seems to have decided that the mother was hopeless, and that little would come of his analysis of the situation. The psychologist, in quoting the mother's interpretation of the battery charge, seems to be arguing that such conduct and her explanation of it is merely a manifestation of "deeper" and more serious "problems." The mother argues the boy's behavior was appropriate in view of the circumstances and consistent with what "we've taught our boys." The law-enforcement officials are now joined by the psychologist in deciding that Drew's conduct is not criminal in intent, but the product of underlying psychological problems that manifest themselves in delinquent conduct. The differentiation is between criminal intent as part of a defective moral and social character, as opposed to a mental condition that is beyond the control of the individual.

I now shift to comments by Drew's teachers in response to the P. O.'s request for an evaluation. Drew's grades for the first quarter of the fall term and a nonacademic evaluation is presented, followed by the teachers' remarks.

Has good work habits	Below average	English	C
Gets along well with others	Average	World Cultures	D
Accepts responsibility	Below average	German	C
Uses his abilities	Below average	Basic Art	B
Has good manual coordination	Average	Geometry	B
Has good health habits	Average	English Review	C
Is obedient and cooperative	Average	P. E.	B
Brings work material regularly	Below average		

Counselor	Have had only one meeting with Drew. Seemed quiet but friendly. Had meeting with mother recently discussing tests that were given Drew. Mother seemed defensive and hard to talk to.
Art teacher	Quality of work: Above average when he works, but he shows inconsistency—some work is very sophisticated, some very immature.
	Attitudes: He works hard on what he likes, but is inclined to reject what he doesn't like or understand by doing it quickly to get it over with.
	Behavior: Often talkative—often distracts others from their work.
World Cultures Teacher	Quality of work: slightly above average.
	Attitudes and behavior: OK most of the time.
	Preparedness: Does some assignments. Does not work to capacity.
German teacher	Quality of work: Very uneven—can do well one day and then can fail the next.
	Attitudes: Withdrawn.
	Behavior: Quiet—no problem.
	Preparedness: Very uneven—makes little effort outside of class. Has trouble keeping up with class due to lack of preparedness.
Geometry teacher	Quality of work: Average.
	Behavior and Attitudes: Good.
	Preparedness: Could be better.
	Strong points: Participates in class discussion more than most students. He does have an aptitude for geometric abstractness.
English teacher	Quality of work: "C"-average.
	Attitudes: Not too responsive to class activities.
	Behavior: Not a class problem—talks too much at times.

Drew's conduct in class is not considered to be offensive. There is no reference to any unusual behavior, for even the German teacher's reference to Drew being "quiet" and "withdrawn" does not square with all of the other teachers who say he is talkative to the point of overdoing it at times. The idea that there are "deep underlying problems" to account for Drew's violation of legal rules and his behavior with the teacher he struck does not fit the school's report, and the teachers' remarks do not provide a strong case for saying "something is wrong" with the boy. Yet Drew's case leads law-enforcement officials to a recurrent interpretation: psychologically disturbed.

The P. O.'s report is lengthy. I begin with the P. O.'s remarks about the "Cause of Court Hearing":

> On December 9, 1964, a supplemental petition was filed in behalf of Drew Timmons, alleging that the previous disposition ordered by the Court had not been effective in his rehabilitation in that the said minor violated an order of the County A Juvenile Court dated December 26, 1963, in that he did on or about the 23rd day of November, 1964, at and in the City of A, County of A, State of California, wilfully and unlawfully use force or violance upon the person of [teacher] at [name] Junior High School, thereby violating Section 242 of the California Penal Code, and because of these circumstances said minor is in need of the continued care, control and supervision of the Juvenile Court of County A.

Throughout the P. O.'s report he attempts to present all of the interpretations given in the police report about "what happened." The report states that the victim "went over to the boy and asked him who he was and what he was doing. Drew told Mr. [teacher's name] that it was none of his business and continued to try to walk away with the girl. Mr. [teacher's name] stated that he grabbed the boy by the arm and that the boy turned and hit him, knocking him to the ground. Mr. [teacher's name] thought that Drew might have hit him with a large book that Drew was carrying." The reconstruction does not state explicitly the different police versions disagree, but provides a continuous dialogue that implies "that's the way it happened" or unfolded. The report states the vice principal "tried to get Drew to tell him who he was and what he was doing on the school grounds with the girl. Drew refused to give him any information, and Mr. [vice principal] reached for the book, hoping to find a name in it. Drew became belligerent and combative and it took three teachers to subdue him and take him to Mr. [vice principal]'s office." The P. O. states Drew revealed to him that the teacher was not hit with the book but with his fist after grabbing his shirt, tearing it, and then grabbing his arm. The officer notes the parents felt the teacher should not have grabbed Drew's arm.

Drew further claimed that he was sorry for hitting Mr. [teacher] and stated that he would like to remain at home and attend [name] High School, where he feels he is making a satisfactory adjustment. . . .

A report from . . . vice principal at [name] High School, indicates that Drew is enrolled in the 10th grade. . . . His attendance at school had been satisfactory. It appears that Drew has poor work habits, does not accept responsibility and is not working to the best of his ability. . . .

The characterization of Drew's performance in school uses phrases like "poor work habits," does not accept responsibility," "and is not working to the best of his ability," to close any equivocality contained in the remarks of the teachers to create unequivocal sets for classifying the juvenile. There follows a portion of the psychologist's report that ends with his remark that Drew is in "need of psychiatric help." (See above) The P. O.'s report then includes the following:

This officer has read several letters that Drew wrote to [name of girl friend]. In these letters he indicates that he feels all mixed up and would like to have [girl friend] forgive him for the embarrassment that he caused her as a result of his hitting Mr. [teacher]. Although Mr. and Mrs. Timmons have refused to allow him to see [girl friend], he sent [girl friend] and her mother a Christmas card and a letter, requesting their permission for him to see [girl friend]. Mrs. [girl friend's mother] and her daughter do not wish to see Drew and are concerned about his continuing to write letters to them.

It appears that Drew considers himself to be a coward. Up until this present incident he has taken his frustrations out by taking things that do not belong to him. It would appear that he needs professional help in order to acquire more satisfactory outlets to release these emotional tensions. Although Drew verbalizes sorrow over the hitting of Mr. [teacher], it is this officer's feeling that he felt that he was justified in doing what he did and that his sorrow is over the embarrassment caused to his girl friend because of the incident. Drew does not express a desire to repay Mr. [teacher] for his loss. He has, however, expressed a willingness to cooperate with a professionally trained person in attempting to find out why he reacts in the manner that he does. Mr. and Mrs. Timmons are extremely defensive of their son but yet also show a desire and a willingness to seek professional help in understanding Drew's problems. It has been clearly pointed out to them by the undersigned that this type of behavior cannot continue.

Since Mr. and Mrs. Timmons and Drew are willing to seek professional help in order to correct Drew's wrong behavior pattern, it is believed that he should be given an additional opportunity at home.

One of the conditions of probation was the explicit reference to "cooperate with his parents and the P. O. in seeking the help of a qualified psychologist or psychiatrist." In stating that "Drew considers himself to be a coward," the P. O. seems to be endorsing a milder clinical view than the one reported by the psychologist, and offers an explanation of Drew's past thefts by saying he "has taken his frustrations out by taking things that do not belong to him." The P. O.'s ambivalence seems apparent in the remark that Drew's sorrow over hitting the teacher is mitigated by "this officer's feeling that he felt that he was justified in doing what he did and that his sorrow is over the embarrassment caused to his girl friend because of the incident." This last remark about the girl friend ties in with the earlier statement about Drew's letters to the girl. The remark that "Drew does not express a desire to repay Mr. [teacher] for his loss," is followed by the comment there is "willingness to seek professional help." The latter apparently offsets the former. It is not clear what is implied by the remark, "this type of behavior cannot continue," but could be viewed as a warning to justify a course of action the parents were anxious to avoid: placement outside of the home. The P. O. suggests the boy sees himself as a "coward," or someone with "frustrations" in need of "professional help," yet there is the reference to serious offenses and a lack of parental agreement as to the "problem." This view is confounded by the P. O.'s contention that Drew is more concerned with the embarrassment he caused his girl friend than over what he had done to the teacher. The possession of the "right attitude" is at stake here, for the P. O. seems to be troubled that "Drew does not express a desire to repay" the teacher. The language of the report does not reveal the unofficial remarks urging the juvenile to adopt a "better attitude," or a disposition recommendation tied to an informal agreement by the parents and the juvenile prior to the court hearing—a commitment to seek "professional help." The concern with finding "out why he reacts in the manner that he does" provides the clue to pushing the imputation toward the clinical pole, and thus enables everyone to cooperate in reading the thefts and recent incident as the manifestation of a "sick" juvenile and "over-protective" home, rather than defective moral and social character that would imply criminality. The notion of a "bad attitude" or "incorrigibility" imply the juvenile is beyond salvation in the community and requires punishment so that he will become amenable to "treatment" and a recognition that he "needs help." The social categories that are available, acceptable, and binding on the action of others provide relevant parties with the imagery to pass judgment, particularly since not everyone is exposed to the phenomena upon which initial interpretations are made. Subsequent encounters, such as those with the P. O., provide occasions where initial imputations are reviewed. Therefore, the P. O.'s remark about Drew's concern with embarrassing the girl friend (as opposed to the act of hitting the teacher *per se*), coupled with the parents' reluctance to accept the P. O.'s interpretation of "what happened" and "why," supply this official with the documentary evidence necessary for him to indicate a slight disclaimer ("this type of behavior cannot continue") to his clinical imputation. For then he can apply stronger pressure on the parents to accept the necessity of therapy, and also warn them that continued infractions by Drew can lead to placement outside of the home. The clinical transformation achieved by the cooperation of all parties, although not by open discussion and agreement, fits a major policy intended by the juvenile court law.

The P. O. must convince the parents and the juvenile the suggested course of action is "best" for all concerned, but this usually occurs in a context where the alternatives are generally posed as threats. Thus the P.O. utilizes the threats both as a means of getting his recommendation accepted, and as a means of enforcing parental and juvenile conformity with the consequences of the terms of the disposition. In return for this cooperation, the P. O. then commits himself to defending his recommendation before the judge. But the burden of "reform" remains with the juvenile and his parents because the report provides the P. O. with an outlet for voicing doubts about the recommendation he suggests and the conditions under which the suggested agreement as to disposition might be forfeited so that it leads to an alternate arrangement.

My following of Drew's case ends about six months after the juvenile court hearing. The P. O.'s informal notes reveal the family began attending therapy sessions but "they were not eager." The importance of the clinical imputation lies in the fact that subsequent infractions can still be "explained" by reference to the "underlying problems." A juvenile can therefore maintain a special liaison with the law-enforcement officials and "survive" until he is eighteen years old, thereby enhancing the possibility his environment will be altered by leaving school and leaving the circumstances where a variety of activities routinely engaged in by juveniles will be labeled "delinquent" by community members.

Before presenting the final case from City A, I want to briefly note a "less serious" type of case that I encountered frequently (and one related to the final case to be presented), but one which seldom involved continual contacts with the police because the juveniles are not caught, and the parents are able to intervene more forcefully to avoid future problems. The case is that of a physician's son (living with his family in a fashionable section of City A), who at sixteen years of age was picked up for shoplifting by the police. The mother was called and she stated that it was the first time he had been "in trouble." The officer and I spoke to the boy alone and after some questioning (". . . now you're a normal boy, don't tell me you haven't done this before . . .") admitted to having engaged in similar activities on fifteen previous occasions. The mother appeared somewhat indignant and told the officer the store where the shoplifting was done should have called her directly instead of the police because the boy is not a "common thief." The officer disposed of the case with the familiar "counselled, warned and released." There were many similar cases in upper middle-income (and for City A upper-income) families where the problem was continual drinking, including the parents' admitting that they have encountered their child drunk at home on various occasions. The police would enter the case after encountering the juvenile drunk in a public setting, and then seek additional information about the frequency of such behavior.

Donald

This final example ("Donald Desmond") from City A is a routine case of what happens when a family is capable of mobilizing considerable resources in helping their child avoid enforcement agencies' labeling of their offspring as "delinquent." The significance of such cases is the absence of the usual conditions (broken home, poor school record, "bad attitude," etc.) associated with "delinquent types." The police record for Donald Desmond is as follows:

2/ 2/63	IOD (314.1 PC) [nearby county Sheriff's Dept.]	Warn & Rel to parents
6/12/63	415PC (Balloons)	Warn & Rel (Patrol)
6/14/63	Mal Misch [Shopping Center Mall] last day of school	Warn & Rel (Patrol)
7/24/63	Susp. Veh. & Occupants (parking lot)	Warn & Rel (Patrol)
2/21/64	415 fight with [name of juvenile]—Hall	Warn & Rel to parents
6/28/64	Battery witness	
9/ 2/64	Miscl traffic (companion to [name])	Contacted by patrol
9/26/64	ADW [Assault with Deadly Weapon]	Pet. filed
10/17/64	Possible Indecent Exposure—Suspect—denied (exposing buttocks out of car window) (not able to locate any victims)	
11/16/64	Juv. Ct. Order—Continued as ward—rel to parents	

To the above summary must be added another incident that was not recorded. Donald and several other juveniles were involved in a petty theft charge in another city about 45 miles away. The items were recovered, and the juveniles were later released to one of the parents. I shall avoid detailed quotations whenever possible, and briefly indicate a few relevant excerpts from some of the police reports.

> (2/2/63) On passing the lodge on a second occasion one of the boys had removed his pants and exposed his rear end out the window of the car. On apprehending the boys it was Desmond who admitted hanging his back side out the window of the car . . . There is no request for follow up this dept [City A]

but the information is recorded for possible future use. [No follow-up because the girl involved would not sign a complaint.]

(6/12/63) Stopped for throwing water filled balloons at a group of other white males.

(6/14/63) ... hundreds of juveniles running around the streets and mall itself, some with shaving cream on them, others throwing balloons, eggs, etc.

(7/24/63) Suspects state they saw hood open & were simply closing it. Advised of curfew & left area. [Police questioned one of Desmond's companions because of several police contacts and the Juvenile Officer states:] This situation, his attitude and everything about him was discussed in length trying to point out to him that he was getting himself in trouble and that he has used up any break he might have thought coming from the police.

(2/21/64) The parents of the Hart boy [who fought with Desmond] arrived. . . . The boy appeared to be a pretty good sort of lad, he has no past contacts with this department except for a school suspension and one truancy contact. The boy was counselled, warned and released and at that time instructed to refrain from fighting for any reason except in self defense. . . .

Donald continued to maintain that the Hart boy had a wrench in his hand as previously stated and that was his reason for returning to continue the matter. The boy was advised that under the circumstances his record of past contacts would indicate that he better begin to think seriously about his actions if he was to keep out of serious trouble. The boy admitted that his mother and father didn't see eye to eye and after talking to the mother it was apparent that it was a typical case of two parents whose ideas do not conform. Mrs. Desmond reported that her husband just didn't seem to have time and felt the boy should be allowed to do as he pleased. She stated it was impossible to get him to agree to any counselling and he would be seriously offended if she called in an outsider to assist in their problems. The boy was counselled regarding this case and his getting along with both parents, he was then released with the understanding that he would forget the matter.

(6/28/64) [*Note*: Desmond part of fight but other juvenile not injured. But his friend Harry injured the juvenile he was fighting.] It was explained to Harry and his father that mainly the Blacks are interested in getting the dentist's bills paid; that if they can get this done and satisfy the Blacks, the family did not intend to pursue this any further. However, if they cannot reach some satisfactory conclusion, this office will file a petition.

(9/2/64) [Friend of Donald's driving the Desmond car without license, but with Donald's permission and presence.]

Before going on to the next offense notice how the City A Juvenile Bureau would have been concerned with the first indecent exposure had the victim signed a complaint, yet the officer states the "information is recorded for possible future use." The event takes on indeterminate significance depending upon future occurrences. The next three contacts are difficult to label as "serious," but the police felt the report labeled "susp. veh. and occupants" should read "tampering with vehicle," and changed it accordingly to conform with their belief the juveniles were actually trying to damage or steal something from the vehicle. Notice that Donald's companion was singled out because of his past record and that the officer notes his "attitude," suggesting that from now on he can expect trouble from the police rather than "any break." The case might never have received the investigative attention of the Juvenile Bureau if one of the juveniles did not have several previous contacts with the police. Curfew was not made an issue. The remarks about the juvenile's "attitude" and "he has used up any break" from the police require further comments because my experience suggests such a statement is uttered as a "final warning" or in exasperation by the police over their failure to document what they feel they "know" about the juvenile's criminality. Whatever "attitude" the juvenile presented to the officer is viewed as "evidence" for the underlying pattern presumed to make up a "punk." The police seem to be saying the "next time" they will utilize whatever discretion at their disposal to maximize the seriousness of any subsequent offense or possible offense. The reference to a "break" implies the trust relationship that may have existed or that may be imputed to have existed has now been completely discarded. Such a conception by the police makes up the relevant background expectancies for deciding the disposition in the next encounter; the official record does not describe conceptions employed by the police with different juveniles, nor the changes that can occur in such presuppositions over time.

The incident of 2/21/64 further reveals the relevance of police conceptions in making decisions about juveniles when the officer states the Hart boy "appeared to be a pretty good sort of lad." Whereas something is said about the Hart boy, little is said about Desmond's demeanor. The Desmond boy's "record of past contacts" generates a strong reprimand by the officer. Reporting that the family does not "see eye to eye," that the father "just didn't seem to have time," and the assertion that the boy is permitted "to do as he pleased" (plus the father's resistance to "counselling") shifts the blame from the boy to the family, but does not reveal how such information emerged in the interview between the officer, the boy, and the mother.

The incident of 6/28/64 indicates Donald is included in a follow-up investigation (but Donald did not injure the boy he was fighting). The police threatened to file a petition if the Hart family did not agree to pay for the dental fees. Some incidents are pushed, whereas others almost identical in nature are not (unless certain conditions are met). The differential consequences of police action depend upon contingencies surrounding each encounter or offense. All of the families involved in this incident are from middle-income (and above) areas of City A. The juvenile officer's remark,

"If they cannot reach some satisfactory conclusion, this office will file a petition," in reference to the dental bill, suggests the matter was not being viewed in criminal terms; an informal settlement could be reached if payment were made. But the threat of a petition automatically implies a transformation of the incident into something "serious" with punishment overtones. I stress the income level of the families because I believe everyone involved wanted to define the incident as "normal" adolescent activity, and avoid any further intrusion by the police. The police were willing to accept such a definition providing a settlement could be reached. The difference between an incident where one juvenile is labeled the "victim" and two juveniles "playing around" in a fight is not clear but includes discretion by the police and the parents. The consequences can be quite varied. In the incident of 9/2/64, the police chose not to cite Donald even though he had given his friend permission to drive his car without a license.

The incident of 9/26/64 led to a charge against Donald of assault with a deadly weapon, and became defined by everyone except Donald's father (as will be noted below) as quite "serious." The police reports are rather lengthy and I shall only provide the reader with a brief picture of what happened as described by the police. The importance of this incident lies in the probation department's disposition recommendation and the court's final action. The patrol officer's report implicates Donald because his nickname was heard being used by his friends: "Stop kicking him Dizzy," and "he's unconscious, let's get out of here." The officers asked several persons standing around who "Dizzy" could be, and they responded with the name Desmond. Another boy had been implicated, a Bob Lew. Lew contacted the patrol officers at the police station to tell them he was there but not involved in the fight.

> Bob [Lew] was advised that it was known that Dizzy did the kicking. He at first stated he didn't know what had happened. He then conceded that Desmond had been doing the kicking and that he had walked away and didn't know if anyone else had kicked or not. He stated that he didn't know the others involved. After a discussion on where loyalty to his friends ended and being mixed up in a dirty mess he stated that Vernon Ness had been the one that took the hat and started the fight. Bob didn't want it known that he had mentioned this name. Bob again stated that he at no time hit or kicked victim and that he had told others not to hit him. He seemed genuinely ashamed that he had even been with the group.

Police concern with establishing the "facts" requires various forms of interviewing (including threats, traps, and negotiations) as to the informant's responsibility, and subsequent police action if he "comes clean." When the police told Bob Lew "that it was known that Dizzy did the kicking" the informant was led to believe this statement was an established fact. The confidence with which the police can utilize such strategies forces the informant to entertain the possibility that his reluctance to "talk" is both foolish and a danger to him because of what the police "know." The following remarks suggest how the dialogue must have gone back and forth with the police trying to convince Lew that they "knew" what happened, and therefore it would be "better" for Bob to simply "come clean." The report states: "He at first stated he didn't know . . . then conceded that Desmond had been doing the kicking . . . [and] after a discussion on where loyalty to his friends ended and being mixed up in a dirty mess he stated that Vernon Ness had been the one that took the hat and started the fight." The comment "Bob didn't want it known that he had" been the informant provides others who may read the report with the suggestion this juvenile was "helpful" but "afraid" of retaliation, or he was after all a "fink" in the final analysis. The additional remark about seeming to be "genuinely ashamed that he had even been" at the scene could be read as supportive of the idea that here is "basically a good kid."

The following quotations (first from police reports, and second from the P. O.'s report) are intended to reveal further problems in establishing a legal version of "what happened" when conditions of due process and adversary services are not afforded the juvenile. After the patrol officer's initial report the incident was described as follows:

9/26/64. 3:30 p.m.—Desmond: Stated he had gone to the football game at Tech [high school] and attended the dance afterward. He was with a date, a [name] (12 Grade Tech lives on [name] Ave.). After the dance was over they walked up the stairs from the gym area towards [names of two streets]. He stated he noticed Ness fighting with victim Slate. Slate and Ness were wrestling on the ground and Slate had grabbed Ness by the testicles and Ness was yelling. Desmond stated he went to Ness' aid and pulled them apart. He denied at this time kicking the victim, or hitting him. He stated guys unknown to him did come up and start kicking Slate. He stated that a large crowd was all around and they got out of there as soon as he separated Ness and Slate.

Ness: Stated he had attended the game with two buddies: [names, date of birth, and school given]. After the football game they went to the dance and as it broke up they walked up the stairs from the gym area towards [same street names given above]. Slate was in front of them and someone in the large crowd of people brushed against Slate's cowboy type hat. Slate turned around and pushed Ness telling him to cut it out. Ness stated he then got mad and punch Slate in the face with his fist. They then started to wrestle around and both went to the ground. He was then grabbed by the testicles by Slate and he hurt so bad he started to yelling. At this time guys, not all known to him came up and started to kick Slate. He knew Desmond came up and pulled them apart but did not know if he actually kicked Slate. His feelings were that Desmond, [friends he came with] had no part in the kicking. . . .

Desmond was again questioned and asked if he had anything further to add to this officer's investigation. He did not know what Ness had stated, he hesitated for a few moments and then stated that when he had talked a few minutes before to this officer that he felt as if he should tell everything. He stated that when he had come upon the fight and saw who was fighting he could tell that his friend was being hurt by being grabbed on the testicles by Slate. When he separated them he had kicked Slate hitting him on the chest and possibly his foot glanced on up onto Slate's chin. He stated he may have kicked him twice but felt he only had once. He further said that he was not the only one who did the kicking, there were others, one being a friend who has been in trouble with the Police before. He did not want to give the name of this friend but stated that he would contact him later this date and talk to him about coming to the Police Station and talking to this officer. . . .

The investigating officer told me he was certain Desmond had done all of the damage to Slate and after the boy's initial remarks "knew" he would "break down" and tell the "truth." The officer was annoyed with what he felt was Desmond's refusal to implicate himself completely initially, but he did not become harsh (in my impression) when urging the juvenile to "come clean." This officer is soft-spoken and, in my opinion, always seemed rather gentle even when telling the juvenile he was "sure" the boy was lying. The officer was annoyed with Desmond for not "coming clean" immediately and because the boy's parents, particularly the father, were not willing to concede their boy could have done something so "bad." For the police, in their informal discussion, this was a case of a "vicious" beating without provocation. The officer indicated how he was suspicous of Desmond's initial remarks ("and asked if he had anything further to add . . ."), while noting Desmond was unaware of what his friend had said. The officer implied he had "other" information that implicated Desmond directly, but would give the juvenile "another chance" to tell his story. The report does not reveal the imputations and prodding that took place.

On 9/28/64, the juvenile officer contacted five presumed witnesses, two of whom were named by Ness as his companions the night of the incident. Relevant excerpts are presented in their order of occurrence in the report.

The first boy . . . stated he was present . . . and that Desmond may have done the kicking of Slate. . . . It was apparent that he was leaving out names other than the ones he had given as being present. Reliable information had been obtained that [name of one of the five being interviewed] was present but he would not admit seeing him at first.

[Second witness] was talked to and it was learned that he had come [with three juveniles not previously mentioned, yet Ness had stated that this second witness was with him and the first witness]. . . . The others decided to tell that [second witness] was with them and it was felt that they were using him to protect the name of a guilty party. [This second witness] was dismissed to go back to class. No action was to be taken on him by the school officials.

[First witness] was talked to again and he admitted that [second witness] was not with him in Ness' car when they came to the game. He stated that [third witness] was instead. Mr. [school official] felt that his lying had implicated him enough along with the others to draw a suspension from school. [Third witness] was then talked to and the following learned after much questioning. There had been a small fight in the gym during the dance . . . [and] word that a rumble would occur after the dance. . . . Someone had pushed victim's hat and then Ness grabbed at it. Shortly he saw Ness hit victim with his fist and then hit him a couple of more times before they wrestled. . . . He saw Desmond come up and kick victim a couple of times. . . . After talking further he admitted that a third boy had been involved . . . named Wally Stevens . . . he saw Stevens lay into victim after Desmond had kicked him. He saw Stevens hit victim in the face several times. [This juvenile also suspended from school.]

[Fourth witness] was questioned. . . . He also observed Desmond kick victim two times in the face. . . . It was apparent he was there because of the suspected rumble and he was hiding the name of Stevens. [Also suspended.]

[Fifth witness] was questioned and . . . he had been drinking earlier on the night of the fight . . . he saw Desmond kick victim and it made him sick so he left. . . . He would not admit seeing Stevens kick victim. [Also suspended.] After being given their suspension orders by Mr. [school official] both [first witness] and [fourth witness] admitted seeing Stevens at the scene and [first witness] had been the one who pulled Stevens off of Slate after he had put in his punches. . . .

Ness was talked to and he would not implicate Stevens. He stated he was at fault for hitting Slate but he had been pushed first. He also stated he had pushed Slate's hat and thrown the first punch. [Also suspended.] Desmond was then questioned. He still would not give Stevens' name at first but when advised that the officials present knew of his actions he then told that Stevens had been there. Desmond stated he kicked victim two times . . . he observed Stevens standing over victim and kicking victim in the face. Desmond was asked if he had been drinking and he admitted having shared a 6 pak of beer with someone (he would not name the person.) . . . To summarize, a small fight had occurred during the dance. . . . The two involved decided to have it out after the dance with the friends coming along. Victim . . . just happen to come along at the wrong time and were attacked on the spur of the moment. . . .

Stevens could not be contacted. . . . Word did reach he and his father during the day by way of some unknown source and Mr. Stevens called this officer . . . and an appointment was set up. . . .

[A description of victim's injuries and conversation with father of victim.]
9/29/64—[Remarks about conversation with Stevens' father and son.] . . .
he was the first one to Ness' aid, he kicked victim Slate in the seat of the
pants (he was sure his kick was in the rear end of Slate) and started to pull
the two apart . . . he observed a foot, later learned by him to be Desmond, kick
victim 4 times (he states he definitely saw 4 kicks) in the face. He observed
that the first kick made victim unconscious. After this he then went to victim
and pulled him onto the lawn and observed his face to be bloody and victim
being still unconscious. At this time he left the area. . . . [Petitions filed on
Desmond, Ness, and Stevens.]

The quoted texts reveal something of the strategy employed by the juvenile officer investigating the case. He interviewed the suspects before a
school official empowered with the authority to suspend any juvenile immediately, and sought to fill in what for him was "a pretty good idea of
what happened." The discussion revolves around the presence of the suspect,
those he witnessed inflicting injury on the victim, and the sequence of what
happened as the event unfolded. When the officer states (with the first
witness) that "it was apparent that he was leaving out names other than
the ones he had given as being present," we cannot pinpoint how the officer
decided it. "was apparent," but assume this assessment was viewed negatively
by both the officer and the school official. The latter then suspended him for
the "lying." When the officer notes that "reliable information had been obtained . . . ," there is no way of deducing from the report how the officer
decided his information was "reliable." In this particular case the officer
had "relied" upon the remarks of other informants. The interrogation of the
second witness led the officer to conclude that considerable collusion as to
"stories" had occurred among the various juveniles present at the incident.
By calling back the first witness, the officer confronts him with information
(its verification not being an issue) that the interviewee cannot check out independently, and which is presented to him as "inside" or "factual" information. In reporting his success with the third witness the officer notes that
"the following learned after much questioning." My interpretation of this
remark, based on my own observations and asking "how it went" when
asking about interrogations I could not attend, assumes the juvenile is told
over and over again his comments will not be accepted "because we know
better" or "the grapevine tells me." Therefore, "much questioning" suggests
a successful "breakdown" of the juvenile's original stance to the officer's
questions. As the officer obtains more and more detailed information, he
feeds the juvenile "loaded" questions including built-in motivational causes
for each participant's actions. (For example, "Did Ness grab his hat because
he was trying to be funny?") Thus, "after talking further he admitted that a

third boy had been involved." The report does not reveal how the officer might supply the witness with the name of the suspect he felt was being protected. The third witness was suspended for not telling the story "straight," in a direct manner, and for not wanting to reveal the name of Wally Stevens as an aggressor. The fourth witness was suspended because "it was apparent he was there because of the suspected rumble and he was hiding the name of Stevens." Thus, admitting an intent to participate in the "rumble" and not revealing Stevens' name were the apparent grounds used for suspension. Notice the fifth witness could be charged with drinking, attending the possible rumble, but "would not admit seeing Stevens kick victim." The disclaimer of watching Desmond kick the victim so that "it made him sick" was not honored by the officer, and the suggestion is he would not admit to something he "knew" about. Then the officer notes the first and fourth witnesses "admitted seeing Stevens at the scene" after they were "given their suspension orders. . . ." Some negotiation can occur because the officer can tell the juvenile that the "worst" is over as far as punishment is concerned and, therefore, the juvenile should reveal what "really happened." Other negotiations occur routinely if the officer and school official (or one of them) agree not to implicate the juvenile any more for a "straight" story. Implicating a juvenile, however, also involves the officer's evaluation of the former's "attitude" and past record. When the officer finally speaks to Ness he cannot obtain a direct implication of Stevens, but does secure an admission of hitting Slate first. The interview with Desmond is now set up for obtaining further details because the officer can invoke all of the testimony of the previous juveniles as established factual information. Desmond admits to drinking and then directly implicates his friend Stevens whom he would not name in the first interview (quoted earlier) because his friend "has been in trouble with the police before." But the interrogation of Stevens states Desmond kicked the victim "4 times (he states he definitely saw 4 kicks)," while Stevens claims to have only kicked the victim in the "rear end." The officer did not make further remarks about the discrepancies in the information he obtained, but he was satisfied that he had the necessary information on the principal aggressors. The probation officer's report provides additional information based upon his own interviewing of the suspects.

I now want to shift the discussion to the victim and his family. This was one of the few cases where I was able to obtain some information about the victim. This is a sore point with the police; the victim is seldom considered while the offender is viewed as being treated "softly." The investigating juvenile officer contacted the victim and his parents several times to inquire about suspects and the condition of the juvenile. The police officer encouraged the parents to "push" the matter to insure that the offenders "got what was coming" to them. The juvenile officer refers to the victim's father as follows:

> Mr. Slate is very upset over this beating and states he will go the full extent in seeing the guilty ones prosecuted criminally and civilly. He has already consulted an attorney and has been advised his civil rights.

A few days after the juvenile officer reported the above information I visited the Slate home with the P. O. handling the case. The parents were told that we were both probation officers interested in the victim's condition, and that we wanted to know the parents' feelings about how the case should be handled. During the visit the father stated that he had called a local lawyer, and was told that he should definitely bring civil action to the case. Then he stated he called the same lawyer a few days later and was advised he probably "didn't have a case." The father became suspicious and began making inquiries about the lawyer. He stated he had "heard" this lawyer was contacted by the Desmond father, and he was told the Desmond father was seen leaving the lawyer's office. The Slate father stated that he would seek an "out-of-town" lawyer, since he felt the Desmond family had more "pull" in City A, while they (the Slates) were relative newcomers. I made separate inquiries of lawyer acquaintances and several police officers. I was told the lawyer in question is the head of one of the largest firms in City A and known for a "winning" record of acquittals in court cases. The police were openly hostile toward this lawyer stating he was a "shyster" and not to be "trusted." The police indicated this lawyer was always able to obtain reduced sentences in cases the police "figured were air-tight." Finally, I was told the Desmond family has often retained the lawyer in question for both family and business matters. The P. O. was quite concerned about the victim's injuries, sympathized with the parents in my presence, and felt the Desmond boy should be punished for his acts. It is rare for probation officers to even know or meet the victims in juvenile matters; therefore this contact is not typical. It was my impression that the police and probation officers were particularly sympathetic with the victim because of the extensive injuries and the social and political influence of the suspect's family.

Before the P. O.'s report was written there were many extensive contacts between the Desmond family and various probation officials, as well as many meetings among probation officials, to discuss the possible disposition. The Desmond family sought to avoid any possibility of sending Donald to a county or state institution, while the P. O. favored a disposition leading to placement in the county's boys' ranch. At one point, several of the P. O.'s superiors asked me if sending the boy to the county ranch would jeopardize his chances of entering a university the following fall. My response was that perhaps a private school might be concerned, but state schools would not reject the juvenile on that basis. I was told the mother of the boy belonged to the same woman's organization as the wife of a high ranking probation official, and that the latter official became involved in the case because of the contact between his wife and Mrs. Desmond. The P. O. told me he was under considerable pressure not to recommend placement at the boys' ranch; his immediate superior was opposed to this latter placement, but the chief of the juvenile section told the P. O. it was "his decision" and everyone would support him. The P. O., however, felt it was clear to him everyone was opposed to the boys' ranch placement. The P. O., in his remarks to me, found the Desmond father's "attitude" particularly annoying. The probation officer concluded that the father was of the opinion Donald had not done anything "wrong," but that it was an accident. Further, a little drinking and fighting "was normal when I was a boy." Mrs. Desmond told the P. O. she felt the boy was difficult to control because of the father's "attitude." (Recall the earlier quotations from a police report where a similar statement was made about the father.) Yet the mother was also quite upset over the possibility of a boys' ranch placement. Everyone seemed concerned that Donald's educational and general future would be influenced negatively by placement at the boys' ranch. The school report revealed the following information:

English	B	Has good work habits	Superior
History	A	Gets along well with others	Average
Math (adv)	C	Accepts responsibility	Average
Biology	A	Uses his abilities	Superior
P. E.	A	Has good manual coordination	Superior
		Has good health habits	Superior
		Is obedient and cooperative	Average
		Brings work material regularly	Average

Donald is a student who is well liked by his peers. He has a tendency to gravitate toward group companionship, thereby being reinforced by "gangs." Although he has been no behavior problem in the classroom, he seems to get "involved" outside the classroom. Some of this appears to be immature behavior and some a strong lack of self-discipline. He became involved in a serious fight after one of the school dances this year which called for strong disciplinary action. Dizzy probably lacks the sterner type of discipline at home; the relationship between Dizzy and his mother seems to be ineffective in matters of behavior.

During a parent conference, the mother expressed great concern for the kind of company "Dizzy" enjoyed.

The school report clearly suggests a better than average student (the "C" was in advanced math), while the remarks accompanying the report indicate that the school officials have decided to join the "community" in denouncing Donald's extracurricular activities. Yet the report notes the boy "has been no behavior problem in the classroom." The categories "gangs," "immature," and "strong lack of self-discipline" seem to be *post hoc* evaluations, even though the remark about the parent conference seems to support the mother's consistent concern with the juvenile's boy friends. This juvenile's school record seems to have played an important part in mitigating the seriousness of the offense, but my impression was that if the offense were considered less serious, the school report would probably neutralize the entire incident.

The P. O.'s report describes the Desmond family (for 1963) as having an income ranging from $12,000 to $18,000 per year, depending upon the father's business returns. The home was described as large, new, and exceptionally well-furnished. All of the family members seem to be or have been active in various community groups. Donald was a member of "Cub Scouts," "Little League," and similar groups. The petition allegations against Desmond and Stevens read as follows:

> On October 1, 1964, identical petitions were filed in behalf of Donald Desmond and Walter Stevens alleging that the said minors come within the provisions of Section 602 of the Welfare and Institutions Code in that the said minors did on or about the 26th day of September, 1964, commit an assault upon the person of Stanley Slate with a deadly weapon, to wit: their feet on which they were wearing shoes, at . . . by kicking said victim with their feet . . . thereby violating Section 245 of the Penal Code of California; and, because of these circumstances, the said minors are in the need of the care, control and supervision of the Juvenile Court. . . .

The allegations against Ness were that he had used his fists to "wilfully and unlawfully use force or violence upon the person of Stanley Slate. . . ." The P. O.'s description of the incident is as follows:

> . . . a minor . . . stopped Slate and asked him why he was dressed in that western outfit. Before Slate could answer, Victor Ness grabbed his cowboy type hat, which Slate promptly recovered from him. Immediately Ness started swinging at Slate. Slate did state that Ness had an odor of alcohol about him and that he (Slate) backed away from Ness to prevent being hit. Immediately, Ness grabbed his western type shirt by the shoulder and ripped the sleeve nearly off. At this point the victim became extremely angry, grabbed Ness by the arm, and also by his testicles. Ness did manage to hit the victim on the face two or three times. As both were scuffling, one of the boys grabbed Slate by his hair, pulled his head, and delivered a blow below his right ear which left him unconscious. It has not yet been determined who did this.

> The Stevens minor denies delivering the first kick. He did state that as Slate and Ness were struggling on the grass he endeavored to separate them by shoving Slate with his feet. Stevens also denies using his fist. Investigation re-

veals that as Slate and Ness were on the ground, Desmond arrived at the scene and immediately started kicking Slate on the face numerous times.

Desmond admits to this stating that he kicked him two or three times. The victim, Slate, was left there by the culprits, and they did not even think of offering some type of assistance. When the victim regained consciousness, the police were there. . . .

[Then follows a paraphrasing of remarks by the minors.]

. . . when he [Desmond] saw that his friend Ness was in great pain . . . he became extremely angry, saw red, went over and started kicking Slate. Desmond did state that he did not aim for Slate's head and that he kicked him two or three times. He also admits that he did not see Stevens kick the victim. Desmond also admits that he knew what he was doing even though he was somewhat intoxicated. . . .

Ness stated . . . Stevens came to his assistance. Ness did state that he saw Stevens kick the victim in the rear. After the victim was knocked unconscious, Ness took a look at him, thought he was dead, did not assist and left the scene in a hurry.

. . . Stevens . . . endeavored to separate them by pushing Slate in the rear with his foot. Immediately, Stevens saw Desmond kick Slate in the face and head with full force approximately three times. . . .

The above remarks suggest Desmond was responsible for any serious damage to Slate, and Stevens did not kick the victim in the head. The P. O. implicates all three boys, charges them with being callous about the victim's condition after the fight, while placing the brunt of the damage on the actions of Desmond, whose behavior is depicted as under the condition of alcohol but where he "knew what he was doing." The statement from Ness did not mention his observation of Desmond as responsible for kicking Slate.

The P. O. utilizes the information in the school report quoted above to say that Desmond "has a tendency to gravitate toward group companionship which is reinforced by 'gangs.' Although he has been no behavior problem, he seems to get 'involved' outside the classroom. Some of this appears to be immature and a strong lack of self-discipline. . . ." The P. O.'s remarks are not quotes from the school report, but rather a paraphrasing of the report. But the school report was requested after the incident and thus the school officials were not only aware of the incident, but suspended Desmond because of it. Yet the P. O. invokes the school report as documentary evidence that "others" are aware of the problems of "group companionship" and "reinforced by 'gangs'."

When Desmond was expelled from school, the parents enrolled him in a local Catholic high school. The P. O.'s report continues by noting that the previous popularity Desmond enjoyed "in school and in the community" had been seriously affected by the incident, he was "ostracized by many of his friends, and his status in the community is below average." Desmond is described by the P. O. as "a minor who is very intelligent, self-assured, and somewhat aggressive. He is the type of individual who is not happy unless he is the top man in any endeavor. Even though Dizzy excels in most of his endeavors, he does not brag about them." This depiction could be read as a general description of the American ideal type of adolescent. Donald is an honor student, polite. "good-looking," and from a "good" family. The categories "intelligent," "self-assured," "somewhat aggressive," "top man" oriented (but not a braggart) do not resemble standard lay or professional depictions of juvenile offenders. Faced with an incident no one in the community could take lightly, the P. O. constructs a biography and something of a legal brief to justify his recommendations. The "hard facts" for both police and probation in a case of this type is that "under the influence of an alcoholic beverage, he unmercifully and without care, and with the intent to hurt the victim severely, kicked him." This last statement is softened by one that follows: "Dizzy appears to be remorseful for his actions and advised this officer that this will never happen again and that he will endeavor to curtail his drinking." The juxtaposition of the two statements permits the P. O. to be both justified in his recommendation of some form of modified punishment (though it will be termed "treatment"). The P. O.'s decision-making can be discerned from the additional remarks made before making his recommendation:

> Both parents have verbally expressed sincere concern for their son and will go to any lengths to continue assisting him in any way whatsoever. Because Mr. Desmond is constantly busy with his business endeavors, the mother actually has been the disciplinarian in this family. When she becomes aware that she could not control Donald, finding out that she was ineffective, she advised Mr. Desmond that it was his obligation to assume the responsibility of disciplining Donald. Even though Mr. Desmond had the best intentions, he actually failed Donald. What was needed at that particular time was for the parents to unite, assisting each other and being firm with Donald. The difficulty was that Mr. Desmond shunned his responsibility and did not take a firm stand in this matter.
>
> Mrs. Desmond approximately two years ago became aware that Desmond was gradually drifting away from their values and standards and that he obviously needed constructive counseling and guidance. She contacted the Welfare Department for assistance, and, when they advised her that they could not help her, she became somewhat frustrated. She then contacted the Family Service Agency in [City A] and was refused assistance not because the agency was unwilling, but because Mr. Desmond could not afford to make time. The parents are in agreement that their son should remain at home, as he is already attending a private school, [name of Catholic high school in City A]. They also

promise that they will be strict with him, that they will endeavor to know where he is at all times, and that he is to curtail his association with the other minors appearing in Juvenile Court today and with some of the other boys who belong to the "organization" [an informal "club" Donald associates with].

To a degree Mrs. Desmond is not realistic in this matter. Donald needs constant supervision and if he remains in the community, he will undoubtedly involve himself in further difficulty. Donald has the innate ability to become a substantial and constructive citizen if only he would change his attitude. This officer, after giving serious thought to this matter, feels that the minor should be removed from the community for the following reasons: the seriousness of the offense, the strong reaction from the community school and the victim, demanding that something be done, the past conduct on the part of the minor within the community and his pattern of fighting and, as he stated to the Probation Officer, "It seems like everytime I drink I get into a fight." [The P. O. then recommends that the juvenile go to a boys' ranch run by the county probation department, stating the screening committee has accepted him.] However, if they [the parents] can present an alternate plan, placing the minor in a private or military school away from the community of [City A], this officer will reluctantly follow their plea. If such is the case this week, this officer then recommends that the allegations be found true and that this matter be continued to November 5, 1964. This is in order to permit the parents to look for a suitable school for the said minor.

The P. O.'s remarks begin with the observation the parents "will go to any lengths to continue assisting" their boy, but quickly notes that the father is "busy with his business," and the "mother actually has been the disciplinarian in this family." The P. O. is fairly pointed in stating that both parents were "ineffective" and had "failed Donald." Although we cannot objectify how the parents both had "good intentions" and yet managed to "fail" their son, it seems clear that the P. O. felt the parents had "failed." The P. O. told me he spoke primarily to the mother because the father felt the matter was not "serious" and that his son had not done "anything that wrong." The P. O. appeared quite annoyed with the juvenile's father, implying to me the father regarded fights and similar activities as "normal" adolescent behavior and part of "growing up." The father was also reportedly not concerned about the juvenile's drinking, and this also displeased the P. O. The father's views are not inconsistent (except for the fighting) with what any "good" fraternity boy might be expected to do in college, or any "good" member of an adult fraternal order when at a convention or private party. The P. O. seems to support the depiction of the mother's dilemma by reference to the latter's attempt to seek help from community agencies. The P. O. then shifts to the disposition problem, and what I felt was continual parental pressure (based upon my impressionistic conversations with the P. O. and his supervisors) to keep their boy at home. This pressure is masked by the remark, "The parents are in agreement that their son should remain at home. . . ." The presumed parental remarks about being "strict" and keeping him away from the others involved in the incident and companions of the juvenile gang or "organization" do not seem to satisfy the P. O. The P. O. counters with the comment, "Mrs. Desmond is not realistic in this matter." The P. O. seems convinced that the boy would continue to "involve himself in further difficulty," and blames the minor's "attitude." The "reasons" for recommending removal from the community mention the "strong reaction from the community [that is, the police, this particular P. O., calls by 'people'], school [for instance, after being told by the police and probation departments] and the victim [for example, the victim protested to the police and probation, and the P. O. was sympathetic with the victim's parents' insistence that 'something be done'], . . . the past conduct on the part of the minor within the community and his pattern of fighting," and the admission of drinking leading to "a fight." The P.O. was under continual pressure not to recommend placement at the boys' ranch. The report hints at the compromise when it flatly states the boy was accepted for ranch placement, but the P. O. acknowledges that he would "reluctantly follow" the parents' "plea" to have the juvenile placed "away from the community." The P. O. told me the priviso of placement outside of the community was something he insisted upon, while the parents preferred to retain the juvenile at the Catholic school in City A.

An indirect source of pressure came from the vice principal of the City A Catholic High School. The vice principal stated the following in a letter to the judge (quoted in part):

Now it has been brought to our attention that Donald is scheduled to appear before Your Honor. I hope that I am not presuming by giving the following facts: During the past month Donald has shown to possess a very good attitude toward school and his studies. He has, in addition, manifested a healthy spirit with regard to the school's activities, and he has shown due respect in every way toward the teachers. Furthermore, there has been no lack of cooperation on his part in anything that he has been asked to do.

Please accept my sincere interest in this young man for I feel that he has shown evidence of a salutary attitude while at school. If he were to remain at [school], I would personally see to it that he received the necessary aid and guidance in the hope of making him a worthwhile citizen.

The official appeared interested in having the juvenile remain at the new school, writing a positive report of the boy's activities. Recall that we are discussing a "nice-looking boy" who can present himself well to others, does not express the "wrong attitude," comes from a "nice home," and is an honor student. While imputations of criminality were not made, neither were there attempts to characterize the juvenile as "sick." The parents did not retain private counsel for the court hearing, but relied upon a variety of contacts to soften the P. O.'s intention of placement in a county facility.

The P. O. told me that for several weeks after placement in another school some sixty miles from home, the juvenile repeatedly violated the terms of probation by returning home and staying out late with friends and at parties. The P. O. warned the juvenile of possible consequences, but took no further action. About four months after placement, Donald was home for the weekend and, on Saturday night, went out with a friend, Lenny Greer (also upper middle-income family) to a lower-income section of City A where a party was said to be in progress. Donald's account of "what happened" is as follows:

After we had danced for a couple of hours this guy Marty Hall came out and said that the party was over and that all of us would have to leave, this was at approx. midnight or twelve thirty. None of the people at the party wanted to leave. Then this subject Marty Hall said "I'll make you leave" at this time he turned and ran up the stairs. At this time Lenny started up the stairs. Lenny was ahead of me as I started up the stairs when I was two thirds or half way up the stairs I heard what I thought to be an Air Rifle shot, it did not sound like a shot gun or rifle to me. When I entered the room that is at the head of the stairs Lenny was on the floor on his side with his feet toward the stairs. Lenny was on his side holding his stomach and when I ask "Are you alright" he said "OH NO" and I repeated a couple of times are you alright and all he would say is "OH NO."

There are some slight variations as to how the suspect Hall decided to go after his rifle (claiming Desmond and Greer were not invited and refused to leave the party), but everyone is agreed, including the suspect, that Hall did fatally shoot Lenny.

The P. O. held a "conference" with Donald and his mother two days after the shooting incident. The following remarks are from the P. O.'s informal record:

Conference with Donald and his mother at P. O. office. Minor did state that on [date], he and three boys and three girls were to see the [circus in a nearby city] but didn't. Art Somer bought some wine and beer and Donald admits to drinking half bottle of wine at party on [name] street. Around 10.30 p.m. this party arrived at Hall's residence and according to Donald, he didn't drink even though the others were drinking. For more detail information, see [City A newspaper with dates] in file and [City A] P. D. report. P. O. could file on Donald for curfew, drinking and attending party without his parents' permission; however, the minor was ordered to abide by the following:

1. Not leave school without permission of P. O. and the only time he will be permitted to return home without permission of P. O. is during spring vacation and summer vacation;

2. When home he is not to stay out after 6:00 p.m. unless he is with his mother or father;

3. Report to P. O. twice a month in writing while at school;

4. Abide by all reasonable directives of the P. O.

Donald and Mrs. Desmond concur with these stipulations. Later I called school and advised Father Gary and Maloney about Donald's episode during the weekend. I also wrote a letter to Donald in regards to the stipulations mentioned above. Even though I have been trying to get [City A] P. D. report in regards to the shooting, I have not been successful. Det. Albert working on this case.

I was contemplating writing modification of Court Order; however Sr. D.P.O. Jones said that this was not necessary and that a letter would be sufficient.

The P. O.'s remarks about Donald's activities were not concerned with how the incident "happened," but with Donald's participation. Newspaper accounts did not mention Donald as on probation, and the police were not concerned with Donald's drinking and curfew violation. The shooting was too "big," apparently, to attend to Donald's participation. The P.O.'s reaction was softened by his supervisor, but this is revealed indirectly when the P.O. points out how the supervisor ("Sr. D.P.O.") told him not to write a modification of the court order, "that a letter would be sufficient." The modification of the court order could be written as a serious violation of probation, and easily constituted grounds for ranch or Youth Authority placement. The Desmond boy could not have received a more lenient "punishment" for his violation of probation. The weekends he had been spending at home violated every condition of probation, and clearly contradicted the trust relationship presumably implied by the terms of probation in the previous serious case. But the P. O. did not establish a trust relationship with the juvenile. If there was a trust relationship it was between the P. O. and the mother. The supervisor negotiated the case for the P. O. My impressionistic observations here have influenced my interpretation of the case because I see the supervisor as an ideal typical middle-class P. O. The supervisor appeared to me as an ideal typical representative of the "respectable" people in City A. His religious and social views could be described as "puritanical." The P. O. could be described as the obverse of this image. The P. O. stated he was "sorry" for the mother because of the father's "attitude," and his feeling that the juvenile was "like his father."

The police and P. O. indicated to me the previous assault case narrowly missed being a tragedy because a few more kicks by Donald might have killed the victim. The case was considered "serious." The mobilization of family resources proved critical in transforming the incident into "something that shouldn't have happened," where the imputations are not pushed in the directions of illness or criminality, but left ambiguous as to neat categorical reference. Everyone agreed it was a "serious" matter, but despite remarks about the family "problem," both parents closed ranks by using every resource available to influence the Probation Department and the Court so as to achieve a disposition that would leave the juvenile's family and himself relatively untouched by the consequences of incarceration in county or state facilities. The P. O. could not interview the parents (as in other cases) because he indicated to me that "they" were "hard to talk to." The father would not accept the P. O.'s depiction of the case. The mother seemed overly anxious to find faults and would agree there had been "problems," but refused to listen to any possibility of incarceration in a county or state facility.

I want to argue Donald's case occurs frequently among middle-class families. The police of a nearby large metropolitan area gave me unofficial statistical materials they claimed demonstrated the point about family resources, law-enforcement policy, and the contingencies of exchanges between juveniles and officers, officers and parents, and the like. The relevant table consisted of a case-load report for the Juvenile Bureau of the large city in the metropolitan area. Four divisions of the city were called to my attention as being "high" income areas. All four areas were outside of the central districts of the city, and I was told considerable discretion was given to local commanders as to disposition policy with juveniles. Area A was listed as having a numerical case load of 1463 for 1964, Area B with a case load of 1340, Area C with a case load of 2430, and Area D with a case load of 2393. The explanation given to me by the senior officers of the Juvenile Bureau was as follows: each commander utilizes discretion in deciding how his juvenile unit will handle cases so that many juveniles never reach court, or the case is not investigated because the parents are allowed to send the juvenile away under the tacit agreement the minor will not be returned except for vacation periods or until he has reached eighteen years of age. A further interesting element in the table was the consistency of the population size for each division, the number of juvenile officers assigned, and the similarity in the types of offenses recorded.

In the next chapter I show a variation of the above theme by focusing on how middle-income families mobilize resources to fight law-enforcement officials in cases where direct community influence is not attempted or possible. I refer to negotiations with probation and court officials. Thus, if the police refer the case to probation, the negotiations and resources impinge upon different ideologies, organizational procedures, and what "anyone" knows about juveniles presumed to be delinquent or "good kids."

Chapter 7

COURT HEARINGS: THE NEGOTIATION
OF DISPOSITIONS

I have chosen the final cases from City B because the volume of court hearings is greater, more like the hearings I have observed in large cities in California, and more likely to reveal problematic decision-making vis-à-vis the juvenile's future based upon open courtroom discussion. City B utilizes a full-time referee for the bulk of its juvenile cases. The judges in City A were less likely to conduct hearings that make dispositional and allegational matters problematic in the courtroom. The hearings in City A appeared more perfunctory, with less interest on the part of the judge, and I had the feeling matters were often settled prior to the hearing. The judges barely had time to read the P.O.'s report, and were usually filled in by the P.O. and his supervisor prior to beginning the hearing.

In City B, the referee had more time to study each case, consult with the P.O. about questions concerning "what happened," how the parents "feel," and would also consult with the P.O.'s supervisor. The explanation of the right to counsel was explained more carefully in City B than in City A, and the referee seemed more interested in drawing the parents into an active discussion of the "problem" and the disposition.

In this chapter I shall take more liberties with police and probation documents (presenting selected portions of them in truncated form), and I shall concentrate on probation-juvenile-parent interaction and the conversational exchanges in the courtroom. The materials cover three juveniles involved in the same case. The court hearings of one of the male juveniles in this case are particularly revealing because of the interchanges between the private counsel and the referee. The case is unusual vis-à-vis routine court hearings in both City A and City B, but I think indicative of what is likely to occur in future juvenile hearings as more elements of the adversary system are incorporated into the juvenile court.

I shall begin the discussion at the point of my entry into the case, and then try to follow the events as they unfolded. I was sitting in the Juvenile Bureau office of City B on a Monday morning in the middle of December 1964, when the Sergeant began telling me of a juvenile case being handled by the Detective Bureau. The case was described as "juicy," and the juvenile officers implied the detectives in the Vice Squad became very interested in the sexual activities involved. The police materials provided a rather lengthy account of the "sexy" details, but I shall only quote a section of the report to summarize "what happened."

Mrs. Peters drove her daughter and 14 year old son to a Christmas Dance at [name] Jr. High School at 7:00 P.M. [date]. The girl was last seen conversing with one Robert Bean in front of the auditorium and it was known that she had a date to meet a 16 year old boy at the dance. The date, Ronald Jones, showed up, but was unable to locate the victim and when Mr. and Mrs. Peters arrived at the dance at 10:00 P.M., their daughter was not to be found. The girl did not attend the dance and was not seen after 7:00 P.M. The girl did not return home as of 7:43 A.M. [next day] and a missing persons report was filed. Investigation failed to turn up the girl, however, at approximately 9:00 A.M. [two days later] victim called a friend and requested that he walk her home. This friend, one Ron Jones, age 15, met the girl at [streets of meeting], walked her to the [bowling alley] where he called his father, and the girl was then transported to her home. Victim related that she had been coaxed from the dance by one Robert Bean, age 13, [address of Bean], and one Tyrone Tryon, age 15, [address of Tryon], and one Denis Bond [address of Bond], age 15. Victim related that she had promised to get drunk with them and that if she loved him, she would get drunk and let him engage in intercourse with her. The four young people then walked to a liquor store on south [address], where Denis Bond stole a 1/5 of bourbon. The four young people then walked to this riding club on south [address], to which Tyrone Tryon and his parents belong, where the girl was given much bourbon to drink, approximately 3/4 of the bottle, and during the drinking engaged in sexual intercourse with Robert Bean. Victim then became violently ill and passed out, at which time the boys carried the girl into the tackle room, laid her on a blanket and called their friend, one Gregg Burns, age 19, [address], who assisted the boys in making the girl comfortable.

Burns, Tryon, and Bean returned the following morning, at which time Burns advised the other two boys to buy the girl a new blouse as she had vomited on the one she was wearing. Burns kept the young girl company throughout the entire day and evening of [next day], brought her some Listerine mouth wash and some apples and oranges to eat. Finding the girl's hose in a trash can, Burns got rid of this evidence as he did not want anyone to know the girl was staying in the tack room. Burns also assisted the girl in being comfortable during the night on [next night] and on the morning of [two days later] gave her a dime so that she could call her parents. The girl did not recall that Burns had intercourse with her. At no time did Burns make any attempt to get the girl home, nor did the other three boys involved. In fact, Robert Bean was contacted by the victim's father on two separate occasions on the evening of [dance night] at which time he denied knowing where the girl was. Robert Bean called the Peters residence three separate times during the afternoon of [next day] wanting to know if the girl had been found as yet. Evidence of the girl's presence was retained by Detective Morris as evidence. On the morning of [two days later] victim was examined at the County Hospital Clinic by Dr. Jensen and smears obtained from the girl's vaginal canal. Dr. Jensen indicated that the girl had indulged in sexual intercourse in the past.

The police account of "what happened" remains fairly consistent through many pages of interrogation. Robert Bean was considered the "organizer" and the only one to have had actual sexual contact with the girl. The police and probation both seem convinced of Gregg Burns' story of not "touching" the girl. The police report did state the following:

> This suspect [Bean] leads one to believe that he was led astray by the older boys and this more experienced female, and that he was merely a victim of circumstances. However, it might be noted that this suspect was the first one to partake in sexual intercourse with her.

The probation view placed most of the blame on Bean. Notice how the officer suggests the boys viewed the girl as "more experienced." The interrogation of Gregg Burns suggests this point: "Burns stated that the conversation continued, although he was unable to say which suspect said what, to the effect that the victim was a 'slut' and had readily consented to the acts of sexual intercourse." The males sought to depict the girl as a "slut" who wanted to have sexual intercourse with them. Subsequent events supported this view, but I want to underscore the following: the police viewed the girl as an "attractive" victim with no prior record and family appearances to support a positive perspective. My impressions support this view. The girl's appearance, clothing, hair styling, voice intonation were interpreted by the writer as "middle-class." She belonged to a teenage auxiliary of her father's fraternal order. The girl was polite, in my opinion, giving the impression of a "sweet" girl. It was difficult for the police to impute negative imputations (e.g., "slut").

The case became complicated a few weeks later because of another incident in which the Peters girl (Linda) was the principal figure. The police report states the following:

> Received a call at 7:45 P.M. [date, approximately two months later] to see the man at [address]. Upon arrival contacted a Mr. Brent Peters who stated that his daughter, Linda Peters, age 13, had run away from home on [day before] and that he knew that she was at this time at a big party at [address] and according to his information there was quite a large amount of drinking going on. The U/S followed Mr. Peters and his wife Barbara, to [address] and as we

approached the house approximately 30-40 juveniles ran out and jumped the back fence. Three others, a [names, age, and addresses] were seen coming out of the back door of the residence. The three were asked back inside with the officers. Upon going into the house, it was observed that every room had half empty bottles of beer and a number of empty cases stacked up in the kitchen plus empty wine bottles. Once inside the house, U/S observed Linda Peters coming from the bedroom, putting her clothes on and she was in a very highly intoxicated condition. Coming from the bedroom next to her was another runaway, Mary Ronson, who was also putting on her clothes and in a very highly intoxicated condition. Miss Peters stated that she had had sexual intercourse with ten boys. She stated one was her boyfriend, Robert Bean, and another named Mark, who later stated that his name was Robert. Miss Peters stated that all ten boys told her their name was Robert. Miss Ronson denied having any sexual intercourse. . . .

From the police report it could be suggested that Linda Peters "thought" she was having intercourse with Robert Bean each time, although Bean was in Juvenile Hall on the other matter at the time. My remark is based upon the assumption that all the juveniles at the school Linda attended became aware of the previous incident and decided she was an "easy lay." Getting the girl drunk was the first step and then each male told her he was "Robert Bean." My interpretation must be modified to include remarks made by the Peters girl to the P.O. stating she propositioned one of the boys at school, known to have been at the party, and had given thought to running away from home and staying with a friend. When I spoke to the girl in Juvenile Hall the next day she was "afraid" of what " might" have "happened" to her.

I have not followed the chronological sequences of the case because the P.O.'s report was not completed after an interview with the parents and girl (reported below), but was rewritten after the party incident and another examination by a psychiatrist prior to the court hearing. The original hearing was delayed for several weeks because of the party incident. I shall now return to the sequence of events after the dance incident. The following material is taken from an interview in the P.O.'s office between the P.O., Linda Peters, and both parents. My notes are not always complete, but almost all of the material presented is verbatim. The girl was well-dressed, a neat appearance and, in my opinion, "attractive." She was always soft-spoken, polite, attentive, and seemed to "blush," appeared sincere, and "interested" at the appropriate occasions. The P.O. interviewed Linda first and began by reading off the charges filed by the police.

JUVENILE. I'm the one that really drank the liquor. [Slight smile, no apparent shame, a slight smile. Linda claimed she has seen or known the boys slightly.]
PROBATION OFFICER. How do you like school?

JUV.   I like school. I miss it.

P.O.   How are your grades?

JUV.   Not that bad. I usually get good grades, but since all this mess I haven't been able to do much concentrating.

P.O.   [Question about] Best girl friend or maybe one or two.

JUV.   Lisa Manson, we ditched once together. Bonnie Berner too.

P.O.   Who is your best boy, not for loving, but for friends?

JUV.   . . . Charlie Dubay [The girl appears to be uneasy at this time.]

P.O.   Who did you have intercourse with first?

JUV.   Ronnie Jones? I did it to keep him. He said he really didn't care. He wanted to just kiss me here and kiss me there.

P.O.   Have there been any other boys since the episode?

JUV.   No. That's all dropped.

P.O.   How did it all start?

JUV.   There was Robert Bean. We were talking about it at school and he said "you gotta prove it." Well, I didn't want to lose him just like with Ronnie Jones. I was scared but didn't want them to think I was chicken. But I thought it was kinda cool.

P.O.   Did Gregg ever bother you?

JUV.   No, he just wanted to help me.

P.O.   You're not pregnant?

JUV.   No.

P.O.   Have you ever used anything to prevent a pregnancy?

JUV.   Once he used one of those things.

P.O.   Did you ever feel scared about getting pregnant?

JUV.   No, I was always trying to get even with my parents.

P.O.   You sort of wanted to [get] even with them.

JUV.   Yes, I always wanted to get even with other people. My mother gets mad at me. I love my rather. I know that's what wrong with me. I talk about this with my parents. I don't know why. [The manner of speaking appeared "sincere."]

The conversation shifts at this point. The P.O. begins the interview by telling the juvenile the charge against her; she is "in danger of leading a lewd and immoral life." The opening gambit appears to be an invitation to the girl to give an accounting for her past actions. The response was immediate and accompanied by what I took to be a grin signifying "mischief" that an adolescent could label "fun." The juvenile's direct reference to her drinking the liquor implies blame on her part and the P.O. does not seek to push the matter further. The references to school and grades appeared to be stock questions designed to elicit "revealing" information about the girl. The question about close friends appeared to me to be calculated to establish something "odd" about the juvenile. I cannot explain my impression that the girl began to feel uneasy. The P.O. did not pursue the "friends" line of questioning, but focused directly upon sexual experiences. It was my impression the P.O. felt she "scored" when the juvenile stated the name of the boy with whom she had first had intercourse and added: "I did it to keep him. He really didn't care . . ." The first part of the response ("I did it to keep him") is a stereotyped expression for suggesting a standard "reason" for the girl to hold "her man." The entire response, including "He said he really didn't care," was stated in a casual voice, in the manner of one girl gossiping with another. The juvenile gave no indication she felt the second remark undercut the first about the fear she could not "keep him." Nor did I feel she sought to "wipe out" the implication of the first remark with the "didn't care" statement and the follow-up of "He wanted to just kiss me here and kiss me there." I stress this apparent casual group of expressions because the reader might infer that, in the absence of clues as to voice intonation, the juvenile "slipped" when making the first utterance and tried to recover the situation by the follow-up remarks. Motives may or may not be imputed depending upon how the voice intonation is "read." The P.O. does not dwell on this past experience but moves to "other boys since the episode?" The juvenile seems to have understood the question as it appeared intended, that is, has she had sexual intercourse with other boys since the dance-evening episode with Robert Bean and the others? The P.O. then seeks to obtain an accounting of how it all "happened." The juvenile provides a truncated summary by suggesting that the incident revolved around the classic utterance "you gotta prove it." The following remarks "Well, I didn't want to lose him just like with Ronnie Jones" all imply the juvenile and Bean had discussed "being in love" or something to that effect. But there is no indication the girl had been seeing Bean, nor any suggestion from my conversations with her to indicate a "serious" interest in the boy. Nor did the P.O. question her about this possibility. It is not clear, therefore, what the referent for "it" might be in the remark "We were talking about it at school. . . ." Another interpretation emerges when the juvenile states "I was scared but didn't want them to think I was chicken." Yet the suggestion of intimidation seems contradicted by the subsequent remark "But I thought it was kinda cool" suggesting the girl might have perceived the proposed affair as "fun," or as prestigious activity. There was no indication of how the other juvenile males were brought into the picture. I call attention to the structuring of the interview to suggest how the P.O. can provide her own conclusions by the kinds of questions she asks and the topics omitted. Some responses are considered "adequate" despite apparent ambiguity in the immediate "answer." The P.O. moves on through the incident by asking "Did Gregg ever bother you?" This last question about Gregg Burns seems to be an attempt by the P.O. to "check out" doubts about Burns' story. The remark "You're not pregnant?" seems to be a statement of fact as well as a possible question. The P.O. seemed to imply some examination had been conducted for determining if conception had occurred. Notice the P.O.'s question about possible use of contraceptives is answered implicitly as "no" by stating "he used one of those things." The questions about pregnancy appear to be the P.O. attempting to determine if the juvenile had "feelings" about the "dangers" and "seriousness" of pregnancy. When the juvenile responded with "No, I was always trying to get even with my parents," I felt the P.O. was again convinced she had "found" the "underlying problem." The "no" seems to presume the juvenile was well aware of consequences and actually was hoping "to get even." The P.O. seemed to encourage an elaboration of the "get even" remark and the girl cooperates to produce a complicated response. At the time I heard the juvenile's remarks they seemed to be contextually appropriate but, later on, I felt the statement was confusing. The response is "ideal" for clinical imputations, but seems undercut somewhat by the remark "I know that's what's wrong with me. I talk about this with my parents." What is not clear is when the "talking" took place, both before or after the incident, or recently, and when did the juvenile decide she has "always wanted to get even with other people," much less her parents or, particularly, her mother. The P.O., however, did not seek an elaboration of the remarks. The conversation continues.

PROBATION OFFICER. I understand you are a [member of adolescent auxiliary to a fraternal order].

JUVENILE. Since Dec. [day], 1963.

P.O. I understand you're going through the . . . [a reference to ritual activities].

JUV. Yes.

P.O. Why do you like it?

JUV. You can meet friends there. You can talk together and have lots of fun. You can act like a lady. You can meet lots of friends there.

P.O. You belong to the ["high" Protestant] church. Did you go to another church one time?

JUV. Yes, [fundamentalist church]. Bonnie's father is a Pastor there. It's different. You know you say [pray] out loud.

P.O. Did you go up there?

JUV. Yes. When [evangelist minister and author of book on Christianity and the adolescent of "today"] was there. I really like what he said. Bonnie knows how much trouble I am in. So I did. You know I used to say "bitch" and smoked. That night I felt so good.

P.O. When did you go to this church? Before it all happened with the boys?

JUV. Before this happened with the boys.

P.O. Do you think God forgives you?

JUV. I think God forgives me.

P.O. You think God understands?

JUV. Yes, I think he is forgiving me and I'm better more each day.

P.O. So you think it was wrong?

JUV. Yes, I talked to my parents.

p.o. Do they know at school?

juv. Yes. You see, Robert Bean made me mad cause he told everybody at school that I took all my clothes off and let them do it. I got mad cause that's not right. [I could not record all of the exchange. She alleged a girl at the high school in her district told "everyone" she was supposed to be pregnant. The juvenile stated this information was repeated at the junior high school and everyone treated her "funny." The girls at the fraternal order also heard about the incident and she indicated how it was necessary to deny the story.]

p.o. What do you think will happen with the boys now?

juv. I'll just tell them no, that if that's all they want from me then they can go. [The conversation shifted quickly to the juvenile's remarks about spending summers in another city in southern California with her grandmother.]

p.o. Will you wait until you get married?

juv. Yes. I don't want my husband to know.

p.o. Will you change then?

juv. Oh yes, I'm trying to change all the time and I'm trying as hard as I can.

p.o. Well, if you are really trying hard that's what we want. I'll be checking with you every so often and you'll be on probation. The object of probation is to help you solve your problems. [The conversation closes with the P.O. telling the juvenile she had better "straighten out" because with each case "it gets worse."]

The P.O. shifts the conversation by mentioning the auxiliary of the fraternal order to which the juvenile was known to belong. Each question appears to be an attempt to obtain "routine" information about the juvenile's "interests and activities," but the P.O. had told me most of the same information about the girl prior to the interview. The P.O. seemed interested in the fact that the girl repeated the remark, "You can meet friends there." The remark was later interpreted to me as documentary evidence of the juvenile's exaggerated "need" for "friends." The calculated character of the questions appeared most obvious to me when the P.O. began asking about religious interests. Prior to the interview I was told by the P.O. about the juvenile's apparent interest in a fundamentalist sect. The P.O. reasoned the religious change was part of an imputed underlying "sick" pattern. Asking "Did you go to another church one time?" was only possible in this context because of the P.O.'s prior knowledge about the fundamentalist participation. The juvenile "cooperates" with the P.O. by supplying her with relevant items of information that appear to "fit" the P.O.'s reasoning: "You know I used to say 'bitch' and smoked. That night I felt so good." At this point in the interview my impression of the exchanges suggested the girl was not certain of her audience, appearing to be suspicious of the line of questioning. The answers sounded mechanical and the recorded version appears to exhibit this quality. I felt the P.O. was trying to turn the juvenile's religious interest into something bizarre.

The statement "I talked to my parents again" suggests a managed orientation to the juvenile's remarks. The P.O. was not "jovial," nor did she appear to be "sympathetic" (but rather detached) while asking questions. The juvenile's responses suddenly became intense when the P.O. mentioned school. The response ". . . he told everybody at school that I took all my clothes off and let them do it" suggests considerable interaction among various groups of adolescents about the incident, and seems to leave little doubt as to the juvenile's awareness of how she might be viewed by others. The juvenile's angry reaction (as it appeared to me) did not imply any impropriety in what she admitted to doing, but in what was felt to be an exaggeration damaging to her character and general reputation. The juvenile's conception of herself as someone misrepresented by "the boys" is elaborated when she responds with "I'll just tell them no, that if that's all they want from me they can go." The additional remark about not wanting her "husband to know" appears to acknowledge the wrongful nature of her acts after the P.O. has led her into the "appropriate" answers. The P. O.'s remark "Will you change then?" and the juvenile's response that she is "trying to change all the time and I'm trying as hard as I can" seems calculated to bring the interview to a "successful" close, and the P.O.'s final remark suggests such a conclusion although there is a warning about things getting "worse" with each subsequent encounter. The P.O. provides the leading questions designed to "test" for the "right" response, and suggests its satisfactory accomplishment.

My reaction to the above interview was based upon prior conversations with the P.O. where I obtained the impression the case had been "doped out" by the P.O. The interview seemed to be a formalized setting for searching questions to document the P.O.'s theories about "what happened" and the juvenile's motivation for her actions. Thus each question was not a probe searching for basic information, but a follow-up of unstated assumptions about what "really happened," calculated to elicit the documentary evidence to support the preestablished theories. The P.O.'s final remarks telling the juvenile about being on probation is revealing because they imply handling the case in a fairly routine manner. The P.O. acknowledges that the juvenile has "problems" in her final remarks, a stance she avoided throughout the interview. Notice my reaction to the P.O.'s remarks does not imply the establishment of a trust relationship with the juvenile. My interpretation of the case suggests the P.O. could not establish such a relationship because of personal revulsion over the entire family including the juvenile.

The interview quoted above does not reveal all of the features discussed in Chapter 4, but both probation officers entered the interview with independent knowledge and theories about "what happened" and used the occasion to obtain information to document what was felt to be "known." The juvenile was not asked for detailed descriptions of her perspective of "what happened," but the P.O. did raise general policies or strategies of conduct (e.g., "Do you think God forgives you?" "So you think it was wrong?" "Will you wait until you get married?" "Will you change then?"), with the implication she was not merely asking questions, but providing the juvenile with a guide for "proper" answers. The effect of my presence during the interview is difficult to assess. Perhaps the P.O. would have interviewed differently if I had been absent. Recall the interview of Chapter 4 where I was not present. I think both interviews support my inferences about the imposition (and managed articulation) of general policies or rules upon particulars not necessarily in correspondence with the ideals implied in the general policies or rules. The P.O. (and the police) employ theories in their practical reasoning about the particulars of how events occur, or how members accomplish tasks or general activities, but to terminate cases they must utilize organizational criteria and legal propositions to provide truncated and idealized or general policies and rules about the nature of behavior.

Following the interview with the juvenile, the P.O. then interviewed the parents. I shall only report a small section of the encounter because I was unable to record all of the exchange. Once again I felt the P.O. was rather negatively impressed with the parents because of her prior inquiries. The parents appeared to be young and "nice-looking." Consider the following exchange:

PROBATION OFFICER. How is she at home?

MOTHER. She's not wild. She just changes. She doesn't know why she's doing it. You say 'why are you doing that?' and she doesn't know why.

P.O. Does she feel sorry for what she did?

MO. Always.

FATHER. What's happened to Linda is caused by an emotional factor. After these tests we should know what is wrong. She may need psychiatric help. Why this hearing if there is something wrong with her? We are more interested in her than the court.

MO. She does this, but she doesn't know why.

P.O. This is a legal proceeding, nothing more.

MO. Then this is a routine thing.

P.O. Yes, it's a long word. That's all.

FA. Does she have to be a ward?

P.O. I'll recommend that and the judge may not agree. You can ask him to dismiss it.

The P.O.'s remark about the "home" leads to a suggestion by the mother that the juvenile "doesn't know why she's doing it," implying that the girl is not responsible for her actions. The P.O.'s next remark about the juvenile feeling "sorry for what she did?" suggests the officer is searching for evidence as to the appropriateness of the remorse expressed earlier or in general by the juvenile vis-à-vis her activities, or is seeking information to document an imputation of illness based on some notion of irresponsible behavior stemming from emotional instability. The mother's response could also lead to the interpretation of the girl as someone who engages in "impulsive" behavior for which she is "sorry" after the "episode" or incident. I felt the P.O. was convinced the girl was "sick." The father then enters the scene and crystallizes the picture by reference to the incident as being "caused by an emotional factor," and adding "she may need psychiatric help." The father questions the relevance of a hearing if "there is something wrong with her?" that would negate criminal implications about the girl's conduct. I assume that the father intended the psychiatric reference to be placed in opposition to a criminal notion of what is "wrong" with the girl. The mother seems to support this interpretation when she stresses once again the girl's not knowing "why" she engages in the drinking and sexual behavior implied but not stated. The P.O. then seeks to establish the proceeding as perfunctory, but notes she will recommend that the girl be made a ward of the court. The P.O. suggests that the parents seek to have the judge dismiss the formal probationary arrangements, but does not indicate she would change her position.

Notice how the parents and the P.O. seek to negotiate the conditions under which each will become involved in the case. My impression of the interview suggests the P.O. tried to document her preconceptions about the negative nature of the family, yet leaving open the possibility that the parents appear to seek a change in the P.O.'s recommendation by asserting their own interest in their daughter and stressing the emotional basis for her actions, with the implication of clinical assistance independent of the court. I stress the importance of "why" did it all "happen," as opposed to some direct correspondence being established between some act, a legal rule, and some disposition from a predetermined set of alternatives. The act itself can lead to a variety of actions by law-enforcement officials, but the seriousness or triviality of the act depends upon officials' practical decisions and not the researcher's hypothetical typology based upon criminal law, or something called the "community reaction." The important point is how the juvenile's future is conceived because of readings of his past and present behavior. Notions like "bad attitude," "poor home" environment, "emotional" problems, and the like, transform the juvenile into an object prepared for disposition, irrespective of the "seriousness" of the acts themselves. Acts viewed as "very serious" may accelerate the process, but I want to stress how acts viewed as trivial from the perspective of the criminal law can lead to equivalent dispositions.

The P.O. told me after the interview that the parents of the spouses had

had marital "difficulties." The P.O. noted the mother's parents had been divorced, with the mother remarrying and the father's mother having been married twice. The P.O. seemed very concerned with establishing the "stability" of the parents' respective home environments prior to their present marriage. The "search" for "stability" or "instability" is part of the P.O.'s attempts to estimate the advantages of alternative dispositions. I am not questioning the P.O.'s interest in the stability of the home, but how she decides "stability" or "instability." The P.O. calls various persons who may know the family. The information obtained is used to construct estimations of "stability" or "instability." The P.O. told me she felt the father and mother were both concerned with their social position vis-à-vis their parents and peers: "You see the status problem. The stepfather [of the mother] couldn't make it past [military rank]. The father's father was [occupation], but sometimes a [presumably lower occupation]. You see he's trying to make it and has always told the girl, ever since she was knee high to a grasshopper, to make others like her." Recall the girl's remark about joining the fraternal auxiliary because "You can make friends there." I assume the P.O. took this statement as indicative of the parents "pushing" the girl to "make friends"; further, the girl seeks to have sexual intercourse with males as a means of "holding on to them." The parents mentioned Linda's association with Ronnie Jones to the P.O., and stressed his membership in the male counterpart to the fraternal auxiliary. The P.O. had already been told by Linda of her frequent sexual activities with this juvenile. The P.O. told me the parents' reference to this boy's membership in the auxiliary was an attempt to "push" the girl into "proper" associations, and hence indicative of the parents' concern for "status." The P.O. suggested the girl's association with a friend active in the fundamentalist sect has undermined her participation in her own church.

Because Linda participated in a second incident involving sexual intercourse with several male juveniles, the P.O.'s report not only covers the conversations quoted above, but many additional encounters with the parents and the juvenile. After the second incident, Linda was placed in Juvenile Hall. The P.O. spoke to the juvenile several times and told me the girl stated her father gave her "drinks" at home. The father spoke to another P.O. at Juvenile Hall and was alleged to have said he was an "amateur psychologist" and had "read" considerably in psychology and psychiatry. Furthermore, he was supposed to have told the P.O. he had "practiced hypnotism on Linda." The P.O. told me Linda stated her father asked her to describe "in detail" her sexual experiences with "the boys." The two probation officers exchanged further remarks in my presence and stated they were not "sure who is sicker," the father or Linda. At this point the outside P.O. told Linda's P.O.

she felt Linda should go to a particular state mental hospital. The two probation officers were agreed on this suggestion, and yet both had read a psychologist's report on Linda which indicated the juvenile would "go" (have
a psychotic break) immediately if institutionalized. Then Linda's P.O. stated
she felt the psychologist's report warranted a recommendation of placement
in a foster home.

The P.O.'s report describes the family's income as $750 per month from
the father and $160 per month from the mother, and states, "Their home
represents an average middle-class family, striving to present a nice home
for their children." The report states:

> He [the father] has told the Officer and the school that he has studied psy-
> chology. According to Linda, he reads numerous books from the library and buys
> books on psychology constantly. He has studied hypnotism, and has practiced
> on members of his own family. The father has been most interested in Linda's
> actions. He is quite fearful that any of the blame will be laid onto his wife and
> structures all interviews to present him and his family in a favorable light. He
> openly states he feels his child is "Schizo." He paid for the psychologicals by Dr.
> Mitchell which are included in the case, but only after requesting that the
> County do it. When told that his income was sufficiently high enough to not war-
> rant this, he paid for it. He was somewhat disgruntled by this. He has a copy of
> the psychologicals and has read them verbatim to Linda and has told her what
> he does accept and what he doesn't and has interpreted them to her. He does not
> feel that Linda is as seriously disturbed as the psychologicals state and he feels
> that he can handle most anything. The father claims a Protestant [name of
> particular] affiliation, but several statements that he made would make one feel
> that he is probably quite liberal and does not adhere to the church's creed or
> doctrines. The marital status of this family is stable. This Officer is of the opin-
> ion that they are very much impressed with each other because of their physical
> beauty and their ability to get ahead with material things.

The P.O. jumps from one topic to another in her report; she mentions the
father's interest in psychology, but then refers to the girl for support of this
point, noting the father purchases books "on psychology constantly." A series
of negative references follow: hypnosis being practiced on "members of his
own family," the interest "in Linda's actions," the reference to presenting
the family "in a favorable light," stating his child is "schizo," reading the
psychological report to the juvenile with "corrections," Mr. Peters' "liberal"
church views, and remarks about the couple's physical appearance. The
statement that the "marital status of this family is stable" does little to
counteract the negative remarks. Notice how the family's "face-sheet" picture would presumably denote a "nice middle-income family," while the
P.O. supplies interpretive information to demolish the idea that the family
is "stable," lives in "nice" surroundings, and maintains "high status" church

affiliation. A few lines were devoted to the other two children, suggesting everything was "fine" with them at school and at home. The P.O.'s report also states: "According to Linda, her mother works as a model on occasions at the [a bowling alley] for their luncheons and at the [a restaurant]." Nothing more is stated about this last remark, but the P.O. had told me independently how she had heard that Mrs. Peters was "modeling" before men during the noon hour. My impression of the P.O.'s remarks suggested that Mrs. Peters was engaging in "questionable" activities for a "mother." The remark about the "modeling" seems calculated to paint a negative conception of the parents as types who would "produce" a girl like Linda. The "objective" information about "middle-class" appearances also lends itself to the possibility of positive remarks about the family, and, therefore, one could simply allege the "problem" must be located in the girl's "head," or with her peers.

The report states the following on the juvenile:

Linda, the minor, had a normal birth, and according to her family has always been attractive and well mannered. She is a very nice appearing child, giving one the impression that she is immature and a somewhat giddy teenager. There is no history of any particular illness other than the normal childhood diseases. Her present health at this time is good. Linda offers no particular interest in hobbies other than boys. Her attitude toward her parents is one of "When I'm mad at one, I tell that one I love the other and vice versa." She says, "I like to hurt my parents. I really love them but sometimes when I'm mad I like to hurt them." Linda's attitude toward this offense is one of ambiguous feelings. She entered into this episode with the feeling that anything goes in order to keep her boyfriend. Now her father and mother have told her that this is not right so she thinks that maybe this isn't right now. She is very mixed up about when is a thing right and when is it wrong. The minor does not exhibit any defiance to authority in an outward way. The minor's religious affiliations and teachings have been very offhand and practically nil. Linda has demonstrated a real interest in the Fundamental Church which her girl friend's father is minister of, but her father has told her that the idea that God can forgive her is a lot of bunk, and this has served to further mix up this child.

The P.O. begins her description of Linda with several pleasantries: "She is a very nice appearing child" but switches to "the impression that she is immature and a somewhat giddy teenager." The P.O. seems to undercut those features a reader might easily take as "positive." The juvenile's only interest is said to be in "boys." The P.O. suggests the juvenile manipulates her parents, and quotes her as saying: "I like to hurt them." The juvenile's implied confused "attitude" is described in several senses: vis-à-vis the offense, boys she presumably "likes," her parents, suggesting the girl does not know "when is a thing right and when is it wrong." Stating "The minor does not exhibit any defiance to authority in an outward way" suggests appearances are misleading in the case of this juvenile, and her conduct should be viewed as some form of "defiance," although not in an "outward way." The search for "causes" leads to the religious participation of the girl, but the account is truncated because it does not unequivocally state the implication I obtained from the P.O. to the effect the fundamentalist leanings were "dangerous." Earlier in the report the P.O. stated that the father's religious beliefs were probably "quite liberal," implying that the father's advice is clearly "wrong," and "this has served to further mix up this child."

In approaching her recommendation the P.O. states:

> Linda's behavior is one of extreme. She is either very happy and lively and giddy, or she withdraws completely and is very moody. She is quite capable of stealing or lying according to whatever pressure is put upon her.
>
> Linda has an IQ overall of 100. Her reading scores are down in the fourth grade level. Her arithmetic is around sixth grade. At the present time, Linda is in the eighth grade at [junior high]. She is not doing well and is constantly reminded by her teachers to get down to business. Dr. Moreau [psychiatrist] has stated that Linda has self-destructive impulses and fantasy to an alarming degree. He feels that this suggests a latent schizophrenic reaction and intensive and prolonged psychotherapy is strongly recommended. The Officer has discussed with him his recommendation that this psychotherapy should be with her parents' participation and that institutionalization at this time could be harmful. The officer in this discussion stated that the money factor here was going to be a problem. He, in turn, stated that the only other alternative would be to place Linda in an institutional setting, such as [state mental hospital] or the adolescent area of [another mental hospital]. The Officer, in turn, talked this over with Mr. and Mrs. Peters and, according to Mr. Peters, he felt that it would be best to place Linda under the Department of Mental Hygiene for a three to six month period with intensive therapy and then try her at home.

The P.O.'s opening remark on Linda begins with a clinical orientation: "lively and giddy, or she withdraws completely" and noting the juvenile "is quite capable of stealing or lying according to whatever pressure is put upon her." The interpretation of the psychiatric report supports the clinical imputation given earlier (if not based upon it), and the psychiatrist's suggestion is viewed as impractical because of financial problems, but it is the P.O.'s estimation of monetary problems, not the parents' statement. The P.O.'s remarks to me implied she preferred the state mental hospital solution to the therapy suggestion of the psychiatrist because she wanted to remove the girl from the home situation. The psychiatrist suggests the parents participate in the therapy, and the P.O. had earlier commented on how "sick" the father was, yet the P.O. did not seem interested in including the entire family in some therapy program.

Many negotiated encounters between Linda's parents and the P.O., the P.O. and her supervisor, the judge, probation officials at Juvenile Hall, teachers, and the like, preceded the court hearing. After the initial interview with the parents the P.O. was prepared to recommend routine probation for the juvenile. The subsequent incident with the boys at the party led to a rereading of the father's remarks about the psychiatric report, the father's presumed use of "hypnosis" on the girl, his "interest and reading" in "psychology," the "religious" problem, and convincing the P.O. she should abandon routine probation and seek incarceration in a state mental hospital. The P.O. at one point intended to have the girl placed in a Youth Authority installation, but the psychiatric report was too strong to push for a criminal characterization of the girl. The following dialogue was recorded during my presence at the court hearing, and reveals elements of prior encounters as quoted in materials presented above. The regular referee was absent and the Chief Probation Officer presided at the hearing.

REFEREE. You're Linda Peters, you're Mr. Peters, you're Mrs. Peters? How old are you Linda?
JUVENILE. 13.
REF. You know you can have an attorney? [The parents acknowledged this question and indicated they did not want one.]
REF. Linda you know the court hearing says you were in danger of leading a lewd and immoral life. That you have had intercourse with some boys. [The girl nods her head in agreement.]
REF. [Looking at the parents.] Has Linda always been this way or is this something new?
MOTHER. I would say she has always had an inferiority complex.
REF. Let's use plain English, huh.
FATHER. She's always had trouble holding friends, ever since she was born.
REF. How about you, Mrs. Peters?
MO. Well, I always thought it was normal, they say you haven't lived until you have a teenager, then suddenly you realize that what she's doing isn't normal.
REF. Could you be more precise?
MO. Well, it's like he [Mr. Peters] says, about making friends. She always makes one friend at a time. Let me give you an example. There was an article in the paper a couple of years ago about the police saying to be careful about men picking up girls and taking them away. Linda said she didn't give "two hoots." I spanked her for her comment and she sure remembered it too. My mother was down at the time and she agreed.
REF. How did you handle sex instruction?
FA. Well, along about 9 we noticed that her breasts were starting to form. We took her to [hospital] for an examination and the doctor said she should be given sex instruction, especially about menstruation. I gave her most of the instruction. Now I find she has a kind of Jekel and Hyde effect—she's a sweet girl

for a long time and then suddenly was a nasty brat. [pause] Before she ran away her mother mentioned that maybe there was something wrong with her mind and that we wondered if there was anything that was bothering her. We talked about this for a while.

REF. What about the hypnosis part, Mr. Peters?

FA. I've never practiced it at home on my family though I've known hypnosis for a long time. I used to go over to [nearby city].

REF. What about the liquor serving at home?

FA. I believe in letting my children tasting liquor but I never gave her a drink.

REF. Well, what was it, let's not change the words.

FA. I gave her a little taste. It was like a shot glass, that's all.

MO. She's never been out on a date by herself. [Much discussion between mother and child I could not hear.]

MO. She's never been out before.

REF. These two episodes are pretty far out.

MO. I know, but this could happen to anyone, she's not a wild girl.

[The parents attempted to convince the referee the girl left home the night before the originally scheduled court hearing because of her fear of court and what might happen to her. They felt the girl was concerned about the parents and had good intentions because after spending the night in an open area, someone told the girl she was dirty, and the girl responded she didn't want her mother to see her dirty and went somewhere to wash herself. There were a few more rapid exchanges I could not record about the court's decision to place her at the mental hospital and the remark that the P.O. would explain the details.]

The referee's questions followed what he had read in the P.O.'s report and what he had been told by the P.O. and her supervisor. The parents spoke in low voices and my impression of the hearing was it was handled routinely, with the referee providing the direction to the dialogue. The parents tried to say something sympathetic about the girl's plight. (". . . she has always had an inferiority complex.") The mother seemed to be suggesting that the girl was not that "sick," although there were "problems." The mother's remarks imply the girl's activities were seen as "life as usual" until "then suddenly you realize that what she's doing isn't normal." When the referee asks the mother to "be more precise," she responds with a story about the newspaper article on "men picking up girls and taking them away." The mother's implication is the girl's "attitude" was not "right," and a "spanking" was in order. The mother cites the grandmother's presence and agreement to her actions. But the mother's initial remarks about doing something not considered "normal" suggests a more "serious" incident like having intercourse with boys. When the referee asks about sex instruction, it is the father who responds with the remark "I gave her most of the instruction." But notice the father's subsequent remark shifts immediately to his observation about a

"Jekel and Hyde effect—she's a sweet girl for a long time and then suddenly was a nasty brat." Presumably the father was suggesting the girl was "normal" throughout the instruction period and some unspecified time thereafter, but then "suddenly" she was a "brat." The father then suggests that Mrs. Peters thought "maybe there was something wrong with her mind," and added that the two of them discussed the possibility of something "bothering her." The referee does not probe this answer but moves on to the hypnosis and liquor allegations. The mother, however, continues to view the girl as someone who has been properly reared ("She's never been out on a date by herself") and, presumably, a "typical" adolescent; "but this could happen to anyone, she's not a wild girl." The mother seems to acknowledge that something is not "normal," but suggests that there were exaggerated imputations of "badness," and that her actions are perhaps situational and partly due to "routine" problems of an "inferiority complex." The referee's remarks about the two episodes suggest that he was not convinced by the mother's comments.

The mother's remarks about the child seem to describe two different objects. Conceptions of adolescent social life held by the police in both City A and City B or other parts of California and the country, are probably consistent with this ambivalence. The police told me the case of the second party was routine. I doubt if many readers of this case would be surprised with the details. To explain the girl's participation as a sign of individual psychological problems does not explain or account for the routine organized character of both male and female adolescent participation in such activities. If Linda's appearances, and those of her parents and home life, were characterized as "bad" and "cheap," then it is unlikely the court personnel would have imputed "sick" properties to the girl and her father. The girl would be sent directly to a Youth Authority installation for incarceration. Throughout the study the police broke up many parties where considerable drinking and sexual activity was known to have taken place, but where the charges were minor and the action minimal. So long as there are no victims in such cases, there is no occasion for invoking either criminal or ill categories to explain participation. Linda told the psychiatrist she had had sexual intercourse with another boy on ten occasions prior to the dance incident. The girl also suggested her parents were aware of this activity. Despite all of the incidents, the mother is capable of viewing her girl as someone with difficulties (for example, "an inferiority complex"), but "not a wild girl." Nor does the mother insist the juvenile is "sick."

The juvenile spent approximately one month at the state mental hospital and then returned home. The P.O. did not have direct information on the case after incarceration at the hospital, for the girl was no longer a ward of the court. Approximately three months after the juvenile returned home, the police received a missing person report from Mrs. Peters on Linda. The police report states the girl was at a party but did not mention drinking or sexual activities. The P.O. told me she had heard the girl was involved in another drinking-sexual intercourse episode, but there was no police record or petition filed.

In the case of Linda, the parents accepted the court's actions. In the next case the parents were more resistant initially. My presentation of materials shall be restricted to how the P.O. interrogates the parents and the juvenile in order to gather material for her report. The court appearance, however, was routine with neither parent contesting the court's conclusions or recommendation. The matter had been decided prior to the hearing with conversations between the P.O., the regular referee, and the P.O.'s supervisor.

Denis

The case of Denis Bond suggests how the P.O. seeks to develop general theories about the family and juvenile in order to reconstruct how the participants could have produced actions leading to "trouble." Denis' part in the Peters case was described earlier. Here I will merely focus on the exchange between the P.O., the juvenile, and the parents at the Probation Department. I was present throughout the interview and the following dialogue is based upon my notes.

[The P.O. begins the interview by asking the juvenile about his courses and the grades he has received. She then asked the boy to tell why he chose the courses he is now taking, and the kinds of activities he is involved in at school. The P.O. then shifts the conversation sharply.]

PROBATION OFFICER. You have quite a lengthy history of stealing. I'm interested in why the stealing.

JUVENILE. I don't know why.

P.O. You have lots of free time?

JUV. Yes.

P.O. Do you do it alone?

JUV. Yes.

P.O. What do you usually steal, you know, objects, money, clothes?

JUV. Oh, I don't know, money, I guess.

P.O. What do you do with it?

JUV. I keep it and spend it.

[The P.O. seemed somewhat lost at this point on how to structure the interviewing. After the P.O.'s opening remarks, she began by asking for face-sheet information on income, occupation, education of the parents, birth places, and the like. The mother interrupted to say "They have all that information." Her remark seemed "cold" to me, as if she were irritated with the questioning. I felt the parents were resentful about being called in for the interview, with the P.O. somewhat uneasy as to how to proceed.]

The remarks about "stealing" seemed awkward to me and my impression of the P.O.'s voice as she uttered the questions suggested she was uncertain about what to ask. The father seemed to view the scene with boredom and disinterest. As the P.O. persisted in asking questions about the "stealing," I felt she was "testing" the boy's "attitude." The P.O. then turned to the parents and continued her questioning.

PROBATION OFFICER. Did you know he was stealing?

MOTHER. No.

P.O. Would you say that part of Denis' trouble is lack of supervision or what?

MO. Yes, part of it is that and part of it is age. There are a lot of things boys his age do and don't seem to care about.

P.O. What would you attribute it to Mr. B?

FATHER. About the same thing.

P.O. But stealing is arbitrary?

FA. We all did it when we were kids, even the best of families, Doc Jones' kids (the twins) did it from the nurse's desk and their father could buy and sell the city. We stole apples, money. It wasn't right either in those days, but everybody did it.

P.O. Well, maybe you think it is sort of normal and things, but Denis doesn't seem to know why he steals. [The P.O. seemed lost for words at this point.]

P.O. Would you say your family life is pretty stable?

FA. It was the depression of course, and everyone was in bad shape.

P.O. What kind of education did you get?

FA. I finished high school.

P.O. What kind of work did you do before you came to City B?

FA. I worked in [mass media] for 14 years [five years in city B and 9 in another area. The father stated he could not work in the same occupation now because he was "too old" now.]

P.O. [To mother] How would you say your family was, average, above average, or below average?

MO. I don't know how to answer that. We ate well. [The mother stated her father owned two general stores.]

[The P.O. appears to be asking redundant questions because of not knowing the area the family came from. I felt the parents were annoyed with the questions, as if to suggest they were naive and irrelevant.]

When the P.O. asks the mother if she was aware of her boy's stealing, the P.O. seems to be searching for family conditions influencing the juvenile's conduct. The mother's response leads to a direct suggestion by the P.O. implicating the mother because of lack of supervision at home. The mother seemed to acknowledge "lack of supervision" as "part of it," but I felt her remark "that and part of it is age," was more in line with the bored emphasis I sensed in her voice. The remark by the mother "There are lots of things boys his age do and don't seem to care about," suggests the juvenile's conduct is part of being "young." This point was raised in earlier chapters and touched upon in the discussion of Linda Peters. The general point is some parents find it difficult to agree with police and probation officials about the "seriousness" of offenses not involving physical harm to others. The father's responses make this point even more sharply, despite the P.O.'s suggestion (in the form of a question "But stealing is arbitrary?") that stealing is motivated and, presumably, by reference to "problems." The P.O. contrasts the parents' viewing of "stealing" as "sort of normal and things," with the statement, "Denis doesn't seem to know why he steals." My feeling that the P.O. was lost for words at this juncture assumes she was surprised by the parents' acceptance of Denis' activities as "the way kids are." Rather than press the morality of the issue implied in her remarks and tone of voice (which I took to mean the P.O. could not believe parents would react to something so "obvious" as "stealing" with such indifference), the P.O. shifts the conversation by asking additional loaded questions about the father's family. The question about family stability receives an answer that is difficult to probe without implying the P.O. directly seeks information to support an apparent suspicion the father's family may have been "unstable" in view of his indifference to "stealing" by juveniles. Notice how the P.O.'s question about the stability of the father's family was answered by reference to the depression and the remark "everyone was in bad shape." The father's remark seems to undercut the P.O.'s search for "problems" by suggesting the question is meaningless given the era. The P.O. seemed quite interested in the father's remarks about his occupational background because she knew the father was presently unemployed, and had already indicated to me her feeling the father's occupational experiences signified something "important" for explaining the juvenile's delinquency. The question posed for the mother ("How would you say your family was . . .") reads as if the P.O. had copied the question from a survey questionnaire. The mother's responses seemed directed at pointing out the foolishness ("I don't know. . . . We ate well.") of the question, but I could not record verbatim the additional remark about the father owning two general stores. The remark about the father's business seemed to complete the undercutting of the P.O.'s loaded question. Notice, therefore, how the mother's response directly avoids the abstract categories posed by the P.O. By this point in the interview my impression was one of uneasiness for myself, the P.O., and the parents, with the latter feeling indignant at the line of questioning. We were all in a small room for five persons. There were few pleasantries, and no one seemed interested in "softening" the remarks being exchanged. At this point the P.O. shifted her questioning back to Denis.

PROBATION OFFICER. How long have you drank, Denis?
JUVENILE. About six months.

P.O. Did you just decide to experiment? [No response by the juvenile.] Who decided to take Linda out?

JUV. Robert.

P.O. Does she have a good reputation, a poor reputation?

JUV. I wouldn't know, I didn't know her before.

P.O. How did you get to the horse farm?

JUV. Walked.

P.O. Were you aware you were going to be in hot water?

JUV. No, well, kinda. I don't know, it's hard to say.

P.O. Well, the girl was away all night, wasn't she?

JUV. Well, I thought maybe her parents would be mad.

The P.O. continually poses loaded questions, but the juvenile does not respond "appropriately." Questions are ignored or answered evasively, but continue to be leading. An obvious suggestion here would be that the parents have established an atmosphere that contradicts the P.O.'s imputations. The question about knowing his actions would result in being "in hot water," is answered with a "No" that changes to "well, kinda." Then the juvenile states "I don't know, it's hard to say." The equivocality of the response did not suggest deference to me, but could have implied that the boy was taking the line begun by his parents that the incident, as it was viewed at the time, was typical adolescent activity of "just trying to have some fun." The response to the question about the girl being "away all night" suggests that the juvenile was well aware of possible consequences, although there is no indication the consequences were viewed as "serious" and to be avoided. Notice how the P.O. seeks to establish the incident as revealing a lack of moral character on the part of the juvenile, implying he "should have known" from the outset the consequences of his acts and their "wrongness." But even admitting he knew the girl was a "slut" or "cheap" implies as much "seriousness" to his participation as saying the girl's reputation was "good." The juvenile did not seek explicitly to explain his actions as if they "sorta happened that way," implying a gradual unplanned sequence of events culminating in activities "known" to be "bad"; yet such an explanation might appear plausible. The juvenile's responses imply he did what "anyone" would do under the circumstances. The juvenile's responses seem to be oriented by the parents' indifferent responses, for my observation of similar interviews almost always found the juvenile admitting the "wrongness" of the acts (at the P.O.'s insistence). The line of questioning did not seem to produce the desired results of remorse, admission of wrongdoing, and the like, and the P.O. shifted her remarks again.

P.O. What were you planning on doing with your education, what do you want to do?

JUV. I'd go to college, you see, it'll be open by then [a new college planned for

City B]. I'll take four years and then go into the service as an officer. Then I can go to work for an airline company and pilot flights, or else be an architect or a doctor.

P.O. You know this charge could jeopardize your career in the service?

JUV. Yes.

P.O. In one year you've managed to get yourself in an awful peck of trouble. How do you expect to get out of it?

JUV. Stay at home, I guess.

P.O. This is no one-shot deal. You have a whole list of things. [Reads off a list of past offenses.]

JUV. Well, . . .

[The P.O. began to speak very quickly about several subjects that ranged from telling the juvenile he does well in school, obtaining good grades, with a high I.Q., and then rambled on about the dangers of his present conduct.]

The P.O. begins to ask about the juvenile's education and utilizes his response to point out how "this charge could jeopardize your career in the service." The string of remarks by the P.O. again focuses upon the seriousness of the offense, but the question "How do you expect to get out of it?" does not elicit remorse, stereotyped remarks about avoiding "bad" companions, recognizing "trouble" and avoiding same, but what to me sounded like a weak and casual "Stay at home, I guess." The P.O. seemed annoyed with this remark and attempted to emphasize how the present incident is merely part of a larger pattern. The juvenile begins to say something, but lapses into silence. At this point the P.O. seemed to search for "good things" to say about the boy, but ended with additional remarks about the seriousness of his recent activities. The P.O. then returns to the incident, as if her last remarks about its seriousness triggered off additional questions she might cover.

P.O. How did you come to steal the liquor?

JUV. I owed Bob some money and he said he'd forget about it if I stole the liquor. [A few rapid general remarks followed on how the boys had expected to obtain the liquor from Bob's house, but were unable to do so, and therefore Bob asked Denis to steal the liquor.]

P.O. You did assault the girl or you did not?

JUV. I did not.

P.O. Robert did and the other boy? You just watched?

JUV. Yes.

P.O. What happened to Linda?

JUV. She sort of got raving.

P.O. A drunken rave. Did she holler, yes, no?

JUV. Just a rave.

MO. Were you drinking?

JUV. No.

P.O. Did you drink at all?

JUV. No.

[The juvenile now appeared to be rather passive and reticent, not indifferent to the questions. The mother also seemed to be "concerned" with the P.O.'s questions. The father appeared bored. The mother (and occasionally the father) then began to tell the P.O. how initially they were unaware of what had happened with Linda Peters, noting they thought the "trouble" was about some chalk marks Denis was supposed to have made at school. The mother went to the boys' school and the vice principal told her about the Peters case. Denis was suspended for the chalk incident, despite the school presumably having the information about the Peters case. The parents indicated that they felt they were improperly informed about the incident and seemed annoyed about this. They noted how the City B. P.D. picked Denis up from the Sheriff's Department and did not tell him what he was being held for. The mother continued with the general point that the police told the juvenile he could have a lawyer, spoke to him for about 15 or 20 minutes, and then drove him home in a marked police car. Furthermore, that the juvenile did not tell the parents about the incident with the Peters girl. The P.O. then began asking how the parents became informed about the matter, and what they did with Denis. At this point everyone seemed to have "softened" their strategies, at least my impression of the voices suggested less sharpness to the conversation.]

The questions about stealing the liquor, "assaulting" the girl, drinking, watching the other "assault" the girl, and the girl's "raving" seemed like a turning point in the conversation; the P.O. did not seem to be as insistent about the seriousness of the juvenile's participation, as if to imply Denis' involvement was not as serious as that of Robert. Yet notice how the P.O. continually thrusts leading questions before the juvenile, and each question presumes guilt even when posed as a question in search of information. The subsequent remarks now quoted seemed to be given in a less formalized tone of voice, not searching for pointed remarks with which to implicate the boy.

PRO. At this point, with the record you have, I can keep you on probation. But this is the last time. You'll go to Youth Authority. You've had it. But with this record you'll be there in no time flat if you keep this up. If you go to Youth Authority you then have a record. That record becomes permanent. Maybe the judge will reverse me. I don't know. Believe me, buster, you can get to the Youth Authority by writing on walls again. [Pause]

Do you think it's right to steal?

JUV. No.

P.O. Have you had any religious training?

JUV. Yes.

P.O. What?

JUV. [Protestant church mentioned.]

P.O. Do you attend church?

JUV. No.

P.O. What is the purpose of church? Do you know?

JUV. To . . . [voice trailed off and the P.O. didn't give him much time to answer before asking:]

P.O. Have you read the Bible?

JUV. No.

P.O. Why don't you look at it. Look at the proverbs. (pause) You're on your own now. I can't stop you from doing these things. [This line continues another few minutes with rapid delivery.] Many mess up in their youth. Now you've had your chance. You've done a real swinging job of messing up. (pause) You're hurting your parents, you know, when you go down. (pause) It's all water under the bridge now. But all of this means you're the best candidate for Youth Authority I have on my desk. I don't mean to threaten you, I'm just stating the cold facts. The Youth Authority is no bed of roses. If you have any profession for your religion, I'd look at it. I'd take the time to read some of it like Solomon. He was supposed to be the wisest man that ever lived. You go back to school and behave yourself now. [The P.O. signified abruptly the end of the interview. She now exchanged pleasantries with the parents and Denis, particularly the mother.]

The P.O.'s opening line after shifting the conversation suggests that she will not press for a disposition beyond continuance of probation, yet she seems to use strong language to underscore the tenuous character of her decision. She mentions the Youth Authority as a threat, for writing on walls suggests that even a minor infraction will be treated as serious. My feeling was the P.O. wanted to make it clear her decision to recommend probation did not diminish the seriousness of the boy's predicament. The P.O. seemed to feel additional remarks were necessary to reprimand the juvenile once more before closing the interview in order to insure the juvenile of her annoyance with his conduct and the fortunate consequences of her decision for the boy. She seemed somewhat at a loss for words and the remark "Do you think it's right to steal?" and the comments about religion appeared to be variations of previous themes. It was as if the P.O. felt something "appropriate" had to be "said," and all she could manage were the remarks on stealing and religion. The threats about the Youth Authority are couched in direct terms with only a brief mention of the possibility the judge would overrule her. The threats about the Youth Authority seemed as directed to the parents as to the juvenile, yet my feeling was that the father was unimpressed by the entire interview. I felt the mother and the juvenile evidenced some "concern," and "cooperated" with the P.O. to avoid any confrontation challenging the threat about the Youth Authority. When the P.O. terminated the interview, I felt she did it so as to preclude further remarks from the parents, signaling the end by rising and then simulating pleasantries apparently tied to her decision to recommend probation and not placement outside of the home. My use of the term "negotiation" seems relevant here; the P.O. continually suggests her version of "what happened" and its significance to the juvenile and the parents, and she seeks to encourage the juvenile and the parents to indicate their "responsibility" in the matter. The line of questioning provides direct and indirect guidelines for eliciting the "proper" answers. The present case deals with parents who did not "cooperate" with the P.O. in agreeing about "what happened" and the juvenile's responsibility, much less that of the parents. The juvenile seemed to pick up this resistance, and the P.O. seemed somewhat startled by it. The P.O. seemed to find it necessary to keep talking about anything that seemed "appropriate" despite the indifference of her audience. The soliloquy she carried on seemed for her own benefit. But both sides (with the possible exception of the father) seemed to "soften" a bit at the end of the conversation, and I felt the P.O. sought to close the interview abruptly by getting in "the last word." The mother and juvenile seemed to be more willing to go along with the final P.O. salvo; perhaps the threat of Youth Authority incarceration encouraged less resistance. The boy's school record and activities could be viewed as "softening" the P.O.'s view of what should happen to the boy, while the parents' remarks about their family environment and their willingness to challenge the P.O., may have convinced the P.O. she should not push for Youth Authority incarceration, but underscore it as a possible future disposition if there was no improvement. The P.O. expressed considerable annoyance with the father's "attitude" after the Bonds had left, but I could not obtain further impressions about how the P.O. arrived at her decision.

Her personal feelings about the case as expressed to me included many remarks about the father and the boy: "Poppa wants glamour, the kid wants glamour. Poppa got kicked in the head with that [mass media] job. He probably began drinking. He failed and shows no responsibility now for that child." The P.O. linked the Bond case with the Peters case by observing the fathers in both families wanted "glamour" and have passed this on to their children. Notice how the P.O. ties the loss of the job to "probably began drinking." The P.O. did not seek direct information from the father but invented an explanation. At the hearing the referee seemed impressed with Denis' school grades, yet remarked "This Bond seems as disturbed as the Bean boy." The P.O. remarked: "Not quite. He's doing better. He's doing okay in school and his dad now has a better job than [last one, considered "unstable"]. His mother seems all up in the air and feels everything is great. He [the Bond boy] sure changed Probation Officers easily. Boy, he writes me notes that are real corkers."

In each case, contingencies continually come up among the P.O., the supervisor, and the referee because the decision is based upon collective interpretations, and no one flatly states an unequivocal position, challenging all others to refute it. Instead, each makes suggestions about what he or she "thinks," allowing for others to disagree or modify the initial statement. The referee does take the lead in reaching what is designed to be mutual "consensus" about the disposition but, even here, contingencies possible in the court scene could lead to further changes, although in my observations such changes are not very common. The following and final case reveals how the court scene can occasionally generate contingencies changing the recommendations agreed upon by the P.O., the supervisor, and the referee.

Before closing the case of Denis I want to note how the P.O.'s report claims the boy "admits to drinking some of the alcohol and encouraging the 13-year-old minor girl to drink most of it. He also admits to attempting intercourse with her, but she had passed out by that time, but he did sit on the sidelines and observe the two other boys attempting intercourse with her." I cite this passage to note how the P.O. can state many "facts" to the court not contained in the allegations (which for Denis referred to violation of probation and petty theft), and which the parents would never see (or know about) unless they retained a lawyer. The document "manages" or masks the original conversation because it was clearly implied in the materials quoted above that Denis did not drink nor attempt any sexual contact with the girl. The P.O. asked: "You did assault the girl or you did not?" The response was "no." It was the mother who raised the issue of drinking to which the answer was "no." Notice the statement in the P.O.'s report that parallels the interview again:

> He [Denis] has ambitions of being an architect or going into the service and being an officer. The officer pointed out to him that his record at this point would not be officer candidate material, and he felt that he was changing and that he was making every effort to live a better life. His attitude towards the offense and authority and society in general is such that "I'm smarter than you are and I only get caught occasionally." He has no real religious affiliation or feelings. His attendance has been poor and his training has been very little. Denis will steal and lie with an amazing ease. He is bright enough to cover and give a very likely story. He only admits when he thinks it is to his advantage. [Cites good grades.] The school feels that they know that he is at the bottom of a good many of their petty thefts. They have never been able to catch him at it, but he always seems to be on the fringes of these incidents.

The P.O. truncates her reaction to Denis' remarks about career ambitions by stating the boy "felt that he was changing . . ." yet pointedly notes "his attitude" in negative terms. The reference to church is couched in negative terms. The school "view" is quite negative, although his grades are good, but there is no reference to the school's view of his "attitude" toward "authority." The recommendation "that Denis remain in his home" seems rather paradoxical given the P.O.'s remarks. The reader should return to the material on Smithfield in Chapter 5, and should compare the two records. Denis' past record lists eight burglaries and the present incident with the Peters girl. There is also a case of arson, which the juvenile admitted. Smithfield was committed to the Youth Authority repeatedly. Denis is able to obtain "another chance" each time. (Notice I am not covering the case of Tyrone Tryon nor that of Gregg Burns because they were handled routinely as cases where the boys acknowledged making "mistakes" in their conduct. The parents were very "responsive" to the P.O.'s and the court's view of "what happened," and neither was viewed as a "serious instigator"; they did not have "bad" past records.)

Robert

The case of Robert is of interest because the family mobilized considerable resources to prevent the boy being sent away from home to the Youth Authority or a state mental hospital. The family is described as a "middle-income" home. The mother has remarried, and the natural father has provided some support since the divorce eight years prior to the present incident. The natural father lives nearby. The P.O. was aware of many incidents at school in which Robert was considered to be "incorrigible." The probation file contains information from the school on fifteen incidents prior to Robert's court appearance. The incidents including "smoking," "continual talking even though he has been asked to keep quiet several different times," leaving "his speech class without permission," interrupting other classes, exposing a "switch blade knife" before other students, "continued defiance," and the like. I was unable to attend the P.O.'s interview with the parents and the boy. At the time the P.O. wrote up her report for the court hearing, she indicated there was no attorney for the minor and parents. Robert was detained at Juvenile Hall until the first hearing. The P.O.'s report contains remarks of the following type:

> According to both husbands, Mrs. Bean has periods of quite severe depression, not talking for a day or so at a time. She also is reported to be disturbed by windstorms, which are frequent in this area, and calls her mother to come and get her or to come and stay with her. Mrs. Bean also will not listen to news broadcasts because, if the news is pessimistic, it causes her a great deal of emotional stress. The overall impression of this woman would be one of great instability and running away from reality. . . .
> The marriage of Penny and Ralph Bean took place [date], and according to Mr. Bean, it has been relatively stable except for these periods of depression that Mrs. Bean gets into, and that Robert has seemed to have been the thorn in the side of their present marriage. . . .
> His [Robert] attitudes are generally hostile, with a plea for leniency when

caught and a promise to do better. Robert is not too happy about placement away from home but, seemingly, is coming around to acceptance. Robert's behavior has been one of complete lack of responsibility toward society. He will steal, lie, hit, use various objects to prod or jam into people with no forethought as to the danger or harm that might be brought about. [I.Q. given as 75.] . . .

At the present time, Robert's principal at [junior high] is asking for expulsion due to numerous infractions of school regulations. . . . He disrupts classes and refuses or is unable to cooperate. . . . Robert has also showed signs of deep emotional disturbance by spitting great wads of phlegm on the clothing and faces of the students for no apparent reason. According to his natural father, [name], Robert has never gotten along in any school he has ever been in, Mr. [natural father] tried to get Mrs. Bean, Robert's mother, to get psychological help three or four years ago but she refused, saying he doesn't need help.

The officer recommends that Robert be placed in a school or state hospital, as the psychologicals indicate. The psychological tests have been ordered and will be administered on [date].

The P.O. establishes a condition of "severe depression" for the mother; several types of conduct are included presumably because the reader would take them to be documentary evidence of the mentioned "depression." Thus the mother is "disturbed by windstorms," "will not listen to news broadcasts because, if the news is pessimistic, it causes her a great deal of emotional stress." To say the mother suffers from "great instability and [is] running away from reality" establishes the home as a locus of "difficulties" for the juvenile. The previously mentioned divorce was the first negative home condition. The vague use of the term "home," to include also categories like "unstable mother" or "unstable marriage," provides the reader with implications not clearly spelled out by the P.O., so that the reader "fills in" what appears to be an "obvious" "negative" or "positive" or "whatever" state of affairs. The P.O.'s use of categories to describe Mrs. Bean could, if employed by a psychiatrist, terminate with some explicit diagnosis of mental illness, complete with documentary evidence of same. Insofar as the court decides a case on such information, the formal validation of a psychiatrist is not necessary for the various personnel at probation to base their recommendations on a juvenile by reference to implied allegations of mental illness on the part of the mother or father or guardian. When the P.O. states the present marriage of Mr. and Mrs. Bean "has been relatively stable except for these periods of depression . . . and that Robert . . . [had] been the thorn in the side of their present marriage," the reader can hardly give serious consideration to this marriage as something "stable." The P.O.'s remarks continually provide apparent "positive" qualities about the boy or the mother or the home, but the reader's credibility is taxed before completing the sentence, or is undermined by subsequent sentences.

The P.O. shifts to Robert by noting the juvenile's "attitudes are generally hostile," and then provides an interesting generalization about his character—"a plea for leniency when caught and a promise to do better." The reader could interpret the P.O.'s remark to mean the boy manipulates or tries to manipulate others when in "trouble," with the hint of insincerity to the declaration "to do better." Other interpretations are possible obviously, but I want to stress how the ambiguous or vague remarks (whose appearance may at first glance seem clear) form a collection of suggested thoughts or depictions offered as "clear" to the reader, yet it is for the reader to "close" the collection, thereby creating a "set" of elements that would enable a reader to classify the juvenile's behavior as "psychopathic," "pre-psychotic," "immature personality," and the like. The P.O. occasionally employs terms to pinpoint an apparent lack of parental "responsibility," a defect in the juvenile's "character," and so on, but most of the report is devoted to categories whose import for a reader is not explicit, but require a "filling in," a "closing" to create unambiguous sets in which objects and events can be counted and placed. But the "rules" for assignment, closing, counting are not always given clarity by language usage (e.g., the mother suffers from "severe depression" and is often "disturbed by wind-storms," "pessimistic" news broadcasts, etc.), but juxtaposed in sentences where seemingly positive and negative elements are included, but no further explication is given. Vague sentences are also presented, hinting at "mental states" in the object but where it is difficult for the reader to assess the hints: "Robert is not too happy about placement away from home but, seemingly, is coming around to acceptance." The reader must fill in remarks attributable to the juvenile to understand the meaning of "not too happy," or "coming around to acceptance." Thus if the referee asks himself "how does the boy feel about placement outside of the home," and the report is being consulted, then he might easily conclude the boy is not that opposed. But the problem is quite serious in the case of the allegations against the mother, for the referee can easily ask the boy himself about his feelings on placement away from home, but is not as likely to ask the mother to verify the P.O.'s remarks about her "severe depression." (In the present case, a lawyer representing the Bean family used the mother's problems to advantage. See below.) But then it is difficult to imagine a situation where adversary rules could be enforced so strictly that leading questions and decisions would expose the tacit knowledge and information exchanged unofficially, but integral to evaluations and recommendations.

The P.O. does not leave much room for doubt vis-à-vis her view of Robert when she states the juvenile's "behavior has been one of complete lack of responsibility toward society." There is little of an equivocal nature in the sentence "He will steal, lie, hit, use various objects to prod or jam into people with no forethought as to the danger or harm that might be brought about." When the boy's I.Q. and test scores are given in the following paragraph, they are not connected to any of the previous material. The reader is confronted with direct statements "convincing" him of how "bad" Robert is, then is exposed to low test scores and a low I.Q. Does the reader conclude the boy's behavior is to be accounted for by divorced parents, a depressed mother, an unstable marriage to which he has contributed, and low native abilities for comprehending his environment? Notice how the sociological researcher could easily code each of the above statements so as to produce numerical representations of the "factors" associated with the juvenile's "problems." The sociologist's measurement would bear a striking resemblance to the P.O.'s reasoning, but objectification and the P.O.'s method of verification are seldom problematic issues in conventional usage of official records. If we add the P.O.'s remarks about the school problems, we have one more "variable" or "factor" to explain the juvenile's behavior. But such a line of reasoning misses the practical reasoning of the P.O. and those with whom he talks, and does not address the properties of the objects and events the P.O. and other actors attend when making decisions. The attributes the sociologist wishes to "freeze" for measurement and cross-tabulation are being transformed by the actions of the members involved in the social organization under study.

The case of Robert suggests how the P.O. depicts the boy's family—divorced, the mother depressed, the juvenile as having a generally "hostile" attitude and complete lack of responsibility toward society," "deep emotional disturbance by spitting great wads of phlegm on the clothing and faces of the students for no apparent reason," continual trouble in school, and a mother who refuses to acknowledge the natural father's advice "to get psychological help three or four years ago." The P.O. clearly indicates placement outside of the home is necessary and indicates she has spoken to the boy about this.

A few days before the court hearing I was at the police station in City B, speaking with the juvenile sergeant about the Bean case. I was told the family had retained the services of a young lawyer and that the police department of a nearby suburb had furnished the Probation Department with information about three prior burglaries by Robert. The lawyer had apparently been to the City B police station inquiring about the possibility of further incidents. The sergeant described the lawyer as "quite annoyed" with the Bean family for not informing him of the burglaries. I went to see the P.O. on the case and she informed me the case took on "new light" because of the burglaries. She now felt the boy should go to the Youth Authority rather than a boys' ranch or the state mental hospital.

The lawyer had been very busy building up his case and had obtained several letters from neighbors and one of the juvenile's teachers to support his contention the family was a "good one." Consider the following excerpts:

[Science teacher] I have, on several occasions, had the opportunity to visit with Bob's parents, Mr. and Mrs. Bean. In my opinion, Bob has a wonderful mother and father. They were of great assistance to me in helping orient Bob at the first school. I am not saying that Mr. and Mrs. Bean are not capable of making a mistake. However, I am saying there has been mistakes made by many, including Bob, which can be amended.

[Friend] I have been a friend of Penny Bean for about two years and have known her much longer. The Beans have a very lovely home always neat and clean. The children are well behaved and mannerly. Penny and Ralph are very good parents and very concerned about the welfare of their children. Robert has always been very polite. He is especially considerate of his sister. My neighbor of the same age as Tina told me she wished her brother was that nice to her.

[Friend] Robert has always conducted himself as any other child would at his age. I cannot say that this is a calm, quite polite child who never has any outbursts of anger or self pity but then no normal young boy is placid at all times. . . .

I have noticed Robert being hi strung and sometimes things are said and done before thought, but this has never reached any level to cause any trouble at home that has been out of the norm. Just being a boy seems to be most of Roberts trouble.

The science teacher seemed interested in making the point of "mistakes" by both the family and the juvenile, but trying to balance this with strong assurances of the "goodness" of the family and the boy, and the assertion things "can be amended." The first friend was positive from beginning to end. The second friend acknowledges "anger," "self pity," "hi strung," but seeks to establish such difficulties as what any child of Robert's age would do. "Just being a boy seems to be most of Robert's trouble," according to this friend. The psychologist at Juvenile Hall tested Robert, and the P.O. summarized the report as follows:

The test results show that he had a full I.Q. of 101 on the Wechsler Bellview, a verbal score of 101, and a nonverbal of 100. He has a moderate scatter which suggests academic retardation. The Rorschach shows aggressiveness with a potential for explosive behavior and a great deal of anxiety.

The statement on the I.Q. contradicts the earlier cited report from the school records by the P.O. The testing occurred after the P.O.'s report was written.

The P.O. and referee were surprised at the retention of a lawyer and my impression was that the lawyer was viewed with some amusement, as if to say he had been retained "for nothing." The case was viewed as "clear," and the referee seemed convinced of placement outside of the home, and seemed responsive to the P.O.'s changing her recommendation to Youth Authority incarceration. When the hearing opened I sensed the lawyer was uneasy about the proceedings. Prior to their beginning he tried to elicit from the referee some statement about how the hearing would proceed. The referee treated the matter as "life as usual," implying it would be routine and straightforward. The lawyer apparently had never attended a juvenile court hearing and did not appreciate the referee's "explanation." The referee went over how "serious" the case was, and emphasized the three burglaries and the continued difficulty at school. The exchanges were rather quick and I could not record much of it. The lawyer introduced the letters (cited earlier) as supportive material for his client. The referee suggested the boy would have to be placed outside of the home because of the "seriousness" of the present incident, the past burglaries, and school record. The lawyer began to protest, and the referee seemed surprised. There were some awkward silences in which both the referee and the lawyer seemed to be thinking about their next move. I was able to record the following:

LAWYER. Now just a minute here. It is my understanding that all parties being helped here have been aided by psychological tests. I feel my client should be exposed to the same help. I would like a continuance on the case.

REFEREE. Now you understand that there is a question of establishing the jurisdiction of the court and then there is the problem of disposition. First there is the question of evidence. Now if you want the boy to remain silent, then we could subpoena witnesses.

LAWYER. Now the psychologicals could affect the evidence of the case and therefore the disposition.

REFEREE. As far as the jurisdictional part of it is concerned, I (pause), the court will have to deny it.

LAWYER. Is the court ready to present evidence?

REFEREE. We can continue it for a week. Then have witnesses if you dispute the jurisdictional side.

LAWYER. Well, I will have to ask for that.

REFEREE. Well, now you are concerned with whether the boy will be placed outside of the home. What is it you want? Can you clarify it?

LAWYER. Well, the whole case may change depending upon the psychologicals.

REFEREE. You realize Robert will have to be detained [in Juvenile Hall].

LAWYER. I will have to go along with that.

REFEREE. I still can't see how things are going to be helped.

LAWYER. If you let me speak to Mr. [natural father] and the others for a minute maybe we could speed things up some since I have delayed things.

After the conference, the lawyer asked for the continuance and received a two-week delay. My interpretation of the dialogue and the accompanying nonverbal behavior suggested the referee was confident he could clearly establish Robert as the "leader" of the incident and the principal offender. The other juveniles involved were all handled in a less severe way and were readily available. I felt the lawyer was not about to contest "what happened." The demand for psychological tests was an expression of dissatisfaction with the court psychologist's report. The Peters girl obtained the services of two psychiatrists paid for by the parents. The lawyer knew (in my opinion) the court was not prepared to present its evidence and, therefore, did not have to ask for a continuance on the basis of wanting the psychological examination. The referee calls explicit attention to the problem of placement outside of the home and seeks to elicit the lawyer's view ("what is it you want?") about disposition. The lawyer does not state his view, but refers to the "psychologicals" again. The referee does not push for an answer to his question about "what is it you want?" The mention of detention produced noticeable (to me) grimaces from the juvenile and his mother. The referee continued to push for some kind of clarification from the lawyer as to his view with the remark: "I still can't see how things are going to be helped." The implication of the last remark seems to be that the referee cannot see how further psychological evaluation will influence the disposition of the case or the evidence to be presented.

Before the subsequent hearing, the lawyer spoke to the referee and apparently agreed the evidence in the case was not something he could or should contest. But the lawyer went ahead and arranged for a psychiatric examination. My understanding of the referee-lawyer discussion was an agreement to accept the referee's view on the jurisdictional elements of the case and to decide the disposition after considering the psychiatric examination. The second hearing established the "seriousness" of the charges and the necessity for firm action. The psychiatric examination was obtained prior to the third hearing. The psychiatrist's report is fairly routine:

> It is my conclusion that Robert has repressed earlier in life a considerable amount of hostility and anxiety and that this has lead to the development of an emotional unstable personality and that coupled with his lack of judgment and control have lead to his aggressive behavior. There also appear to be many other mechanisms involved such as a rather low self image with over compensatory strivings for attention and/or approval of his peer group. Contributing to this has been lack of consistent discipline and proper manifestation of the authoritarian role of the stepfather.

The psychiatrist acknowledges speaking to, and examining the reports of, the P.O. and the psychologist who tested Robert. He also spoke to the parents. The report provides all of the necessary validation necessary for a psychiatric gloss to the material from the P.O. and the psychological testing. The psychiatric pitch is unequivocal in saying "something is wrong," but equivocal as far as knowing what one is to make of the abstract language unless the reader "fills in" and "knows" the boy's "history." The psychiatrist recommends therapy for the entire family.

During the third hearing I felt the lawyer made a brilliant defense. He carefully reviewed each of the allegations, along with the various incidents said to have contributed to a picture of "complete incorrigibility," and suggested the court was imputing motivated connections between each difficulty, but he argued the incidents could also be seen as independent events arbitrarily connected by the court. The lawyer pointed out there were no explicit references to occasions between incidents when the juvenile presumably was "doing well." The referee was not swayed by the lawyer's arguments, and insisted there "was too much" evidence to make such an argument. Finally, the lawyer argued the case would best be settled if the boy changed schools, the family moved to another neighborhood, and the entire family participated in a therapy program as suggested by the psychiatrist. The lawyer sought to convince the referee the course of action suggested by him was covered by the juvenile court law. The referee seemed to hesitate, but could not muster an argument to refute the lawyer's calculated appeal to those elements of the court often forgotten when it has been decided tacitly (by adopting a criminal view of the case) that the juvenile should be "sent away" for "his own good." I interpret the referee's and P.O.'s perspective to be one which included some form of punishment in their insistence that the boy be sent away, particularly to the Youth Authority. The disposition suggested by the lawyer was agreed to by the referee and arrangements were made for the family to begin therapy sessions with the psychiatrist.

The P.O.'s supplemental report anticipated the lawyer's suggestion for keeping the boy at home (with the family in therapy) because she spoke to the psychiatrist three days before the third court hearing. But the P.O. notes Robert had difficulties during his stay in Juvenile Hall leading to three occasions in which the boy had to be isolated because of "his attitude and overacting out." The officer is of the opinion that Robert is still in need of being placed in an institution that has definite limitations and restrictions." The last statement is vague about "institution," but the P.O. told me personally the juvenile should be sent to the Youth Authority or at least to the boys' ranch. Two months later Robert was arrested for violation of probation (taking an auto without consent of owner). The psychiatrist came to his defense with the following statement:

> It is indeed unfortunate that he has broken his probation, for, at this time, I feel he had moved toward significant improvement and that his further progress would be assured in the home and school environment and the therapy regime which he now has. Disruption of these factors at this point, in my opinion, could preclude benefit from future attempts at therapy with the minor and precipitate

a regression. Certainly his violation of probation cannot and should not be minimized, but in dealing with this issue, I recommend careful consideration of the improvement he has made and the effort that has been expanded by him and all concerned in achieving this.

Robert remained at home, but I was informed of further difficulties by Robert, but did not follow the case after the spring of 1965.

The psychiatrist's remarks could be made about anyone in therapy if the juvenile were fortunate to receive this kind of defense rather than Youth Authority incarceration. The police and probation view subsequent offenses as documentary evidence of criminality, but the psychiatrist's report forces a clinical interpretation that cannot be objectified or verified. A judge faced with a lawyer arguing as persuasively as the one quoted above would find it difficult to deny efforts to place the entire family in a therapy program. Parents seeking to mobilize resources to help their children under the juvenile court law are encouraged to do so by law-enforcement agencies. Such action saves the county and state considerable monies, avoids the assumed negative influence of incarceration in an environment likely to expose the juvenile to the "worse" elements, and minimizes the stigma presumed to be forthcoming from the "community."

The presence of a lawyer who makes it his business to challenge all or parts of a case makes it difficult for the police, probation officials, and the court to invoke their conventional practical reasoning in handling cases, but does not resolve the question of who are the "delinquents" and how do they "get that way." The cases in this chapter reveal how the entire process is managed and negotiated by socially organized activities amenable to direct study and observation. It should be clear how the object (the delinquent) or delinquent act can be transformed by invoking an ideology to reread the "facts," character structure, family structure, mental stability, and the like. The rereading highlights theoretical issues inherent in all decision-making, and reveals the problematical structure of social control and judicial procedures.

Chapter 8

CONCLUDING REMARKS

In previous chapters I tried to show how conventional sociological research must be altered to include invariant properties making up the background expectancies members use in everyday decision-making. The background expectancies, as invariant properties, have been discussed elsewhere in some detail,[1] and their relevance is presupposed throughout the research discussed in earlier chapters.

The police, like all members of a society, operate with background expectancies and norms or a "sense of social structure" that enables them to transform an environment of objects into recognizable and intelligent displays making up everyday social organization. The special skills, which the police acquire to enable them to decide "normal" and "unusual" circumstances, become crucial elements of their sense of social structure. The general rules and policies governing day-to-day bureaucratic and administrative activities become intelligent and recognizable features amenable to implementation because of the application of the background expectancies. Therefore, general policies and rules are implemented within a context of unfolding contingencies attached to actual social scenes. When the police discover or are called to the scene of a supposed violation of the legal order, their sense of social structure and memory of past events in the neighborhood provide initial interpretations as to what happened. The general policies or rules, derived from police department directives and standing orders, are connected to legal statutes and practices by the background expectancies and remembered experiences about the neighborhood, its residents, and the information given to the officers by the station or upon encountering the scene on their own. The contingencies of the unfolding scene provide the officers with the raw material for generating practical solutions.

The officers' attempts to comply with departmental and legal requirements, through written and oral reports, initiate an accounting system I have labeled loosely the "creation or generation of history." I have attempted to describe how the historicising features of the legal system (as it is implemented in a particular community) determines the nature of social control, the judicial procedures that are likely to follow, and the kinds of delinquent or nondelinquent products officially recorded or not recorded. A researcher utilizing official materials cannot interpret them unless he possesses or invents a theory that includes how background expectancies render everyday activities recognizable and intelligible. In addition, the researcher must be familiar with the implementation of organizational policies and day-to-day procedures of law-enforcement agencies and the administration of juvenile justice activities that can follow.

In my discussion of who are the delinquent juveniles, I stressed the organizational influences of day-to-day policy implementation. I noted that when the initial samples described in Chapter 3 were obtained, there was a large discrepancy between the number of cases contained in the two cities studied, despite almost identical populations. I attributed the differences in the number of cases to policy differences and the number of personnel assigned to the Juvenile Bureau. The situation in City B was linked to the mayor's office and the Chief of Police, favoring the Captain of Detectives' interest in controlling juvenile investigations. The structure of juvenile law enforcement in City B changed with a change in mayor and Chief of Police at the end of my study. Two new officers were added. The number of cases increased because all units were directed to send juveniles to the Juvenile Bureau. In City A, however, the change in the chief, due to normal retirement, did not change the Juvenile Bureau operations. I was told informally, however, that the new Captain of Detectives appointed by the new chief wanted to change the Juvenile Bureau, but felt the time and circumstances were not right. I was also told by a juvenile officer that the Juvenile Sergeant did not like the new Captain of Detectives, but was so confident of his standing with the Chief and juvenile officers' professional associations, that he disregarded or ridiculed all directives from the Captain of Detectives. The situation became crystallized after my study terminated, but an informant revealed that after the Sergeant lost an election in an important juvenile officer's association, the Captain of Detectives and Chief (both of whom, I was told, followed the election closely), agreed to his being removed from the office and given a complete change of assignment. The Juvenile Bureau's general operations changed drastically. The number of personnel was reduced to three and one-half officers and a supervising sergeant, as opposed to the previous number of seven when the Bureau was at maximum strength. The new sergeant was told to confine his duties entirely to the office, thus eliminating the investigative work done by the previous sergeant. Furthermore, most of the initial investigative work was turned over to the Detective Bureau, as had been previously the case in City B. Particular types of cases (for example, possession of alcohol, truancy, curfew) were now being handled by patrolmen who would issue citations referring the juvenile directly to court for informal hearings. Whereas, in City B, such policies and actual practices stemmed from political interference originating in the mayor's office, in City A the situation changed because the juvenile sergeant was deposed because he had (so my informants revealed) been in trouble within the department for violating departmental rules and having been indiscrete in his personal affairs and conduct.

Extra and intrapolitical interference in City B and internal problems relating to a single man in City A (indiscretion and also a long-standing inability to satisfy routine criteria for promotion) led to similar consequences. The absolute number of cases handled in City A was reduced, the types of cases investigated changed, and the view of juvenile offenders as "needing help" became compromised because the Detective Bureau became responsible for most of the investigations. *Organizational policies and their articulation with actual cases, via the background expectancies of officers differentially authorized to deal with juveniles, directly changed the size of the "law-enforcement net" for recognizing and processing juveniles viewed as delinquent, and determined the size and conception of the "social problem."* The sociologist, therefore, cannot take community or law-enforcement definitions of deviance and their routine organizational processing, as "obvious" in his description and analysis of "social problems."

Attempts to estimate crimes not known to the police are exceedingly difficult, but it is also difficult to evaluate the cases that are uncleared in police files and for which there are no suspects. Add to this the crude and ambiguous classificatory and descriptive materials making up police and probation files, along with the practical circumstances governing the assembly of official statistics, and the reader can only wonder how the conventional literature can use official materials after only the usual perfunctory remarks about their drawbacks. Yet researchers of crime and delinquency continue to identify "problem areas" and then generate *ad hoc* theories to explain official depictions of the problem or design studies to find out why certain groups already designated as deviant by fiat engage in illegal activities. The issue is not the ultimate or even short-range usefulness of statistical materials from official or researcher-governed surveys, but that such materials cannot be interpreted unless the observer is able to demonstrate the theoretical and empirical grounds for assigning sense to both the members' activities and his own coding operations that produced the "data." The activities of police and probation officers are governed by practical circumstances. The same practical circumstances orient field research and researchers' coding of law-enforcement and legal materials that are disengaged from the daily unfolding action scenes leading to their assembly.

In Chapters 4, 5, 6, and 7, I reported extensive accounts based primarily upon my participant observation as police officer and probation officer. The materials reported in those chapters reveal the contingencies associated with day-to-day police, probation, and court activities. The particular cases described reveal how the officers managed their interrogations of juveniles. Of specific interest is how differences in the official's relationship to the juvenile influence immediate disposition and the youth's long-range career consequences. Within the same community, differences in law-enforcement personnel perspectives on juveniles, who are in "defiance of authority" or possess a "bad attitude," can lead to accelerated incarceration away from home. The officer's estimation of the home can lead to recommendations favoring incarceration where the fact of incarceration itself becomes a serious negative entry on the juvenile's record, despite the motives (to "protect" the juvenile from his family) leading to this disposition. Middle-income families, because of their fear of the stigma imputed to incarceration, mobilize resources to avoid this problem. The family's ability to generate or command resources for neutralizing or changing probation and court recommendations, as in adult cases, is a routine feature of the social organization of juvenile justice.

The General Problem

Throughout the book I have stressed how members of socially organized activities, through their practical reasoning, *seek* order in their perception and interpretation of an environment of objects to articulate the particulars of an unfolding action scene with some general policy or rule. The general policy or rule may be an ideal norm like "be kind to elders," or a written statute called part of the adult penal code or juvenile court law. I have stressed theoretical and methodological issues because conventional sociological theories and procedures on crime and delinquency emphasize the "facts," the "real" substantive issues, while taking for granted what is presumed to be "known" and how something is "known," viewing such problems as irrelevant or minor obstacles to understanding the "pressing" problems at hand. Thus for years sociologists have complained about "bad" statistics and distorted bureaucratic record-keeping, but have not made the procedures producing the "bad" materials we label "data" an object of study. The basic assumption of conventional research on crime, delinquency, and law is to view compliance and deviance as having their own ontological significance, and the measuring rod is some set of presumably "clear" rules whose meaning is also ontologically and epistemologically "clear." Recent advances, recognizing the problem of how members of a group or society come to be labeled as "deviant," "strange," "odd," and the like, have not explicated in detail terms like "societal reaction" and "the point of view of the actor," while also ignoring the practical reasoning integral to how members and researchers "know" what they claim to "know." Sociologists have been slow to recognize the basic empirical issues that problems involving language and meaning pose for all social research.

In calling attention to a basic problem of how conversations are transformed into documents or reports, and how members walk away from initial observations with "impressions" or "knowledge" about "what happened," as opposed to meanings derived from a later oral or written account of "what happened," I emphasize the significance of how any oral or written (or combination of the two) tradition(s) serves as a stable and changing depiction of the social structures. Notice the problem of "creating history" is integral to the study of such depictions, as touched upon in Chapter 4. But the implicit obvious problem addressed throughout the book is how dossiers are created by members of any socially organized collection of activities (the "community," the family, the police, the Probation Department, the courts, etc.), and how such dossiers provide members with "correct" depictions of character structure, morality, justice, legality, criminality, and illness. The social organization of juvenile justice reveals both oral and written dossiers. The oral dossier may be activated by a passing reference in the written dossier, or the former may lead to a formalization in written form.

My concern with the problem of "creating history" and interpreting "what happened" as historical depictions is similar to how dossiers are created and then interpreted as "correct" designations of members of a group as social types. The related problems of "history" and dossiers are similar to the study of rumor or collective behavior. The idea of history and the use of documents, reports, or dossiers are presumed to be rooted in institutionalized practices of a society; events and objects routinely practiced and known in socially prescribed and proscribed ways. Yet the material discussed throughout this book bears a striking similarity to remarks contained in a recent work on rumor.[2] The difficulty with sociological studies of the family, work groups, and complex organizations is the presumption of idealized regularity and the search for features to account for variations in the regularities. The contrasting view followed in this book is to view the assembly of a product (for example, a statistic, a juvenile labeled "delinquent"), recognized by societal members as "routine" and called the "social structures" by sociologists, as being generated by practical decision-making. The truncated reports, documents, questionnaire results, tables, and the like (produced by routine administrative work, censuses, and surveys) are treated as manifest regularities of "underlying patterns," but the manifest content is viewed as containing "factual" or cognitively "obvious" meaning. When researchers seek the "underlying patterns" to manifest materials, they employ an implicit abstracting procedure for discovering a few ideals to explain large masses of unintelligible manifest data, rather than develop a theoretical apparatus that would explain and generate everyday behavior. The present work has sought to avoid a search for "underlying" ideals by seeking to discover those thoughts and taken-for-granted elements participants of conversations and documents utilize for producing utterances and making decisions they routinely honor as "communication." Consequently, how members "fill in" equivocal utterances to "close" their meaning, state they "know what you mean," assume they "see the point," has been the central concern of the present study. The search for hypothetical "underlying patterns" precludes the discovery of social meaningful action by invoking the researcher's ideals as an unobservable explanation.

I earlier referred to rumors and collective behavior because I want to underscore the problematic features of the social organizations I have discussed throughout the book. The policeman's conception of "typical" juveniles, "punks," "good kids," his recognition of typical ecological arrangements,[3] family organization, and the like, are integral to understanding how behavior comes to be labeled "delinquent," and how some general policy or rule is to be invoked to dispose of the case. Therefore, institutionalized behavior has critical problematic features that seldom are underscored as in the case of rumor and collective behavior, despite conventional sociological reference to the relevance of stabilizing dominant norms and values. The "delinquent" is an emergent product, transformed over time according to a sequence of encounters, oral and written reports, prospective readings, retrospective readings of "what happened," and the practical circumstances of "settling" matters in everyday agency business. The following remarks could easily be used to explain earlier descriptions of the social organization of juvenile justice:

The work of Allport and Postman (1947) is the most comprehensive study of this kind. They summarize their findings in terms of three concepts: leveling, designates the tendency of accounts to become shorter, more concise, and more easily grasped; sharpening, the tendency toward selective perception, retention, and reporting of a limited number of details; and assimilation, the tendency of reports to become more coherent and more consistent with the presuppositions and interests of the subjects. Their experiments not only confirm previous findings, such as those of Bartlett (1932), but have also been replicated by several others with substantially the same results. Repeated tests show, then, that testimony by serial transmission is rarely accurate, that most persons are unable to repeat verbatim what they had heard from others, that comprehension depends upon the frame of reference of the perceiver. These are demonstrated facts, and they have been explained in terms of limitations of human perception and memory. . . .

From this standpoint it is not easy to make clear distinction between communicative processes and the product of communication. Rumor content is not viewed as an object to be transmitted but as something that is shaped, reshaped, and reinforced in a succession of communicative acts; as Turner (1964, p. 398) puts it, rumor is not so much the dissemination of a designated message as the process of forming a definition of a situation. In most cases one can speak of rumor content only heuristically.[4]

The notions of "leveling," "sharpening," and "assimilation" suggest how members of a community and law-enforcement personnel seek short, concise, and easily understood conceptions of juveniles as "punks," "troublemakers," and the like, for it is not necessary to be explicit about the behavioral elements others presumably can verify. The speaker's intentions and "what he means" is augmented by the listener's "of course," "uh, huh," "I see," and by the listener's assuming he "knows" what the speaker intends, and conversely when it is the listener's turn to speak, that is, the use of a reciprocity of perspectives. The "sharpening" is revealed continually in the study of juvenile justice when conversations between officers and juveniles recurrently make reference to selective elements perceived and interpreted, truncated by both participants either to mask their thoughts or intentions or simply to "get to the point" faster, or to "trap" the "kid" and "break" his story. The "assimilation" could refer to reports becoming more "coherent" by use of abstract language to "close" the collection of terms and create unambiguous sets with which to classify and count objects and events, and bring accounts into line with general organizational policies, rules, and interests of the participants. Throughout the book I have repeatedly used the phrase "what happened" to refer to delinquent acts as labeled by the police and probation officials, and to stress the ambiguity or problematic character of "facts" and presumed "evidence." I have sought to document a perspective that parallels a statement by Shibutani that "most persons are unable to repeat verbatim what they had heard from others, that comprehension depends upon the frame of reference of the perceiver." But I have also stressed how the researcher's descriptive accounts are not any more "objective" than the member's version, as long as both trade upon implicit common sense or folk knowledge, for the observer must rely upon his own observations to recommend an analysis of "what happened." The contextual setting, the properties of juveniles "seen" as "delinquent," how members of the community or law-enforcement agencies employ language categories and gestures to depict the behavioral environment making up the activities labeled "delinquent," "good homes," "defiance of authority," and "a bad attitude," all constitute contingent features of institutionalized conduct. I have described the police officer's interrogation procedures as an apparatus designed to produce delinquency, "something that is shaped, reshaped, and reinforced in a succession of communicative acts," in Shibutani's words. There is no denial of "something done," that is, acts members could describe as delinquent, but the issue of how that "something" can be objectified for the reader by the observer's procedures, and how members communicate the "something" to each other as part of their practical circumstances (leading to inferences and action) is seldom addressed in conventional research. The generation of official documents, oriented by general policies or rules, enables members to construct acceptable legal "definitions of the situation," but they are definitions disengaged from the behavioral scene of occurrence. Shibutani continues:

> Rumors exist only in the communicative acts of men, but they cannot be identified in terms of any particular set of words. What is identified as a "rumor" is usually a shorthand expression summarizing the general sense of many different verbalizations. A particular message may be stated as an affirmation, or it may be part of a question. It may be a direct statement, or it may be implied in what he said. In each universe of discourse certain things are taken for granted and need not be said at all. . . .
>
> The basic unit of analysis becomes the ambiguous situation, and the central problem is to ascertain how working orientations toward it develop. If rumors are viewed as the cooperative improvisation of interpretations, it becomes apparent that they cannot be studied fruitfully apart from the social contexts in which they arise.[5]

The various expressions used by the police, probation, and school officials for depicting juveniles do not depend for their meaning on some dictionary or literal interpretation of lexical items, but require an open texture of what "anyone knows" and assumes "others know." The social contexts in which situations unfold over time can be perceived and interpreted by members as "clear" or "ambiguous," or "clear" or "ambiguous" until "further notice." "Further notice" may be forthcoming immediately and lead to "cooperative improvisation of interpretations" and successive transformations on later occasions in sequentially relevant social contexts. The characterization of delinquent objects over time is conditional upon subsequent acts, evaluations of "the family," "school adjustment," "psychiatric evaluation," reexamination of past acts or descriptions of past acts, prospective changes imputed to the object, and so on. Accounts contained in various documents and reports and their reading or rereading by the same or different officials over time augment the possible transformations available on some *assumed* starting point. The extent to which documents become "frozen" accounts remains an empirical issue; any reference to a past written account becomes part of the process of either "creating history" or the "discovery" of "history" or "delinquency" (or whatever). The significance of the notion of "natural social order" is not to be found in the presumption of predetermined or divine forces, but in how members (laymen and scientists) decide order, make decisions, assert "facts," label and depict moral character, "good families," "defiance of authority," a "bad attitude," assume a policy or rule applies, and so on.

The study challanges the conventional view which assumes "delinquents" are "natural" social types distributed in some ordered fashion and produced by a set of abstract "pressures" from the "social structures." The central assumption of the alternate views is that members' categories, the things to which they refer, members' objectification and verification procedures for deciding delinquency, and members' rules for expressing and deciding "what happened" become the source of data. The existence of delinquents as "natural social types" assumes their known (that is, taken for granted) existence in the community, with the sociologist's task to be one of identifying those attributes "that correlate" with the "social fact" of delinquent boys. Police and probation statistics serve as documentary evidence for the existence of delinquents as "natural social types," despite problems of error, sampling, and the like. The methodological strategy of sampling some population and finding the attributes to explain as much of the "variance" as possible assumes that law-enforcement identification of "natural" delinquents produces the relevant population. I have tried to show the relevant population is like a rumor, and that its generation is a negotiable enterprise within a socially bounded arena of discourse. How members of the community and law-enforcement agencies identify attributes of "delinquency" and utilize linguistic and paralinguistic properties to both recognize the phenomena and express this recognition to others became focal points of the research.

My substantive discussion of delinquency focuses upon community political organization as setting the stage for the development of police activities and policies on handling juveniles. Within police and probation departments there are additional conditions of advancement, job routinization, and theories about those juveniles who are likely to become delinquent, from what types of families, and the like. I have focused upon the significance of officers applying general policies or rules, based upon legal criteria and augmented by a sense of social structure and properties of the interaction scene, to designate acts of delinquency and criminal or ill character structure. The interrogation procedures and written reports constitute oral and written dossiers of juveniles, and provide the conditions for justifying evaluative and dispositional action. Abstract, statistically correlated information on age, sex, ethnicity, income or class level, school "adjustment," type of offense, number of offenses, age at first offense, and the like, do not provide the researcher with material for understanding how delinquency is produced. Such information (often termed "objective") represents truncated indices of "what happened," and is divorced or disengaged from the day-to-day occurrences of actual school, police, probation, and court practices. The negotiated character of phenomena labeled delinquency by community and law-enforcement members cannot be shown by merely examining statistical information on administratively produced accounts, unless the researcher can utilize a theory of social organization which would generate both the statistical materials and the activities that such materials truncate and transform.

NOTES

1. Harold Garfinkel, "A Conception of and Experiments with 'Trust' as a Condition of Stable Concerted Actions," in O. J. Harvey (ed.), *Motivation and Social Interaction* (New York: Ronald Press, 1963) pp. 187-238; Garfinkel, "Studies of the Routine Grounds of Everyday Activities," *Social Problems*, (Winter, 1964) **11**, 225-250; and Aaron V. Cicourel, *Method and Measurement in Sociology* (New York: Free Press, 1964).
2. Cf. Tamotsu Shibutani, *Improvised News: A Sociological Study of Rumor* (Indianapolis: Bobbs-Merrill, 1966).
3. Cf. Harvey Sacks, "Methods in Use for the Production of a Social Order: a Method for Warrantably Inferring Moral Character," unpublished manuscript, n.d.
4. Shibutani, *op. cit.*, pp. 5 and 9.
5. *Ibid.*, p. 16 and pp 23-24.

NAME INDEX

SUBJECT INDEX